# VIRGINIA WOOLF & COMMUNITIES

Selected Papers from the Eighth
Annual Conference on Virginia Woolf

Saint Louis University
Saint Louis, Missouri
June 4-7, 1998

Edited by Jeanette McVicker and Laura Davis

Pace University Press
1999

**Pace University Press**
**One Pace Plaza**
**New York NY 10038**


Printed in the United States of America

**Library of Congress Cataloging-in-Publication Data**

Conference on Virginia Woolf (8th : 1998 : St. Louis University, Saint Louis, Mo.)
Virginia Woolf & communities : selected papers from the eighth annual conference on Virginia Woolf, Saint Louis University, Saint Louis, Missouri, June 4-7, 1998 / edited by Jeanette McVicker and Laura Davis.
p. cm.
Includes bibliographical references.

ISBN 0-944473-47-4 (pbk. : alk. Paper)

1. Woolf, Virginia, 1882-1941—Criticism and interpretation Congresses. 2. Woolf, Virginia, 1882-1941—Political and social views Congresses. 3. Feminism and literature—England—History—20th Century Congresses. 4. Women and literature—England—History—20th century Congresses. 5. Community life in literature Congresses. I. McVicker, Jeanette. II. Davis, Laura. III. Title.
IV. Title: Virginia Woolf and Communities.

PR6045.072Z5787 1998 99-21636
823'.912—dc21 CIP

# Contents

# Abbreviations

| | |
|---|---|
| *AHH* | *A Haunted House* |
| *AROO* | *A Room of One's Own* |
| *BP* | *Books and Portraits* |
| *BTA* | *Between the Acts* |
| *CDB* | *The Captain's Death Bed and Other Essays* |
| *CE* | *Collected Essays* (4 vols.) |
| *CR1* | *The Common Reader* |
| *CR2* | *The Common Reader, Second Series* |
| *CSF* | *The Complete Shorter Fiction* |
| *D* | *The Diary of Virginia Woolf* (5 vols.) |
| *DM* | *The Death of the Moth and Other Essays* |
| *E* | *The Essays of Virginia Woolf* (6 vols.) |
| *F* | *Flush* |
| *FR* | *Freshwater* |
| *GR* | *Granite & Rainbow: Essays* |
| *JR* | *Jacob's Room* |
| *L* | *The Letters of Virginia Woolf* (6 vols.) |
| *M* | *The Moment and Other Essays* |
| *MEL* | *Melymbrosia* |
| *MOB* | *Moments of Being* |
| *MT* | *Monday or Tuesday* |
| *MD* | *Mrs. Dalloway* |
| *ND* | *Night and Day* |
| *O* | *Orlando* |
| *PA* | *A Passionate Apprentice* |
| *RF* | *Roger Fry: A Biography* |
| *TG* | *Three Guineas* |
| *TTL* | *To the Lighthouse* |
| *TW* | *The Waves* |
| *TY* | *The Years* |
| *VO* | *The Voyage Out* |
| *WF* | *Women & Fiction: The Manuscript Versions of* AROO |
| *WH* | *The Waves: The Two Holograph Drafts* |

# Introduction

**Georgia Johnston**

## Raising Community

This introduction is dedicated to Jerry Troxwell, 1937–1998, friend and colleague.

What is community? For the Virginia Woolf Conference, which has convened annually since 1991, each year at a different location, community has become a gathering to which many Virginia Woolf scholars return and new participants are welcomed. The conference goal is to enrich and exchange ideas about Virginia Woolf and revive energy after the year of writing, teaching, administering, creating, reading, and research.

In order to diversify perspectives, to incorporate discussion, to step aside from conference hierarchies of presenter and listener, and to promote communication, each conference has experimented with traditional conference structuring. This conference sponsored "Conversations." Brief initial 20-minute staged conversations opened up into full-audience impromptu discussion in an Artists' Conversation and in a Conversation in response to the documentary film, *Paris Was A Woman.* The conference included a panel of high school students to give insight into "First Encounters" with Woolf. The conference also experimented with "Chat Rooms," scheduled at the center of the conference as a way for participants to come together in small groups to discuss what they had brought to the conference, what they had heard, what ideas had most stimulated them, and to exchange information about panels that had already taken place.

For this conference, community building was not only part of the ongoing experimentation with conference structuring, but the theme was thrown into relief as the text of the conference. One goal of focusing this conference on community was to instigate thinking and conversation in order to foster renewed thinking about Woolf in terms of communities. The aim of the conference was not to delegate Woolf to one community, but to discuss Woolf as an artist who mediates between pluralities of communities, who redefines communities and the individuals who inhabit them, who creates communities of readers.

Bonnie Kime Scott's introduction to *The Gender of Modernism* influenced my initial formulations for the theme of the Eighth Annual Conference. Re-gendering modernism, she multiplies readings of modernist texts and redefines the modernist agenda beyond the traditional canonical (masculine) definitions. By means of reminding readers of Virginia Woolf's metaphor of the web, Scott reconstructs connections between modernists (conversations, reviews, letters)—connections that have been ignored because critical work in modernist studies has been blindered by a universalizing of modernism as masculine (9-12). Scott's revelations about connections between modernists, the communities of writers fostered by those connections, as well as the "interrupted careers" influence our readings of the "politics of literary production, a politics," Scott reminds us, "we enter in our recovery work" (7). I hope that the Eighth Annual Conference has participated in this "recovery work," rethinking Woolf in terms of communities (both those associated with her and not) that, on an abstract plane, the work done at the Eighth Annual Conference has participated in the politics of rethinking community through Woolf.

The call for papers encouraged presentations that re-explored communities of which Virginia Woolf was a part—for example, Female Modernists, the Memoir Group, the Bloomsbury community, the feminist community, communities of artists, communities formed by letter writing, lesbian and gay communities, the British community, the pacifist community; and not a part—for example, the Apostles, the working class. Presenters could analyze communities that Woolf describes in her writings—for example, the community of the "outsider," of the woman writer, of the village pageant, of the Dalloways' party, of *The Voyage Out* travelers, of Orlando's biographers; or could focus on textual communities outside the spheres in which Woolf is generally explored—for example, the Harlem Renaissance or Socialism. Community could be interpreted as national, geographical, editorial, pedagogical, sexual, gendered, ideological, economic, racial, cultural, psychoanalytical, colonial, postcolonial. Community was not restricted to Woolf's own era; presentations of future, current, or past communities in terms of Woolf, for example, evaluating current communities of critics (Woolf and lesbian studies, for example) were applauded.

By means of concurrent panel presentations, the idea of community was analyzed and explored in diverse ways. In between these concurrent presentations, keynote events pulled the community together for joint experiences. Beginning with Marianne DeKoven's opening lecture, and ending with Patricia Moran's closing presentation, the conference provided four days to focus upon Woolf and her writings through this focus—Woolf and community.

* * *

How can any conference be remembered in total? The papers included in these *Selected Papers* will be one historical record. To remember the conference as it was, however, is an impossible task. Each year the introductions to the *Selected Papers* attempt this task—a group memory from a director's overall perspective, an historical account from someone who was present, at least, from beginning to end. The memories will be fragmented; some events will be highlighted; names will float—through a linear thread that cannot hope to capture a totalizing experience.

Such an all-impossible, imagined omniscience cannot be written. Closest comes the schedule of events, an official historical version of the conference, but even this, as is the way with official documents, cannot be counted upon to give an accurate rendition. For instance, Suzanne Diamond, listed in the schedule, suffered a ruptured appendix and faxed her introduction to Marianne DeKoven's beginning lecture, to be read in absentia. Jane Marcus, because of illness, and Shari Benstock, because of gale-force Massachusetts winds, were not able to attend. Shari Benstock express-mailed the movie *Paris Was a Woman*, so that it could be shown, with her comments for her Conversation, but keynote events for Friday and Saturday were all rescheduled to allow time for the movie to arrive.

Most events, of course, proceeded as planned. Marianne DeKoven spoke about liminal feminine spaces and audience. Awiakta illustrated how narrative can create community. Vara Neverow historicized textualities through photographic artifacts. Rachel Bowlby examined metaphors of material cultures in Woolf's writings. Tuzyline Allan revealed the impact of colonialization on Woolf studies. Patricia Moran analyzed the theories of sexologists in *A Room of One's Own*.

Sponsored artists—Awiakta, Cherokee poet/essayist/story-teller, Suzanne Bellamy, Australian visual artist/sculptor, and Sigrid Nunez, whose novel *Mitz: The Marmoset of Bloomsbury* revisions Virginia and Leonard Woolf in the company of Mitz—under the leadership of J. J. Wilson, gave insights into art and cultures. By conversing about the effects Woolf has had upon them and their art, and by witnessing to the relationships they have with Woolf's writings, they inspired discussion about ways Woolf's writing affects readers outside academic constraints.

Morris Beja and Bonnie Kime Scott rose to the occasion in the second Conversation, "Filming the Left Bank," to enact a cafe scene and, with their conversation, to lead a rousing discussion about the problems and merits of the documentary *Paris Was A Woman*. Debate turned to the film's audiences, lesbian politics, and representations of modernism.

This volume of *Selected Papers* will help us to remember the textual dynamics of the panel and keynote presentations. But who will recall the tables of the *Virginia Woolf Miscellany*, Left Bank Books, the *South Carolina Review*, the International Virginia Woolf Society, Suzanne

Bellamy's art? Who will remember the temporal, fleeting experiences that are not things in themselves, but help to create communities, that help, as Woolf writes, to light, "halfway down the spine . . . the more profound, subtle and subterranean glow, which is the rich yellow flame of rational intercourse" (*AROO* 11)? Rain, food, conversations, post-panel discussions, introductions, the shaking of an umbrella, a shared cab ride, a shared bottle of wine, a walk—how can these be contained in a history of this conference community? Who will recall that the map sent some participants toward the arch, instead of towards a desired restaurant? (They were picked up by campus police and returned.) Though a conference can be divided into its beginning, middle, and end through a rendition of its events, a conference is also, always, in its middle as it proceeds.

And then it is done.

* * *

I have great gratitude to the students, colleagues, and friends who helped oil the wheels of this conference. First to the Women's Studies Program, and especially Mandi Schauble, its work study student, to the Women's Studies students, especially Jen Hoef, who took on the Virginia Woolf Conference as her Women's Studies Capstone project. To Nita Pettigrew, who put together the high school panel. To Hal Parker, Duane Smith, Colleen McCluskey, Toby Benis, Tony Hasler and his mother, Joan Hasler, Kathleen Nigro, Helen Mandeville, Martha Baker, Lisa Ives, and Martha Fiklen, staunch helpers at registration. Thank you Ellen Jones and Murray Beja for your wisdom and advice while the conference was in preparation stages and for your strength and help in carrying this conference while it convened. Thank you, Jerry Troxell, Laura Patton, and my Research Group for helping with stamps and advice. And a special thanks to Paige Canfield, integral to the Eighth Annual Virginia Woolf Conference, and our friends, Beth Dockery, Dru Dockery, Sue Fleming, Cheryl Franz, Nancy Reiter, and Margaret Tucker for your support and labor throughout the year.

As in every year, the Conference Steering committee (made up of past directors) and a Program Committee (chosen each year) were indispensable. Thanks go to Mark Hussey (1991), Vara Neverow (1992), Jane Lilienfeld (1993), the late Paul Connolly (1994), Beth Rigel Daugherty (1995), Wayne Chapman and Elisa Sparks (1996), and, especially, Jeanne Dubino (1997). And thank you, Judith Allen, Suzanne Diamond, Leslie Hankins, Andrea Harris, Patricia Moran, and Pierre-Eric Villeneuve, ready to help whenever called upon, even with the most trying problems.

Towards the end of the conference, the seven-week-old Xena the Warrior Kitten Canfield-Johnston was found under a bush, rescued by a stalwart crew of intrepid Woolf scholars, and given to me to raise (and bring to all forthcoming Woolf conferences). She is doing well and has taken over the household, assaulting with affection dogs, people, and, even, the senior cats. She is sleeping here at the side of the computer while I finish this introduction.

## Works Cited

Scott, Bonnie Kime. "Introduction." *The Gender of Modernism: A Critical Anthology*. Ed. Bonnie Kime Scott. Bloomington: Indiana UP, 1990. 1-18.

Woolf, Virginia. *A Room of One's Own*. New York: Harcourt, 1929.

# Note from the Editors

Poking around in an antique/junk store with her mother last summer, Laura's eye lighted on pocket-sized cigar tin featuring the brand-name Between the Acts. Her brain flooded with possibilities, inarticulate, but pulsating with the idea that not only is nothing ever just one thing, but that meaning can be discovered turned 180 degrees away from one's original thinking.

That shift took on palpable meaning when we met at the Cleveland airport at 8:00 a.m. for the brief flight to St. Louis. "Express" means small, not fast, we realized as our non-hub jet was grounded in flawlessly blue-skied Cleveland, too small to land in the torrential St. Louis weather. (Ours would be just one of many weather stories at the conference.) During our thirteen-hour wait in the Cleveland airport, we picked up another stranded Woolfian, Carol Niemczura (she would miss her 4:30 presentation); shared nachos (amazingly Jan produced a Shouts wipe her dad had supplied her with when Laura inevitably dropped them on her khakis) and margaritas at Cheers; were tricked into thinking that the buttons on the jukebox worked because a song we punched in quickly came up—but after four hours of punching buttons and waiting expectantly for "Build Me Up Buttercup" realized we had been taken in; resisted the allure of the Victoria's Secret saleswoman stationed in the walkway who tempted us with unitards "nice to wear under suits"; and didn't resist the balms and potions of the Body Works and t-shirts commemorating the Psychedelic Era at the Rock and Roll Hall of Fame shop. Punchdrunk from false hopes and promises broken as we sat twelve hours after our originally scheduled departure at our third gate of the day (now night), we struggled to remember line two of "My Baby Does the Hanky Panky." A woman looking like anyone's cousin—a tad matronly, yet pleasant, but surely no Tommy James and the Shondells fan—leaned in from the row behind with "You know I saw her for the very first time": shift. Finally, in St. Louis, "atmosphere" took on a new meaning. Prepared for the hot weather that seems to first come with the Woolf conference—even in Plymouth, New Hampshire!—Laura found herself layering her bed at night with spare clothes in an effort to keep warm. (Jan, more sensibly, had brought flannels and socks.)

* * *

When arranging the selected papers for the previous volume, we tried to put ourselves in the position of "listening" to the papers—"hearing papers in conversation with each other." That seems, too, what Georgia Johnston put into action with the St. Louis conference, "Virginia Woolf & Communities, which Georgia imagined around the notion of clustering people—big groups and small groups. Our arrangement of the volume this year tries to be in keeping with the same principle and commitment: let's see what happens as we let the papers come together and "speak" in community with each other. Both Georgia's conference theme and Jeanne Dubino's, "Virginia Woolf and Her Influences" (VW-7), easily lent themselves to—seemed almost to demand—an arrangement for the selected papers that was generated by the conference theme dynamic.

A conference, by its nature, raises common questions: What does it take to feel community? Does there have to be a sense that there are others outside the community? Is "outside" the condition for the possibility of community? Plymouth, New Hampshire was descended upon by two kinds of outsider communities—motorcyclists and Woolf conferees—seemingly emblematizing the two ends of a spectrum, yet visually brought together for Woolfians in the conference poster image of Woolf astride a motorcycle and by such realities as Beth Rigel Daugherty's being a weekend motorcyclist. In an effort to counter the possible outsider feelings of conference attendees in St. Louis, Georgia arranged for "chat room" conversations among participants in the early days of the conference during which these feelings might be addressed and new communities founded. In the end, however, the notion of community that may work best for Woolf is coming together momentarily, dispersing, wavelike. Jan kept seeing the image throughout the conference of Woolfian flocks of birds—typically rooks—that come together as if part of one great mind, then disperse as if responding to some invisible signal. The conference participants, too, seemed to come together, disperse, be "inside and outside" some determining center much like those flocks.

We found the St. Louis conference both extending and reversing the Plymouth conference in significant ways. For instance, we were both struck by the way that last year's *Selected Papers* section we called "Acts of Reading" seemed to extend itself into this year's conference papers, but with the kind of reversal of perspective we've been describing. Our perspectives on Woolf and her work are always shifted by the annual conference; the St. Louis conference did this overtly by helping to nurture, construct, and encourage alternative reading communities. Several of the papers we've included pick up on this idea: Anna Snaith's discussion of the *Three Guineas* respondents to Woolf; Terry DeHay's alternative "punch bowl" communities; Elisa Kay Sparks's construction of the "virtual" community established in the pages of *The Dial*. Each year, the annual Woolf conference—unique among academic conferences—attempts to encourage innovative offerings, such as Stephen Pelton's dance-theater production of *The Death of a Moth* at Plymouth and the collaborative reading-writing project of Lana Hartman Landon and Laurel Smith in St. Louis. This effort offers at once both continuation and a conscious attempt to preserve difference of perspective.

One more manifestation of the relation between this year's and last year's conference, but with some distinct twists, was the function of historical perspectives and historicity. Our experience last year was that the theme gave us many wide-angle historical shots of Woolf and her influences; this year, the historical perspective was akin to the zoom lens. "Virginia Woolf & Communities" lent itself interestingly to what seemed to us a heightened focus on cultural constructions of narrative as opposed to last year's socio-historical rootedness. Perhaps the most striking example of this was the way that Georgia attempted to put into practice the web-like cluster arrangement used by Bonnie Kime Scott's anthology *The Gender of Modernism*, which Georgia hailed as her inspiration for the conference theme. Scott's book is exemplary in developing "reversals in perspective" that we came to feel so strongly in St. Louis. (Perhaps it is more than serendipitous that the 1999 conference will be organized by Bonnie at the University of Delaware?) The visual metaphor of webs/clusters (as opposed to "historical threads weaving themselves together"—how the papers from the Plymouth conference arranged themselves) readily lends itself to new ways of imagining communities; at the same time, it alters our sense of a writer/reader's location in quite variable ways, as the selection of papers here variously attests.

In a volume characterized by the notion of reversal, the reader will experience many, beginning with Beth Rigel Daugherty's new way of seeing the effect of Woolf's relationship with her father on her education and culminating in Judith Allen's application of performance theory, which provides a final turning, moving from the rhetorical to the social/historical/cultural, closing the ends together. Finally, this volume will point the community of Woolf readers to the Ninth Annual Conference—"Woolf Turning the Centuries." In its very title, the Ninth Annual Conference brings full circle the idea of turning around, suggesting both completion and an opening back out to future-directed reading/thinking/writing, providing an open-ended closure, convergence with community, not fixed but fluid.

* * *

As last year, we selected papers for the volume according to a number of considerations: recommendations from conference attendees, the theme and sub-themes of the conference, representation by contributors in past conference volumes (again listening for new voices), range of critical approaches, and our effort to capture the range of creative and intellectual exchange that characterizes the annual conference. A total of 143 session papers, presentations, and special events comprised the conference program, with 72 session papers submitted for consideration. Twenty-nine session papers are included in the volume, representing 22 of the 48 concurrent panel sessions, along with four of the five featured addresses delivered at the conference and the two Featured Conversations.

Grateful appreciation goes to all of the participants in the Eighth Annual Conference on Virginia Woolf: those who presented their work, shared in the conversations that followed, and offered suggestions for this volume. Special thanks, too, to the contributors to this volume, which aims at extending those conversations. All of us are deeply grateful to Georgia for her monumental effort in putting on the conference as well as her beatific calm in the face of the conference's literal storms and the stresses that accompany any such event. Thanks yet again to Mark Hussey for his leadership in Woolf studies and willingness to allow us a second time to discover the alternative plan in which we found the papers emerging. For support of her travel to the Woolf conference and work on the volume, Laura would like to thank Dean Suzanne Fitzgerald, Kent East Liverpool, and, on the Kent Campus, Gordon Keller, Interim Provost, and Dean Joseph Danks, College of Arts and Sciences. Laura would also like to thank Tom Clapper for his steadfast support and Jan McVicker for the joy and deep satisfaction our collaborative work has brought. Jan wishes to thank the English Department, especially secretary Diane Bohn, her Fall '98 students at SUNY-Fredonia, and United University Professions for a PDQWL award to cover expenses on this project. She especially wishes to thank William V. Spanos for his insights into the nothingness in addition to his constant support. Lastly, Jan would like to thank Laura Davis for her friendship, imagination, fastidiousness, and the opportunity to spend some wild nights at the Conneaut, Ohio Days Inn these past two years.

**Jeanette McVicker and Laura Davis**

# Isolation and Community

**Beth Rigel Daugherty**

## Learning Virginia Woolf: Of Leslie, Libraries, and Letters

My work on Woolf and education will eventually include four sections: Woolf's education; Woolf's teaching; Woolf's essays as education; and the implications of Woolf's pedagogical practices for teaching literature. This essay combines "what I did on my summer vacation" with some preliminary conclusions and is a working draft for a small part of the section on Woolf's education.

In the summer of 1997, I traveled to Pullman, Washington, to visit the Library of Leonard and Virginia Woolf housed in the Manuscripts, Archives, and Special Collections area of the New Holland Library at Washington State University. With the help of Diane Gillespie, Laila Miletic-Vejzovic, Leila Luedeking, and Julie King, I isolated Leslie Stephen's library (over 1,000 volumes) from the more than 6,000 volumes in the collection. Going through the card catalog drawers for the Woolf Library, I noted what *surely* belonged to Leslie Stephen and what *probably* belonged to him. I also noted books that belonged to Julia Stephen, books that belonged to Virginia Stephen, and books related to education (did the young Virginia ever consult the huge *Catalogue of the London Library* before going there, for example?). Then, I actually looked at many of Leslie Stephen's books, holding them, opening them, finding and transcribing some of his notes, enjoying his drawings, and annotating my bibliographic notes.

As I sat in the Reference and Research Room, surrounded by Bloomsbury books, Hogarth Press books, Bloomsbury-related pictures and art, *and* Leslie Stephen's annotated copy of the 63-volume *Dictionary of National Biography*, I thought about what it meant to handle someone else's books. How excited I was to discover, for example, that an anecdote in *To the Lighthouse* may have a factual basis: in *The Works of George Eliot*, volume 3 of *Middlemarch* is missing! What did it mean to Virginia Stephen, though, to walk into her father's library and to walk out with one of his volumes? What did it mean to Virginia *Woolf* to pull down one of his books from a shelf in *her* library? To see the notes in his hand, so like her own? To see the many amusing drawings? To see the inscriptions to Laura Makepeace Stephen? To come across volume 2 of an early edition of *Hours in a Library*, as I did, a volume with all its front matter and back matter, every free inch, even 36 pages into the first essay on Sir Thomas Browne, crammed full of quotations about books, libraries, and reading? (These notes became the preface to the second edition.)

I went to Pullman to learn more about the young Virginia Stephen's education in Leslie Stephen's library, but something else happened as well. As I handled Stephen's books, my opinion of the man who had owned them began to change. Jeremy Bentham said, "A man may be judged by his library" (qtd. in Stephen, *Hours* xxv), and J. J. Wilson, after her first visit to this collection, said something similar, "the books on our shelves do characterize us" (6). Certainly the books on Leslie Stephen's shelves and the marks he made in them reveal a different facet of him. Perhaps another reason Vanessa and Virginia had differing views of their father, that Virginia "preferred [her] father" to her mother (Bell n. pag., 7), that Virginia vacillated between hate and love and expressed more ambivalence about him than Vanessa did, was that she literally handled and continued to handle his books.

My work supports Leila Luedeking's claim that, given the titles she mentions in her own work, Woolf must have read most of the books belonging to her father (5); her essay on Addison in the *Common Reader*, for example, mentions Richard Hurd, the editor of *The Works of the Right Honourable Joseph Addison* that Leslie Stephen owned. She also consults *his* work, saying, "I always read *Hours in a Library* by way of filling out my ideas, say of Coleridge, if I'm reading Coleridge; and always find something to fill out; to correct; to stiffen my fluid vision." Though she reads him "medicinally," she feels "a reader's affection for him" and notes that "[t]hrough his books I can get at the writer father still" (*MOB* 115-6). Handling his books, those he owned and those he wrote, may be why Woolf reports feeling "in league" with him (*MOB* 111).

As *I* handled his books, I became more curious about and more sympathetic toward Woolf's "writer father." I dipped into Leslie Stephen's biographers, F. W. Maitland and Noel Annan and David Zink, consulted Gillian Fenwick's bibliography, read some of Stephen's essays (including "The Study of English Literature," delivered as a talk to school boys), reviewed the arguments of Katherine Hill and Louise DeSalvo (was he a loving mentor or an abusive tyrant?), and read the essay by Jane Elizabeth Fisher that says "both" and explains how his daughter worked against, with, and through those dynamics. As a result, the ranting patriarch still exists, but in a palimpsest of many layers. His rages about money, so inexplicable and inexcusable, are surely related to his great grandfather's imprisonment for debt, for example, and are another version of the conflict between knowledge and behavior that we see in his daughter's statements about class on the one hand and her behavior on the other. Surely much of his patriarchal posturing—his Alpine climbing, long-distance walking, and reliance on the term "manly" in his criticism—goes back to his sickly youth and having to be protected from bullies by Fitzjames at the school where the brothers were "day boys." He loved poetry as a child, loudly reciting it on the streets, and might have become a poet, but a doctor told his mother to nip such tendencies in the bud: send him to a boys' school, he said, deprive him of poetry (Maitland 28), and prevent him from getting too emotional; doctors would later deprive the daughter of reading and writing in an attempt to rid *her* of extreme emotions (DeSalvo 81). Leslie and Virginia have similar handwriting, love to walk, and can be hysterically funny. They place emotional demands on others, are insecure about their talents, and work compulsively (the aging, sick Leslie says that he goes on writing "as a habitual drunkard goes on drinking" (Rosemary Hill 25; see also Katherine Hill 352 and Luedeking 3 for more similarities). Too, they both use newspaper clippings to build an argument they feel passionately about, he, in his arguments for the North in the American Civil War, she in her arguments for equality in *Three Guineas*. Virginia Woolf internalized more of both the tyrant father and the writer father than she may have realized or desired at the same time she rebelled against both.

Woolf's mixed feelings about her father naturally extend to the education she received from him (see Hill 361n15 for further discussion of this ambivalence). She writes with affection about going "up to father's study to fetch a book" (*MOB* 157) and praises his "wisdom" in allowing her fifteen-year-old self the "free run of a large and quite unexpurgated library" (*CE*4 79). But she also resents not receiving a formal education, of having maybe £100 spent on the education she did have, of being sacrificed to "Arthur's Education Fund." It does seem strange that even though Julia had persuaded Leslie to give up his more progressive ideas about their girls' education (Annan 121) it did not occur to him later, after Julia's death, to consider Cambridge for his daughter. Particularly given his friendship with Henry Sidgwick, an educational reformer and a founder of Newnham, and with Henry Fawcett, husband of another founder! Knowing how damaging the educational system had been to the males in her life, saying that to explain her father's brutality, for example, "one would have to discuss the crippling effect of Cambridge and its one sided education" (*MOB* 146) or that she could not "think of [her male relations] as natural human beings" because they had all been "shot into that [great patriarchal] machine" of male education "at the age of ten" (*MOB* 153), she was still angry.

What angers her the most is the isolated nature of her education. In an August 24, 1940 draft of a letter to Ben Nicolson, she writes that her "education (alone among books) was a very bad one" (*L6* 420). Although she calls his Eton/Oxford education bad, too, she always resented having to "delve from books, painfully and all alone," what Thoby and his friends got in the evenings in front of the fire. "Theres nothing like talk as an educator I'm sure" (*L1* 77), she wrote in 1903 (see also *L3* 247). The reactions of the first women to attend Hitchin College for Women, the college that became Girton, make Virginia Stephen's comments about her loneliness even more poignant. There, late evening cocoa parties quickly became "virtual institutions," and as Perry Williams notes, though many an ostensible purpose was always named, the really important thing was that "students met and talked" (179-80). So that when Emily Davies asked the first five students about their experience at the end of the first year (1869), "'Miss Lumsden said that before she came, she used to feel fearfully solitary. . . . Now, she feels herself belonging to a body, and has lost the sense of loneliness'" (176). Williams notes, "What they received from higher education, then, came partly from their academic studies, but more especially from their . . . life in a community of women" (177). Leslie Stephen, grateful to a university that had given him, a delicate and sickly youth, not only an education but also health, friends, and fun (Maitland 62), understood the benefits of such a community. Yet he gave his daughter, the one who "is certainly very like me, I feel" (letter to Julia, 25 Jan. 1891; qtd. in Hill 352), an education "alone among [his] books."

What was that education like? When students walk into a school, they walk into a context that provides structure and support: a campus with buildings and rooms, a divided day, a curriculum that names or implies cultural value, that divides a body of knowledge into topics for study and reading lists, a pedagogical theory that assumes how learning should occur, and most important, a community of teachers and learners. When Virginia Stephen walked into Leslie Stephen's library—her school—she, too, walked into a context, a room that named a curriculum, reflected a pedagogy, and implied a community.

The room itself was large, with "three long windows at the top of the house" (*CE4* 76), probably making it more light-filled than the rest of the house. Books were scattered around Leslie's low rocking chair, where he reclined, rocked, and wrote, and the room must have been ringed with shelves. How his books were arranged, we cannot be sure, but surely there was some system because in Woolf's memories, he easily finds and replaces books when she visits. Rarely disturbed there, reading and writing for at least two or three hours a day even near the end of his life (Maitland 485), he demonstrated daily the advantages of having a room of one's own. To a girl whose own room could be entered at any time by anybody, who read everywhere in the house and was delighted to discover a "back room" that was somewhat private, Leslie Stephen's library must have seemed like a haven. The presence of the library and Leslie's particular use of that space communicated respect for reading and writing, represented privacy and safety, and reflected a refreshing combination of unpretentiousness and seriousness.

My conclusions about this library's curriculum must remain somewhat tentative, since what exists at Pullman is not all that would have existed in Leslie Stephen's study. Some of his books were auctioned off, others are still owned by descendants and collectors, some may have been sold when the Woolfs pruned their library for the move to Mecklenburgh Square in 1939, and many must have been destroyed by the bombs that hit their home there in 1940. For example, some titles on Virginia Stephen's reading list in her 1897 journal, along with some books she says her father read out loud to them, are not in this collection. There seems to be no Austen, though Stephen took her books to the nursing home with him in 1902 (Maitland 485). There's no Dickens, Shakespeare, Sterne, or Trollope, but are we really to believe that Leslie Stephen owned no books by these authors? In addition, some titles, though in the Library of Leonard and Virginia Woolf and with a publication date that suggests Leslie's library, lack his inscription, notes, or drawings: there's no proof of Leslie Stephen's ownership. Thus, the present lack of a certain author or a certain title may not have been a lack then.

Having stated these qualifications, however, some conclusions about the curriculum reflected in Leslie Stephen's library can still be reached. First, what DeSalvo and Hill and others have surmised about the presence of numerous histories and biographies is borne out by this collection; titles such as *The Constitutional History of England from the Accession of Henry VII to the Death of George II* abound, and many titles are a variation on *The Life and Works of Robert Burns* or *The Prose Works of John Milton, With a Life of the Author.* Stephen's sociological approach to literature, his belief that works existed in the context of the times and of a man's life, communicates itself in the physical proximity of biography to collected works. Second, it is primarily a humanities curriculum in history and political science, philosophy and religion, and eighteenth- and nineteenth-century literature, for example, Goldsmith and Pope, Fielding and Richardson, Coleridge and Shelley, Thackeray and Meredith, Lowell and Emerson. Third, his love for eighteenth-century literature is apparent; he owned the eight-volume set of the *Illustrations of the Literary History of the Eighteenth Century*, for example, and duplicate copies of Boswell's *Life of Samuel Johnson.* Fourth, qualifications notwithstanding, it is startling to see how few women appear. Leslie Stephen's library makes it easy to understand why Woolf would claim there was no women's tradition; it existed, as Margaret Ezell has shown, but not there, not on Leslie's shelves.

Perhaps most important, however, this library represents an adult, not a children's curriculum, and it represents a curriculum unchanged for the female student. Thus, it reflects Emily Davies' Cardinal Principal, instituted at Girton, rather than Henry Sidgwick's philosophy at Newnham. That is, the curriculum offered men at Cambridge may not be the best curriculum, Davies said, and it probably should be transformed, but women must be expected to master it, and in the same way; she would not have people assuming women could not achieve as much or as well (Bryant 86-87). The debate between those demanding access to the same education and those insisting that the education offered must be different (a debate that sounds quite familiar) was complicated by what both Deborah Gorham and Felicity Hunt note: reading lists and curricula designed specifically for girls and women were often used to reinforce women's social role (Gorham 39-59; Hunt 18-21). Paradoxically, then, Leslie Stephen's curriculum assumes that male writers have more value than female ones, thus reinforcing traditional gender roles, but it also assumes that women do not need a different curriculum, thus providing a rationale for the *breakdown* of those roles.

The numerous sets of authors' complete works in Leslie Stephen's library make a strong pedagogical statement: literature should *not* be taught from anthologies! We also know his pedagogy was based on freedom. At first, Leslie Stephen assigned books to his daughter, and when she returned one, he would give her another. But soon, "all his books, 'mangy and worthless', . . . were to be had without asking" (*CE*4 80). "Read what you like," he told her. His lessons? "To read what one liked because one liked it, never to pretend to admire what one did not—that was his only lesson in the art of reading. To write in the fewest possible words, as clearly as possible, exactly what one meant—that was his only lesson in the art of writing. All the rest must be learnt for oneself" (*CE*4 80). To encourage such independent thinking, he used a simple teaching strategy: when Virginia returned a book to the library, he asked her "gently, kindly; 'What did you make of it?'" (*MOB* 157). In fact, Woolf uses the word "gentle" twice to describe her father's attitude toward her in the library: he is also "very gentle and pleased" when she comes to the study (*MOB* 112). In contrast to what he did in the rest of the house, Leslie Stephen does not seem to have thrown temper tantrums in the library.

Finally, Leslie Stephen's books and the notes and inscriptions in them reflect a community of letters, a world of reviewing, corresponding, sharing with friends. Whenever Virginia Stephen picked one up of Leslie Stephen's books, she joined a conversation. After all, she might read something like: "All this seems to me to be very like nonsense" or "What, I think, Hume really meant was . . ." (Morley 17, 114).[1] Whenever Virginia Stephen chose a book from among the many sets of complete works that Leslie Stephen owned, she gazed at a writer's whole career. Whenever Virginia Stephen read the inscriptions in Leslie Stephen's books from friends, editors, and loved ones (Henry James giving him a copy of his brother's *Will to Believe* or Hardy sending him a copy of *Wessex Poems*, for example), she experienced literature as an ongoing process with readers. Every time she stepped into that library, she saw and heard, quite literally, in those books and on those shelves, a literary conversation. It might be a male conversation in a male community, but she had access to a literary community at work.

Still, for Virginia Stephen, it was a community on paper. Not only must "all the rest be learned for oneself," but her father had decreed, at least for *her*, it must be learned *by* oneself. Her experience of how painful and lonely it is to piece it all together by oneself, her isolation "among [her father's] books" (*L6* 420), her sense of deprivation, even in the midst of such wealth, compelled Woolf, even more than the ideas and approaches suggested by the library's content did, to provide context and conversation in her own essays. She uses her essays to create a community of learning. "Theres nothing like talk as an educator I'm sure," she writes to Thoby in 1903, and in her essays, she never quit trying to talk her way out of loneliness into community. Ironically, then, Virginia Stephen's loneliness in her father's library may have taught Virginia Woolf, essayist, her greatest lesson: how to create community, "talk as an educator," in and through writing.

### Notes

[1] Grateful acknowledgment is given to Washington State University Libraries for their permission to reproduce these two examples of Leslie Stephen's marginalia. John Morley's book, one of the many Leslie Stephen scribbled in, is in the Library of Leonard and Virginia Woolf at the New Holland Library.

### Works Cited


Annan, Noel. *Leslie Stephen: The Godless Victorian.* New York: Random House, 1984.

Bell, Vanessa. *Notes on Virginia's Childhood.* Ed. Richard F. Schaubeck, Jr. New York: Frank Hallman, 1974.

Bryant, Margaret. *The Unexpected Revolution: A Study in the History of the Education of Women and Girls in the Nineteenth Century.* London: U of London Institute of Education, 1979.

DeSalvo, Louise. "1897: Virginia Woolf at Fifteen." *Virginia Woolf: A Feminist Slant.* Ed. Jane Marcus. Lincoln: U of Nebraska P, 1983. 78-108.

Ezell, Margaret J. M. "The Myth of Judith Shakespeare: Creating the Canon of Women's Literature." *New Literary History* 21.3 (1990): 579-92.

Fenwick, Gillian. *Leslie Stephen's Life in Letters: A Bibliographical Study.* Aldershot: Scholar Press, 1993.

Fisher, Jane Elizabeth. "The Seduction of the Father: Virginia Woolf and Leslie Stephen." *Women's Studies* 18 (1990): 31-48.

Gorham, Deborah. "The Ideology of Femininity and Reading for Girls, 1850-1914." *Lessons for Life: The Schooling of Girls and Women, 1850-1950.* Ed. Felicity Hunt. Oxford: Blackwell, 1987. 39-59.

Hill, Katherine C. "Virginia Woolf and Leslie Stephen: History and Literary Revolution." *PMLA* 96 (1981): 351-62.

Hill, Rosemary. "The pressure of the unsaid." Rev. of *Selected Letters of Leslie Stephen*, by John Bicknell. *Times Literary Supplement* 14 Feb. 1997: 25.

Hunt, Felicity. *Gender and Policy in English Education: Schooling for Girls 1902-*

*44*. London: Harvester/Wheatsheaf, 1991.
Luedeking, Leila. "'Hours in a Library': Virginia Woolf's Exposure to Leslie Stephen's Books." Unpublished paper. Pullman, WA.
Maitland, F. W. *The Life and Letters of Leslie Stephen*. 1906. Detroit: Gale Research, 1968.
Morley, John. *On Compromise*. London: Chapman and Hall, 1874.
Stephen, Leslie. *Hours in a Library*. 1892. 2nd ed. Vol. 1. London: The Folio Society, 1991. 3 vols.
——. "The Study of English Literature." *The Cornhill Magazine* 8 (1887): 486-508.
Williams, Perry. "Pioneer Women Students at Cambridge, 1869-81." *Lessons for Life: The Schooling of Girls and Women, 1850-1950*. Ed. Felicity Hunt. Oxford: Blackwell, 1987. 171-91.
Wilson, J. J. "My First Visit to the Woolf Library and Bloomsbury Collection in Pullman." *Virginia Woolf Miscellany* 22 (1984): 6.
Woolf, Virginia. "Leslie Stephen." *Collected Essays*. Vol. 4. New York: HBJ, 1967. 76-80.
——. *The Letters of Virginia Woolf*. 6 vols. Ed. Nigel Nicolson and Joanne Trautmann. New York: HBJ, 1975-80.
——. *Moments of Being*. 2nd ed. Ed. Jeanne Schulkind. San Diego: Harvest, 1985.
Zink, David D. *Leslie Stephen*. New York: Twayne, 1972.

## Lana Hartman Landon and Laurel Smith

### A Community of Correspondences: Two Women, Letters, and *The Voyage Out*

> [W]e might remind ourselves that criticism is as inevitable as breathing, and that we should be none the worse for articulating what passes in our minds when we read a book and feel an emotion about it, for criticizing our minds in their work of criticism.
> —T.S. Eliot, "Tradition and the Individual Talent"

Our project is a collaborative, critical reading of Virginia Woolf's major novels, beginning with *The Voyage Out*. This reading takes the form of letters exchanged between us—one scholar-teacher, one poet-teacher. We focus on issues of community for two women characters and two women readers. Our epistolary reading of *TVO* provides an unusual opportunity to look at the reading process as exploration, engagement, and reflection in the real time in which the reading occurs. Our project is meant to serve as a model for discussion of Woolf's work as alive and vibrant; our approach corresponds to Woolf's own model of the experimental mode in fiction: the novel's unfolding as questions and response in the course of each chapter. The novel exists as a community endeavor between writer and active reader, rather than as an artifact of authoritarian, one-way expression.

Each exchange of letters was based on the reading of three chapters in *The Voyage Out.* The two exchanges included here present our discussion of chapters 13 through 15 and 16 through 18. The epistolary form is a hybrid of conversation and reflection, while at the same time exemplifying the principle that reading is an intimate activity. This project recognizes that, especially for women, narrative is always embedded in real life and that the author and reader relationship is as real and human as any other.

*Smith to Landon*

10 January 1998

. . . Woolf considered herself uneducated, yet she read widely, intently, and she tells a young May Sarton that poetry is interesting, but novel writing is so much more exciting for the possibilities of experimentation (Lee 689). Observation was to Woolf what music was to Rachel, an immersion and a gift she perhaps took for granted. From these observations such unusual, beautiful fiction comes forth. When she gives up her journals at different points—a breakdown is coming on or the doctor prescribes no writing—it is a "danger signal" according to Hermione Lee (190). How does one observe without writing down?—from an individual activity to the possibility of sharing, of using something later. This *improvisation based on knowledge* seems different from Eliot's *tradition and the individual talent*—and the difference seems connected to community in the new creation (reader and author? something else?).

. . . Hewet wonders what it is to be in love as well—Hirst asks him point blank if he is in love. Hewet tries "reasoning" the answer of being in love, but it will not do. Hewet becomes not a soldier, then, but an unconscious spy. He imitates Rachel and Helen's game of "seeing life" (by the way, this expression was used by Virginia and Vanessa as children). He wanders to the Ambrose villa and listens to Helen and Rachel. After they have gone in, without discovering his presence, he is satisfied: "An exquisite sense of pleasure and relief possessed him"—sounds sexual to me (172). Yet the chapter itself ends with Hewet wondering why human relations are usually so dishonest. If Evelyn M. is the new woman—direct, independent—only her style has changed from generations of women who cannot survive without flirtation with men (another version of Lydia Bennet). Sexual conquest is finally not satisfying by itself. No kidding.

I think one of the wisest passages of the novel comes in the beginning of chapter 15: "When two people have been married for years they seem to become unconscious of each other's bodily presence so that they move as if alone, speak things aloud which they do not expect to be answered, and in general seem to experience all the comfort of solitude without its loneliness" (179). What a wonderful insight into marriage as community—the *comfort* without the *loneliness* of solitude. I suppose this idea could conjure up couples who stay together out of habit more than anything else, but Ridley and Helen are portrayed very affectionately here. I see the mutual comfort derived from very real friendship and sexual chemistry; each of them is truly an independent spirit, too. This marriage seems unthreatened by Hirst's crush on Helen. In fact, Helen can be flattered by Hirst (she blushes when he calls her the most beautiful woman he's ever seen), and she can still advise him to leave Cambridge and be part of a "pattern" that includes herself, a more sensual world, possibilities he has not imagined (190, 192). Again, the improvisation—woman as artist, not muse!—is seen in Helen's view of a pattern of visual images joining the pattern of talk.

*Landon to Smith*

16 January 1998

"Improvisation based on knowledge" is not what Eliot meant by the relationship between the individual artist and tradition; you are absolutely right. In fact, "improvisation based upon knowledge *gleaned from observation*" is a fine and true definition of intuition—altogether different from Eliot's description of art as a series of formal variations. To my mind, intuition is the microscopic observation of detail and nuance and then the basing of conclusions upon the observations. It is what women do. It is the reason women notice details of another woman's dress or a man's behavior—men reject the intuitive conclusion because they have not been able or willing to make the observation. It is, in fact, not an emotional rejection or transcendence of reason, but a fine application of it in a smaller field of vision. It is what Woolf does so very well in print: like fine needlework, it requires attention to detail.

Chapter 13 is a meditation on Rachel and on the question, What is it to be in love? It, too, could be considered an epistemological question—how does one know when one is in love? By conforming to traditional expectations (Eliot)? Or observing the self and the other relentlessly? The men (Dalloway, Hirst, and even Ambrose) are pushing for tradition (Greek, Gibbon, Burke). Helen wants Rachel's education to be something else, an education of the emotions—which is a form of self-knowledge.

. . . The design that Woolf has created now repeats like the pattern on wallpaper—Hewet outside listening, occupying the place that Rachel and Helen had earlier. Your comparison of Evelyn M. to Lydia Bennet is very illuminating—Woolf (looked at from Eliot's point of view, alas!) is rewriting Austen. She seems to have lifted elements from Austen's design (emphasis on marriage and its permutations) without reaching the same conclusions. There is such a variety among the couples, and I agree that Helen and Ridley come off seeming very happy in chapter 15. Helen and Ridley are a strong vision of what is best in marriage: the comfort without the loneliness. It is what I felt from the beginning with my husband Dennis. Helen's comment that she "spoils" Ridley with praise is interesting (191). It is hard to imagine her doing so, and we are given an insight into the marriage. Since we have not seen her do so, it suggests that their intimacy is something even the reader can not be privy to.

I agree that, in many ways, Woolf's most radical idea is that women are the artists and not the muses of life.

. . . The best way I can think of describing the author and reader as a community is that, while reading, I experience all "the comfort of solitude without its loneliness" (179). It is, I suppose, what it is to be in love with reading.

*Smith to Landon*

29 January 1998

. . . It would seem that falling in love is about raising consciousness, along with the very real desire to kiss and be kissed, regardless of what is said. The notion of silence is interesting: Hewet wants to write a novel about Silence, "'the things people don't say'" (204). That ambition seems related to his awareness that women have been silent so long, that men are bullies, that the treatment of brothers and sisters is so different: the contrast of St. John's education and St. John's sister feeding rabbits is grim (197), and it foreshadows something of Woolf's imagining of Shakespeare's sister. When Hewet speaks of his art (or desire to make art), Rachel is depressed—he seems "impersonal" (204). Rachel's description of her music has a similar depressive effect on Hewet. He sees that her art gives her a self-sufficiency which may exclude him. So in the silence between them, each of them is falling in love with the individual who can find some freedom, some identity separate from others—independence is attractive (it is why our husbands love us, *n'est-ce pas*?). Yet Rachel asks herself why they haven't "done with this searching and agony? Why did they not kiss each other simply?" (203).

. . . Chapter 18 shows the agony of Hewet in love—angry that Hirst might be a rival, certain of his feelings for Rachel, but very unsure about marriage. He is right to value his unique devotion with a challenge to convention: "Even the Ambroses, whom he admired and respected profoundly—in spite of all the love between them, was not their marriage too a compromise?" (229). Of course. All marriage, all real friendships (all communities) involve some compromise if we define that term to mean sharing, considering others as well as oneself. Compromise does not have to mean one-sided sacrifice or dissolution of one's identity. And then there is the wonderful chance for enhancement and enrichment because of an additional personality besides one's own. Eventually he imagines a shared freedom. Not a bad image—a worthy life's work.

*Landon to Smith*

8 February

"'[S]cratching on the matchbox'"—what a wonderful way to describe writing! (196). All of chapter 16 charms me, I must admit. Woolf truly seems to have captured the wonder of those first conversations, those falling-in-love conversations, when the beloved is still an undiscovered country, uncharted territory. Of course, the Amazon is, too, and I thought of Conrad as Mrs. Flushing and Mr. Flushing describe the area. Perhaps getting to know a person has the potential for a kind of emotional imperialism. I think that is the case with Hirst—of course, Rachel is in love with him, he thinks; after all, he has TALKED with her. How could she resist his superiority? How civilized and civilizing of him!

I, too, have the feeling that I have been feeding the rabbits for 24 years (I entered graduate school in '74). Somehow feeding the rabbits is the perfect description of gratuitous or undervalued activity. It seems to me that chapter 16 is a kind of early draft of *A Room of One's Own*. The mention of St. John's sister, Hewet's 600 pounds a year, and Hewet's desire to write about silences: Hewet wants to be a female novelist without being female. Hmmm.

"'A house takes up a lot of time if you do it properly'" (198). A wonderfully ambiguous phrase! Does it mean the obvious, that doing housework properly is time consuming? Or does it mean, more subversively, that if it takes up a lot of time, one is then doing it properly? This, dear Laurel, is the sixty-four-thousand dollar, Martha Stewart question! (You know, even her name is perfect: "Martha" was the scurrying, dutiful, household-tending sister Jesus rebuked in Luke's gospel; "stew-art" as in "making an art of stew" is also apropos. If she had not been born, she would have to have been invented! Especially since Stewart is her married name; that is, *stew-art* came to her with marriage!) ANYWAY, the statement is a great insight into how women approach many of life's tasks, consciously or unconsciously. In "Aurora Leigh," Elizabeth Barrett Browning talks about how unnecessarily labor-intensive women's work becomes. It, too, like novel writing, involves a lot of scratching on the matchbox!

. . . Hewet's examination of marriage is key, I think, to any understanding of community in the novel. He is right about marriage transforming people, but I would not agree about compromise. I think that people change as they age, and our relationships (all of them) shape us. Marriage shapes us most of all (only our parents have more influence, I guess). Dennis and I have not *compromised* I don't think, we have *metamorphosed*. Now, I may be nit picking over words, but I do think there is a connotation of loss in "compromise," and I think a good marriage, at least, helps us become more who we are to begin with. (Note that we agree about the concept—we simply don't agree about the word compromise.) I think the beauty of marriage is what he says about Rachel: "there had never been any one like her for talking to" (230). It certainly describes my marriage, our relationship as man and wife, and it describes community, too. Milton (dare I mention the great bugbear of Woolf and others?) wrote eloquently about the need for true conversation as the foundation for a real marriage. It is Buber's "I and thou."

It is finding the ideal reader, after all.

Clearly, correspondence is an impulse toward community through the exploration of similarity and, as such, represents an interpretive endeavor. Through responding and corresponding, we have established that collaboration is what it means to read actively, whether between colleagues, students, or the author and reader. Our experiment in a new form of writing about literature resulted in a new form of reading literature, one which restored the intimacy and pleasure of the reading process while leaving room for critical interpretation.

Community, in the case of Virginia Woolf, as in the case of most authors, refers to the joint ownership of the text as a common location for writing and reading. Reading is a collaborative activity; there is no interpretation without it. To learn from what someone else has seen or found in writing is the foundation of the entire field of literary study. While it may be more obvious in our case, every reading of a literary work establishes a tension between the tradition as author and the reader as individual talent.

**Works Cited**

Eliot, T. S. "Tradition and the Individual Talent." *The Norton Anthology of English Literature*. Vol. 2. 6th ed. Ed. M. H. Abrams. New York: Norton, 1993. 2170-2176.

Lee, Hermione. *Virginia Woolf.* New York: Knopf, 1997.

Woolf, Virginia. *The Voyage Out.* 1915. New York: Penguin, 1992.

## Pierre-Eric Villeneuve

### Communities of Desire:
### Woolf, Proust, and The Reading Process

> The world that I regard is myself; it is the microcosm of my own frame that I cast mine eye on: for the other I use it but like my globe, and turn it round sometimes for my recreation.
> —Sir Thomas Browne, *Religio Medici*

> Proust hardly knew English. From his heroic effort to translate Ruskin he may have picked up something. But what is there common to Ruskin's verbiage and Proust's press of words—each corresponding to some twist or start of the mind?
> —Clive Bell, *Proust*

Virginia Woolf and Marcel Proust. The combination of these two writers is overwhelming for any scholar: where do we enter their work, approach it, how can we not generalize in summing up, how do we compare them, elaborate a dialogue? Certainly, we find in Woolf and Proust different and also similar communities of selves in relation to the somewhat same exhausted world. This might explain my interest in both writers, who speak to my own historicized positionality as a francophone, alienated by the motherland, living in what was formally a British colony, and daily reminded of my anglicized subjection.[1] Indeed, through this specular scope of analysis, my affinity to and for Woolf and Proust raises issues of the exiled's central need for belonging, issues that also serve the theorization of the reading process and help one to understand the forms of alterity these writers experienced in the act of reading their own selves, their own worlds.

My investigation focuses mainly on two short essays which engage with the fluctuations of the reading process, namely Proust's "On Reading," written as an introduction to his French translation of Ruskin's *Sesame and Lilies*, published in 1905, and Woolf's essay titled "Reading," written in 1919. I choose them not only because they both offer insights into what will become their respective conception of the activity of reading as an act of rememoration, but also because they embody a philosophical quest for freedom through reading.

It is important to remember that Proust's career was to end with his death at fifty-one years of age in 1922. Woolf, of course, was at the same time entering what would become her golden years, starting with the radical shift of *Jacob's Room* with its exploration of memory and desire, deeply connecting her to Proust. Other connections exist as well. Let us also consider Woolf's and Proust's common admiration of the Greeks and their exploration of the character's soul in fiction. The importance of speech and the rigor of rhetorical strategies found, for instance, in the dialogue of *Phaedrus*, not only by Plato but in Racine's play as well, were very important to both authors. This admiration also implies a sacralization, allowing a form of identification ranging beyond anything ever experienced by Woolf for any of her contemporaries, where the substance emerging from the reading process is what ultimately matters. We are all too familiar with the tunneling expression of bodily sensations and tears while she was reading the first volume of *La Recherche du temps perdu* in October 1922: "My great adventure is really Proust . . . . How, at last, has someone solidified what has always escaped—and made it too into this beautiful and perfectly enduring substance?" (*L2* 565). How can we not foresee, in this last passage, what will be synthesized some years later in Woolf's examination of the creative process as represented in her own remembering of things past, that is, her elegy *To the Lighthouse* ?

By exploring what my title refers to as communities of desire, I am referring to the role *pathos* plays in the transfer carried out through reading—especially with respect to a breaking away from the regulations of pleasure in language.[2] For instance, Proust's essay "On Reading" already suggests all the paradigms that we will later find in the beginning of *La Recherche*: an exploration of the self as seen from the outside world and the body transmuted by the alterity embodied by written words. For Proust, the direct approach to the alterity of Ruskin's language raises various questions in the act of reading which can be compared to Woolf's own investigation, especially in her coming to terms with the act of reading as *translation*,[3] as she explored her mother tongue within the frame of her familiar yet foreign "outlines of things" offered by the English language. Indeed, her essay "Reading" is an analysis of the conflicts opposing a common unconscious of the English tongue and the individual response foreclosed in the written word as appropriated by the self, in various spaces and times. As different as she is from Proust in her approach, he locating the act of reading from the scope of the narrator outward, and she proceeding from the outside inward, their examination is strikingly similar in the way they construct the self as an extension of print. In fact, the concept of community is relevant to the reading process as a result of the layers the self displays in the depth and the surface of the reading time. For instance, Proust's very direct and specular approach subtly establishes as a survey of the pleasure of reading, including the annoying interruptions and the more frightening moments of loss, evoked by the ideal spectrum of childhood memories:

> There are perhaps no days of our childhood we lived so fully as those we believe we left without having lived them, those we spent with a favorite book. Everything that filled them for others, so it seemed, and that we dismissed as a vulgar obstacle to a divine pleasure: the game for which a friend would come to fetch us at the most interesting passage; the troublesome bee or sun ray that forced us to lift our eyes from the page or to change position. ("On Reading" 99)

Proust juxtaposes the reading process and the figurative time of childhood memories, drawing his community of readers to himself, to the reader he was and is becoming. He also draws attention to the space of interruptions which become patterns of resistance within the secure and comforting place of the text, dialogical in its opposition of inner and outer self, conscious and unconscious drives. The reading process becomes then a metaphor for the body and the unconscious:

> If we still happen today to leaf through those books of another time, it is for no other reason than that they are the only calendars we have kept of days that have vanished, and we hope to see reflected on their pages the dwellings and the ponds which no longer exist. ("On Reading" 99-100)

Woolf, on the other hand, proceeds differently. While we find the same concerns with readership, her attention is more focused on the actual construction of scenes, results of shocks that break in, making her aware of her dislocated and shifting place in relation to her surroundings and situating her as an extension of the outside view. One can argue that this form of phenomenology carries an *ethos*, such as described by Julia Kristeva in her analysis of Proust's use of *le caractère* in the tradition of La Bruyère. What Woolf seeks in the opening of her essays is to direct our attention to the act of reading as a ritual of sensations conflicting with the Law—constructing our vision through hers, a particular *ethos*, indeed capable of analyzing how cultures are constantly changing:

> Why did they choose this particular spot to build the house on? For the sake of the view perhaps. Not, I suppose, that they looked at views as we look at them, but rather as an incentive to ambition, as a proof of power. (*E3* 141)

Like Proust's metaphor of the page to describe, to some extent, the unconscious, Woolf sees the room of the library as a reflection of her own contradictory body in history, time, and space:

> Here they all are; Homer and Euripides; Chaucer; then Shakespeare; and the Elizabethans, and following come the plays of the Restoration . . . . I liked that room. I liked the view across country that one had from the window, and the blue line between the gap of the trees on the moor was the North Sea. I liked to read there. (*E3* 141)

With paradoxical complexity, she draws parallels between the actual physicality of the library where fiction and reality coexist, and her own drives as a reader welcoming new sensations, making them resonate and be part of the patterns that she discovers in the actual world that the books invite.

Contrary to Proust's vision, Woolf is not disturbed by the ongoing energy of the outside world, as we can see in her description, which recalls the movements of "the shadow of the gardener," " the tall ladies that used to come out of the house," or "the butterflies." This is even more evident in the following passage:

> None of these things distracted me in those days; and somehow or another, the windows being open, and the book held so that it rested upon a background of escallonia hedges and distant blue, instead of being a book it seemed as if what I read was laid upon the landscape not printed, bound, or sewn up, but somehow the product of trees and fields and the hot summer sky, like the air which swam, on fine mornings, round the outlines of things.
>
> These were circumstances, perhaps, to turn one's mind to the past. (*E3* 142)

In this case, the "outlines of things" turning Woolf's mind to the past are fraught with the problem of incorporating the written word as she reads.[4] By looking carefully at her various digressions, we—through her narrator—can see the sharp interest she has in the oral traditions found in the works of the Elizabethans, as foreign as their language is to her present reality in many ways. She says: "In all this there is no doubt much exaggeration, much misunderstanding. One is tempted to impute to the dead the qualities we find lacking in ourselves" (*E3* 149). Moreover, her particular dialogue with Sir Thomas Browne is most revealing, and the appropriate choice of *Vulgar Errors* speaks for itself: "pictures of malformed elephants, baboons of grotesque and indecent appearance, tigers, deer, and so on, all distorted and with a queer facial likeness to human beings" (*E3* 153-4) Once again what seems foreign rouses desire and identification. Woolf goes further by trying to find the right place for such sensations in her encyclopedic mind and bodily memories. If she does not altogether understand, she then translates and frames it within her present realities; she adds: "We enter into their shades acquiescent and hopeful, convinced that if light is lacking the fault is ours" (157). How logical becomes then her shift of analysis from Sir Thomas Browne to Cervantes?

Some explanation of my use of the term "translation" is required to define the reading processes. From Proust's dialogue with Ruskin's foreign imagination to Woolf's direct questioning of meaning, a failure to grasp in their own language the concerns they raise gives rise to communities of interpretation. In reading Cervantes, Woolf argues: "Yet what with our natural reverence and inevitable servility, we seldom make our position, as modern readers of old writers, plain. Undoubtedly, all writers are immensely influenced by the people who read them" (*E3* 157), as such modalities of translation also conflict with the question of authorship. In this respect, Woolf is less romantic than Proust, more ready to engage with the status of the writer as a cultural stigma of his or her time, where translation indeed becomes *appropriation*. While Proust sees a direct relation between the written word and the "personality" of the author, Woolf questions what makes whatever elements of that personality *relevant* to her, in her cultural location of reading. Yet Proust, like Woolf in her complex response to Sir Thomas Browne, is also nostalgic and immensely aware of the possibilities raised by the alterity of reading in one's own language. In the world of Racine, for instance, he finds lost sensations, lost bodies:

> It is the very forms of the syntax, laid bare, revered, embellished by his chisel so frank and so delicate, which move us in those turns of phrase familiar to the point of singularity and audacity, and whose abrupt pattern we see, in the sweetest and most touching passages, fading like a swift arrow or coming back again in beautiful broken lines. It is those completed forms, true to the very life of the past, that we go to visit in the work of Racine as in an ancient city which has remained intact. ("On Reading" 127)

My interest in these communities of desire as a way to conceptualize the translation in reading the inside or outside reality of language is more about finding the semiotic potential of affect enclosed in the search for meaning. This gives an interesting coloration to Woolf's response to Proust in *A Room of One's Own* as "wholly androgynous, if not perhaps a little too much of a woman"(*AROO* 93), or her use of the terms like "saturation," "vibration," "intensification" to describe her feeling, to the point that "theres [sic] something sexual in it" (*L2* 525). Since such terms are all expressed in relation to the effect of reading suggested by her definition of poetics.[5] Indeed, can the reading process be understood as a threshold of sexual crisis?

The plurality of desires conflicting in the reading process are not as interesting in their origins as in the effect they produce upon the reader. That is where the issue of translation becomes a complex space of dislocation of meaning, and in this light Woolf's comments on the Russians certainly remain the most illuminating. Ultimately, there is something happening beyond the boundaries of language to make possible the *osmosis* between Proust and Woolf. I refer to the colonizing effect of reading, that is, a cultural process so marvelously interrogated by the young Virginia Stephen, against essentialism, in her essay "The Feminine Note in Fiction." It is reading as an alienating regime that they both want to break away from, a common ground for the unusual freedom Proust probably finds in literally translating the very moralist Ruskin or Woolf in her reading of Proust.

**Notes**

1 See here Butler in her recent book *The Psychic Life of Power: Theories in Subjection* and her definition of subjection: "Subjection consists precisely in the fundamental dependency on a discourse we never choose but that, paradoxically, initiates and sustains our agency" (2).

2 This question of *pathos* in the reading process was extensively theorized by Barthes thoughout his work in the late seventies. His essay titled appropriately "On Reading," in *The Rustle of Language,* contains a section called "Desire": "This certainly confirms that the reader-subject is a subject entirely transposed into the register of the image-repertoire; his whole economy of pleasure consists in nursing his dual relation with the book (i.e., with the image), by shutting himself up alone with it, fastened to it, like the child fastened to the mother and the Lover poring over the beloved face. The iris-smelling bathroom is the very closure of the Mirror, the site of the paradisiac coalescence of subject and Image—of the book."(39). Via the use of Barthes' theory of reading, one can offer a different interpretation of the relation between Proust and Woolf than Mares in her interesting essay "Reading Proust: Woolf and the Painter's Perspective," where she is not afraid to qualify Woolf's appropriation of Proust's *La Recherche* as "misreadings" (67). Another way to look at the location of pleasure in reading can be seen in Cramer's recent essay on Proust's influence on Woolf's *The Years.*

3 The term *translation* is taken here in its English and French definitions. In English it suggests the passage from one language to the other, and in French it problematizes a shift of meaning—very close to the function of the metaphor.

4 This most serious question of how Woolf read Proust is interestingly overlooked by Mares, whose work has paradoxically focused on Woolf's interest in Proust. Mares says: "But the fact that she was reading Proust in translation does not

explain why her reading of individual volumes was so selective, so prolonged, and apparently so haphazarded" (186). Firstly, Mares seems to claim that Woolf only read Proust in translation (which is easily arguable); more importantly she does not answer the ultimate question: how can we verify what Woolf really assimilated in her intense reading of Proust, in the various periods of her intellectual life?

5 Once again, I find Mares's comments on that most celebrated passage of *A Room of One's Own* to be arguable, from the point of view of Woolf's understanding of androgyny. Isn't the fact that she finds Proust "too much of a woman" what makes him, in her reading, ultimately appealing to her, in the specific context of *A Room of One's Own*?

**Works Cited**

Barthes, Roland. "On Reading."*The Rustle of Language*. Trans. Richard Howard. Oxford: Blackwell, 1986. 33-46.

Bell, Clive. *Proust*. New York: HBJ, 1929.

Butler, Judith. *The Psychic Life of Power: Theories in Subjection*. Stanford: Stanford UP, 1997.

Browne, Sir Thomas. *Religio Medici. Works*. Ed. Simon Wilkin. Vol 2. London: Pickering, 1835.

Compagnon, Antoine. *Proust entre deux siècles*. Paris: Seuil, 1989.

Cramer, Patricia. "'Pearls and the Purpoise': *The Years*—A Lesbian Memoir." *Virginia Woolf: Lesbian Readings*. Ed. Eileen Barrett and Patricia Cramer. New York: New York UP. 222-240.

Deleuze, Gilles. *Proust et les signes*. Paris: PU de France, 1964.

Duchêne, Roger. *L'impossible Marcel Proust*. Paris: Robert Laffont, 1994.

Kristeva, Julia. *Le temps sensible: Proust et l'expérience littéraire*. Paris: Gallimard, 1994.

Mares, Cheryl. "Woolf's Reading of Proust."*Reading Proust Now*. Ed. Mary Ann Caws and Eugène Nicole. New York: Peter Lang, 1990. 185-195.

——. "Reading Proust: Woolf and the Painter's Perspective."*The Multiple Muses of Virginia Woolf*. Ed. Diane F. Gillepsie. Columbia: U of Missouri P, 1993. 58-89.

Proust, Marcel. "On Reading." *Ruskin*: *Prefaces to* La Bible d'Amiens *and* Sésame et les Lys. Trans. and ed. Jean Autret, William Burford, and Philip J. Wolfe. New Haven: Yale UP, 1987. 99-165.

——. *Sur la lecture*. Paris: Actes Sud, 1989.

Woolf, Virginia. "The Feminine Note in Fiction."*The Essays of Virginia Woolf*. Ed. Andrew McNeillie. Vol. 1. New York: HBJ. 15-17.

——. "Reading."*The Essays of Virginia Woolf*. Vol. 3. Ed. Andrew McNeillie. New York: HBJ. 141-61.

——. *The Letters of Virginia Woolf*. Ed. Nigel Nicolson and Joanne Trautmann. Vol. 2. London: Hogarth, 1976.

——. A Room of One's Own *and* Three Guineas. London: Penguin, 1993.

**Marilyn Zucker**

## Virginia Woolf and the French Connection: A Devotion to Language

Virginia Woolf's relationship to contemporary French-inspired literary criticism (deconstructive, poststructuralist, Lacanian, French feminist) has been more than uneasy since Elaine Showalter chided Woolf for her "aesthetic" disconnection from real-life concerns. Condemning Woolf for the tragedy of her personal life and for betraying her literary genius (264) Showalter characterized Woolf as the exemplar of the "female aesthetic" (240), detached from and denying worldly concerns and living the renunciatory life whose room of one's own became the grave (297). Showalter's harsh, and I believe inaccurate, assessment of Woolf's work polarized Woolf studies for years and reconfirmed the art/life opposition Woolf expressly rejects. Showalter paints the Woolfian aesthetic as anaesthetic, without feeling, and an-aesthetic, without a vital poetics, cut off from a healthy relation with both the world of experience and the world of art. Unproductive in her divisiveness and rather wrongheaded in her undifferentiated rejection of language-oriented criticism, Showalter nevertheless intuits something important about the relation of Woolf to the late-nineteenth-century Symbolist decadent aesthetic. Thus, it is here that I begin my discussion of that imaginative community—Woolf, the French Symbolists with their "high priest," Mallarmé, the twentieth-century New Novelists and the French-inspired critical approaches, which attend to the varied transparencies and opacities of language and that grew in concert with these literary movements. I'm not looking to ascribe origins and direct precedents, nor to account for every poem, novel, and essay of this complex and diverse field of study. Rather, I'll lightly sketch a larger context of appreciation to suggest how some features of the French literary and critical landscape might enhance our understanding of Woolf's self-reflexive style, whose feminist moorings are nevertheless well oriented outward toward the world, to the reader, for full consummation.

Before I continue, I ask, as I do each time I posit a topic for consideration, why does this matter? Why does what Woolf herself called the "esthetic view of fiction" (*CE*1 109)—the attention to style and language—matter? It matters, I think, because analyzing and understanding the processes of creating meaning in literary works gives access to the processes of making meaning in culture in general. The way we human beings conceptualize frameworks of signification gives foreground and background, contour and nuance to all discourse, from small conversations between individuals, to the shape and scope of academic disciplines, to the cultural conversations that dictate, enforce and liberate our ways of thinking about all manner of subject: about nature, about science, about technology, about issues of class, of race, of gender—and even ideas about ourselves.

Though the aesthetic is often posited in opposition to the political—that which considers power relations in the world—we could think about the two in a more resonant and complementary manner. The political nature of the aesthetic dimension of art has been noted by critics with apparently divergent approaches to literature. John Sturrock, critic of the French New Novel, noting that "to change aesthetic stereotypes *is* ultimately to help in changing reality" (11), sounds like Marxist critic Herbert Marcuse: "The political potential of art has only its aesthetic dimension. There may be more subversive potential in the poetry of Baudelaire and Rimbaud than in the didactic plays of Brecht" (xii-xiii). So, with inspiration from materialist critic Marcuse, I turn briefly to the Symbolists as we think about Woolf's efforts to revise prose fiction to convey "truth or spirit, life or reality" in literary form, reaffirming the role of language as agent, creator, expressor of the real.

* * *

Yes, Elaine Showalter was on to something. Virginia Woolf's writing indeed shows resonance with the nineteenth-century French Symbolist aesthetic. And here I'm interested in the literary movement larger than the one called Symbolism, the Paris-based literary school of the decade 1885-1895. The work of Woolf and the Symbolists (among them, Baudelaire, Rimbaud, Mallarmé) moves to restore emotional power and music to language—for her, to prose, for them, for the most part, to poetry—and shows a preoccupation with words, with the radiance and shimmer of language. Their work attempts to convey an elusive reality-behind-appearances and a belief in the nondiscreteness of "categories of being" or as Robert Cohn says of the Symbolists, a sense of "the universal analogy, [in] the ultimate harmony or connectivity of all reality" (3) and its consequent expressions of synaesthesia and transformation. Woolf, for example, knows of Rimbaud's famous poem "Vowels"—"Black A, white E, red I, green U, blue O . . ." (123)—as she ascribes colors to words in *The Waves*: "Rough black [NO], the golden [come]" (*TW* 298). Woolf and the Symbolists practiced the accretion of image upon image creating dense webs of radiating meaning, the exploration of the prose poem form, and the intimation of things by suggestion and nuance rather than by denotation and naming. Woolf's idea that it is fatal for the vitality of words to pin down meaning echoes the great Symbolist Mallarmé who believed that naming an object destroys its poetic enjoyment. But Mallarmé took this to heart so completely, weaving intricate cryptic webs of abstraction and ambiguity, that he spent his life working "on his meager harvest of poetic survivals, polishing and repolishing them, and dreaming of the Great Work which was never to be written because the plane of perfection on which he places it in his imagination forbade the possibility of its ever becoming a reality" (Balakian 74). Severed from vital connection with the world, the symbolism of Mallarmé devolved into a decadent, hermetic, art-for-art's-sake movement, withering and dying like des Esseintes, the renunciatory hero of the period's most well-known novel, *A Rebours* and a figure Showalter obliquely refers to in her condemnation of Woolf and other "female aesthetics."

The theme of the simultaneous necessity and danger of the study of the self in solitude permeates both the Symbolists' poetry and Woolf's work. The tendency to reclusiveness apparent in the decadent heroes appears in several of Woolf's characters, but the temptation to withdraw and retreat from the world is tempered in her work by the call back to the activity of daily life. Bernard, for example, becomes distracted from self-reflexive mediation: "What did the hairdresser see on the street? It is thus that I am recalled. For I am no mystic; something always plucks at me—curiosity, envy, admiration, interest in hairdressing and the like bring me to the surface" (*TW* 371). Woolf and the Symbolists, however, finally part company, for not only do their respective literary characters deal differently with the call to reclusiveness, but the authors and their language do as well. Woolf, like Mallarmé, recognized the limitations of language for conveying reality and the appeal of solitary, isolated reflection required for its experience. Yet she, instead of trickling words out in precious couplets as he did, faced the world with a proliferation of books, thus demonstrating the faith that although language is less than adequate for the job of conveying "truth and reality," its exploration in literature is, as Sturrock says, "the objectification of the only freedom we possess" (33).

It seems important to stop here to reemphasize the "speaking to the face of nothingness" that Woolf undertakes. Whatever her feelings about silence, absence, and non-being, all suggesting a repudiation of the real world, her work, by its sheer abundance let alone its genius, affirms her connection to that world; the person who writes a dozen novels, hundreds of essays, thousands of letters and diary pages clearly believes in the value of the written word for conveying something, if not everything, of reality. Woolf believed that the writer as seeker of truth need partake vigorously of the world of experience: "It is not to the cloistered disciplinarian mortifying himself in solitude that we are to turn, but to the well-sunned nature, the man who practises the art of the living to the best advantage, so that nothing is stunted." (*CE*1 9), unlike Mallarmé, who used cigarettes "to put some smoke" between the world and himself. Poetry indeed had grown "aloof in the possession of her priests" as Woolf notes (*GR* 17), but their devotion to language was not lost on her.

Shortly after the Continent produced a literature that prefigured some of Woolf's language-oriented explorations, it saw the birth of a critical mode that would give access to some of her more opaque literary creations, confirming Vico's notion of the rather simultaneous development of the art form and its critical apparatus. Ferdinand de Saussure's influential work—a series of lectures given between 1906 and 1911, and published posthumously in

1915—provides the departure point for contemporary structuralist criticism. The linguistic principle Saussure formulated of pertinence to my discussion reveals the arbitrary nature of language: at its simplest, the notion that the word and its referent (the "sound pattern" and its "concept") are not related by any necessary or causal sequence, by no "natural connexion in reality" (Saussure 69). The application of the word *cat* to a furry four legged creature inheres in the word's difference from other words (mat or cap, for example) and not in any intrinsic relation between word and object. Woolf herself understood the creation of a word from the admixture of sound and sense, as she rephrases this primary point of Saussure:

> [L]et a sufferer try to describe a pain in his head to a doctor and language at once runs dry. There is nothing ready made for him. He is forced to coin words himself, and, taking his pain in one hand, and a lump of pure sound in the other (as perhaps the people of Babel did in the beginning), so to crush them together that a brand new word in the end drops out. (*M* 11)

The arbitrariness of the sign implies that meaning is not inherent in words themselves but agreed upon by "collective habit or on convention, which comes to the same thing" (Saussure 68). This single feature of Saussurean linguistics suggests the created quality of sign systems, language being one of them, and shifts the relation between perceiver and perceived from one of simple objective detection to one of collective agreement. That language conveys meaning by collective habit or convention attests to biases, prejudices and power relations tacit and implicit in its underlying structures. Disruptions of those biases, prejudices and power relations permeate Woolf's writing. And of course, detection of those disruptions motivates the application of certain aspects of structuralist criticism to her writing.

Unfortunately the appropriation of Saussurean linguistics by male-biased theorists (among them, Lévi-Strauss, Derrida, Lacan) has produced a body of thought hostile to the exploration of female textual presence, which is very much at the heart of Woolf's *oeuvre*. Theories in several disciplines—anthropology, literary criticism and psychology, for example—highlight poststructuralism's loyalty not to Saussure's first principle, "the sign is arbitrary" (67), but to extrapolations that focus on the gap of difference (the absence) that creates signification rather than the multiply suspended resonances (the plenitudinous presences) that create meaning. Focussing on the internal dynamics of sign systems, these theorists *have* produced a hermetic view of literature obsessed with the machinations of language: a twentieth-century critical version of the decadent art-for-art's-sake. But by rejecting or neglecting the power dynamics inherent in the structures of language because of ahistoric, female-excluding movements of the prevailing literary critical mode some critics have thrown the baby out with the bathwater, thus missing a significant aspect of Woolf's feminist effort. I note that the burgeoning field of feminist narratology finally offers a productive analytic matrix for exploring the interrelationship of sound and sense, of word and concept, of form and content or the myriad ways that duality has been posited.[1]

Leap forward now to 1985, to Woolf's centenary celebrated in Paris and in New York with a staging of *Freshwater*, with performances by Alain Robbe-Grillet, Eugene Ionesco and Nathalie Sarraute. These stars of France's literary life—the surrealist Ionesco and the New Novelists Robbe-Grillet and Sarraute—pay homage to Virginia Woolf, acknowledging the connection of their work to hers. In the work of New Novelists, story and plot are no longer coherent; things happen, but the relationship between events and scenes is problematic. Robbe-Grillet, for example, has said that he finds it impossible to tell a story. Characters, too, never come to life as they do in realistic novels but remain creations in words, projections of the novelistst's personal concerns and obsessions. Sturrock sums up the New Novel, which, he says, deprives its readers of the "consolations of a mechanistic sequence of events, with its confident marriage and causes with effects, and of an essentialist psychology which lends a spurious coherence to the activity of unknowable other minds" (9). Here we think of Woolf's comments on her "characters" in *The Waves*: "Odd that they (The Times) shd. praise my characters when I meant to have none" (*D*4 47); on her own inability to "make up plots" (*D*3 160); on her refusal of the conventions of realistic narrative, which supply a series of mechanistic "gig lamps" to guide and support the reader; and the causality-questioning comment of Lily Briscoe: "How did one add up this and that and conclude that it was liking one felt, or disliking?" (*TTL* 24). The New Novelists, continues Sturrock, focus on the creative process, challenging the notion that there are absolute forms of representation and questioning all attempts to pretend so (5). Their challenge addresses conventions of ordering, representing and projecting reality but is often considered an attack, a rejection of reality itself (Sturrock 10).

The fierce literary materialism of the Symbolists and the French New Novelists, and the Surrealists, whom I've not discussed, foregrounds the role of language in creating as well as in expressing what we understand as reality. The word *materialism* might surprise us in this context. As in other instances regarding the literary work, the word *materialist* indicates concern with the conditions in the real world, in the case of *A Room of One's Own*, for example, with the relation between a good meal and inspired thinking. Even Woolf herself, as she calls the Edwardians "materialist" writers, locates her disagreement with them in their attendance to qualities and features of the objective world, instead of the real subject of fiction, "truth or spirit." In most cases, "materialist" or "material" applies not to the medium and its manipulation in the form or style of the work of art but to the world that work describes, portrays, represents.[2] If we call Marxist literary critics materialists for their concern and attention to the material quality of life depicted in the literary work, we might see poststructuralist literary critics as materialists for their attention to the actual material that constitutes the literary work. Sturrock mentions a similar point regarding the New Novel: "I use this Marxian term [material evidence] deliberately because it can be argued that with the narrative structure of the New Novel the novel has entered a materialist phase: Claude Simon, indeed, was quick to claim that Robbe-Grillet's *La Jalousie* . . . was 'the first truly materialist novel'" (28-9).

The literary materialism of Woolf has its gender-inflected contour. Words matter as matter, stuff, the building blocks of literature—with words printed on the page, traced in the sky, etched in the stone, feathered in the imagination—and in this way, her materialism connects with that of the French literary and critical tradition. But for her, words also matter as *mater*, as mother, perhaps an idealized and sentimental essentialist association, but I use the word here to suggest a matrix, a motherbed of wholeness among all aspects of reality that Woolf created out of the material of her life's work—language. Writing helped cure her sense of injury and hurt: "It is only by putting it [some real thing behind appearances] into words that I make it whole; this wholeness means that it has lost its power to hurt me" (*MOB* 72). Her writing addressed also the "second severance from the body of our mother" (*TW* 261) that patriarchal culture and language inflicts upon its daughters and its sons.[3] Woolf's deeply feminist material language invites us to reject that which has been posited as the irreconcilable duality of the form of the literary work and life-in-the-world but rather to apprehend their irrevocable similarity and connectedness.

## Notes

[1] See, for example, Mezei.

[2] Moi, generally astute in her insistence on the need to study Woolf's language, blurs the same boundary between world and text. She notes Michèle Barrett as the exceptional critic who indeed attends to the "material" aspect of Woolf's writing, taking into account "material conditions which have structured women's consciousness" (16).

[3] See Kristeva, whose analysis of symbolic/semiotic language in the work of avant-garde writers (all male) neglects, I believe, important feminist aspects of Woolf's radical writing and of the intelligible rather than irruptive aspects of her semiotic language. In so doing, Kristeva forwards the androcentric Lacanian perspective rather than offering a way of understanding the comprehensible maternal presence of a feminist writer such as Woolf.

## Works Cited

Balakian, Anna. *The Symbolist Movement.* New York: Random, 1967.

Barthes, Roland. "Lecture in Inauguration of the Chair of Literary Semiology, College de France, January 7, 1977." Trans. Richard Howard. *October* 8 (1979): 3-16.

Cohn, Robert. *Toward the Poems of Mallarmé.* Berkeley: U of California P, 1963.

Kristeva, Julia. *Revolution in Poetic Language.* Trans. Margaret Waller. New York: Columbia UP, 1984.

Marcuse, Herbert. *The Aesthetic Dimension.* Boston: Beacon, 1978.

Mezei, Kathy. *Ambiguous Discourse: Feminist Narratology & British Women Writers.* Chapel Hill: U of North Carolina P, 1997.

Moi, Toril. *Sexual/Textual Politics.* London: Methuen, 1985.

Rimbaud, Arthur. *Complete Works.* Trans. Paul Schmidt. NY: Harper, 1975.

Saussure, Ferdinand de. *Course in General Linguistics.* Ed. Charles Bally and Albert Sechehaye. Trans. Roy Harris. London: Duckworth, 1983.

Showalter, Elaine. *A Literature of Their Own.* Princeton: Princeton UP, 1977.

Sturrock, John. *The French New Novel.* London: Oxford UP, 1983.

Woolf, Virginia. *Collected Essays.* Ed. Leonard Woolf. Vol 1. London: Chatto & Windus, 1966.

——. *Moments of Being* Ed. Jeanne Schulkind. 2nd ed. San Diego: Harvest, 1985.

——. *Granite and Rainbow.* New York: HBJ, 1958.

——. *The Moment and Other Essays.* New York: HBJ, 1974.

——. *To The Lighthouse.* San Diego: Harvest, 1989.

——. *The Waves.* San Diego: Harvest, 1959.

# Trauma and Loss

**Michelle N. Mimlitsch**

## Powers of Horror and Peace: Abjection and Community in Virginia Woolf's *Between the Acts*

In *Powers of Horror*, Julia Kristeva defines abjection as the disarming mix of attraction and loathing one feels for objects that remind us of our own fragility and mortality, of the terrifying permeability of the boundaries that separate one's "clean and proper body" (72), and one's "*own and clean self*" (65), from others, the Other, nature, and death. Thus bodily fluids and excretions, food, birthing, or a corpse all are signifiers of the abject, sucking us into a vortex of fascination and dread. Kristeva writes that abjection is caused by "what disturbs identity, system, order. What does not respect borders, positions, rules. The in-between, the ambiguous, the composite" (4).

Although several critics have used Kristeva's theory of the semiotic to read Woolf's novels successfully,[1] little has been written about the presence of what Kristeva calls "abjection" in her work. *Between the Acts*, however, explores abjection at several levels; much of its darkness comes from the different shades of fear and horror threatened boundaries of all kinds engender. Nevertheless, in what Mark Hussey has described as "a *rhythm* between the individual center and the public circumference" (145) the novel also asserts the possibility for ambiguous personal boundaries that engender peace and community rather than isolated horror. Certainly, the novel examines abjection and the need people feel for a meticulously distinct body and subjectivity; however, the momentum toward the breakdown of borders in a quest for unity in the novel cannot be ignored. Woolf's novel attempts to face abjection and then write beyond it, to inscribe the "'We' . . . composed of many different things" that Woolf pondered in her diary while planning *Between the Acts* (*D*5 135).

Abjection in *Between the Acts* centers on the need for a distinctly bordered self. Things that threaten those borders become the horrifying obsessions that plague the characters in the novel. The reactions of Isa and Giles to the day's newspaper provide an early hint of this kind of abjection. Isa reads a story about a rape, the abject violation of a woman's body, the attraction of sexuality written over by the horror of violence (20). Giles, on the other hand, is enraged by news of the war in Europe (46), war that threatens to transform the body into a corpse, to violate national and cultural boundaries, and to destabilize the world as Giles knows it. Both Giles and Isa will come back to these stories in their thinking throughout the day, nursing the "attraction and repulsion" (Kristeva, 167) inherent in the abject. For each of them, these distant bits of news carry an idea that threatens intimately, yet fascinates.

The drive to separate oneself from that which is strange, ugly, or even simply other is also apparent in the guests who participate in the pageant. The emphasis placed on names throughout *Between the Acts* incessantly reminds us of the distinctions between individuals. Virtually every performer in the pageant is named, marked out as a discrete individual. Similarly the audience is named, in passing references and single quoted comments. Often the rush of names is confusing; a descriptive phrase would help the reader identify the character better, but would lessen the sense of distinction.

The reactions to Albert, the village idiot, are another indicator of the need to separate, to cast off that which is strange or threatening to one's conception of oneself as a normal, "clean and proper" person. When he first appears in the pageant there is immediate concern in the audience: "Suppose he suddenly did something dreadful? . . . [Mrs. Elmhurst] half covered her eyes, in case he did do—something dreadful" (87). Significantly, she only *half* covers her eyes: she is horrified but also intrigued, her abjection evident in her pretense of not wanting to see. A half-covered eye, after all, *does see.* The discomfort the audience feels in the presence of the village idiot becomes clearer at the close of the novel, when Albert carries a collection basket out among the audience while the rector concludes his interpretation of the pageant, advocating community, a sense of wholeness among all the people present, including the disturbing idiot: "He too . . . is part of ourselves. *But not a part we like to recognize*, Mrs. Springett added silently" (emphasis added;194). Because of his disability, Albert represents a part of people—the infirm, the fragile, the incomplete—they do not care to recognize. He marks a point of contact with abjection, a defilement some wish the Reverend Streatfield to "excorcise" (*BTA* 194) in a ritual of cleansing that would re-establish the boundaries between the self one identifies as "me" and that which one would cast away.

Perhaps the strongest marker of otherness in *Between the Acts* is homosexuality—whether real or simply rumored—as it appears in both Miss La Trobe and William Dodge.[2] Kristeva posits that all taboos, such as that against homosexuality, function to mark the boundaries of the "clean and proper" from that which is abject. Concomitantly, she argues that an individual's abject hatred of Others "to the extent that it settles the subject within a socially justified illusion [of identity]—is a security blanket" (136-137). In *Between the Acts*, Giles's homophobia, manifest in his loathing for William Dodge, allows him such a security blanket—an illusion of an abjection-free self, and a clearly marked social and individual boundary. Kristeva writes: "when reason attempts to *globalize*, *unify*, or *totalize* . . . the crushing anarchy or nihilism of discourse topples over and . . . an object appears—an object of hatred and desire, of threat and aggressivity, of envy and abomination" (178). For Giles Oliver, that object is the homosexual. Giles's negative response to William is almost immediate:

> *His expression . . . gave Giles another peg on which to hang his rage* as one hangs a coat on a peg, conveniently. A toady; a lickspittle; . . . not a man to have straightforward love for a woman . . . but simply a ——— At this word, which he could not speak in public [even in this unspoken sentence], he pursed his lips. (emphasis added; 60)

Already mired in abjection—feeling his own boundaries threatened by the danger of war—and already trying to totalize that threat by connecting it to all his other grievances ("the conglomeration of things [that] pressed you flat" [47]), all the things that defy his idea of himself, Giles's reason "topples over," finding William a "peg on which to hang his rage." Even Giles himself recognizes that his loathing shores up the boundary of his own self: he thinks later in the novel how lucky it is that he can hate William rather than himself (111). William's homosexuality, lying as it does in the ambiguous space of abjection, the space which marks the permeability of borders and the fragility of laws, poses a threat Giles must exorcise with his hatred.

We see the vehemence of this hatred and the profundity of his fear when Giles, walking toward the barn and thinking, among other things, about "Dodge (perversion)" (99), comes upon and kills the grotesquely intertwined snake and toad in the grass. As Barbara A. Babcock has observed (103), all of the elements of abjection are here: consumption of food (in this case food that really does destroy the consumer), blood and the image of birthing, made more abject by its inversion, death. It is this complex of abjection Giles feels he must stamp out, this physical instance of violated borders (the bodies of toad and snake) which represents the violation of sexual taboo as well.

The link between the abjection of the toad and snake and the sexual abjection that lies at the center of William's character is made clear if we remember that Giles has thought of him as a "toady" (60) and that William identifies himself as a snake in his imagined coming-out to Lucy Swithin. In his "painful history of abjection" (Barber 425) he declares, "I'm a half-man . . . a flickering, mind-divided little *snake in the grass*" (emphasis added;

73). Kristeva comments that "abjection is above all ambiguity" (9); if so, William Dodge, "half-man," and "mind-divided," is essentially abject. Taught by his school companions to view his own desire as repulsive, William is at the center of his being the kind of ambiguity Giles cannot allow in his psychological framework.

In spite of all this abjection, however, *Between the Acts* resists the idea that horror is inherent in every breakdown of distinction. Often, in fact, the sense of connection or community, of a blurred boundary with a positive connotation, grows directly out of a character or circumstance that at first appears to function only as an agent of abjection. In the process of naming cited above there exists, along with the tendency to mark distinction, a tendency to note relationships. When we read that the fishmonger's delivery boy's name—like those of his customers—is in the Domesday Book (31), we are reminded of the heritage a name can carry, of the historical connections between people and places, and of the ways in which names *join* as well as separate. These ideas surface again in the question of a roll call at the pageant, at which, had there been one, half of the people present would have declared they were there in place of their parents or grandparents (75).

Also, the verbal gesture of naming oneself acts as a catalyst for connection at critical points in the novel. When William realizes Lucy has forgotten his name, he longs to tell her, "I'm William" (70). When he finally does, it initiates a moment of shared intimacy between them in which Lucy explains that she has taken him away from the others to ease her own tension. His imagined coming-out follows immediately, ending in the phrase, "you've healed me . . ." (73). Each has found relief, albeit briefly, in the other's company, connected by the sharing of a name. Similarly, a simple exchange of names precedes the intimacy between William and Isa: " 'I'm William,' he said . . . 'I'm Isa,' she answered. Then they talked as if they had known each other all their lives" (114).

Much of the impetus toward community comes from three of the central female characters in *Between the Acts*: Isa Oliver, Lucy Swithin, and Miss La Trobe. Isa, who feels throughout the novel torn between love and hate for Giles, is, unlike her husband, able to accept this fundamental ambiguity and look beyond it. Isa's "love and hate"(66, 90, 92, 215) parallel Kristeva's "attraction and repulsion," yet despite this abjection inspired by her husband Isa is able to envision peace as "the third emotion" (92), and at times to practice it. In contrast to Giles's need to stamp out the threat of William's homosexuality, Isa accepts it too:

> Isabella guessed the word that Giles had not spoken. Well, was it wrong if he was that word? Why judge each other? Do we know each other? Not here, not now. . . . but somewhere surely one sun would shine and all without a doubt, would be clear. (61)

Where Giles perceives the border marked by the abjection of William's homosexuality as intolerable, Isa, perfectly aware of the crossing between "pure" and "impure," believes that within this here and now of abject ambiguity there lies the possibility for reconciliation, for community, for a time when "*one* sun would shine" (emphasis added), and "all would be clear."

Lucy Swithin, too, is able to find connection in the murk of abjection. She is able to "heal" William Dodge, at least for a moment. Her brother, although unable to share her religious faith, identifies her as a unifier (118). Assuming Bart imagines her thoughts correctly, she ponders two of Isa's three emotions, but remains unconflicted by hate or repulsion. Unlike all the others, she is spared the failure of religion Kristeva identifies as a hallmark of the modern, and is therefore able to eliminate all boundaries in peace, a universal harmony (175). Others in the novel dismiss her thinking as quaint, simple, a self-deception. But Lucy, too, is aware of people's need for boundaries and distinctions. It is telling that she seeks her private vision in the lily pool—murky and obscured by the potentially strange threshold of plants growing on water. She looks into this darkness for a glimpse of the fish which she connects to "'Ourselves'" (205). She knows her brother would ridicule her. Nevertheless, "She [returns] to her private vision; of beauty which is goodness; the sea on which we float. Mostly impervious, but surely every boat sometimes leaks?" (205). Like Isa, who finds potential for reconciliation in the threat to bordered identity, Lucy searches for beauty and goodness not in imperviousness, but in the thought that "surely every boat sometimes leaks." William accuses Lucy of not believing in history because she supposes the Victorians were just like themselves but wearing different clothes (175); yet it is Lucy who reads a history of England that begins in prehistory, populated by mammoths, mastodons, and primeval forests. Unconcerned with the minute distinctions between people, her sense of history is as all encompassing as her sense of harmony. Her "one-making" (175) asserts connections *in spite of* vast spaces of difference.

Miss La Trobe's vision is far more ambiguous, but no less ambitious than Lucy Swithin's. The play she writes (like Woolf's novel) attempts to create community out of fragments—to violate borders just enough to show the connections between individuals. The whole pageant is a patchwork of literary fragments culminating in the textually ambiguous "Ourselves" on the program (177). Her audience fiercely resists this idea. Waiting for her attempt, "All their nerves were on edge. They sat exposed. . . . They were neither one thing nor the other; neither Victorians nor themselves" (178). In this state of ambiguous identity, however, each person in the audience struggles to maintain the boundaries of his or her discrete self, to fend off abjection by thinking that it is impossible that Miss La Trobe could capture "me" (179). Each believes him- or herself to be resistant to categorization or connection. But this belief requires a conscious effort; the thought process is labored through. And as the audience fidgets, Miss La Trobe waits, wanting to expose them to real, present time. But the experiment goes wrong, the audience begins to evade her design, and only a fortuitous rainshower falling like "all people's tears" (180) brings them back together again. Earlier in the pageant music had performed this service, preventing the audience from being broken up prematurely. Ultimately, though, fragmentation proves to be the grand gesture of the pageant: Miss La Trobe's use of mirrors to show the audience "Ourselves" shows them, in fact, only parts (184). The audience perceives this as cruel, for she has forced a kind of abjection upon them, in which they must perceive themselves as non-unified, not securely bounded as one whole "clean and proper body" but rather as "*orts, scraps and fragments*" (188). Miss La Trobe's purpose, however, is to lead them to a community on the other side of abjection. Fearing they won't understand her vision, she tries to explain from the bushes to the side of the stage, encouraging them to see how "civilization" can indeed be built by "orts, scraps and fragments like ourselves," and encouraging them to hear "*the gramophone affirming*" (188). Thus once again we have a movement toward connection and community, toward a breaking down of boundaries of whole and discrete selves that is gratifying rather than laced with horror.

Significantly, in all of these cases, this unity comes not from a denial of abjection, but from a recognition, even an elaboration, of it, *followed by* an attempt to move beyond it into a community where boundaries need not be impermeable for people to feel comfortable. Isa hopes for "one sun" to rise on all separate people; Lucy for a larger harmony in which each individual simply adds to the whole; Miss La Trobe for a unity made up of fragments. Furthermore, we must remember that Miss La Trobe is also located in the abject because of her possible lesbianism; her vision of fragmentary unity is a "gift" (209) from within abjection. It is a "triumph" (209) which comes directly out of abjection—a victory not unrelated to the peace William Dodge is able to bring to Lucy Swithin. The triumph may fade—Miss La Trobe believes her gift fails (209)—but the gift is given, coming from no other source than the primary site of abjection in the novel.

Kristeva identifies a "dizziness" that "leads [Céline] to the fulfillment of a kind of challenge to abjection; it is only thus that he can, by naming it, both have it exist and go beyond it" (190). However, where Céline's movement beyond the signification of abjection "opens out on the *void*" (191), in Woolf it leads to a kind of connection within the space of fragile boundaries, a momentary indistinctness of the separate self which is, nevertheless, horror free.

The ultimate depiction of this moment in *Between the Acts* occurs as the pageant's audience disperses. The unifying, affirming gramophone continues to play, its music repeating the refrain, "*Dispersed are we*" (196). This simple phrase, in fact, sums up the message: dispersal (separated subjectivity marked by boundaries operating independently) is capped by "we"—unity has the last word, even in a phrase that reinforces fragmentation. Similarly, the five pages that follow of polyphonic greeting and farewells, gossip and conversation are all joined, all one, connected by the ellipses between each sentence or phrase, even as they represent the distinct thoughts and ideas—the discrete subjectivities—of the dozens of now and only now unnamed speakers. Woolf's ellipses shore up language's ability to signify a community in which borders between subjects are unclear yet in which neither the characters nor the reader seem threatened with the horror of abjection.

Even the last scene of *Between the Acts* emphasizes the possibility for a space beyond abjection that is productive rather than destructive. The novel closes with Isa and Giles, and a coming to the fore of the love and hate that have drawn them together yet torn them apart throughout: "Alone, enmity was bared; also love. Before they slept, they must fight; after they had fought, they would embrace. From that embrace another life might be born" (219). Before peace, in the form of sleep, there is hate, in the form of fighting, and love, in the form of the embrace. But the conflict between attraction and repulsion, love and hate, can lead to peace, and can produce new life, extending the human community. Kristeva does not really discuss the pleasure-filled, (re)productive version of human sexuality in *Powers of Horror*—it does not fall into the category of abjection. And yet it is a space wherein we can experience what might in another context be abjection as pure pleasure, even joy. By ending *Between the Acts* with the first words of the fight that will precede an embrace, Woolf reiterates the message that such community can exist—that one can embrace a self not wholly distinct from all others, and find not horror but joy.

## Notes

1 For example, Bonnie Kime Scott has applied Kristeva's theories about women and feminine writing to *Between the Acts* specifically, while Makiko Minow-Pinkney has written extensively about the semiotic and subjectivity in Woolf's fiction.

2 William Dodge is more often identified by critics as doubtlessly homosexual than Miss La Trobe. See for example David Eberly's "Woolf and Gay and Lesbian Modernism."

## Works Cited

Babcock, Barbara A. "Mud, Mirrors, and Making Up: Liminality and Reflexivity in *Between the Acts*." *Victor Turner and the Construction of Cultural Criticism: Between Literature and Anthropology*. Kathleen M. Ashley, ed. Bloomington: Indiana UP, 1990. 86-116.

Barber, Stephen. "Lip-Reading: Woolf's Secret Encounters." *Novel Gazing: Queer Readings in Fiction*. Eve Kosofsky Sedgwick, ed. Series Q. Durham: Duke UP, 1997. 401-43.

Eberly, David. "Talking it All Out: Homosexual Disclosure in Woolf." *Virginia Woolf: Themes and Variations: Selected Papers from the Second Annual*

*Conference on Virginia Woolf.* Vara Neverow-Turk and Mark Hussey, eds. New York: Pace UP, 1993. 128-34.

Hussey, Mark. ""'I" Rejected; "We" Substituted': Self and Society in *Between the Acts.*" *Reading and Writing Women's Lives: A Study of the Novel of Manners.* Bege K. Bowers and Barbara Brothers, eds. Ann Arbor: UMI Research Press, 1990. 141-52.

Kristeva, Julia. *Powers of Horror: An Essay on Abjection.* Leon S. Roudiez, trans. New York: Columbia UP, 1982.

Minow-Pinkney, Makiko. *Virginia Woolf and the Problem of the Subject.* Brighton: The Harvester Press, 1987.

Scott, Bonnie Kime. ' The Word Split Its Husk': Woolf's Double Vision of Modernist Language." *Modern Fiction Studies.* 32:3. Autumn, 1988. 371-85.

Woolf, Virginia. *The Diary of Virginia Woolf.* Vol. 5. Ed. Anne Olivier Bell, assisted by Andrew McNeillie. San Diego: Harcourt, 1984.

Woolf, Virginia. *Between the Acts.* 1941. San Diego: Harcourt, 1970.

## Marlene A. Briggs

### Veterans and Civilians: The Mediation of Traumatic Knowledge in *Mrs. Dalloway*

How does traumatic knowledge become transmissable—
how can it extend into personal and cultural memory?
—Geoffrey Hartman, "On Traumatic
Knowledge and Literary Studies"

A re-examination of *Mrs. Dalloway* raises many questions central to the developing discourse of trauma theory, a body of critical literature which has arisen in response to the literary, psychological and ethical legacies of recent historical catastrophes. For instance, how does *Mrs. Dalloway* textualize the aftermath of the Great War? Specifically, how does combat trauma problematize fictional representation? And how do the dynamics of transference configure the reception and transmission of trauma? Moreover, in what ways does Woolf's fiction both critique and inevitably participate in the contests which attend the cultural transmission of traumatic knowledge? In post-war London, interpretation is the only explicit connection between Clarissa Dalloway and Septimus Smith, civilian and veteran, respectively, in a text which poses the nature of their connection as its major problematic. My discussion of *Mrs. Dalloway* destabilizes the familiarities of their fictive relationship through its exploration of Clarissa's role as a "belated witness" (Felman 108) to the traumatic aftermath of combat. Septimus does not reassimilate into civilian life after his war experience; rather, his death disperses his traumatic experience into traces, which are then (re)configured by civilian communities. Such (re)configurations are the objects of cultural contestation in *Mrs. Dalloway*. Issues of trauma, narrative and community, then, will be discussed in relation to the political and ethical contests which constituted membership in civilian or veteran communities in the aftermath of the Great War.

Focus on Clarissa's "reading" of Septimus's death has predominated in critical discussion of the novel. Literary critics have traditionally privileged Woolf's own assertion that Septimus is intended to be Clarissa's "double" ("Preface" vi), and they have often failed to acknowledge the discursive contexts which work to undermine such a comparison. For example, one critic declares, "The bond between Septimus and Clarissa should be understood as a common sense of victimization by the war and by patriarchal values" (Usui 151). Civilians and veterans, however, require greater differentiation: what are the similarities between surviving the Front and surviving the cumulative, daily repressions of civilian life? Such a general comparison elides the dynamics of traumatic knowledge produced under combat on the Western Front, highlighting the ethical and representational challenges which traumatic experience poses in the process of its translation into narrative contexts.

Yet, precisely because traumatic knowledge exceeds narrative representation, assimilation and communalization of trauma for the survivor requires enabling narrative contexts. "Massive trauma precludes its registration" (Laub 57); the witness, then, is crucial to the survivor's ability to configure overwhelming events. Because *Mrs. Dalloway* is a fiction, however, its representation of traumatic knowledge is not configured by the dyad of witness and survivor in the urgent act of testimony. But Woolf's fictional mediation of trauma is nonetheless implicated in the problems of translation and transmission which attend the aftermath of traumatic experience. Such dilemmas of translation and transmission are foregrounded in the text's attention to the double-edged nature of narrative in relation to trauma; narrative may engender both tyranny and community. As Caroline Webb has observed, "Reading *Mrs. Dalloway* we confront the positive and negative implications of our desire to make sense through connection" (280). In particular, assimilative reading strategies which collapse the distinct cultural locations of Clarissa and Septimus fail to confront the non-congruence of narrative representation and traumatic experience to which the act of witnessing paradoxically pays tribute.

*Mrs. Dalloway* represents the consciousness of Septimus Smith in terms of traumatic temporality: a timeless present, proliferating with dense imagery, metaphor, repetition and hallucination. Combat trauma, like other traumatic events, overwhelms the frameworks of narrative, and the knowledge it produces is disjunctive, non-narrative and temporally dislocated; trauma resists emplotment (Janet). By representing Septimus through the "unassimilable forms" (Caruth 156) of traumatic knowledge, the text acknowledges the exceptional challenge to narrative assimilation embodied by the combat veteran. Chronology and sequence are shattered and distorted: "The word 'time' split its husk; poured its riches over him; and from his lips fell like shells, like shavings from a plane . . ." (75). The troping of secrecy, revelation and transformation is recurrent: "Why could he see through bodies, see into the future, when dogs will become men?" (73). Similarly, texts reveal coded messages to him: "The secret signal which one generation passes, under disguise, to the next is loathing, hatred, despair" (96). He both anticipates and fears narrative, succession, sequence: things are drawn "together to one center before his eyes, as if some horror had come almost to the surface and was about to burst into flames" (14). The text thereby reveals the "perpetual troping" (Hartman 537) of dissociated traumatic experience. Affective sequences are absent; he cannot feel. Septimus's identity is without a temporal frame and instead collapses into simultaneous and overdetermined forms: he is a "lord of men" (72), a "drowned sailor on a rock" (74), as well as "the last relic straying upon the edge of the world" (100). Significantly, he is also described as a "giant mourner," "with legions of men prostrate behind him" (75). As Susan Smith points out, such a mourning is impossible to complete (314). Rezia's hatmaking can only provide a provisional context of sequence and safety (94) to intervene in the veteran's circles of traumatic temporality.

Simultaneously, however, *Mrs. Dalloway* participates in the process of cultural codification (Tal 18-9) of massive historical trauma through its strategic emplotment of the veteran. While traumatic knowledge exceeds sequential contexts of understanding, requiring dense metaphorical registers, the reader is also supplied with a chronological narrative of Septimus's life and given etiological cues to interpret his shell-shock. The reader is offered a physiognomy and class profile for Smith: "angular, big-nosed, intelligent, sensitive profile; but not his lips altogether, for they were loose . . . he was, on the whole, a border case . . . one of those half-educated, self-educated men" (90) reminiscent of Leonard Bast from *Howard's End*, who is also framed within conflated class and eugenic contexts. We are then offered a clear chronology of Septimus's early life and enlistment, followed by an indication of homosexual relationship with his officer, whose subsequent death Septimus is unable to mourn. As Peter Knox-Shaw has pointed out, particularly concerning the loss of Evans, such an incident constitutes a "locus classicus" in contemporary accounts of war trauma (104) and serves to plot a "paradigmatic case" (103) of shell-shock: "At every point his symptoms coincide, indeed, with those listed prominently in contemporary writing on shell-shock" (104). Septimus Smith's "madness" is constructed from composite narratives, which may presumably incorporate Woolf's own experience, serving to emphasize the cultural and textual emplotment of the veteran within existing and often implicit interpretive frameworks.

Yet *Mrs. Dalloway* explicitly probes those institutions which have the capacity to tyrannize through the imposition of narrative: heterosexuality, imperialism, and particularly aspects of medicine. At his death, Septimus retains some awareness of the conventions of the social genre which have come to define his spoiled identity. His last words before suicide, "I'll give it you!" ensure his location within a narrative which defines his disordered state as "cowardice" and "lack of proportion": "It was their idea of tragedy, not his or Rezia's . . . Holmes and Bradshaw like that sort of thing" (162). The veteran, however, defies any imposed norms of integration and Holmes's response to the suicide is couched in terms of narrative betrayal: "Who could have foretold it? A sudden impulse, no one was in the least to blame . . ." (163). The human propensity to impose narrative is referred to as "Human nature," "the repulsive brute, with the blood-red nostrils" (99). Such narrative tyranny is chiefly explored through the categories of Proportion and the more sinister form of Conversion (107-8). These aspects of "monumental time," the product of "all the complicities between clock time and figures of authority," (Ricoeur *Time* 122) constitute a configuration which overwhelms the traumatic simultaneity of Septimus. The translation of traumatic experience into narrative contexts renders it uniquely vulnerable to appropriation or resistance by those in a capacity to receive its transmission. As Tal observes, "For the veteran, the price of reintegration is the revision of memory to coincide with hegemony's newly produced consensus" (14). In *Mrs. Dalloway*, Septimus's traumatic memory defies such revisionary processes in death.

Throughout the novel, Clarissa muses on "a transcendental theory" of unseen life after death, "So that to know her, or any one, one must seek out the people who completed them; even the places" (166). Clarissa's creation of "fictive kin" (Winter 46) may be understood as a mode of response to the "[deepening]" of "older languages of loss and consolation" (Winter 76) in the wake of the Great War. And yet, throughout the text, Clarissa's empathic limitations are often highlighted. Her limitations are particularly pronounced with respect to the political aftermath of the Great War: "she could feel nothing for the Albanians, or was it the Armenians? but she loved her roses (didn't that help the Armenians?) . . ." (130). The conflation of Albanians, Armenians and roses highlights her collapse of public conflict with private consolation, a pattern reiterated in relation to the combat veteran.

Clarissa undergoes a complex series of responses to the veteran's suicide. She feels a fleeting sense of public complicity (202); empathy and compassion are also significant, if provisional, aspects of her response. In fact, her complex reflections in relation to Septimus's death reveal the transferential challenges issued by the trauma survivor to the trauma witness: psychic confrontation with the fundamental facts of existence, particularly in terms of the witness's own relationship to death. The trauma witness must strive to cope with such transferential challenges in the midst of a simultaneous commitment to co-implication and difference with respect to the trauma (cf. Laub 58). Yet Clarissa's response to Septimus suddenly gives way to a rapture which breaches any such poised contention of boundaries: "But what an extraordinary night! She felt somehow very like him—the young man who had killed himself. She felt glad that he had done it; thrown it away while they went on living" (203). Clarissa's substitution of herself for the veteran reveals the imperiled status of traumatic knowledge subject to narcissistic implosion. Her interpretation of the veteran's death can be partially understood as an inability to grieve or confront mortality, arising in complex association with her own role as a traumatized eye-witness to her sister's death (84). The resulting transference culminates in an act of appropriation implicated in the very critiques which the text launches against those who seek to impose, coerce, or confine a particular narrative understanding on those subject to traumatic knowledge.

The dynamics of Clarissa's response raise questions concerning the role of ego boundaries in *Mrs. Dalloway.* As Peter Walsh reflects after his imaginative pursuit as a "romantic buccaneer" (57) through the streets of London, "one makes up the better part of life . . . all this one could never share—it smashed to atoms" (57-8). During such an enactment of fantasy, Walsh, in a manner similar to Clarissa, explores the fundamental investment of subjectivity in its own narrative positions, its own interpretive acts. In Paul Ricoeur's view, appropriation is not a "taking possession" but a "divestiture" ("A" 95) of the ego through the act of reading. Jean Wyatt's perspective on the novel, for instance, corresponds with this view: "[Clarissa] emerges from fusion with Septimus radiant with new vitality and expanded awareness" (125). Certainly, the act of bearing witness to the trauma survivor will involve a demanding affective exchange; such exchange, however, requires the witness's ongoing achievement of a recursive and reflexive self-awareness. Fusion, exemplified in Clarissa's response, displaces any encounter with difference. In my view, then, the issue of ethical engagement with the traumatic experience of the veteran is not adequately addressed in an emphasis on the interpretive interchangeability of narrative positions.

Where is the alterity, the "affront to understanding" (Caruth 154), embodied by traumatic experience to be found in Clarissa's response? In fact, affinities, echoes, and chains of imagery throughout the text link Clarissa with Septimus. Clarissa's bodily imagining of his death actually heightens our knowledge of the suicide (Tate 478). But, as Webb points out, many of the text's other characters are implicated in the chains of imagery they share: "Woolf's narrative interweaving challenges the exclusive parallel she has invited us to construct" (290). Despite this textual mode of communalization, during his distress, Septimus has no consistent or responsive witness. And after death, his "belated witness" (Felman 108), Clarissa, does not function as a "guardian" of his testimonial act (Laub 58); rather, the veteran functions as an enabling narrative context for her own identity. Clarissa's meditations on Septimus's death require contextualization in relation to the struggle of veterans to achieve communalization of their trauma. Her reactions to the suicide transform the "unassimilable forms" of traumatic knowledge into "forms of mediation" for her own subjectivity (Steedman 108). Clarissa's endorsement of his death affirms the "privacy of the soul" (137) against the incursions of coercive narrative, even as her response translates the alterity of his traumatic experience into the terms of her own narrated self-identity.

Contestation over the cultural mediation of traumatic knowledge in the aftermath of the Great War was a momentous and ongoing task, a task subject to explicit and implicit concern in *Mrs. Dalloway*. As Peter Walsh muses, "Those five years—1918 to 1923—had been, he suspected, somehow very important" (77). The Armistice did not signal the end of the war experience but "the beginning of a process in which that experience was framed, institutionalized, given ideological content, and relived in political action as well as in fiction" (Leed xi). The politician Richard Dalloway contemplates the war dead, "thousands of poor chaps, with all their lives before them, shovelled together" and reflects that, in spite of the halting of traffic for the laying of a wreath (54), the war dead, whose ranks Septimus has joined, are already "half-forgotten" (125). So too, in *Mrs. Dalloway*, veterans are "half-forgotten": the narrative's complex interweaving of the issues of individuality and universality (Miller 392) affirms but ultimately collapses difference between the veteran and civilian communities.

Alternately, Allyson Booth concludes that the novel has both cautionary and exemplary status with respect to its representation of civilian-veteran relations: "civilians can at least begin to approach the experience of war by directing imaginative energy toward it. The suggestion is modest but honest: to claim access to more would be presumptuous" (168). Yet, Clarissa's own presumptuous claims regarding the veteran enable the reader to witness her failure to sustain the transferential challenges involved in the affective and ethical stance of bearing witness to trauma. Similarly, critical practices which assimilate the incommensurable experiences of veterans and civilians cannot commemorate trauma's "affront to understanding" (Caruth 154) and may constitute a form of "false witness" (Lifton 142). Because of its textualization of traumatic experience, then, *Mrs. Dalloway* foregrounds the ongoing and difficult role of the reader in configuring ethical contexts for the narrative's translation and transmission of traumatic knowledge.

**Works Cited**

Booth, Allyson. *Postcards From the Trenches: Negotiating the Space Between Modernism and the First World War*. Oxford: Oxford UP, 1996.

Caruth, Cathy. "Introduction: Recapturing the Past." *Trauma: Explorations in Memory*. Ed. Caruth. Baltimore: Johns Hopkins UP, 1995. 151-57.

Felman, Shoshana. "Camus' *The Plague*, or A Monument to Witnessing." *Testimony: Crises of Witnessing in Literature, Psychoanalysis, and History*. Ed. Shoshana Felman and Dori Laub. New York: Routledge, 1992. 93-119.

Hartman, Geoffrey. "On Traumatic Knowledge and Literary Studies." *New Literary History* 26 (1995): 537-63.

Janet, Pierre. *Psychological Healing: A Historical and Clinical Study*. 2 Vols.

1917-25. Trans. Eden and Cedar Paul. New York: Macmillan, 1976.

Knox-Shaw, Peter. "The Otherness of Septimus Warren Smith." *Durham University Journal* (Jan 1995): 99-110.

Laub, Dori. "Bearing Witness or the Vicissitudes of Listening." *Testimony*. Ed. Felman and Laub. New York: Routledge, 1992. 57-74.

Leed, Eric. *No Man's Land: Combat and Identity in World War I*. New York: Cambridge UP, 1979.

Lifton, Robert Jay. "An Interview with Robert Jay Lifton." *Trauma: Explorations in Memory*. By Cathy Caruth. Ed., Intros. Caruth. Baltimore: Johns Hopkins UP, 1995. 128-147.

Miller, J. Hillis. "*Mrs. Dalloway*: Repetition as the Raising of the Dead." *Fiction and Repetition: Seven English Novels*. Cambridge: Harvard UP, 1982. 176-202; 240.

Ricoeur, Paul. "Appropriation." *A Ricoeur Reader: Reflection and Imagination*. Ed. Mario J. Valdes. Hemel Hempstead: Harvester Wheatsheaf, 1991. 86-98.

——. *Time and Narrative*. Vol II. Trans. Kathleen McLaughlin and David Pellauer. Chicago: U of Chicago P, 1985.

Smith, Susan Bennett. "Reinventing Grief Work: Virginia Woolf's Feminist Representations of Mourning in *Mrs. Dalloway* and *To the Lighthouse*." *Twentieth Century Literature* 41 (1995): 310-27.

Steedman, Carolyn. "About Ends: On the Way In Which the End is Different From an Ending." *History of the Human Sciences* 9.4 (1996): 99-114.

Tal, Kali. *Worlds of Hurt: Reading the Literatures of Trauma*. Cambridge: Cambridge UP, 1996.

Tate, Trudi. "*Mrs. Dalloway* and the Armenian Question." *Textual Practice* 8.3 (1994): 467-86.

Usui, Masami. "The Female Victims of the War in *Mrs. Dalloway*." *Virginia Woolf and War: Fiction, Reality, and Myth*. Ed., Intro. Mark Hussey. Syracuse: Syracuse UP, 1991. 151-63.

Webb, Caroline. "Life After Death: The Allegorical Progress of *Mrs. Dalloway*." *Modern Fiction Studies* 40.2 (1994): 279-98.

Winter, Jay. *Sites of Memory, Sites of Mourning: The Great War in European Cultural History*. Cambridge: Cambridge UP, 1995.

Woolf, Virginia. *Mrs. Dalloway*. 1925. New York: Harcourt, 1997.

——. Preface, *Mrs. Dalloway*. New York: Modern Library, 1928.

Wyatt, Jean. "Avoiding self-definition: In defense of women's right to merge (Julia Kristeva and *Mrs. Dalloway*)." *Women's Studies* 13 (1986): 115-126.

Madelyn Detloff

# Imagined Communities of Criticism: 'Wounded Attachments' to the Icons of H. D., Gertrude Stein, and Virginia Woolf

This paper is an excerpt from a longer work in which I analyze the consequences of our retrospective re-tellings of the lives of Woolf, Stein, and H.D.[1] Although they frequented overlapping social circles, each remained relatively isolated from the other. It is only in later constructions of modernism that they seem, with regularity, to cohabit the same space. All three have been regarded as central figures in the story of female modernism, and have taken on overdetermined significance in the community-building work of late 20th century feminist and lesbian identity politics.

While acknowledging the importance of this political work, I argue that many contemporary critics construct H.D., Stein, and Woolf as iconic, even heroic, historical figures. These representations serve important functions, standing for painful issues such as sexual abuse, mental illness, and marginalization. However, such iconic representations also encourage what Wendy Brown calls "wounded attachments" to trauma-produced identities, rather than analyses of the conditions that foster trauma-producing practices (391).

In what follows, I will briefly discuss some of the mechanics of wounded attachments to the icons of Woolf, Stein, and H.D., and then suggest that Woolf herself offers an alternative to wounded attachments in "A Sketch of the Past."

That H.D., Stein, and Woolf left behind major collections of manuscripts and papers, allowing scholars insight into their personal lives, may account for some of their iconic appeal to later generations. Their penchant for autobiography has helped construct the personages that now loom so large in (at least feminist) studies of modernism. We may think that we "know" these modernist writers because they were public personae who revealed many of the details of their lives in their unpublished papers and their memoirs. If the "institution of autobiography," as Elizabeth Bruss notes, helps to form notions of identity, then the identities constructed through the autobiographical writing of Stein, Woolf and H.D. have been particularly germane for feminist and lesbian identity politics of the eighties (Bruss 5).[2] Although, or perhaps because, feminist scholars have disagreed about the meanings of the "lives" of each of these women, they often serve as exempla of evolving feminist issues.

In particular, I am interested in the role sexuality has played in configuring iconic identifications with H.D., Stein and Woolf. I therefore focus on the construction of Woolf's identity as a sexual abuse survivor and constructions of all three writers' lesbianism. I choose these examples because of the resonance they have in feminist discourse today, but also because tracing a history—of social tolerance of abuse, of female-female erotic attachments in the past—has become a powerful political strategy. However, one effect of attempts to revalue the "lives" of women authors like H.D., Woolf and Stein, and to advocate their inclusion in a canon of major writers, has been the creation of a kind of historical fetish, the feminist icon: a symbolic representative of difficulties that women encounter in the present.[3] H.D. has therefore represented the plight of the female author struggling to free herself from heterosexual "romantic thralldom." Stein has—positively and negatively—been represented as the masculinized butch lesbian, while Woolf has been represented as the exemplary radical socialist feminist, and/or the psychologically scarred incest survivor.[4]

Forging identifications that enable more forceful articulations of contemporary cultural issues, the feminist icon memorializes the wounds women have incurred at the hands of patriarchal culture, and thus keeps such abuses in public view. At the same time, it may displace the affect that should be directed toward contemporary struggles with wounding powers. That is, the energy we need to bring about change can become absorbed in a melancholic fixation on the past.

This melancholic fixation fosters, as I noted, "wounded attachments," because identification with the iconic historical figure is dependent on establishing sameness, despite the long interval of time (not to mention the differences in social and geographical location) that separates someone like me from someone like Woolf. This sense of sameness is facilitated by holding constant some notion of identity, and this is done through invoking similar experiences of exclusion, or marginalization, or trauma. As Brown argues, when such shared identities are consolidated through exclusion or wounding, we develop unwitting psychological investments in the condition of woundedness. If the consolidating wound were alleviated, we might feel our consolidated identity unraveling (403).

Moreover, because the feminist icon—through wounded attachment—stands for shared identity, any challenge to the meaning of the iconic life is bound to invoke a great deal of affect.[5] Hence the painfulness of arguments about the sexual identity of historical figures like Woolf, Stein, or H.D., or the painfulness of being reminded, as we were in yesterday's film (*Paris Was a Woman*), of Natalie Barney—the sapphic amazon's—fascist sentiments.

I am not going to address the issue of lesbian identity further today, but will look to another example of the painful effects of wounded attachments—the critical furor that periodically erupts over the interpretation of Woolf's accounts of sexual abuse. There has been so much fighting about Woolf's identity as an incest survivor that I think we have overlooked the lessons that Woolf herself teaches us about how to interpret her autobiographical accounts.

As you know, in "A Sketch of the Past," Woolf recounts her experience of molestation by Gerald Duckworth. She mentions the experience as an illustration of the "complexity" of feelings that make a memory "less strong; or if not less strong, less isolated, less complete" (67).

I am, of course, not the first person to connect Woolf's looking glass scene to her very sophisticated autobiographical practice. Shari Benstock analyzes this scene as Woolf's exploration of the Lacanian "mirror stage" (14). However, by focusing on Woolf's subjectivity and consequent refusal to shore up identity via the consolidating focus of autobiography, Benstock herself consolidates Woolf's gender difference from the male autobiographers ("Authorizing" 16). As compelling as Benstock's reading is, it nevertheless posits Woolf's autobiographical practice as an effect of her female subjectivity, with sexual abuse merely a shock that initiates the process of the mirror stage ("Authorizing" 14).

There may be another way to read the function of Woolf's looking glass scene, though, that doesn't depend on the Lacanian notion of a yearning for wholeness that is expressed in male autobiographies and rejected in female. In this scene we might see the performative dynamics of shame operating. Eve K. Sedgwick suggests that "shame floods into being as a moment, a disruptive moment, in a circuit of identity-constituting identificatory communication. . . . But in interrupting identification, shame too, makes identity" (5). Woolf explores the "dynamic relation" between identity and shame by juxtaposing the problems of memoir writing with a long narrative attempt to explain the "shame which I had in being caught looking at myself in the glass in the hall" (*MOB* 68). Woolf offers the molestation scene, where Gerald Duckworth lifted her onto the "slab outside the dining room door" and "explored my private parts" as a possible source for the shame she felt of her own body (69). But this incident is only one source of a longer genealogy of Woolf's looking glass shame, and the complexity of the affect leads Woolf right back to the difficulties of constituting the autobiographical subject:

> And this [response to Gerald's actions] throws light not merely on my own case, but upon the problem that I touched on the first page; why it is so difficult to give any account of the person to whom things happen. The person is evidently immensely complicated. Witness the incident of the looking-glass. Though I have done my best to explain why I was ashamed of looking at my own face I have only been able to discover some possible reasons; there may be others; I do not suppose that I have got at the truth; yet this is a simple incident; and it happened to me personally; and I have no motive for lying about it. In spite of all this, people write what they call 'lives' of other people; that is, they collect a number of events, and leave the person to whom it happened unknown. (*MOB* 69)

Despite Woolf's evocation of the complexity of her shame-filled responses to the looking glass, Louise De Salvo uses this passage to make a direct link between the boundary-shattering effects of abuse and Woolf's lifelong depressions and mental illness. Through writing about this experience in

"Sketch," DeSalvo argues, Woolf "began to understand that sexual abuse was probably the central and most formative feature of her early life" (101). Moreover, De Salvo directly links the distinction between "moments of being" and "moments of non-being" to incest survivors' frequent practices of dissociation (103).

In her memoir, however, Woolf suggests that "moments of non-being" consist of much more mundane instances of inattention and forgetting. She describes the "misleading" way memories may be taken for a complete "account of my life" and is dismayed that she cannot adequately recount moments of "non-being." This disappointment is connected to her career long re-valuation of the everyday, the domestic—such underappreciated yet necessary activities such as eating and household chores:

> Often when I have been writing one of my so-called novels I have been baffled by this same problem; that is, how to describe what I call in my private shorthand—"non-being". Every day includes much more non-being than being. . . . I have already forgotten what Leonard and I talked about at lunch; and at tea; although it was a good day the goodness was embedded in a kind of nondescript cotton wool. This is always so. A great part of every day is not lived consciously. One walks, eats, sees things, deals with what has to be done; the broken vacuum cleaner; ordering dinner; writing orders to Mabel; washing; cooking dinner; bookbinding. When it is a bad day the proportion of non-being is much larger. (*MOB* 70)

Despite the clear connection Woolf makes between the quotidian and "moments of non-being," DeSalvo attaches overdetermined significance to Woolf's evocation of "nondescript cotton wool." Discounting Woolf's revaluation of the everyday, she interprets this metaphor as a symptom of Woolf's damaged psyche: "This is not an expression of Woolf's philosophy about the nature of existence; rather it is an attempt to describe her own emotional makeup, an attempt to analyze how depression interfered with her sense of connection to experience; it is a description of a continuing fragmentation, disconnection, and detachment" (103)

I don't want to deny the shattering effects of abuse or the way abusers' persistent denials can wreak havoc on a survivor's trust in her memory, but DeSalvo's interpretation here suggests, by implication, that people who have not been abused can and do live continually in the fully present states of conscious attention that Woolf associates with "moments of being." That is, they fix broken vacuum cleaners, "deal with what has to be done," cook dinner, recall what was said over lunch, etc., with the same full conscious attention they devote to extraordinary, or intensely pleasurable or painful, experiences. By depicting moments of "non-being" as specific effects of abuse, DeSalvo has, by contrast, constructed a normative "whole" person with remarkable powers of observation and attention. This is what wounded attachments do: they create and valorize ideal subjects whom we long to be.

While shaming events such as molestation contribute to the sense that one lacks bodily coherence or control of one's physical and psychological surroundings, it seems more helpful to posit these experiences along a continuum of childhood feelings of powerlessness, or lack of bodily integrity, and a continuum of modes of forgetting and remembering experience. This is the rhetorical move Woolf makes in recounting her feelings of "looking glass" shame. She moves back and forth from the particular to the general, all the while analyzing the experiences connected to her feelings as a way to understand the difficulties of producing "an account of my life" (69).

We can regard Woolf's experiences of molestation with the gravity they deserve without constructing a mythical "whole" person (who is subsequently damaged by abuse) by understanding sexual abuse as a particularly intense and invasive shaming experience. In this reading, neither sexual abuse nor female subjectivity is causative of Woolf's awareness of the difficulty of composing a "life" of one's self. The trajectory of causation may, in fact, be in reverse—that her awareness of how characters are constructed through an "institution like autobiography" (to quote Bruss), may give her insight into the subjection, or the disciplinary subject-making, of a person through other institutions and acts. Woolf does, after all, include the looking glass scene as an example of her difficulty creating the autobiographical subject "Virginia." To say this is not to discount the impact molestation must have had on Woolf's early self-conception, only to say that Woolf's rendering of this scene is a conscious act, and not an unconscious symptom, and that Woolf herself understands that the impact of this experience on her later personality is complex rather than etiological or predictable.

Woolf's own depiction of the molestation scene is extremely nuanced, presenting the shaming event as a confirmation of what she describes as an "instinctual" shame about the body:

> I remember resenting, disliking it—what is the word for so dumb and mixed a feeling? It must have been strong, since I still recall it. This seems to show that a feeling about certain parts of the body; how they must not be touched; how it is wrong to allow them to be touched; must be instinctive. It proves that Virginia Stephen was not born on the 25th January 1882, but was born many thousands of years ago; and had from the very first to encounter instincts already acquired by thousands of ancestresses in the past. (*MOB* 69)

Woolf's Lamarckian turn here, suggesting an inheritance of acquired "instincts" passed on through "ancestresses" indicates that, for her, shame has a social genealogy. One's social location—a queer person, in Sedgwick's formulation, a Victorian girl in Woolf's—enhances the performative (or "deformative") force of the shaming incident. In contrast to Woolf's "ancestresses," Gerald and George Duckworth are not shame-filled because they are not in the social position that encourages one to be a person to whom shame readily accrues.

Understanding the highly-charged dynamics of shame allows one to take seriously the way experiences influence one's sense of self, without reifying identity, or retrospectively creating a subject who is forever constituted as damaged. In Sedgwick's formulation, identity is dynamic and interpersonal, connected to a history of experiences, but also part of a continuing process. Shame, for Sedgwick, "generates and legitimates the place of identity—the *question* of identity—as the origin of the impulse to the performative, but does so without giving that identity-space the standing of an essence" (14). More importantly, Woolf's autobiography, as a performative act, can bring about the "misconstrual and misrecognition" that Sedgwick links to "social metamorphic possibilities" (14).

To unpack Sedgwick's argument, let me suggest that Woolf's depiction of the scene of her molestation by Gerald Duckworth illustrates how a girl, a Victorian girl, is produced as a person who is ashamed of her body, of her sexuality, whose body is subject to the controlling forces of older males. The looking glass scene therefore is not so much a depiction of psychoanalytic coming to subjectivity, as Benstock argues, but a depiction of social subjection—her interpellation as a shame-filled person through the invasive actions of Gerald Duckworth. In this depiction, Woolf rhetorically pairs Gerald's actions, "His hand explored my private parts," with her own process of memoir writing, another kind of (certainly more benign) exploration of her "private parts." This pairing is purposeful, for as a performative act, Woolf's memoir writing can be seen to effect its own "social metamorphic possibilities" by interrogating Gerald's own part in the shame-producing dynamics of abuse. That is, through this autobiographical act Woolf produces Gerald Duckworth as "shameless" person while she describes herself as shame-filled. Through this action, too, Woolf makes use of the transitive property of shame to construct Gerald as a person who ought to be ashamed. Woolf enacts this kind of performative redeployment by reversing the trajectory of the utterance "shame on you." Although this reversal does not alleviate Woolf's sense of shame or undo the stigmatizing effects of incest, it does imply a sense of political agency, that of calling a "respectable" Victorian male to account for his abuse of power.[6] This agency may seem purely rhetorical, since Gerald died a year before Woolf began composing "A Sketch of the Past." Nevertheless, Woolf's performative act does have political consequences, opening up the possibility that such abuses will, in future generations, be exposed for their "deformative" power.

Let me end by teasing you with the suggestion that "A Sketch of the Past," through its genealogical tracing of the identity-forming functions of trauma, memory, and autobiography offers us a model for writing about identity without forging wounded attachments. While accountable to the past—and an open discussion of past woundings—Woolf's genealogical practice is more importantly accountable to the future, because it demonstrates the possibility for resistance and change, even in the wake of traumatic experience. Rather than upholding the icon of Woolf as the symbol of a wounded identity, then, we might be better off emulating her resilient practice.

## Notes

[1] While the format and brevity of this paper have made it difficult to incorporate all of their advice, I would like to thank the attendees of the "Traumatic Knowledge" panel, as well as H. Porter Abbott, Victoria Harrison, Judith Raiskin, Brenda R. Silver, and Carla Freccero for their feedback on this essay. The title of the paper alludes to Benedict Anderson's *Imagined Communities,* a study of the conceptual formation of the idea of national community. I refer to his title to emphasize the conceptual grouping of disparate writers under the sign of "female modernism."

[2] Abbott has noted the importance of Bruss' *Autobiographical Acts* for later theorists of autobiography, suggesting that Bruss "was trying to do for autobiography what Austin, Searle, and Strawson sought to do for the study of speech: that is, to move from a static to a dynamic conception of the field, to show how the communicative unit not only states but performs" (600). Bruss' insights have fallen by the wayside in most feminist studies of the genre, which focus more on autobiography as an articulation of subjectivity. Given especially the importance of speech act theory in recent queer theoretical texts, Bruss' work deserves a critical resurgence.

[3] Although I do not have space to elaborate on this here, my analysis is indebted to Silver's cogent examination of the iconic constructions of Woolf in popular culture.

[4] See, for example, DuPlessis, Smith, Cook, Marcus, and DeSalvo, respectively.

[5] For example, at a recent conference on "Virginia Woolf and Lesbian Vision," the question of whether Virginia Woolf identified as a lesbian, or whether there might be some other way to describe and account for her homoerotic attachments to women, was interpreted by many conference attendees as complicit with a homophobic denial of lesbian existence (June 11, 1997, Boston, MA). The affect surrounding such challenges to transhistorical concepts of identity often serves to foreclose efforts to arrive at a culturally and historically particular understanding of someone's homoerotic experiences and attachments.

[6] Sedgwick discusses the politically useful potential of the utterance "shame on you" in "Queer Performativity" (4-5).

## Works Cited

Abbott, H. Porter. "Autobiography, Autography, Fiction: Groundwork for a Taxonomy of Textual Categories." *New Literary History* 19.3 (1988): 597-615.

Anderson, Benedict. *Imagined Communities.* New York: Verso, 1991.

Benstock, Shari. "Authorizing the Autobiographical." *The Private Self: Theory and Practice of Women's Autobiographical Writings.* Ed. Shari Benstock. Chapel Hill: U of North Carolina P, 1988.

Brown, Wendy. "Wounded Attachments." *Political Theory* 21.3 (1993): 390-410.
Bruss, Elizabeth W. *Autobiographical Acts: The Changing Situation of a Literary Genre.* Baltimore: Johns Hopkins U P, 1976.
Cook, Blanche Wiesen. "'Women Alone Stir My Imagination': Lesbianism and the Cultural Tradition." *Signs: Journal of Women in Culture and Society* 4.4 (1979): 718-739.
DeSalvo, Louise. *Virginia Woolf: The Impact of Childhood Sexual Abuse on Her Life and Work.* New York: Ballantine Books, 1989.
DuPlessis, Rachel Blau. "Romantic Thralldom in H.D." *Signets: Reading H.D.* Ed. Susan Stanford Friedman and Rachel Blau DuPlessis. Madison: U of Wisconsin P, 1990.
Marcus, Jane. *Virginia Woolf and the Languages of Patriarchy.* Bloomington: Indiana U P, 1987.
*Paris Was a Woman.* Dir. Greta Schiller. Zeitgeist Films, 1996.
Sedgwick, Eve Kosofsky. "Queer Performativity: Henry James's *The Art of the Novel.*" *GLQ* 1.1 (1993): 1-16.
Silver, Brenda R. "What's Woolf Got to Do With It: Or, The Perils of Popularity." *Modern Fiction Studies* 38.1 (1992): 20-60.
Smith, Sidonie. *Subjectivity, Identity, and the Body: Women's Autobiographical Practices in the Twentieth Century.* Bloomington: Indiana U P, 1993.
Woolf, Virginia. "A Sketch of the Past." *Moments of Being.* Ed. Jeanne Schulkind. New York: HBJ, 1985.

**Robin Paula Silbergleid**

## "We perished, each alone": Loss and Lyricism in Woolf, Maso, and Young

During the writing of *To the Lighthouse* (1927), Virginia Woolf's journal entries show her grappling with the increasingly poetic and experimental form her new novels have taken. In fact, Woolf questions whether the book should be considered a novel at all, suggesting that it might best be characterized as an elegy (*D*3 34). Numerous critics including Mark Spilka, Gillian Beer, and Elissa Greenwald have taken Woolf's comment as a basis for interpretations of the novel, turning to Woolf's biography for examples of her vexed relationship to grief, particularly in regard to her mother and her brother Thoby. Unquestionably, Woolf's sense of loss lies at the heart of *To the Lighthouse*, organized structurally around the death of Mrs. Ramsay. Yet, to my mind, Woolf's generic frustration argues less for an understanding of the novel as personal grief work than a recognition of the impact loss has had on her narrative technique, a recognition that speaks to a larger modernist concern about cultural trauma and representational crisis.[1] It is the form, not merely the content, that marks this novel as elegiac, using poetic structure and discourse to bracket the traumatic experience of war: the wartime death of Andrew Ramsay is literally reduced to a parenthetical in Woolf's haunting, lyrical prose.

But unlike Mr. Ramsay who insists that "we perish, each alone," Woolf is not alone in her search for a new language in which to grieve. Rather, twentieth-century literary production demonstrates a far-reaching concern with loss and the failure of traditional narrative to deal with it. This essay, therefore, considers one effect of loss on narrative, positioning Woolf at the foundation of a community of twentieth-century prose stylists who find in lyricism a way of dealing ethically and aesthetically with loss. In what follows, I would like to sketch the contours of that community, focusing my discussion on contemporary writer Carole Maso and mid-century writer Marguerite Young. Despite the disparate sociopolitical contexts of their work, these three novelists reveal that one effect of unmourned loss is the loss of narrative itself. But rather than mourning the death of narrative, they use a hybrid form, the lyrical novel, to arrive, in the words of Hélène Cixous, at "a language that heals as much as it separates" (qtd. in Conley 146).

As we know, for Virginia Woolf a new historical moment began "on or about December, 1910," the moment that "human character changed"(*CDB* 96). Yet this well-known quotation only begins to hint at the effect of cultural loss on Woolf's work. All her major novels attempt to find a language capable of addressing the crisis of representation that results from war, and all of them reject traditional narrative to do so. In *Mrs. Dalloway*, Septimus Warren Smith embodies the effects of war, suffering from what Freud would describe as the "war neurosis" and serving as a haunting reminder at Clarissa's party that nothing will be the same again. In *The Waves*, the death of Percival enables a larger cultural trauma to make its way into a novel that has been critiqued for being too caught up in personal voice and introspection. But it is *To the Lighthouse* that best enacts the ineffability of loss and turns to lyricism as a way of attempting to address that representational problematic.

The "Time Passes" section of *To the Lighthouse* in particular demonstrates the convergence of formal and thematic losses in Woolf's work. Stylistically a poetic interlude or an extended prose poem, "Time Passes" removes the deaths of Mrs. Ramsay, Prue, and Andrew from the novel's linear flow of time. More significantly, these central losses are told from an omniscient point of view as parenthetical remarks. This is important because it suggests that the experience of loss cannot be conceptualized within narrative logic and time. Instead, loss takes place within a lyrical time-space. Sharon Cameron, in her book *Lyric Time*, characterizes lyric as a struggle to exempt language from temporal progression, giving the illusion of a timeless space, of stasis (212). Such illusion is conducive to a literary experience of loss, or more precisely, a refusal of loss, as it attempts to stave off death by rejecting chronology. For this reason, lyric is, for Cameron, a "language of mourning" and a "grammar of pain" (239). Taking "Time Passes" as exemplary, I would argue that lyricism can be seen as the very site of loss within otherwise narrative texts. Removed from the teleological impulse of narrative, this central section operates by using the Ramsays' decaying summer house as a symbol of loss. The house, filled with objects left by its occupants, is thus haunted by their presence. Woolf writes: "What people had shed and left—a pair of shoes, a shooting cap, some faded skirts and coats in wardrobes—those alone kept the human shape and in the emptiness indicated how once they were filled and animated; . . . how once the looking-glass had held a face; had held a world hollowed out in which a figure turned, a hand flashed, the door opened, in came children rushing and tumbling; and went out again" (*TTL* 129). Here Woolf's lyrical use of enumeration and parallelism to describe the lingering presence of domesticity stands in place of a psychologically motivated description of the Ramsays' mourning process. This substitution of impersonal for subjective point of view in a time of grief suggests the inability of the Ramsays to confront loss head on. Instead, Woolf relegates an overt discussion of grief work to the third section, which details Lily's attempt to grapple with the loss of her surrogate mother figure Mrs. Ramsay.

Whereas "Time Passes" enacts formally the loss (or breakdown) of linear narrative as a consequence of thematic loss, the final section of the novel, "The Lighthouse," restores Lily's narrative of psychological development to suggest the possibility of healing from traumatic loss. This possibility enters through two interrelated registers: the maternal and the poetic. As, according to post-Freudian psychoanalysts, successful artistic production can only occur after a completed grieving process, Lily Briscoe shows working through her relationship to Mrs. Ramsay to be instrumental to her artistic vision. While Charles Tansley insists that "women can't write, can't paint," leaving Lily unable to produce, Mrs. Ramsay acts as a muse for Lily, first as a symbol of ideal femininity and later as a surrogate mother who must be mourned. Although Lily ultimately rejects entrance into the heterosexual economy Mrs. Ramsay offers, choosing instead to move the tree to the middle of her painting, Lily cannot "have her vision" until she has worked through her relationship to this lost mother figure, shifting desire from the maternal to the paternal function and entering a desiring relationship with Mr. Ramsay, bearer of logic from A to Z. We might understand this shift in terms of Kristeva's work on melancholia, which connects a refusal to give up the maternal object with a denial of the function of language. Instead, the melancholic turns to a speech of the depressed, a mode of expression reliant on semiotic processes such as rhythm or tone (33, 64-5). Within this formulation, it is poetic not narrative discourse which approximates the language of melancholia. Thus, Lily's inability to mourn keeps her from entering the paternal realm of the symbolic, figured in the novel by a failure of verbal representation: she says, "For really, what did she feel, come back after all these years and Mrs. Ramsay dead? Nothing, nothing—

nothing that she could express at all" (145). This failure of expression returns for Lily, who thinks a bit later, "Words fluttered sideways and struck the object inches too low. . . . For how could one express in words these emotions of the body? express that emptiness there?" (178).

Yet if Lily shows the failure of representation (or the symbolic) in a time of grief, Augustus Carmichael suggests that it is precisely in such times that writers turn toward poetry. The death of Andrew Ramsay in war inaugurates a poetic rebirth for Mr. Carmichael: "The war, people said, had revived their interest in poetry" (134). That Woolf has one of her characters turn to poetry as a way of solving cultural crisis reveals her own understanding of the psychosocial function of lyricism. For Woolf, as for Kristeva, lyricism becomes a language of ungrieved loss, becomes a language to speak through pain, if not about it. But what, ultimately, is the vision of mourning Woolf presents? Formally, "Time Passes" best demonstrates the possibilities of lyricism in grief work and, for me, best exemplifies the promise of the novel. That "Time Passes" is ultimately recontained within narrative shows the difficulty of moving away from Freudian models in which narrative is cure.[2] Thus, while I agree with Susan Bennett Smith that *To the Lighthouse* offers "a more developed thinking with regard to grief" than, say, her earlier novel *Mrs. Dalloway,* which goes only as far as critiquing the psychoanalytic institution through Septimus (323), I would argue that the novel also betrays a certain ambivalence on Woolf's part, one she only begins to work out in the figure of Lily Briscoe.[3]

Heavily influenced by *To the Lighthouse* in content and form, Carole Maso's first novel *Ghost Dance* (1986) furthers the use of lyricism to create an alternative language of mourning. For Maso, the power of this language stems from its association with the feminine. This association occurs through the novel's central emblem of loss, the protagonist's mother, poet Christine Wing. After Christine's death, her daughter Vanessa turns to lyricism as a form through which to mourn. Like Woolf's "Time Passes," *Ghost Dance* opens a lyrical space in which Vanessa can, in the words of Susan Stanford Friedman, recover a "timeless union with the mother" (165). Maso accomplishes this, in part, by using a spatial structure to organize the book. Rather than progressing chronologically, *Ghost Dance* centers around key scenes between Vanessa and Christine. Divided into five sections, the novel opens in Grand Central Station where Vanessa sees Christine for the last time, set against "a cathedral of light" (6). Part III, the novel's structural hinge, begins with another scene of separation—it is Vanessa's first day of college. After her parents leave her at school, Vanessa goes to the college library where she finds a copy of her mother's book *To Vanessa*, a lyrical connection between mother and daughter. The final movement of the book recounts the events which lead to Christine's death, and Vanessa's direct attempt to work through her loss. It is, in this way, similar to the movements of Woolf's novel, ending by bearing witness, by giving Vanessa the ability to complete her narrative, just as Lily Briscoe can finally have her artistic vision.

But Maso goes a step beyond Woolf in creating a language of mourning, ultimately positing female-female bonds as an alternative to reinvestment in heteronarrative economy. Whereas Lily Briscoe has an ambivalent relationship to Mrs. Ramsay, recognizing her love for the woman but ultimately rejecting her for her husband, Vanessa enters into two lesbian attachments in attempted unification with her mother. Significantly, these relationships are also fundamentally connected to lyricism within the logic of the novel. First, Vanessa transfers desire from her mother to Marta, a college student in a perpetual state of mourning for her own lost lover. Vanessa realizes from the beginning of their relationship that it has everything to do with her mother, and everything to do with mourning. She says: "So it was my mother who had brought me here. . . . She had united us at this wailing wall, this place of the lacerated skin, the shorn hair. She had brought me here, as if she herself had taken me by the hand. She had brought me here to this universe of grief, though I did not know why yet" (164). Maso structurally underscores the connection between Marta and Christine by interweaving the meeting scene with the library scene, returning several times to Vanessa in the library stacks. Thematically, the connection reaches a peak when both women are dying—Marta from a suicide attempt, Christine from a car crash. As Vanessa says, "when the phone call came at three in the morning with its unmistakable ring of death, I thought it was Marta who had finally passed from the last room to the lovely porch where Natalie sat waiting. I was not thinking of my mother" (242-3). If Christine led Vanessa to Marta and grief, Vanessa finds Christine again through a second lesbian attachment, this time with her mother's own lover Sabine. The two women find in each other elements of Christine, and Vanessa vicariously makes love to her mother. But, as comforting as Vanessa's encounter with Sabine is, her process of mourning is still incomplete, her mother still ungrieved.

The final stage of Vanessa's mourning is the Ghost Dance from the book's title. The novel's final scene depicts Vanessa and her brother Fletcher participating in a Native American ritual for the dead. It is this ceremony that finally enables Vanessa to purge herself of grief, to live, as she says, "side by side with the sorrow," much as the Ramsays' trip to the lighthouse allows Lily to finish her painting (Maso 274). The implication of this final gesture is Maso's rejection of the traditional Western psychoanalytic model of mourning—a model in which narrative and heterosexuality signal cure—in favor of a mourning process invested in female bonds, resurrection of ghosts, and lyricism in the form of ritualized chants. But the importance of lyricism for mourning should not be limited to orality. Rather, the novel's rejection of narrative logic reaches a climax in this last scene, allowing linear time to collapse and a synchronic chorus of voices to emerge. To give a fuller sense of Maso's polyphony, I'd like to quote the text at length: :

> We live in the hands of the family that prays. We live in the hidden valleys folded in the hills. We live in the corncrib, in the center of the

> haystack. We live in the song of the woodthrush. . . .
>
> We live in the south and we live in the north; we live in the east and in the west. We live in the past and we live in the present. Let us live in those who wanted only to have a normal lifetime but for whom it was not possible.
>
> "Give me back what you have taken," the DES daughter says from her hospital bed.
>
> "Give me back my life," the Vietnam veteran demands.
>
> "Give me back what you have taken," Black Hawk repeats, turning the television louder. (274)

Here, through synchronic presentation of mourners' voices, Maso suggests the process of mourning is neverending. Lyricism, then, becomes a place where specters may reside and gain voice.

If loss disrupts narrative teleology in *To the Lighthouse* and fosters a synchrony of mourners' voices in *Ghost Dance*, Marguerite Young's 1198-page lyrical novel *Miss MacIntosh, My Darling* (1965) shows that a world of loss is not necessarily a world of emptiness, a world drained of meaning.[4] Rather, the richness of Young's imagination bedecks the novel's interior landscape, complete with phantasmatic symphonies and opium-induced dreams, where loss becomes the very possibility of beauty and knowledge. The novel details Vera Cartwheel's bus trip through the midwest to What Cheer, Iowa, as she attempts to search for her lost governess and darling, Miss Georgia MacIntosh—a woman with a black umbrella and a red marcelled wig who taught Vera the importance of remaining in the real world. Yet real as Miss MacIntosh's death by water probably is, only a quest of the imagination might enable Vera to encounter her lost love once again—a quest without guideposts or a sense of direction. Like Vera's talkative bus driver, Young consistently skirts the reader's narrative expectations, setting up a lyrical landscape in its place. This alternative landscape and epistemology gradually unfolds Vera's tale of loss. After some two hundred pages of digressions, Young reveals Miss MacIntosh to be the very embodiment of loss. Her red wig gone, she is bald and missing a breast—a specter that haunts and sustains the novel. Her loss is everywhere and nowhere, for loss is only recognizable within a narrative framework. But in *Miss MacIntosh My Darling*, the very constitutive elements of narrative—stable characters, recognizable setting, definitive action—are virtually eliminated. Structurally, the novel takes its shape from Vera's mother Catherine, whose opium-induced dreamscapes are more real than life itself. Vera's description of Catherine's mental process works well to characterize the novel as a whole:

> She had no respect for logical sequences, none for the relation of cause to event, none for this web of causality, none for the correct order of time, none for the place, none for the person—confusing noon with purple midnight or the pale moon's setting with the moon's rising like a

> moth over the waves or life's ending with life's beginning or mountainous seas for mountains with foaming crests. (378)

While the novel's relentless fantasy world has been critiqued for its failure to incorporate history—there is no clear time frame for the novel, no politics, no real society to speak of—I would argue that this seeming refusal of the world captures the vestiges of loss more tangibly than realist representation ever could.[5]

One way the novel accomplishes this purposeful avoidance of representation and sets up an alternative notion of mourning lies in its unusual point of view. The central narrative line feigns to be a bildungsroman, though, in the end, it says very little about the development of the narrator as protagonist. Instead, Vera recounts, with the directness of interior monologue, other characters' inner thoughts for hundreds of pages at a time. The voice of the novel is thus Vera's and larger than Vera's. But this choral voice or consciousness creates within the novel a community of mourners, as Miss MacIntosh becomes the overarching figure of loss, her story connected with all the other failed romances and deaths along this novel's antinarrative path. Loss, the novel suggests, is too big to be captured from a single perspective.

It is this point, finally, that suggests the implications of the lyrical novel as a structure for a new model of mourning, a model that refuses to reduce grief to a condition which can be cured if you only tell the right story. As *Miss MacIntosh, My Darling*, *Ghost Dance*, and *To the Lighthouse* reveal, the lyrical novel is communal, maternal, and ethical. For what these novels don't say—their parentheticals, digressions, and stasis—is not a symbol of isolation but reparation.

**Notes**

1 Mepham's article "Mourning and Modernism" begins to address the relationship between Woolf's modernist aesthetic and the cultural trauma of World War I, suggesting that her "obsession with mourning reflected a general cultural malaise" (143). Mepham retains, however, the psychobiographical tendencies he critiques.

2 See, for example, Greenwald's discussion of *To the Lighthouse*, in which she argues that the final section enables narrative to supplant the lyricism of "Time Passes," resulting in the family's recovery from "the narcissistic broodings of melancholia" (52).

3 In her article "Reinventing Grief Work," Smith contends that "In *Mrs. Dalloway* Woolf tells a cautionary tale of the fatal results of the feminization and medicalization of grief, but offers no viable alternative. In *To the Lighthouse* she removes mourning from the realms of femininity and medicine, and provides a positive model for grief work" (310).

4 Shaviro's essay "Exhoritance and Death" discusses the relationship between loss and imagination in *Miss MacIntosh, My Darling*, claiming that "the space of

absence and failure which the novel defines is infinitely full rather than infinitely empty" (122).

5 See Strehle's "Telling Women's Time: *Miss MacIntosh, My Darling*" for a discussion of the novel's rejection of linear temporality and history and for an overview of its critical reception.

**Works Cited**

Beer, Gillian. "Hume, Stephen, and Elegy in *To the Lighthouse.*" *Essays in Criticism* 34 (1984): 33-55.

Cameron, Sharon. *Lyric Time: Dickinson and the Limits of Genre.* Baltimore: Johns Hopkins UP, 1979.

Conley, Verena Andermatt. *Hélène Cixous: Writing the Feminine.* Lincoln: U of Nebraska P, 1984.

Friedman, Susan Stanford. "Lyric Subversion of Narrative in Women's Writing: Virginia Woolf and the Tyranny of Plot." *Reading Narrative: Form, Ethics, Ideology.* Ed. James Phelan. Columbus: Ohio State UP, 1989. 162-85.

Greenwald, Elissa. "Casting Off From 'The Castaway': *To the Lighthouse* as Prose Elegy." *Genre* 19 (1986): 37-57.

Kristeva, Julia. *Black Sun: Depression and Melancholia.* Trans. Leon S. Roudiez. New York: Columbia UP, 1989.

Maso, Carole. *Ghost Dance.* Hopewell, NJ: Ecco, 1986.

Mepham, John. "Mourning and Modernism." *Virginia Woolf: New Critical Essays.* Ed. Patricia Clements and Isobel Grundy. London: Vision, 1983. 137-56.

Shaviro, Steven. "Exhoritance and Death: Marguerite Young's Vision." *Marguerite Young, Our Darling.* Ed. Miriam Fuchs. Normal, IL: Dalkey Archive, 1994. 122-8.

Smith, Susan Bennett. "Reinventing Grief Work: Virginia Woolf's Feminist Representations of Mourning in *Mrs. Dalloway* and *To the Lighthouse.*" *Twentieth Century Literature* 41 (1995): 310-27.

Spilka, Mark. *Virginia Woolf's Quarrel with Grieving.* Lincoln: U of Nebraska P, 1980.

Strehle, Susan. "Telling Women's Time: *Miss MacIntosh, My Darling.*" *Marguerite Young, Our Darling.* Ed. Miriam Fuchs. Normal, IL: Dalkey Archive, 1994. 106-11.

Woolf, Virginia. *The Diary of Virginia Woolf.* Ed. Anne Olivier Bell, assisted by Andrew McNeillie. Vol. 3. London: Hogarth, 1980.

——. "Mr. Bennett and Mrs. Brown." *The Captain's Death Bed and Other Essays.* New York: Harcourt, Brace & World, 1950. 94-119.

——. *To the Lighthouse.* San Diego: Harvest, 1989.

Young, Marguerite. *Miss MacIntosh, My Darling.* New York: Harcourt Brace, 1965.

# Historicized Textualities: Resisting Patriarchy

## Vara Neverow, Featured Speaker

### Thinking Back Through Our Mothers, Thinking in Common: Virginia Woolf's Photographic Imagination and the Community of Narrators in *Jacob's Room, A Room of One's Own, and Three Guineas*

In writing this talk, I was thinking back through my scholarly "mothers"—the critics both female and male who have given birth to the body of Woolf criticism that situates her as a feminist, socialist, activist, pacifist, incest survivor, and radical lesbian and I hope you will hear the murmur of that communal voice, for, as Woolf and her narrators argue, the living body of feminist thought can only be sustained by such communal effort. I must also state that this project is in great measure a joint effort with Krystyna Colburn and that Diane Gillespie's landmark article "Her Kodak Pointed at His Head: Virginia Woolf and Photography" is essential to my argument.

But what, you may ask, does the narrator of *Jacob's Room* have to do with the narrators of *A Room of One's Own* and *Three Guineas*? What I hope to establish is that the narrator of Virginia Woolf's novel *Jacob's Room* (1922), is a sister/self of the narrators in Woolf's two political tracts *A Room of One's Own* (1929) and *Three Guineas* (1938) and that these narrators think in common and speak in unison with her, echoing Woolf's own voice. However, before I explore the connections among these texts, I must discuss a rather unusual photo album from Virginia and Leonard Woolf's estate which I believe is part of this same continuum. The album is part of the Woolfs' extensive collection of photos, the majority of which are gathered into the seven albums (MH1-MH-7) in the Frederick R. Koch Collection in the Harvard Theater Collection at the Pusey Library. In addition to the albums, the Koch Collection also includes a significant number of photos and negatives loose in envelopes. Of the seven albums, five contain primarily the photographs of the Stephen family and the friends of the Woolfs, many of which were used by John Lehmann for *Virginia Woolf and Her*

*World* and by George Spater and Ian Parsons for *A Marriage of True Minds*. There is also one album with just a few photos which was almost certainly intended to showcase Leonard's photos from his sojourn in Ceylon (the rest of the Ceylon photos are loose in envelopes, the project apparently attempted half-heartedly and never completed).

It is the first album of the collection (MH-1) on which I wish to focus. Diane Gillespie describes the album as "Victorian photographs of famous people" (131) and Elizabeth Richardson in her *Bloomsbury Iconography* refers to the album "opening with *cartes-de-visite* from the 1880s" (B5 Appendix B 322). The album is a collection of 142 photographs, primarily consisting of *cartes-de-visite*, some of which are from the 1860s, but also including cabinet photos and a number of formal portrait photos and snapshots from a later era, possibly the 1910s or even 1920s. Instead of being entirely random, the album seems to have a rather powerful rationale underlying its distinctive organizational pattern. I would like to suggest that this collection of photographs may be either a very early precursor of the notebooks for *Three Guineas* or an actual adjunct to Woolf's twelve volumes of *Three Guineas* research (Silver). In either case, the album seems to evidence Woolf's determination to indict patriarchy for heinous crimes committed against humanity using the portraits of famous men not as icons but as mug shots of perpetrators. In fact, as William Welling points out in his *Collectors' Guide to Nineteenth Century Photographs*, "the carte de visite was adopted for police 'rogues' galleries'" (57). Thus, for such a project, photography is an ideal resource, as the photos in *Three Guineas* demonstrate. As Susan Sontag accurately observes, photographs "furnish evidence" and "the camera record incriminates" (5).

Since the heyday of the *carte-de-visite* was in the 1860s, this large collection could easily have come from a family treasure trove. It is also possible that the *cartes-de-visite* were accumulated systematically over a period of time by Virginia Woolf or another family member who collected such mementos. The likelihood, however, is that the *cartes-de-visite* themselves (as opposed to other, later items in the album) were collected by Leslie Stephen since the majority of the photographs are of his contemporaries (Stephen was born November 28, 1832 and died in 1904 at the age of 72). Most of the *cartes-de-visite* of famous or public figures have typeset captions provided by the professional photographer but some of the studio photographs are not identified (for a listing of the photographs in sequence by page, see Table 1). The album begins with two unidentified cabinet photos which have been somewhat roughly cut down to fit into the album; one is of a woman holding a pug dog and the other is of a man and woman standing side by side. In the collection are *cartes-de-visite* of some of Leslie Stephen's friends and acquaintances—for example, the album includes photos of Elizabeth Gaskell, George Eliot, Tom Hughes and Henry James. At least one photo is of a relative—Leslie Stephen's cousin, Edward Dicey, who became the Marquis of Hartington. The photo groupings seem to be, on the whole, thematic. Many of the groupings are organized by the profession of the subjects—clusters of ecclesiasticals or politicians or military men. One grouping, which may attest to Leslie Stephen's visit to the United States in 1863 "at the height of the Civil War" (Annan 52), includes photographs of Abraham Lincoln, General Robert E. Lee, Jeff Davis, Ulysses Grant and William Lloyd Garrison, an abolitionist newspaper publisher. There are also a few clusterings that primarily feature women, one such being photographs of the actresses Sarah Bernhardt, Ellen Terry, and Mrs. Langtry and the writers Elizabeth Barrett Browning, and George Eliot (this cluster also includes Mr. Gaskell).

The clusters seem to be organized so as to comment on each other in rather interesting ways. For example, there is a grouping of ecclesiasticals which consists of Ugo Bassi, the (unnamed) Patriarch of Greece, Cardinal Wiseman and Dean Stanley. Bassi, a priest who supported Giuseppe Garibaldi's revolutionary movement and was ultimately executed on charges of bearing arms though he never carried or used a weapon in the struggle, is implicitly linked to photographs in the album of Garibaldi, the military genius of guerilla warfare who initiated the effort for Italian unification, and to Pius IX, the pope who abandoned his nationalist position and turned against Garibaldi. Garibaldi himself appears in a cluster with Helmuth Moltke and Lord Napier, who was involved in numerous military engagements including the Indian Mutiny of 1857. Another group of photographs includes images of Gambetta, who served as war minister during the Franco-German War of 1870-71, Jules Grévy (1807–1891) and Marie-Edme-Patrice Maurice Mac-Mahon (1808–1893) whom Grévy succeeded as President of France. Also in this grouping is Adolphe Thiers (1797–1877), the French leader who helped elect Louis Napoleon (his *carte-de-visite* image is also included in the album). Thiers was responsible, with the assistance of the Germans, for the slaughter of 20,000 Communards in Paris during the 1871 Commune uprising (*The New Encyclopedia Britannica*).

The album itself closely resembles the scrapbooks Woolf made for her *Three Guineas* clippings. Like the scrapbooks, this album is an improvised affair—a two ring loose-leaf binder with sloppily hand-glued blue cloth boards, not a professionally produced item like some of the other albums. The pages themselves, however, are commercial heavyweight photo album cardstock with brass grommets. In addition to the studio captioning, almost every photograph is captioned on the album page with the name of the subject in a handwriting strikingly similar to Woolf's. These captions themselves strongly indicate an organizational plan especially since many were first written in pencil and then retraced in black or red ink. One caption—that for the photograph of Tyndall—was erased and Herbert Spenser was substituted, suggesting that a particular sequence of images was intended.

Based on multiple levels of physical evidence, I would argue that that this album was assembled (and perhaps even occasionally rearranged) by

Virginia Woolf over an extended period of time and that it reveals a deliberate strategy of sequencing. One must take into account that, despite the apparent haphazardness typical of Woolf's research notebooks, Woolf was very systematic in her organization of certain materials. As Brenda Silver indicates in her introduction to *Virginia Woolf's Reading Notebooks*, Woolf's "notes [are] interspersed . . . with names, addresses, shopping lists, passages from her novels, even drawings, jotted on the backs of pages or interjected into other entries" (26). One thus is not entirely surprised that the fourth album in the Koch collection begins with a newspaper clipping clearly of significance to Woolf's research for *Three Guineas*. The cutting, which is from the 5 May 1938 *News Chronicle*, is captioned "Lady Baldwin addressing wives and mothers who went to the Ministry of Health yesterday to discuss formation of babies' welfare clubs." It is worth noting that, in her *Three Guineas* scrapbooks, Woolf included a letter from C. S. Wentworth Stanley, the Chairman of the House Committee at The City of London Maternity Hospital, to the editor of *The Times*, praising Lady Baldwin for having won the battle to "introduce analgesics (pain deadeners) for normal maternity cases" (MH B.16.f Vol. 3:6; Silver LX13 301), a topic the narrator of *Three Guineas* mentions twice. In the body of the text, she notes that if women had wealth, they would have power—the power, for instance, to "provide every mother with chloroform when her child is born" (*TG* 68). In the footnote, the narrator quotes the letter in its entirety and scathingly remarks that "since chloroform was administered to Queen Victoria, on the birth of Prince Leopold in April 1853, 'normal maternity cases in the wards' have had to wait for seventy-six years and the advocacy of a Prime Minister's wife to obtain this relief" (*TG* n19 163-164).

Like the album of *cartes-de-visite*, Woolf's scrapbooks for *Three Guineas* are organized thematically, clustering newspaper clippings in much the same way as the album groups photographs. As Sybil Oldfield points out in "The Elegaic Artist," "Woolf juxtaposed Hitler's definition of maleness ('A Nation of Men') with a photograph of Mussolini's son-in-law, Count Ciano, smiling above his death's-head emblem, and above Ciano, a cutting about the persecution of Frau Pommer of Essen ('The Thorn of Hatred') for speaking out against anti-Jewish hatred in Germany. She was arrested for 'slandering the State'" (114). In a footnote, Oldfield points out that most of the second scrapbook consists of materials from 1937, stressing that "this particular page," which includes materials from 1935 and 1936, "suggests that Virginia Woolf had made a special point of preserving these items" (114n50), creating a kind of mosaic of information.

Even though Gillespie indicates that in the five albums dealing with Virginia's family and Leonard and Virginia's life together, "the photos . . . often are arranged without regard for chronology or subject, labeling is in different hands and sporadic as well as occasionally inaccurate, and professional photographs and postcards are mixed with Leonard's and Virginia's own [photographic] work" (n33 130-31), the undisturbed organization of the *cartes-de-visite* album (an artifact which has attracted almost no attention from Woolf scholars) indicates that some of this disorder could be due to careless prior use of the collection by such researchers as Lehmann or Parsons and Spater who worked with the albums in the 1970s. The albums offer strong evidence that Virginia was the Stephen and Woolf family archivist. This claim is premised on the relative completeness of the Stephen and Woolf photo albums (despite their comparative disorganization). The family photo albums, even if they were initially compiled by Leslie Stephen or Julia Stephen or one of the other children, were maintained in a consistent fashion for decades by one person. The albums are a critical point of reference for the argument that Virginia Woolf assembled the *cartes-de-visite* album. The final Monk's House family photo album, though it is dated 1939 on the cover and actually begins with photos from 1930, also has handmade boards like that of the *cartes-de-visite* album and is only partially full. The few photos added after 1941 are clearly inserted by another hand. That hand is almost unquestionably Leonard's. The features of Leonard's contributions to the album are distinctive and it is important to note that the album is unfinished, like his Ceylon album, and that most of the photographs taken subsequent to 1941 are loose in envelopes, including the famous portraits of Leonard taken by Gisele Freund late in his life. While whoever maintained the other Monk's House photograph albums had systematically outlined each photograph in thick marking pencil and then inserted the photo into four comparatively neat diagonal matte knife cuts across the corners of the outline, the person who added photographs after 1941 made no outlines around the few additional items in the album before they were inserted. The incisions themselves are crooked and have ragged edges. Prior photos were inserted only on one side of the album page; however, the few final photos are placed somewhat haphazardly on both sides of the page, creating a certain degree of visual confusion since the corners of photos on the other side stick through and distract the eye. Further, several of the final photos are of cats Leonard acquired after Virginia's death.

Additional evidence linking the album of *cartes-de-visite* to Virginia Woolf can be found in the photographs themselves. The album includes uncaptioned portraits of Leslie Stephen and of Sidney Woolf, Q.C. Even if the album was originally Leslie Stephen's, it would be odd for him to place his own uncaptioned cabinet photo portrait among the studio photos of his contemporaries and it is very unlikely that he would have included the photograph of his daughter's father-in-law, who had died in 1892, especially since Virginia did not even meet Leonard until after her father's death. Further, there is a photograph in the album of Leslie Stephen's friend Henry James as a relatively young man which is captioned "Sir Henry"—an honor not bestowed on James until 1916, 12 years after Leslie Stephen's death. Also of interest is the photograph of the unidentified woman with a dog, an image which may be referenced in *A Room of One's Own* when the narrator urges women writers to tell the stories of anonymous women, to "go . . . in the spirit of fellowship into those small, scented rooms where sit the courtesan, the harlot and the lady with the pug dog" (*AROO* 92).

If this is an album consisting of *cartes-de-visite* from Leslie Stephen's collection, Woolf would have inherited the photographs themselves in 1904, the year of his death. Although there is no way to determine when the album was assembled, and it is quite possible that Woolf arranged these images in this handmade album late in her life, it is equally possible that she was engaged in the project of patriarchal critique long before she published her first novel. Whether one sees the organizational pattern of the *cartes-de-visite* album as a visual harbinger of all of Woolf's political statements or, shifting the dating, as an important supplement to Woolf's *Three Guineas* scrapbooks, the album is a political document in the same ways that *Jacob's Room, A Room of One's Own* and *Three Guineas* are political; in other words, like this collection of *cartes-de-visite*, each of these works are virtual photo albums featuring men (and women) whether of actual or fictitious historical relevance to the feminist project Woolf undertook as her life work.

The narrators of *Jacob's Room, A Room of One's Own* and *Three Guineas* share certain features that do not occur as explicitly in any other of Woolf's published works except, perhaps, the biographies, which themselves participate only peripherally in this commonality. *Orlando, Flush* and *Roger Fry* are all texts in which the narrator documents the genesis of a male cultural identity, but Orlando changes sex, Flush is a dog, and Roger Fry was a friend, not the subject of a critique. *Jacob's Room* has much more in common with *A Room of One's Own* and *Three Guineas* than with these biographies. Unlike the biographies, *Jacob's Room, A Room of One's Own* and *Three Guineas* are all full-scale studies of contemporary patriarchal practices presenting views virtually identical to Woolf's own—despite her claims to the contrary. To her friend Jacques Raverat, Woolf wrote a rather disingenuous disclaimer on this subject, remarking: "Women may be worse, or may be better, than men, but surely the opinions of the writer of Jacobs Room on that point, or any other, are not *my* opinions" (quoted in Hussey 128). Since Clive Bell years earlier had chastised Woolf for a similar transgression, criticizing Melymbrosia, the draft of *The Voyage Out*, for its "sharp & marked contrasts between the subtle, sensitive, tactful, graceful, delicately perceptive, & perspicacious women, & the obtuse, vulgar, blind, florid, rude, tactless, emphatic, indelicate, vain, tyrannical, stupid men" (Bell, *Virginia Woolf*, Vol. 1 Appendix D 209), she had learned to be more cunning and evasive (see Carroll 101-3).

While all of Woolf's works offer memorable descriptions of archetypal patriarchs and intrepid female resisters, the narrators of most of her novels do not explicitly identify themselves as critics of patriarchy whereas in *Jacob's Room, A Room of One's Own* and *Three Guineas*, the narrators are openly and specifically antagonistic toward patriarchal culture and deliberately create derisive verbal portraits of patriarchs. In *Jacob's Room*, there are such vivid examples as the fictitious naval hero, Captain Barfoot with his maimed hand and his rubber-shod stick (*JR* 28), "Old General Gibbons" asking "Where are the men?," "Where are the guns"? (*JR* 156) and the "elderly man," with the "bald, red-veined, hollow-looking" head, who, with fifteen other gentlemen, initiate British involvement in the Great European War, "decree[ing] . . . the course of history[,]" "manfully determined to impose some coherency upon Rajahs and Kaisers" (*JR* 172). In *A Room of One's Own*, we have not only the Kaiser, the Czar, Napoleon and Mussolini but Galsworthy and Kipling, Oscar Browning and Sir Chartres Biron, the insufferably misogynistic scholar Professor Von X (who seems to be a caricature of Sigmund Freud) and the enormous pseudo-photographic image of Milton's bogey projected onto the sky itself. *Three Guineas* offers additional real-life dictators, a rogue's gallery that positions Adolf Hitler and St. Paul alongside the overbearing fathers of Elizabeth Barrett Browning and Sophia Jex-Blake.

Like all women writers, the narrators of these texts think back through their mothers (*AROO* 76, 97). All are the daughters of educated men and were "educated by the same teachers" (those teachers, of course, are "poverty, chastity, derision" and "'lack of rights and privileges," a term which the narrator of *Three Guineas* glosses as "freedom from unreal loyalties" [*TG* 68]). All the narrators situate the women who defy patriarchy as members of a Society of Outsiders and gleefully celebrate these women's acts of resistance against the vast impediment of patriarchy. Further, while not all women who resist patriarchy are lesbians, the narrators of these texts make it clear that many members of the Society of Outsiders are, in fact, lesbians whether they are fictitious figures like Betty Flanders and Mrs. Jarvis in *Jacob's Room* or Chloe and Olivia in *A Room of One's Own*, or historical figures such as Mary Kingsley or Sophia Jex-Blake.

As these narrative voices intertwine, they create a narrative genealogy that can—as indicated above—be traced to their literary and political mother/creator, Woolf herself. Although the narrators' arguments are foregrounded differently in each text, all are intimately interrelated and focus on the same agenda. All three narrators are obviously situated as surrogate authors who purportedly "write" the text we read. Further, all three are anonymous (a typically Woolfian gesture), are definitively of the same sex (female) and speak from a specifically gendered perspective frequently using the plural pronoun "we" to invoke the community of women. All three of these narrators situate themselves in a familial relation to patriarchy and, on the occasions when they acknowledge their male readers, they articulate themselves as outraged sisters reproving their more privileged brothers (see Swanson 36). All offer gender-specific double narratives, revealing the profound differences between female and male realities. All are fiercely critical of Oxbridge, especially its enforcement of gender inequity and its investment in the destructive militaristic values of patriarchal culture. All speak in similar registers, though each subsequent voice becomes more caustic, more pointedly critical of patriarchal culture and more emphatically feminist.

*Jacob's Room* can be seen as a prophetic text, predicting the arguments of *A Room of One's Own* and *Three Guineas*. Of the three narrators, the narrator of *Jacob's Room* is probably the least stinging and sarcastic in her depiction of patriarchs and the least overtly political in her articulation of the images of women. This narrator, who as Pamela Caughie observes, "becomes a character in her own story" (69), evidences a significant degree of affection for her doomed protagonist even though he is a patriarch in training. As many critics have noted, *Jacob's Room* is to a degree an elegy for Virginia Woolf's eldest brother, Thoby Stephen (for a concise summary of these critical perspectives, see Hussey 127-128). It was in 1906, that Thoby, Vanessa and Virginia's friend Violet Dickinson all contracted typhoid fever while on an excursion to Greece with Adrian and Virginia. Vanessa and Violet lived but Thoby died, possibly because of medical incompetence, at the age of 26 shortly after his return to England. The narrator's tenderheartedness toward Jacob can legitimately be linked directly to Woolf's memories of her relationship with Thoby. One such moment of reminiscence is the transformation of the young Virginia's diary entry on a "sugaring" expedition with Thoby ("the most scientific way of catching moths") into the account of Jacob's nocturnal pursuit of moths in the woods (*A Passionate Apprentice* 144-5; *JR* 23).

While the narrative link between *Jacob's Room* and these subsequent works must be established, the continuity between *A Room of One's Own* and *Three Guineas* is explicit. For example, Woolf actually refers to the nascent *Three Guineas* (which she began November 23, 1936 [Bishop 188]) as *A Room of One's Own* in a letter to her friend Ethel Smyth in 1936 (*Letters* 6: 44) . Like *Jacob's Room*, which incorporates Woolf's memories of Thoby, *Three Guineas* is an elegy of sorts for Julian Bell, Virginia Woolf's nephew. Julian, named after his uncle Thoby (whose full name was Julian Thoby Stephen) wanted, as Nigel Nicolson and Joanne Trautmann point out, "to take an active part in resisting Fascism" (*L*6 85n1). When the Spanish Civil War began, he joined a team of ambulance drivers and went to Spain where, on July 18, he was struck by a shell and mortally injured, dying just a few hours later. He was 29. As Nigel Nicolson and Joanne Trautmann observe, "Julian's death came at the very moment when Virginia was writing *Three Guineas*" (xv). As Woolf admitted to her sister, "I'm always wanting to argue it with him—in fact I wrote it as an argument with him. Somehow he stirred me up to argue" (*L*6 159). Particularly poignant is that Woolf described in a letter to Julian while he was still in China the hideous photographs of children killed in the Spanish Civil War, photographs which she deliberately omits from *Three Guineas* (*L*6 85).

Woolf found Julian's fatal urge to fight just as incomprehensible as her childhood confrontations with Thoby: "We were pommelling each other with our fists. Just as I raised my fist to hit him, I felt: why hurt another person? I dropped my hand instantly, and stood there, and let him beat me. I remember the feeling. It was a feeling of hopeless sadness" ("A Sketch of the Past" 71). Woolf's letters and diary entries over the years indicate that Julian always reminded her strongly of Thoby. In a letter to Judith Stephen, the daughter of Adrian and Karin Stephen, written more than a year after Julian's death and subsequent to the publication of *Three Guineas*, Woolf, who had once described Thoby as "a charming great inarticulate creature, with torrents of things shut up in him" (*L*1 74), remarks that "Julian was a magnificent creature. What would he have done, I wonder. He had such an immense store of life in him, and God knows why he went and threw it away. But I daresay it was better in Spain than in Flanders" (*L*6 372). As the reference to Flanders suggests, it seems that *Jacob's Room* had become—following Julian's death—a unintended prequel to the epistolary *Three Guineas*. *Three Guineas* appears to be addressed to a composite correspondent who fuses both Thoby Stephen and Julian Bell with Thoby's surrogate self, Jacob Flanders, the perfect specimen of the privileged middle- or upper-class male:

> You . . . are a little grey on the temples; the hair is no longer thick on the top of your head. You have reached the middle years of life not without effort, at the Bar; . . . [y]ou have never sunk into the contented apathy of middle life, for, as your letter shows . . . you are writing letters, attending meetings, . . . asking questions, with the sound of guns in your ears. For the rest, you began your education at one of the great public schools and finished it at the university. (*TG* 3-4)

Although *Jacob's Room* is a memorial to Thoby ("pictures of the dead oversee the present in Woolf's novels" [121] as Gillespie observes with regard to *The Voyage Out*, a novel begun shortly after Leslie Stephen's death), it is also a consciously crafted portrait of the generic patriarch. As Robert Kiely points out, the parallels to Thoby, which include "the Cambridge education, love of literature, visit to Greece, intention to study law, even the awkward good looks and the tendency to be tongue-tied . . . as Woolf knew[,]. . . did little to distinguish her brother from hundreds of other young Englishmen of their generation" (208). The composite portrait of Jacob almost certainly draws on Woolf's depressingly conventional and sexually repulsive half-brothers, George and Gerald Duckworth, who molested Woolf (see DeSalvo) and imposed rigid patriarchal standards of female beauty and behavior on both her and her sister Vanessa, an experience Woolf and Vanessa refer to as "those Greek slave years and all their drudgery and tyranny and rebellion" ("A Sketch of the Past" 106). Like Jacob and his infant brother John, George and Gerald were very young at the time when their father, Herbert Duckworth, died suddenly. Even without Louise DeSalvo's argument that the young Virginia's "Terrible Tragedy in a Duckpond" documented the Duckworth brothers' transgressions by intricate punning on their last name (257-60), it seems quite calculated that the narrator of *Jacob's Room* attributes the cause of Seabrook Flanders' death to complications associated with a bout of "duck-shooting" (*JR* 16).

As Caughie suggests, "Woolf draws attention to narrative strategies and thus to the ways in which characters and, by implication, notions of identity are produced" (64). Jacob is a patriarch in the making because the culture codes him thus. He is described as:

> satisfied; indeed masterly; which expression changed slightly as he stood there, the sound of the clock conveying to him (it may be) a sense of old buildings and time; and himself the inheritor; and then tomorrow; and friends; at the thought of whom, in sheer confidence and pleasure, it seemed, he yawned and stretched himself. (*JR* 45)

Later in the book, the meaning of time shifts into a different register when "the master gunner counts the seconds, watch in hand" just before a target "flames into splinters," killing "a dozen young men in the prime of life," young men just like Jacob (*JR* 153; see Handley 122). Unlike the narrator of *A Room of One's Own*, when Jacob reads the *Daily Mail*, he feels free to reflect that "[o]ur fathers at any rate had something to demolish. So have we for the matter of that[.] . . . He would go into Parliament and make fine speeches" and he never once doubts his privilege to do so (*JR* 139). Jacob's very footsteps "ech[o] with magisterial authority" and when he goes to the British Museum to read Christopher Marlowe, he is perceived from the point of view of the feminist scholar, Julia Hedge, as "regal and pompous" (*JR* 107).

The narrator's description of Jacob's casual arrogance is strongly echoed in *A Room of One's Own* and *Three Guineas*. In *A Room of One's Own*, the narrator describes her impression of the novelist Mr. A: "One had a sense of physical well-being in the presence of this well-nourished, well-educated, free mind, which had never been thwarted or opposed, but had had full liberty from birth to stretch itself in whatever way it liked" (*AROO* 103), similarly, in *Three Guineas*, the code term "Arthur's Education Fund" translates for the young patriarch into the affirming experience of a public school and university education much more valuable than the "book-learning" which the daughter of an educated man could glean from her father's library: "games educated your body; friends taught you more than books or games. Talk with them broadened your outlook and enriched your mind. In the holidays you travelled; acquired a taste for art; a knowledge of foreign politics" (*TG* 4-5).

The narrators of *Jacob's Room*, *A Room of One's Own* and *Three Guineas* offer compelling evidence of what I would like to call a photographic imagination, an imagination which is further reinforced by the actual images of the patriarchy published in the first edition of *Three Guineas*. Essentially, these three works are a kind of triptych portraying the dominant male and muted female cultural traditions. This threefold manifestation of Woolf's political vision—early, middle and late in her career—

is also rather like the tripod which supports her photographic imagination as she documents the activities of the Patriarchs and the Society of Outsiders. While only *Three Guineas* includes any actual illustrations, all three works are virtual photo albums of patriarchs. Similar to the missing photos from the Spanish Civil War in *Three Guineas*, these images are printed directly on the reader's mind by the chemistry of the narrator's words. Like Woolf's great aunt, Julia Margaret Cameron, the noted photographer whose technique emphasized highly stylized poses and featured images both of the famous and the obscure, including photographs of Annie Philpott, "a local orphan" and "the long-suffering Mary Hillier, Cameron's maid, model, and photographic assistant" (Roberts 49; see also 50), Woolf herself throughout her entire oeuvre alternates between depicting the famous and the altogether unknown. Countering her father's greatest project, the highly patriarchal *Dictionary of National Biography*, Woolf, particularly in *Jacob's Room*, *A Room of One's Own* and *Three Guineas* (as well as in her biographies), has assembled a kind of illustrated, deliberately oppositional, multi-volume work offering a radically alternative version of history and reality.

Woolf was intrigued by the cultural impact of photography and was herself an amateur photographer. The young Virginia's interest in photography is evidenced by her diary entries from 1897 when she was only 15; in the diary, she makes repeated references to pictures she has taken and developed (see, for example, the entries for 10 and 11 August 1897 in *A Passionate Apprentice* 121). After Virginia married, she and Leonard often photographed their friends, and Virginia's sister, Vanessa Bell, was also an avid photographer as documented by the published album of her photographs compiled by Quentin Bell and Angelica Garnett.

In *Jacob's Room*, *A Room of One's Own* and *Three Guineas*, Woolf consistently links the record provided by visual representation such as photographic and painted portraits to the written record provided by history and biography. The narrator of *Jacob's Room*, describing Jacob's lodgings, notes that near the "photograph of his mother," lies "paper ruled with a red margin—an essay no doubt—'Does History consist of the Biographies of Great Men?'" (*JR* 39). The narrator of *Three Guineas*, in a passage that refers to the suppressed photographs from Spain, notes that, "besides these pictures of other people's lives and minds, these biographies and histories, there are also other pictures, pictures of actual facts; photographs." In this same passage, the narrator also comments somewhat artfully that "[p]hotographs, of course, are not arguments addressed to the reason; they are simply statements of fact addressed to the eye" (*TG* 20). She equates this visual record not only with history and biography but with daily newspapers and radio broadcasts and argues that the existence of the somewhat fugitive Society of Outsiders—a "model [which], far from sitting still to be painted, dodges and disappears," is documented "by history and biography in the raw, by the newspapers that is, sometimes openly in the lines, sometimes covertly between them" (*TG* 209).

As these passages suggest, the narrators in *Jacob's Room*, *A Room of One's Own* and *Three Guineas* repeatedly advance the argument that real history is a record of the forgotten and the oppressed, not just an account of the oppressors' triumphs. To make this claim, each narrator interweaves photographs and portraits with newspapers and radio broadcasts as well as published biographical and historical materials. In *Jacob's Room*, the narrator compares newspapers to a nightmarish quasi-photographic process—"thin sheets of gelatine pressed nightly over the brain and heart of the world . . . take the impression of the whole." She comments bitterly: "[h]ow miserable it is that the *Globe* newspaper offers nothing better to Jacob Flanders" than accounts of "a strike, a murder, football, bodies found" (*JR* 98) and remarks on the venerable history of patriarchal domination: "[w]hen a child begins to read history, one marvels, sorrowfully, to hear him spell out in his new voice the ancient words" (*JR* 98). The narrator of *A Room of One's Own*, who, before she received her legacy, made a living in part by "cadging odd jobs from newspapers" (*AROO* 37), reads similar news items in the daily paper as she eats her lunch, and observes angrily that "the most transient visitor to this planet . . . who picked up this paper could not fail to be aware, even from this scattered testimony, that England is under the rule of a patriarchy" (*AROO* 35). The narrator of *Three Guineas*, echoing the narrator of *Jacob's Room*, observes with regard to contemporary history that "the uproar [on the wireless] . . . is such that we can hardly hear ourselves speak [,] [A]s we listen to the voices we seem to hear an infant crying in the night, the black night that now covers Europe[.] . . . But it is not a new cry, it is a very old cry[.] . . . [It] is the voice of Creon, the dictator" whom Antigone defied at the cost of her life (*TG* 141).

Despite his university education, Jacob, who is "not much given to analysis" (*JR* 139), is oblivious to this ancient tradition of patriarchal violence. He does not recognize that his patriarchal privileges depend on the inevitable exercise of patriarchal aggression and that he is contractually obligated to participate in the inevitable slaughter. Judy Little comments that Jacob is "a brutally deceived heir" of the patriarchy (112) while William Handley observes that Jacob is ultimately just another commodity in the patriarchal marketplace, as much a prostitute as Laurette or Florinda (116). Woolf's "portrait" of Jacob is an obvious expropriation of James Joyce's quintessentially patriarchal *Portrait of the Artist as a Young Man* (Lawrence; Hussey 126) and a parody of the male *bildungsroman* (Little). Stressing the scopophilic aspect of the novel, Karen Lawrence notes: "Unlike Joyce's cool and unobtrusive narrator who shares Stephen's experiences, Woolf's narrator serves as a kind of voyeur of the male personality," for "the main interpreter of this novel of education is a woman, . . . excluded, as was Woolf, from the very kind of education he is free to obtain" (Lawrence 33-4). This voyeuristic perspective is, of course, profoundly photographic. As Sontag argues, "To photograph people is to violate them, by seeing them as they can never see themselves, by having knowledge of them that they can never have; it turns people into objects that can be possessed" (14). Lawrence contends that "exclusion from Jacob's mind forces us to develop our skills of observation and to learn to read a face or gesture" (34) and, in a different register, Gillespie specifically notes that *Jacob's Room* foregrounds Woolf's "verbal snapshot" technique (144).

The photographic and visual imagination of the narrator in *Jacob's Room* is gendered female as are the photographers who are specifically mentioned in the text. Thus, there is a conscious narrative emphasis on the female gaze. Julia Eliot, the spinster photographer, seems to be a deliberate invocation of Julia Margaret Cameron as she enthusiastically sets up her tripod and camera equipment on the lawn of her hostess, Mrs. Durrant, to photograph Joseph Clutterbuck, another house guest, as Jacob is leaving for London. The other photographer—Madame Lucien Gravé—actively preempts Jacob's scopophilic male privilege as the one who looks. Further, though old Mrs. Pascoe is not a photographer but a lonely working class woman living in an isolated cottage, she represents the variant female gaze of a woman looking at another woman. Mrs. Pascoe particularly enjoys "the picture papers" that are "delivered punctually on Sunday" and "she pore[s] long over Lady Cynthia's wedding at the Abbey" (*JR* 54).

While some of the images in *Jacob's Room* are like blurred snapshots, others are remarkably like posed photographs. Snapshots include such scenes as the Guy Fawkes bonfire at which Florinda is first seen. "Of the faces which came out fresh and vivid as though painted in yellow and red, the most prominent was a girl's face. By a trick of the firelight she seemed to have no body. The oval of the face and hair hung beside the fire with a dark vacuum for background" (*JR* 74). A posed description of Lady Rocksbier verges on photographic portraiture. She has "[a] discriminating nose . . . for scents, prolonged, as if in quest of them; her underlip protruded a narrow red shelf; her eyes were small, with sandy tufts for eyebrows, and her jowl was heavy" (*JR* 100). While Lady Rocksbier is definitely ugly by patriarchal standards, a topic I will return to, the narrator suggests that beauty itself is so ephemeral that it is best captured by the camera: "if you talk of a beautiful woman you mean only something flying fast which for a second uses the eyes, lips, or cheeks of Fanny Elmer, for example, to glow through" (*JR* 115). Fanny, as she poses for the painter Nick Bramham, suddenly looks remarkably like Lady Rocksbier: "she [is] not beautiful[.] . . . [H]er underlip too prominent; her nose too large; her eyes too near together" (*JR* 115). Disturbingly morbid is the framed and posed photographic image evoked by the description of Seabrook, Jacob's father, "dead these many years; enclosed in three shells; the crevices sealed with lead so that, had earth and wood been glass, doubtless his very face lay visible beneath, the face of a young man whiskered, shapely, who had gone out duck-shooting and refused to change his boots" (*JR* 16).

The verbal images of Jacob are deliberately enigmatic and, as many critics have noted, Jacob is known only superficially. To intensify this sense of the superficial, the narrator offers the reader snapshot glimpses of Jacob as he is seen by those around him. "'Extremely awkward,' [Mrs. Durrant] sa[ys], 'but so distinguished-looking" and the narrator herself chimes in, remarking that "[s]eeing him for the first time [distinguished-looking] is the word for him"; Julia Eliot, the photographer, refers to him as "the silent young man"; "Timothy Durrant never made any comment at all"; "Mr. Sopwith's opinion was as sentimental as Clara's, though far more skillfully expressed"; "Captain Barfoot liked him best of the boys, but as for saying why . . ." (*JR* 70, 71; ellipsis in text). In addition to such photographic metaphors, the narrator and other characters repeatedly compare Jacob to classical sculpture. Florinda babbles to him "[y]ou're like one of those statutes [in the British Museum]" (*JR* 80); Fanny Elmer, having had the misfortune to fall hopelessly in love with Jacob, goes to the museum to alleviate the ache of desire by looking surreptitiously at the statue of Ulysses (*JR* 170). Clara Durrant also subconsciously links the doomed Jacob to the siege of Troy, associating him involuntarily with the statue of Achilles (*JR* 166) in Hyde Park. In addition to statues, the narrator uses tombstones and epitaphs, tombs and monuments to fix the fleeting moment much in the same fashion as photographs. Aside from the fantastic glimpse into the grave, Jacob's father, Seabrook Flanders, is represented only by the epitaph on his tombstone: "'Merchant of this city,' the tombstone said" (*JR* 15). Combining the photographic and the sepulchral, the prostitute Florinda had "for parents . . . only the photograph of a tombstone beneath which, she said, her father lay buried" (*JR* 77). The narrator also offers the reader a photographic glimpse of "a mason's van with newly lettered tombstones recording how some one loved some one who is buried at Putney. Then the motor car in front jerks forward, and the tombstones pass too quick for you to read more" (*JR* 112).

The text of *Jacob's Room* functions as a rather disorganized photo album in which, to use Sontag's terms, "[a] photograph is both a pseudo-presence and a token of absence" (16). The narrative technique in the chapters before Jacob goes to Cambridge seems to be based on an album arranged by Betty Flanders, Jacob's rather helter-skelter mother, a woman whose organizational skills are suggested by the passage in which, after "ferreting" for a stamp in her bag, she must "h[o]ld it up mouth downwards" and rummage in her lap" (*JR* 8). At the beginning of the novel, the reader knows that Betty Flanders, a woman of perhaps 35, has been a widow for two years and that Jacob, who seems to be about six, has wandered off down the beach. The reader's first glimpse of Jacob is like a blurry photograph in which, syntactically, the little boy seems to emerge from a huge "primitive" rock: "Rough with crinkled limpet shells and sparsely strewn with locks of dry seaweed, a small boy has to stretch his legs far apart, and indeed to feel rather heroic, before he gets to the top" (*JR* 9).

In the second chapter, more snapshots of Jacob's early life are jumbled together. The reader must guess Jacob's age based on information about his mother. At the beginning of the chapter, she is "a widow in her prime[,] . . . halfway between forty and fifty" (*JR* 17)—about ten years older than she is at the beginning of the first chapter which begins two years after her husband's death (*JR* 8). Since her husband died when Jacob was perhaps four, and has been dead for at least a decade, Jacob must be about sixteen. Without warning, the narrative flashes back to an earlier stage in Betty's life. She is again a widow in her thirties with three sons she must educate and she remembers her deceased husband vividly as she briefly considers the marriage proposal of the unprepossessing Mr. Floyd, who "out of kindness" tutored Jacob and his brothers in Latin "for three years in his spare time" (*JR* 20). At this point, Jacob, who, at the mention of his tutor, exclaims "Oh, bother Mr. Floyd" while "switching off a thistle's head," cannot be much more than eight. Jacob at about eleven is seen with his brothers as they select something from Mr. Floyd's study before he leaves for a new parish. There is a glimpse of Jacob, again at perhaps sixteen, seen "helping himself to jam," as Mrs. Flanders reads aloud from the paper that "Rev. Andrew Floyd . . . had been made Principal of Maresfield House" and later, Jacob is described examining "the upper wings of [a] moth . . . undoubtedly marked with kidney-shaped spots of a fulvous hue" and "choosing a very fine pen" to make "a correction in the margin" of an expert guide to moths. That Jacob has gone to public school is suggested primarily by a reference to "the last day of the Easter holidays" (*JR* 24).

By the end of the chapter, however, Jacob is abruptly at least eighteen and will to go off to Cambridge "in October of 1906." When, at the beginning of the next chapter, "a powerfully built young man jump[s]" on board a train to Cambridge, the reader continues to see Jacob from a dual female perspective—that of the narrator and of Mrs. Norman, "fifty years of age," with "a son at college," who recognizes "[n]evertheless, it is a fact that men are dangerous" and is fearful to "be shut up alone, in a railway carriage, with a young man." In this difficult situation, she "decide[s] the question of safety by the infallible test of appearance." What does she see? "Taking note of socks (loose), of tie (shabby), she once more reached his face. She dwelt upon his mouth. . . . One must do the best one can with her report. Anyhow, this was Jacob Flanders, aged nineteen" (*JR* 30). This highly photographic passage illustrates Sontag's caveat that, "[s]trictly speaking, one never understands anything from a photograph" (23). The "snapshot" of Jacob as a potentially dangerous man is repeated when the narrator herself describes in vividly photographic terms Jacob's paralyzing rage after he has seen Florinda, his lover, "turning up Greek Street upon another man's arm": "The light [from the arc lamp] drenched Jacob from head to toe. You could see the pattern on his trousers; the old thorns on his stick; his shoe laces, bare hands, and face" (*JR* 94). As the narrator observes, "[w]hether we know what is in his mind is another question. Granted ten years seniority and a difference of sex, fear of him comes first; this is swallowed up by a desire to help" (*JR* 94-95). Clara Durrant, too, though she writes in her diary "I like Jacob Flanders," adds the qualifier "though he is frightening because" and breaks off because she "was not the one to encroach upon Wednesday [in her shilling diary]" (*JR* 71).

Jacob, whether he is perceived as tongue-tied but distinguished or as potentially dangerous, fully epitomizes the privileges of the middle- to upper-class male and evidences the patriarchal tendencies Woolf particularly despised. He has a public school and university education and, as a consequence, a room of his own at Cambridge; he has a flat of his own when he goes down to London where, apparently, he practices law ("Head bent down, a desk, a telephone, books bound in green leather, electric light. . . . 'Fresh coals, sir? . . . 'Your tea, sir." . . . Talk about football, [ . . . ] six-thirty *Star* brought in by the office boy [ . . . ] while letters accumulate in a basket" [90; bracketed ellipses mine]). Like the narrator of *A Room of One's Own*, who inherited money from an aunt, Jacob too is the recipient of a legacy which he uses to pay for a grand tour of Europe. However, while the narrator's legacy liberates her from economic dependence on men, allowing her to think for herself and live without flattery or fear (*AROO* 38), Jacob's inheritance is used to maintain an upper-class patriarchal tradition.

Despite his father's premature death, Jacob somehow manages to acquire the patriarchal mindset, perhaps from Captain Barfoot or Mr. Floyd or his public school education, proving that men think back through their cultural not only their biological fathers. The university system reinforces the tendencies of a rather awkward and uncooperative boy and molds him into a misogynistic and somewhat arrogant undergraduate, contemptuous of his elders, "insolent . . . and inexperienced" (*JR* 36). The narrator, in her snapshot descriptions of the Cambridge community, strongly implies that Jacob, although he may be rebelling against his elders, is also very much a willing participant in a homosocial conspiracy to exclude women from the precincts of male privilege. Jacob himself evidences a sustained and unrepentant contempt for women. This scorn is illustrated by the narrator's description of a worship service in King's College Chapel (a passage which is rife with motifs that recur with a vengeance in *A Room of One's Own* and *Three Guineas*). Emphasizing the critical female gaze, the narrator encourages the reader to "[l]ook, as they pass into service, how airily the gowns blow out, as though nothing dense and corporeal were within. What sculptured faces, what certainty, authority controlled by piety, although great boots march under the gowns," a freeze-frame image strongly reminiscent of news photos. The women attending the service are seen as trespassers, defiling the sacred space: "[f]or one thing, thought Jacob, they're as ugly as sin" and "[h]e caught Timmy Durrant's eye; looked very sternly at him; and then, very solemnly, winked" (*JR* 33), demonstrating both the abhorrence of women that infects the collective male consciousness and the secretive conspiratorial exchanges between men which reinforce their patriarchal privilege.

Again focusing on the visual, the narrator reveals, in the few fleeting moments when the reader has access to Jacob's internal monologue, that Jacob's attitude toward individual women is determined almost entirely by their physical appearance. The one exception is Florinda, for "it did occur to Jacob, half-way through dinner, to wonder whether [Florinda] had a mind," and later, when he realizes that "[b]eauty goes hand in hand with stupidity," he "ha[s] a violent reversion towards male society, cloistered rooms, and the works of the classics" (*JR* 79; 82). Even though Florinda is "straight and beautiful in body," when she "la[ys] her hand upon his knee," Jacob offers her the archetypal alibi—"[h]e told her his head ached," thinking that "[a]ny excuse serves a stupid woman"; but he is, of course, wrong; Florinda does understand (*JR* 82), and it is just a chapter later that Jacob sees her with another man. By contrast, when Jacob purchases sexual services from another prostitute, Laurette, "put[ting] so many shillings on the mantlepiece," as he leaves, he thinks patronizingly "[a]ltogether a most reasonable conversation; a most respectable room; an intelligent girl" seemingly because "her skirts were short, her legs long, thin and transparently covered." He is interrupted in his pleasant self-congratulatory musings when "Madame herself, seeing Jacob out had about her that leer, that lewdness, that quake of the surface . . . which threatens to spill the whole bag of ordure, with difficulty held together, over the pavement" (*JR* 103-104). Jacob reveres Sandra Wentworth Williams for her loveliness, a viewpoint she unabashedly shares ("there remained with her a sense of her own beauty, and . . . luckily, there was a looking-glass" which allowed her to reflect "I am very beautiful" [142]). While at the Erechtheum, he "look[s] rather furtively at the goddess on the left-hand side holding the roof on her head. She reminded him of Sandra Wentworth Williams. He looked at her, then looked away. He looked at her, then looked away. He was extraordinarily moved" (*JR* 151). Jacob finds the statues which Woolf in her Greek journal describes as "fat Maidens" (*Passionate Apprentice* 323) very appealing and even sexually stimulating, but when he sees "perched on a block of marble," not unlike the statues, "Madame Lucien Gravé" with "her kodak pointed at his head," and watches her leap down from her pedestal, "in spite of her age, her figure, and her tight boots—having now that her daughter was married, lapsed with a luxurious abandonment, grand enough in its way, into the fleshy grotesque," Jacob reacts with disgust: "Damn these women—damn these women! . . . How they spoil things." It is Madame Gravé's physical unattractiveness, not merely her temerity in taking the photograph, that stirs in Jacob the "violent disillusionment" that the narrator assures the reader is typical "in young men in the prime of life, sound of wind and limb, who will soon become fathers of families and directors of banks" (*JR* 151).

Of course, although Florinda may well be pregnant with Jacob's child (*JR* 168), Jacob never becomes the father of a family or the director of a bank. Instead, he dies, offstage, in an unspecified fashion, one among millions (Handley 132), in the Great War, as if "driven by an unseizable force" (*JR* 156). Prior to the actual onset of the war, while Jacob is still in Greece, the narrator provides, in present tense, a non-specific and absurdly sanitized snapshot of generic military conflict: "Like blocks of tin soldiers the army covers the cornfield, moves up the hillside, stops, reels slightly this way and that, and falls flat, save that, through field-glasses, it can be seen that one or two pieces still agitate up and down like fragments of a broken match-stick" (*JR* 156).

Slyly, the narrator explains that "these actions, together with the incessant commerce of banks, laboratories, chancellories, and houses of business, are the strokes which oar the world forward, they say. And they are dealt by men as smoothly sculptured as the impassive policeman at Ludgate Circus" (156). This postcard image of a rigid and emotionless patriarchal figure corresponds precisely to the tyrants and dictators described in *A Room of One's Own* and *Three Guineas*. Like Hitler and Mussolini, "far from being padded to rotundity [the policeman's] face is stiff from force of will, and lean from the efforts of keeping it so. When his right arm rises, all the force in his veins flows straight from shoulder to finger-tips; not an ounce is diverted into sudden impulses, sentimental regrets. . . . The buses punctually stop" (156).

In counterpoint to this patriarchal system, the narrator weaves an oppositional, alternative reality into *Jacob's Room*. The novel has typically been read as a work focused on Jacob himself. However, the snapshot album of Jacob's life is interspersed with fleeting images of women. Countering the sporadic semi-chronological narrative which centers on Jacob is another entirely de-centered, mythic narrative pattern through which the narrator fuses thinking back through our mothers with the ancient matrifocal culture of the Great Goddess, thereby inverting patriarchy in the novel. The women in the novel—spinsters and widows, maidens and mothers, marriage and remarriage resisters or married lesbians, tutors, feminist researchers, tourists, photographers—all are members of the Society of Outsiders. As Josephine O'Brien Schaefer notes, "Jacob occupies an unimportant position in each stage of his own career. In the section on his childhood, his mother holds the center of interest" (*Three-fold* 68).

This female-focused counter-narrative preempts the history of male dominance and situates Jacob as the rising and dying god, the son-lover of the goddess. Jacob is linked to Dionysus in several passages but most explicitly when, after the Guy Fawkes bonfire, "two of the dancers, . . . bowing profoundly before him" declare that "you are the most beautiful man we have ever seen," wreathing "his head with paper flowers," seating him on "a white and gilt chair," and hanging "glass grapes on his shoulders . . . until he look[s] like the figure head of a wrecked ship" (75). There is strong evidence that the Goddess narrative in *Jacob's Room* is based on Jane Harrison's scholarship, especially her *Prolegomena to the Study of Greek Religion*. In the *Prolegomena*, Harrison argues that militaristic patriarchal culture and religion displaced Goddess-centered civilization when the Olympian pantheon supplanted the "primitive goddesses [who] reflect . . . a relationship traced through the mother, the state of society known by the awkward term matriarchal" (*Prolegomena* 26). The narrator of *Jacob's Room* reinstates these displaced goddesses by playfully tracing the lineage of her female characters to distant origins and alluding to the ancient matriarchy as a profound commonplace of women's community. For example, Lady Rocksbier has "fed upon champagne and spices for at least two centuries (four if you count the female line)" (*JR* 100). When Mrs. Flanders murmurs "Goodnight, Rebecca" to her maid and Rebecca responds by calling her "ma'm," these two women are literally described as members of a secret society, "conspirators plotting the eternal conspiracy of hush and clean bottles" (*JR* 13; see Ruddick 193). Yearning for Jacob, Fanny Elmer is comforted by her roommate who counsels her to give it up, "bringing the whole thing down . . . to a level of mother-wit" at which point Fanny remarks "[o]ne's godmothers should have told one" (*JR* 170).

The novel is crowded with allusions to the Great Goddess. She appears in many guises as maiden, mother, widow and crone and as sacred prostitute. Aspects of the Goddess in the novel include references to the Goddess's traditional activities (e.g., hunting; archery [*JR* 100; 166]), her symbols (e.g., the tripod; the moon; the garnet brooch that signifies the seeds of the pomegranate Persephone ate of in Hades [*JR* 63; 131-34]), and her sacred creatures (e.g., dogs [*JR* 100; 166]). The goddess is also manifest in specific relationships. Thus, there is the obvious Demeter/Persephone pairing of Elizabeth Durrant and her daughter Clara Durrant, a dyad which is also echoed in the more erotic relationship between Elizabeth Flanders and her intimate friend, Mrs. Jarvis, the rector's wife. However, the Goddess is invoked most frequently by the proliferation of her names (for definitions of names, see Cresswell, Hodges and Hanks, and Withycomb). Like multiple prints of the same negative, three characters (Betty Flanders, Mrs. Durrant and Elspeth Siddons) share names derived from Elizabeth, evoking Elizabeth Rex, the virgin queen of England whom Edmund Spenser celebrated in the *Fairie Queen* as an earthly Artemis. Three characters bear names that mean "light" and thus are also linked to Artemis—Clara Durrant, the Countess Lucy and Madame Lucien Gravé, the gallant photographer. Two different women, the photographer Julia Eliot and the feminist scholar Julia Hodge, share a name that means "descended from Aphrodite," a lineage the two prostitutes, Florinda and Laurette, also share. Sandra Wentworth Williams, the married woman with whom Jacob falls in love, is the namesake of Hera, thus making her ineffectual and passive husband a parodic Zeus. Ironically, a number of critics have been puzzled by this profusion of names. Allen McLaurin finds them meaningless (167) while Hermione Lee notes that many of the names are "ludicrously similar" (87; for a more positive discussion of names in Woolf's novels, see Grundy).

In *Jacob's Room*, the matrilineal Goddess narrative is a cyclical counterpoint to Jacob's linear existence—his life and death rigidly determined by a patriarchal plot in which the fathers slaughter their sons. Inevitably, the novel is haunted by implacable *memento mori*. As Sontag notes, "[p]hotography is an elegiac art, a twilight art. Most subjects photographed are, just by virtue of being photographed, touched with pathos. . . . All photographs are *memento mori*" (15). But the *memento mori* in *Jacob's Room* are not restricted to photographs. They include, as suggested earlier, portraits, statues, sculptures, tombs and monuments, tombstones and epitaphs and even found objects like the sheep's skull. Throughout the novel (as in *A Room of One's Own* and *Three Guineas*), references to statues and sculptures occur in militaristic contexts. As Handley indicates, the novel "emblematizes [a] fixated love of past patriarchal greats in the statues of Pitt, Waltham, Burke and Gladstone at Whitehall" (118). The young men in white gowns and heavy boots entering King's College Chapel have sculpted features as does the dictatorial policeman directing traffic at Ludgate Circle. Jacob is explicitly associated with statues of both Ulysses and Achilles, so-called heroes of the Trojan War. St. Paul's Cathedral is "haunted by ghosts of white marble" and "Mrs. Lidgett" goes there every day "to rest . . . by the very side of the great Duke's tomb, whose victories meant nothing to her, whose name she knows not" (*JR* 65). Betty Flanders' musings, as she stands in the cemetery where her husband is buried, are evocative of war graves: "now one of a company, he had merged in the grass, the sloping hillside, the thousand white stones, the decayed wreaths, the crosses of green tin"; "the bell for service or funeral" was to her "Seabrook's voice, the voice of the dead" (*JR* 17).

The opal crab struggling hopelessly to escape from Jacob's little bucket is a particularly cruel *memento mori*. Then, too, early in the novel Jacob speculates that his long-lost Uncle Morty is "feeding the sharks" and, later, the narrator anticipates the carnage of the war as she tells her readers that "a man called Jimmy" "feeds crows in Flanders" (*JR* 38; 96-7). However, the passages alluding to Jacob's moth and butterfly collection are the most fraught with symbolic references to the horrors of war. Daniel Ferrer comments that "[s]ometimes we have the impression that the entire landscape of this novel, strewn with skulls and bones (*JR* 8; 128), peopled with 'death's head moths' (*JR* 21), is a great corpse in the process of decomposing" (43). As the narrator observes, "[t]he stag-beetle dies slowly. . . . Even on the second day its legs were supple. But the butterflies were dead. A whiff of rotten eggs had vanquished the pale clouded yellows which came pelting across the orchard and up Dods Hill and away on to the moor" foreshadows mustard gas shells exploding around men charging through a ruined orchard in a hail of machine-gun fire. Rebecca, the maid of all work, "caught the death's head moth in the kitchen"; when Jacob is out searching for moths, "there had been a volley of pistol shots suddenly in the depths of the woods" the night "the tree had fallen"; when Jacob returns home, he resembles a ghost, "pale, come out of the depths of darkness" and he startles his mother who exclaims "How you frightened me!" . . . She thought something dreadful had happened." While "fritillaries flaunted along the hedgerows[,] . . . [t]he blues settled on little bones . . . and the painted ladies and the peacocks feasted upon the bloody entrails dropped by a hawk. . . . [Jacob] had seen a white admiral circling higher and higher . . . but he had never caught it." An old woman who describes to Jacob a rare "purple butterfly which came every summer to her garden" also mentions that "if you looked out at dawn you could always see two badgers. Sometimes they knocked each other over like two boys fighting, she said" (*JR* 23-4). In a seemingly innocent passage, the narrator juxtaposes a reference to tombstones with a description of two white butterflies circling (*JR* 37). In the penultimate chapter of the novel, Richard Bonamy, suddenly realizing to his dismay that Jacob is in love with a woman, stalks away in a fury leaving Jacob "star[ing] straight ahead of him, fixed, monolithic—oh, very beautiful—like a British Admiral" (*JR* 165), an image which mingles photography, sculpture, and, perhaps most horribly, butterfly collecting. The butterfly box with its neatly labeled specimens is not unlike the rows of crosses in Flanders fields inscribed with the names of the fallen—meticulously arranged corpses that constitute the record of conquests and captures. In Jacob's case, he is one among millions in an inventory of the dead. For the narrators, their works are like albums filled with imaginary photographs documenting the perpetual struggle between the oppressors and the resisters.

**Works Cited**


Annan, Noel. *Leslie Stephen: The Godless Victorian*. New York: Random House, 1984.

Bell, Quentin. *Virginia Woolf: A Biography*. 2 vols. New York: HBJ, 1972.

Bell, Quentin and Angelica Garnett, comps. *Vanessa Bell's Family Album*. London: Jill Norman and Hobhouse, 1981.

Bishop, Edward. *A Virginia Woolf Chronology*. Boston: G.K. Hall, 1989.

Carroll, Berenice A. "'To crush him in our own country': The Political Thought of Virginia Woolf." *Feminist Studies* 4 (1978): 99-129.

Caughie, Pamela L. *Virginia Woolf & Postmodernism: Literature in Quest and Question of Itself*. Urbana: U of Illinois P, 1991.

Cresswell, Julia. *Tuttle Dictionary of First Names*. Boston: Charles E. Tuttle, 1992.

DeSalvo, Louise. *Virginia Woolf: The Impact of Childhood Sexual Abuse on Her Life and Work*. Boston: Beacon, 1989.

Ferrer, Daniel. *Virginia Woolf and the Madness of Language*. Trans. Geoffrey Bennington and Rachel Bowlby. New York: Routledge, 1990.

Gillespie, Diane F. "'Her Kodak Pointed at His Head': Virginia Woolf and Photography." In Diane F. Gillespie, ed. *The Multiple Muses of Virginia Woolf*. Columbia: U of Missouri P, 1993. 113-47.

Grundy, Isobel. "'Words without meaning—wonderful words': Virginia Woolf's Choice of Names." *Virginia Woolf: New Critical Essays*. Ed. Patricia Clements and Isobel Grundy. Totowa: Barnes and Noble, 1983.

Handley, William. "War and the Politics of Narration in *Jacob's Room*." *Virginia Woolf and War: Fiction, Reality, and Myth*. Ed. Mark Hussey. Syracuse: Syracuse UP, 1991. 110-33.

Harrison, Jane. *Prolegomena to the Study of Greek Religion*. 1903; Princeton: Princeton UP, 1991.

Hanks, Patrick and Flavia Hodges. *A Dictionary of First Names*. New York: Oxford UP, 1990.

Hussey, Mark. *Virginia Woolf A to Z: A Comprehensive Reference for Students, Teachers, and Common Readers to Her Life, Work and Critical Reception.* New York: Facts on File, 1995.

Hussey, Mark, ed. *Virginia Woolf and War: Fiction, Reality, and Myth.* Syracuse: Syracuse UP, 1991.

Kiely, Robert. "*Jacob's Room* and *Roger Fry*: Two Studies in Still Life." *ModernismReconsidered.* Robert Kiely, ed. Harvard English Studies II. Cambridge, Mass.: Harvard U P, 1983: 147-66.

Lee, Hermione. *The Novels of Virginia Woolf.* London: Methuen, 1977.

Lehmann, John. *Virginia Woolf and Her World.* London: Thames & Hudson,1975.

Little, Judy. "*Jacob's Room* as Comedy: Woolf's Parodic Bildungsroman." *New Feminist Essays on Virginia Woolf.* Ed. Jane Marcus. Lincoln: U of Nebraska P, 1981.

McLaurin, Allan. *Virginia Woolf: The Echoes Enslaved.* Cambridge, England: Cambridge UP, 1973.

*The New Encyclopedia Britannica.* Chicago: Helen Hemingway Benton, 1974.

Nicolson, Nigel and Joanne Trautmann. Introduction. *The Letters of Virginia Woolf.* Vol. 6. New York: HBJ, 1975. xiii-xxi. 6 vols.

Oldfield, Sybil. "The Elegiac Artist: Virginia Woolf (1882-1941)." *Women Against the Iron Fist: Alternatives to Militarism, 1900-1989.* Cambridge, MA: Blackwell, 1989. 96-130.

Richardson, Elizabeth P. *A Bloomsbury Iconography.* Winchester: St. Paul's Bibliographies, 1989.

Roberts, Pam. "Julia Margaret Cameron: A Triumph over Criticism." In *The Portrait in Photography.* Ed. Graham Clarke. London: Reaktion Books, 1992.

Ruddick, Sara. "Private Brother, Public World." *New Feminist Essays on Virginia Woolf.* Ed. Jane Marcus. Lincoln: U of Nebraska P. 185-215.

Schaefer, Josephine O'Brien. "The Great War and 'This late age of world's experience' in Cather and Woolf." In Mark Hussey, ed. *Virginia Woolf and War: Fiction, Reality, and Myth.* 134-50.

——. *Three-fold Nature of Reality in the Novels of Virginia Woolf.* The Hague: Mouton, 1965.

Sontag, Susan. *On Photography.* New York: Farrar, Straus and Giroux, 1977.

Spater, George, and Ian Parsons. *A Marriage of True Minds: An Intimate Portrait of Leonard and Virginia Woolf.* New York: HBJ, 1977.

Silver, Brenda. *Virginia Woolf's Reading Notebooks.* Princeton: Princeton U P, 1983.

Swanson, Diana. "An Antigone Complex? Psychology and Politics in *The Years* and *Three Guineas.*" *Virginia Woolf: Texts and Contexts. Selected Papers from the Fifth Annual Conference on Virginia Woolf.* Eds. Beth Daugherty and Eileen Barrett. NY: Pace UP, 1996. 35-39.

Welling, William. *Collectors' Guide to Nineteenth-Century Photographs.* New York: Collier Books, 1976.

Withycombe, E. G. *The Oxford Dictionary of English Christian Names.* 3rd ed. New York: Oxford UP, 1976.

Woolf ,Virginia. *The Diary of Virginia Woolf.* Ed. Anne Olivier Bell with Andrew McNeillie. 5 vols. New York: HBJ, 1977-1984.

——. Introduction. *Victorian Photographs of Famous Men & Fair Women* by Julia Margaret Cameron. With Introductions by Virginia Woolf and Roger Fry. Preface and Notes by Tristram Powell. London: Hogarth P, 1973.

——. *Jacob's Room.* 1922. New York: HBJ, 1950.

——. *The Letters of Virginia Woolf.* Ed. Nigel Nicolson and Joanne Trautmann. New York: HBJ, 1976. 6 vols. 1975-1980.

——. *A Passionate Apprentice: The Early Journals: 1897-1909.* Ed. Mitchell A. Leaska. San Diego: Harvest/HBJ, 1990.

——. *A Room of One's Own.* 1929. New York: HBJ, 1963.

——. "A Sketch of the Past." *Moments of Being: Unpublished Autobiographical Writings.* Ed. Jeanne Schulkind. Second Edition. San Diego: Harvest, 1985. 61-138.

——. *Three Guineas.* 1938. New York: HBJ, 1963.

TABLE 1: SEQUENCE OF PHOTOGRAPHS IN MH-1
(ALBUM OF *CARTES-DE-VISITE*)

Compiled by Krystyna Colburn

| Page | List of Photographs ( / indicates separate picture<br>// indicates second line of pictures) |
|---|---|
| 1 | Woman with Pug Dog / Man and Woman Standing |
| 2 | Gambetta / Thiers //<br>M. Grevy (French President) /MacMahon / Rene Gortichkoff |
| 3 | The Rev. L. L. Davies // Mr. Gaskell / Dr. Jowett |
| 4 | Sarah Bernhardt / Ellen Terry //<br>Mrs. Langtry / Elizabeth Barrett Browning / George Eliot / Mr. Gaskell |
| 5 | Hubert Parry / Dr. Michael Costa // Prof. Beasley / Mdlle. Tietjens |
| 6 | Lady Carlisle / Lady Mary Murray // Princess Royal / Edmund Gurney |
| 7 | Pere Hyacinthe / Baboo Keshub Chundersen //<br>Cardinal Newman / Pius IX / Leo 13th |
| 8 | Westcatt / L L. Davies, Scott / F. D. Maurice //<br>Bishop Lightfoot / Newman / Cardinal Manning |
| 9 | Ugo Bassi / Patriarch of Greece // Cardinal Wiseman / Dean Stanley |
| 10 | Gladstone / John Arthur Roebrick / Huxley //<br>Professor Owen / Faraday / Louis Napoleon |
| 11 | Unidentified Man (probably Leslie Stephen) // Charlotte Yonge / Mrs. Gaskell |
| 12 | Renan // Victor Emmanuel / Bismarck |
| 13 | Robert Browning / Tennyson / Tom Hughes / Goldwin Smith |
| 14 | Mrs. Crompton / Ethel Sargent / Mrs. Garrett Anderson |
| 15 | Lincoln / General Lee / Jeff Davis // Lincoln / Grant / Lloyd Garrison |
| 16 | Abraham Lincoln // Emerson / Chase |
| 17 | W. E. Gladstone, M. P. / Herbert Gladstone / Marquis of Hartington //<br>Lord Salisbury / W. M. Bright / Disraeli |
| 18 | Lord Palmerston / Earl Granville / Earl Russell //<br>Earl of Beaconfield / Earl of Canarvon / John Bright |
| 19 | Moltke / Todleben / Lord Napier //<br>Garibaldi / Crown Prince of Germany / Cavour |

| | |
|---|---|
| 20 | Garibaldi / Gambetta // Signature of Garibaldi / Garibaldi |
| 21 | Mr. Gladstone, W. E. Gladstone, Hubert Gladstone / Lord Selvins / Lord Lingen / Alexander II |
| 22 | Garfield |
| 23 | Unidentified Man |
| 24 | Gladstone / Duke of Argyll / Sir Stafford Northcote // R. A. Cross / Forster, M. P. / W. H. Smith, M. P. |
| 25 | Sir Charles Dilk, M. P. / Parnell / Marquis of Hartington / Sir Henry James / Mandella / Cobden |
| 26 | Franz Hanfstaevels Kunstuerlf / Anton Rubinstein // Madame Norman-Neruda / Joachim |
| 27 | M. Stanley / J. A. Froude / Longfellow // Carlyle / Kingsley / James Martineau |
| 28 | Rogs, Gul., Eff., E. M. / J. S. Mill |
| 29 | Darwin / Murchison / Herbert Spencer // Prof. Madden / Kischoff Bunson Roscoe / Tyndall |
| 30 | Mandella / Charles Burton // Washington / Arnold Toynbee |
| 31 | John Dillon // Mr. Justice Grove / Mrs. Langtry |
| 32 | Lady Mary Murray / Lady Carlisle / Princess of Wales / Mrs. Crompton |
| 33 | Unidentified Man (Sidney Woolf, Q.C. ) / Henry Crompton / Mr. Justice Crompton / Henry Crompton |
| 34 | F. J. Furnivall |
| 35 | Arnold Toynbee |

Examples of *cartes-de-visite* photographs similar to those in the MH-1 Album in the Frederick R. Koch Collection in the Harvard Theater Collection at the Pusey Library.

**Nancy Knowles**

# A Community of Women Looking at Men: The Photographs in Virginia Woolf's *Three Guineas*

At last summer's conference, I was sitting in a room very like this one (except for the roar of the motorcycle convention passing outside) and listening to Linda Stewart discussing the photographs in *Three Guineas* when it occurred to me that a profitable dialogue might be constructed between the *Three Guineas* photographs and psychoanalytic gaze theory. The match between participants in this dialogue is perhaps not ideal, but in many ways the juxtaposition *is* intriguing. Namely, gaze theory provides a means of discussing the politics of Virginia Woolf's photographs.

Today, I intend to argue that Woolf's photographs resist the psychoanalytical underpinning of the more modern gaze theory which constructs "gaze" as masculine.[1] Woolf effects this resistance to gaze theory by constructing a community of women gazing at men. Because this community does not share the masculine gaze, particularly with reference to the professions, its existence explodes the biased theoretical connection between gaze and masculinity; it denies that gaze is essentially masculine. In doing this, the community of women gazing illustrates both that the patriarchal bias, which characterizes the masculine gaze as objective, causes war and that women, when armed with similar power, have the potential to be equally oppressive.

In order to demonstrate this argument, I have divided today's paper into three sections: first, I will discuss gaze theory as detailed by Laura Mulvey; second, I will show how Woolf's use of photographs resists this theory; and finally, I will explain the significance of this resistance to Woolf's pacifist argument.

In "Visual Pleasure and Narrative Cinema" originally published in 1975, Laura Mulvey argues from a psychoanalytic standpoint that the traditional cinematic experience reproduces patriarchy. Mainstream film accomplishes this by privileging the masculine gaze which acts not only within the film, through the eyes of the male protagonist, but also in the audience, where the spectator sees from his own perspective and from the perspective of the male protagonist with whom he identifies. In contrast to the active male spectator, the female character is objectified, relegated to "erotic spectacle" (Mulvey, "Visual" 62). Based on this configuration, Mulvey delineates "two contradictory aspects" of the masculine gaze: the *scopophilic* and the *narcissistic*. Mulvey defines the scopophilic as "aris[ing] from pleasure in using another person as an object of sexual stimulation through sight," and we can see this in the protagonist's and the spectator's gazing at the female character. The second aspect of the masculine gaze, the narcissistic, "comes from identification with the image seen." In other words, the spectator identifies with the protagonist (Mulvey "Visual" 61).

Besides the theory's heterosexual bias, which for purposes of brevity I will not discuss here, the obvious problem with this argument, which Mulvey acknowledges in a 1990 article titled "Afterthoughts on 'Visual Pleasure and Narrative Cinema' inspired by *Duel in the Sun,*" is, "'. . . what about the women in the audience?'" (24). In answering this question, Mulvey retains the Freudian paradigm, arguing that, rather than having a gaze of their own, female spectators identify with the masculine gaze "in memory of [their] 'active' [or "tomboy"] phase" ("Afterthoughts" 35). Somehow this answer seems inadequate given the range of even conventional cinematic texts and the range of my own female experience. As we will see, Woolf in 1938 has already challenged the fundamental concepts of this theory.

The 1938 edition of Virginia Woolf's *Three Guineas* contains five black-and-white photographs, which, as Vara Neverow remarked in yesterday's presentation, have been omitted from later editions. These are titled "A General," "Heralds," "A University Procession," "A Judge," and "An Archbishop."[2] The text also includes what Linda Stewart terms "verbal photographs," or photographs constructed in words. I will address primarily the black-and-white photographs.

Although photographs represent an art form different from film—in that, according to Susan Sontag, ". . . they are a neat slice of time, not a flow" (17) and they are not usually experienced in a darkened theater which, as Mulvey states, "promote[s] the illusion of voyeuristic separation" ("Visual" 60)—photographs do possess the potential for a masculine gaze similar to that which Mulvey identifies in the medium of film ("Visual" 59). For example, the "pin-up girl" represents a photographic parallel of Mulvey's "show-girl" ("Visual" 62). However, Woolf's photographs differ significantly from the films discussed in both of Mulvey's articles, and this difference reveals the patriarchal bias of psychoanalytic theory, undermining the potential for gaze theory to generalize about photographic representation. The following analysis of Woolf's use of the photographs in *Three Guineas* will demonstrate that the essentialist psychoanalytic terminology which defines gaze as "masculine" cannot be sustained beyond texts which have both a male protagonist and a man behind the camera. In other words, masculinity and gaze cannot be conflated.

The fundamental difference between Mulvey's films and Woolf's photographs is that in contrast to the films Mulvey discusses, which are directed by men, Woolf's photographs are collected and placed in a linguistic context by a woman speaking for a community of women. We see this perspective explicitly and repeatedly constructed throughout the text through the use of the first person plural to refer to those people answering the letter of inquiry written by the man who wishes to prevent war. As Lynne Hanley indicates, "While *you* in the frame letter means now a man, then Man himself, *we* remains anonymously and collectively female . . ." (58). For example, Woolf writes, "Let us then by way of a very elementary beginning lay before you a photograph—a crudely coloured photograph—of your world as it appears to us who see it from the threshold of the private house; through the shadow of the veil that St. Paul still lays upon our eyes . . ." (26). Not only is Woolf "speaking . . . for many of the daughters of educated men" (Woolf 5), but also she is constructing their perspective in terms of photographs so that others can see through that perspective. The emphasis falls not on the object photographed but on the way of seeing it; speaking to the male letter-writer, she says, ". . . though we look at the same things, we see them differently" (6). This community of women has not coopted "the" masculine gaze but instead views the world through a distinctly feminine gaze shaped by female cultural experience, as signified by St. Paul's veil.

Not only does this gaze differ from the masculine gaze propounded by gaze theory in that this gaze is feminine, but also this gaze lacks the sexual motivation which is the essential component of psychoanalytic theory. Remember, Mulvey classifies the two aspects of the masculine gaze as the scopophilic, where the spectator desires the object represented, and the narcissistic, where the spectator identifies with the object. These aspects derive from the Oedipal moment in Freudian theory where the male child identifies with the father (narcissistic) and desires the mother (scopophilic). Initially, because the black-and-white photographs in *Three Guineas* depict only men, the feminine gaze directed at the photographs might seem to be a feminine version of the scopophilic aspect Mulvey describes in that the women viewing the men might see them as sexual objects. However, this is not the case. Through the communal, feminine gaze Woolf constructs, the men appear ridiculous rather than attractive. Such derisive depiction precludes both scopophilic and narcissistic desire, masculine or feminine.

Let's look at the photograph titled "A General" as an example of this resistance to psychoanalytic structures of desire. This photograph is the first black-and-white photograph to appear in *Three Guineas*. Depicted from his plumed hat to the edge of his medal-encrusted coat, the smiling general squarely faces the camera. The crenelated battlement behind him is out of focus, allowing the emphasis of the photograph to fall on the general himself. Although the photograph seems relatively objective—neither is there a soft haze around the general's face, nor are dead bodies stacked behind him—the details—age, rank, decorations, benevolent smile, jaunty feather, and nothing-to-hide photographic style—reveal a narrative of battlefield success. Seen through the masculine gaze, this photograph would likely have a narcissistic effect on young men, encouraging them to become soldiers as part of an honorable tradition. Similarly, seen through a hypothetical feminine gaze (if gaze theory admitted a female version) the image might have a scopophilic effect on female spectators in that through the fatherly attractiveness of the general, they might be persuaded to approve of the men in their lives going to war.

However, Woolf's community of women looking at men sees something very different. In contrast with the psychoanalytic foundation of gaze theory, their perspective negates both the narcissistic effect the photograph might have on male spectators and the scopophilic effect on female spectators by revealing the military profession as reprehensible. The constructed gaze calls attention to the symbolism of the general's clothing as integral to *causing* war: "Since the red and the gold, the brass and the feathers are discarded upon active service, it is plain that their expensive and not, one might suppose, hygienic splendour is invented partly in order to impress the beholder with the majesty of the military office, partly in order through their vanity to induce young men to become soldiers" (30). Woolf reveals the fact that such costumes not only encourage civilians to support violence but also incite young men to fight and die. According to Woolf, women can see this deception because ". . . we . . . are forbidden to wear such clothes ourselves. . . ."(30). Through the eyes of this community of women looking at men, the viewer begins to see the general as "a ridiculous, a barbarous, a displeasing spectacle" (30-1).

Because the gaze Woolf has constructed is feminine and lacks the structures of desire integral to the psychoanalytic foundation of gaze theory, her text explodes the assumption that gaze theory can generalize the spectator experience. Perhaps when the director and protagonist are male, the theory works, but under other circumstances, as illustrated by *Three Guineas*, the theory fails. This failure insists that we resist the patriarchal bias of psychoanalytic theory and sever the seemingly essential connection between masculinity and gaze so that gaze theory can include the broad scope of photographic texts which actually exists.

Woolf's resistance to psychoanalytic theory's patriarchal bias is significant to her pacifist argument for two reasons: first, because ". . . the public and the private worlds are inseparably connected . . . [and] the tyrannies and servilities of the one are the tyrannies and servilities of the other" (Woolf 217), the valuing of men over women which occurs in Freud's theories, and by extension, theories based on Freud such as gaze theory, must be eradicated in order to eradicate war. And second, because the patriarchal bias which accords men power also accords men responsibility for misuse of that power, such bias obscures the fact that women, too, are responsible for tyranny. Woolf writes, ". . . we cannot dissociate ourselves from that figure [of the Dictator] but are ourselves that figure" (217). I will address each of these ideas briefly in turn.

Although the theory Mulvey describes has limited application, as Woolf's work has demonstrated, both Mulvey and Woolf are engaged in similar efforts to reveal and resist patriarchal bias. Mulvey employs gaze theory in order to reveal patriarchal bias not only in film but also in society; she writes, "Psychoanalytic theory is thus appropriated here as a political weapon, demonstrating the way the unconscious of patriarchal society has structured film form" ("Visual" 57). Similarly, Woolf constructs her communal, feminine gaze, the gaze of the "Outsider," to demonstrate that the masculine gaze, which has seemed objective, is not the only valid point of view and, in considering war, may be particularly handicapped by patriarchal structures of masculinity. The fact that Woolf uses photographs to demonstrate this is significant. Even as the camera lens becomes a metaphor for sight and the photograph, one of the most seemingly objective forms of representation, becomes a metaphor for reality, Woolf reveals the photographic mechanism as biased, exploding what Sontag calls "the fairy tale of photography" (53). Woolf exposes photography's means of production by employing seemingly objective "photographs from magazines and newspapers" (Wussow, "Visual" 51), as we have seen already with the photograph of the general, to make her own arguments. Says Helen Wussow, "Woolf chose the images in order to make the argument that photographs can be manipulated and supposedly hard factual evidence weighted on the side of one's argument" ("Virginia" 2). Because the camera can be manipulated, we must also question the seemingly objective masculine gaze which views war as honorable, and we must insist that it is not objective, that all gaze is not masculine, that other ways of seeing exist, such as that demonstrated by Woolf's community of women looking at men. For this reason, Woolf's resistance to patriarchal bias, particularly that inherent in perception, is essential to her pacifism.

While Woolf's use of photography in the service of pacifism explodes the patriarchal bias of "objectivity," it also demands that women share responsibility for war. We can see this demand in the fact that the feminine gaze still has the power, although not in the sexual terms of psychoanalysis, to objectify what it sees. In what Diane F. Gillespie calls Woolf's "aggressive uses of photographs" (113), the men in the photographs, scrutinized by the feminine gaze, become just as much objects as Mulvey's "show-girl" ("Visual" 62) because the institutions they represent become more important than who they are. The fact that the active gaze has this objectifying capacity reminds us that women are equally, naturally capable, if culturally inhibited, of the oppression the masculine gaze signifies. Remember Woolf's wording—her use of the inclusive, female "we"—when she discusses the dictator: ". . . we cannot dissociate ourselves from that figure but are ourselves that figure" (217). This means that even women, Woolf's "Outsiders," can become ultimate oppressors. I would argue that Woolf does not include a black-and-white photograph of a dictator not only to avoid blaming individuals, as Gillespie argues (139), but also to avoid depicting a man in this role, a depiction which would exclude women. Wary of becoming the dictator, women must be vigilant in maintaining their "Outsider" status even as they join "the tail end of the procession" of professional men (Woolf 66).

By constructing, through the photographs in *Three Guineas*, a community of women gazing at men, Virginia Woolf resists the psychoanalytic foundation of gaze theory which privileges the masculine. This use of photographs is consistent with the text's main argument—that such inequities cause war.

## Notes

[1] While Woolf could not have known gaze theory in the codified way I will detail here, her discussion of perspective, particularly gendered ways of seeing, suggests a familiarity with the concepts on which the theory depends.

[2] The people in these photographs have been identified by Alice Stavely.

## Works Cited

Gillespie, Diane F. "'Her Kodak Pointed at His Head': Virginia Woolf and Photography." *The Multiple Muses of Virginia Woolf.* Ed. Diane F. Gillespie. Columbia: U of Missouri P, 1993. 113-47.

Hanley, Lynne. "The Romance of Oxbridge: Virginia Woolf." *Writing War: Fiction, Gender, and Memory.* Amherst: U of Massachusetts P, 1991. 47-63.

Mulvey, Laura. "Afterthoughts on 'Visual Pleasure and Narrative Cinema' inspired by *Duel in the Sun.*" *Psychoanalysis and Cinema.* Ed. E. Ann Kaplan. New York: Routledge, 1990. 24-35.

——. "Visual Pleasure and Narrative Cinema." *Screen* 16.3 (1975): 6-18. Rpt. *Feminism and Film Theory.* Ed. Constance Penley. New York: Routledge, 1988. 57-68.

Neverow, Vara. "Thinking Back Through Our Mothers, Thinking in Common: Virginia Woolf's Photographic Imagination and the Community of Narrators in *Jacob's Room, A Room of One's Own,* and *Three Guineas.*" Eighth Annual Virginia Woolf Conference. Saint Louis University, Saint Louis, Missouri. 5 June 1998. (See elsewhere in this volume)

Sontag, Susan. *On Photography.* New York: Farrar, Straus and Giroux, 1977.

Stavely, Alice. "Name that Face." *Virginia Woolf Miscellany* 51 (Spring 1998): 4-5.

Stewart, Linda. "The Politics of Virginia Woolf's Photographic Vision: Picturing a World without War." Seventh Annual Virginia Woolf Conference. Plymouth State College, Plymouth, New Hampshire. 15 June 1997.

Woolf, Virginia. *Three Guineas.* New York: Harcourt, Brace and Company, 1938.

Wussow, Helen. "Virginia Woolf and the Problematic Nature of the Photographic Image." *Twentieth Century Literature* 40.1 (1994): 1-14.

——. "Visual Images and Verbal Subtexts." *Virginia Woolf and the Arts: Selected Papers from the Sixth Annual Conference on Virginia Woolf.* Ed. Diane F. Gillespie and Leslie K. Hankins. New York: Pace UP, 1997. 48-56.

**Mónica Ayuso**

# Virginia Woolf in the Spanish-American Female Imagination

The work of Virginia Woolf has been scrutinized by women writers throughout the world. A diverse Spanish-American community of women—who wrote in relative isolation until very recently, "with less writerly contact and less of an eventual audience than their male counterparts" (Miller 23)—responded intimately to Woolf's influential voice because she was interpreted as "the woman writer *par excellence*" (Bowlby 12) and "a textual model for women's writing in general and Spanish America in particular" (Chevigny 155). This study concentrates on the record of two of those writers—Victoria Ocampo and Rosario Ferré—as a means of interpreting the impact that Woolf had among writers who read her work from countries far from Great Britain and admired it. Its purpose is to extend the limits of previous studies—those intuiting, but seldom crafting—the possibility of considering Woolf as a textual model to women who wrote in a language other than English.

Even writers whose ideologies clashed or those aware of the perils of comparative translations of culture recorded encounters with Woolf's writings which are invariably personal—never cool—and intensely passionate. Among the Spanish-American writers who have left such records are Victoria Ocampo (Argentina), Rosario Castellanos (Mexico), Sylvina Bullrich (Argentina), Albalucucía Angel (Colombia), Ulalume González de León (Uruguay), Julieta Campos (Cuba/Mexico), Sylvia Molloy (Argentina), and Rosario Ferré. Among the most frequently adopted metaphors are the writer's room of her own (Kamenszain, 1983; Pampillo, 1989; Ordoñez, 1991), the related metaphor of the closed door that deconstructs the dichotomies inside/outside because it liberates while it locks in (Ordoñez, 1991; Ferré, 1991) and, finally, the metaphor of textuality that figures as "a spider's web, attached ever so lightly perhaps, but still attached to life at all its corners" (*A Room of One's Own* 43).

Among this heterogeneous community, Argentine-born Victoria Ocampo (1890-1979) is clearly the writer who shares explicit similarities with Woolf. To Ocampo, as a world-traveler and an avid reader in English as well as French, the literature of these languages was available as a source of inexhaustible inquiry. Apart from being contemporaries—they were introduced to one another by Aldous Huxley in 1934 at the London opening of the Man Ray photography exhibition and they remained in touch until 1941, the year of Woolf's suicide—they had much to share. At the personal level, both had grown up in "Victorian" households with dominant fathers; they were childlcss; they had feminist convictions. At the professional level, both became essayists, critics and prominent editors, presiding over Hogarth and Sur respectively.

Ocampo's acquaintance with Woolf was so momentous that the first of her ten-volume *Testimonios,* which spans from 1920 to 1934, begins with a prologue of sorts, meaningfully entitled "Letter to Virginia Woolf." The anecdote central to the letter is a visit to Tavistock Square, when the two writers shared the warmth of a fire which dispelled the darkness and cold outside. The anecdote can be read as Ocampo's paradigmatic encounter with a European writer which will then prove fundamental to her own emergence as a writer. In the intimate moment recalled in this letter, the strong emotional affinity Ocampo feels for Woolf seems to foreshorten the physical distance that separated them as citizens and products of two distanced countries (9). Well aware of their circumstances, Ocampo acknowledged with self-deprecation that Woolf, as a consummate artist, had found the key that fitted her safely-locked chest of treasures. She herself had not. Keys were symbolic because they pried open private rooms—the rooms of one's own—and public ones—of libraries and universities—and publishing houses.

Even though Ocampo's social privilege and wealth made the metaphor of the room seem redundant in her case, she still found it amply applicable to her publishing impulses. In spite of the financial hazard that these ventures sometimes represented to her personally, the publishing house Sur "opened up new spaces in the cultural field for women writers, which would benefit subsequent generations" (King 16-18). For example, Ocampo found Jorge L. Borges as translator of *A Room of One's Own* , published from December 1935 to March 1936, and *Orlando*, shortly thereafter. It is quite possible that had her assessment come at the end rather than the beginning of her long and prolific publishing career, she might have acknowledged her own possession of that precious key, for Ocampo was not without achievements of her own. To mention just two, she was one of three founding members of the Argentine Women's Union in 1936 and the first woman to be elected to the Argentine Academy of Letters in 1977.

No other Spanish-American writer profited from contact with Woolf as directly as Ocampo did and, even to her, exchange with Woolf seemed at times regretfully unilateral. In spite of the exchange of gifts, the repeated invitations to travel to South America, and Ocampo's visits to Tavistock Square, Woolf perceived Argentina as a mysterious and remote country, *hundido en el tiempo y el espacio* ("buried in time and space"). It was cryptically described in her diary as a land of savage cattle, fox tails, and gilded butterflies (*Virginia Woolf en su diario* 97).

Writers born of successive generations, in different latitudes and indeed of different aspirations continued in their own time to identify with Woolf's female-centered world, to gloss her directives, and to revise Woolf's dicta as a means of tracing the contour of a vision that began to emerge in Spanish America in later years. At the same time, they personalized her testimony to fit different cultural realities.

With Ocampo, Rosario Ferré—born in 1932 in Ponce, Puerto Rico—shared a trilingualism that allowed her to serve her apprenticeship by reading extensively the French and English women novelists. It is not surprising that, among these, Virginia Woolf engrossed her. Though their voices do not commingle as smoothly as Ocampo's does with Woolf's in "Virginia Woolf in my Memory," the last emotional tribute Ocampo paid to the writer that dark April of 1941, after Woolf took her life ("The Writer's Kitchen" 135-140), Ferré shares with the British writer the conviction that society is overwhelmingly patriarchal. Between these two writers, there is one irrefutable, linear conjecture: Ferré confesses she went "literally crazy" when she first discovered Woolf and read everything the British writer ever wrote. In "La cocina de la escritura," Ferré called Woolf one of her "evangelistas de cabecera" (139). The evangelists not only penned the four Gospels but they were also scribes for those who could not write; in the original Spanish, the noun carries religious connotations lost in its English equivalent, "mentor" ("The Writer's Kitchen" 216).

So undivided is Ferré's attention to Woolf's coaching during the first years of her apprenticeship that even when she disagrees with the British writer, Woolf's advice is never slighted. One such occasion relates to Woolf's admonition to strive for objectivity and distance. In *AROO*, she specifically separated two women from the gallery of writers who made an emotional nuisance of themselves. According to Woolf, only Austen and Brönte succeeded in writing like Shakespeare, "with a mind incandescent and unimpeded" (*AROO* 57).

However, Ferré is repeatedly disturbed by the claim that passion and anger are serious deterrents to artistic production ("La autenticidad de la mujer en el arte" 39). One of the essays added to the second edition of *Sitio a Eros* (1980), entitled "De la ira a la ironía, ó sobre cómo atemperar el acero candente del discurso," is crucial to Ferré's sense that her righteous indignation at the position she occupies as a woman in Puerto Rico has affected, but not necessarily marred, her art. In the essay, Ferré discusses the positive way in which she controlled her anger, as if she had finally come to terms with Woolf's renowned rejection of that emotion. Thus, she establishes a relationship between two apparently dissimilar projects: *Papeles de Pandora* (1976) and *Fables of the Bleeding Heron* (1982), texts she published within six years of one another. She considers both didactic books on the topic of woman. While the first is historical in nature and the second is allegorical, she concedes that the aim of the two projects is quite similar. Both show how women—as historical subjects in one case and mythic in the other—are trapped by two types of commitments: social and personal. It is within the continuum afforded by the two projects that Ferré sees a positive attenuation of her anger through the formal use of irony as a technique that allows her an effective distance between herself and her topic (196-98). Most notably, she works out a major discrepancy of opinion with a writer that she reveres at the same time that she equates Woolf's strategy with her own:

> The fact that Virginia Woolf spoke so energetically against anger in *A Room of One's Own* is ironically proof of the importance of suppressed anger in her own novels. *A Room of One's Own* is an essay built on anger, although of a special type of anger: that which has been refined by the crucible of irony.
>
> ("How I Wrote 'When Women Love Men'" 147)

Among Spanish-American women writers, Woolf fueled a fundamental imaginative act. For both Ocampo and Ferré—who also started her literary career as editor of a journal called *Zona de Carga y Descarga*—Woolf was a foremother. She showed them, as well as many writers after them, ways of thinking critically about and aesthetically warring on the political, religious, and literary traditions that had treated women unfairly. There is no question that Woolf's vision enhanced theirs; it opened a space heretofore unavailable. It told a story differently nuanced and, on occasion, it attenuated their self-doubt. In the '70s and '80s, when Ferré started publication of her creative work as an *engagé* writer, she depicted an overwhelmingly patriarchal Puerto Rican society in transition. In *Papeles de Pandora* (translated in 1991 as *The Youngest Doll*), she painted a grim picture of island life, of women subjected to unscrupulous male doctors, adulterous male chauvinists, and infantile egocentrics. Like Woolf, Ferré equated the flamboyance of the clothes worn by educated men in their public capacities with war. In *Three Guineas*, Woolf had asked,

> What connection is there between the sartorial splendours of the educated man and the photograph of ruined houses and dead bodies? Obviously, the connection between dress and war is not far to seek; your finest clothes are those that you wear as soldiers. (21)

Similarly in "Amalia," Ferré's archetypal story of gender oppression of the '70s and '80s, she links the showiness of gold-braided attire and the havoc of war with sexual oppression in a sexually-polarized society that divides the female (private) from the (male) domain. "Amalia" is an orphaned girl virtually imprisoned in a house by an uncle with an impressive military career. Isolated from the world, the girl witnesses daily a procession of males—ministers and generals—who frequent the house to discuss public matters behind closed doors while she plays with her favorite doll, Amalia. It is onto Amalia that she unloads the anxieties of her existence. As the objectified representation of the girl herself, the doll's destruction foreshadows the girl's demise in a passage in which Ferré, like Woolf, envisions a procession of ambassadors, colonels and ecclesiastical powers bringing destruction to the world. Uncomprehending, the girl listens to the men make war at the same time that the Spanish text erupts in a bilingual staccato that mimics the sound of artillery. Bilingualism is a site of resistance at one in language and across languages. In Puerto Rico, a country polarized by the stalemated debate over its future as free-state associated, literally at war are nations (Puerto Rico and the United States), histories (colony and colonizer), languages (Spanish and English) and genders (woman and man).

Since she wrote this story, Ferré's views have evolved. Through the '70s, her focus seemed to be on the female narrative. Writing in Spanish as a means of preserving her heritage, she asserted her position as the committed keeper of a culture devoured by North American colonialism. The publication in Spanish of *Maldito Amor* and her subsequent translation of the novella into English with the title *Sweet Diamond Dust* mark Ferré's turn to a national narrative and to the task of translator who embraces language as a powerful political tool. This stage involved also the occasional recreation of entire passages as a means of crossing linguistic and cultural barriers (Jaffe 66-77). Finally, with the publication of *The House on the Lagoon* (1995), her first novel in English, she makes a new statement on the still-unresolved destiny of Puerto Rico at the close of the twentieth-century. No longer bent on independence as she was during two plebiscites, Ferré admitted in 1998 that with U.S. recognition of bilingualism and multiculturalism as vital aspects of North American policy, Puerto Rican culture seems no longer in as grave a danger of being engulfed as it had been in the past ("Puerto Rico, U.S.A" A21).

Rendered in Spanish, in English or in the linguistic space between both, Ferré's vision was stimulated by the impact of Woolf's. For three decades now she has combined the recurring and dominant presence of women with an analysis of the historical status of her island divided by the stalemated debate over its future. The Woolfian texts provided her with a pad from which to launch an attack on the objectification of Puerto Rican women.

Like Ferré, other Spanish American women writers separated from Woolf by language, distance and time engaged in fruitful, but unilateral, dialogue with her that stimulated their own thinking. Much of the dialogue involved extending Woolf's advice through the great physical distance that separated them as products of cultural contexts different from Woolf's and admittedly unknown to her: Woolf did not read Spanish; she acknowledged jokingly that she did not even know where Guatemala was; and, in general, the scattered references in the letters reveal her view that South America was a remote and mysterious land. Still, much of the dialogue also reveals that Spanish-American women writers considered Woolf a foremother; they allowed themselves to be tutored by her and felt a strong sense of continuity between her struggles in Britain and theirs in Spanish America (Castellanos 346).

**Works Cited**

Castellanos, Rosario. "Virginia Woolf o la literatura como ejercicio de la libertad." *Juicios Sumarios*. Xalapa: Editorial Veracruzana, 1966.

Chevigny, Bell Gale and Gari Laguardia (eds.) *Reinventing the Americas*:

*Comparative Studies of Literature of the United States and Spanish America.* Cambridge: Cambridge UP, 1986.

Ferré, Rosario. "De la ira a la ironía, o sobre cómo atemperar el acero candente del discurso." *Sitio a Eros: Quince ensayos literarios.* México: Joaquín Mortiz, 1986.

——. "How I Wrote 'When Women Love Men.'" *The Youngest Doll.* Lincoln: U of Nebraska P, 1991.

——. "La cocina de la escritura." *La sartén por el mango: encuentro de escritoras latinoamericanas.* Ed. Patricia E. González and Eliana Ortega. Río Piedras: Ediciones Huracán, 1984.

——. *Papeles de Pandora.* México: Joaquín Mortíz, 1986.

——. "Puerto Rico, USA." *New York Times,* 19 Mar. 1998: A21.

——. *Sitio a Eros: Trece Ensayos Literarios.* 1980. México: Joaquín Mortiz, 1986.

——. *The House on the Lagoon.* New York: Plume, 1995.

——. "The Writer's Kitchen." Trans. Diana L. Vélez. *Lives on the Line: The Testimony of Contemporary Latin American Authors.* Ed Doris Meyer. Berkeley: U of California Press, 1989.

Jaffe, Janice. "Translation and Prostitution: Rosario Ferré's *Maldito Amor* and *Sweet Diamond Dust.*" *Latin American Literary Review* 23, 46 (July-December, 1995): 66-82.

Kamenszain, Tamara. *El texto silencioso: tradición y vanguardia en la poesía sudamericana.* México: Universidad Autónoma de México, 1983.

Ocampo Victoria. "Carta a Virginia Woolf." *Testimonios I (1920-1934).* Buenos Aires: Sur, 1954.

——. *Virgina Woolf en su diario.* Buenos Aires: Sur, 1954.

Ordoñez, Montserrat. ¿Qué le debo a Virginia Woolf? *El Espectador* 413 (24 Marzo 1991): 6-7.

Pampillo, Gloria. "Un cuarto sin límites." *Mujeres en la escritura.* Ed. Sylvia Etkin. Buenos Aires: Editorial Puro Cuento, 1989.

Woolf, Virginia. *A Room of One's Own.* New York: Harcourt Brace Janovich, 1929.

——. *Three Guineas.* New York: Harcourt Brace Jovanovich, 1938.

## Megumi Kato

### The Politics/Poetics of Motherhood in *To the Lighthouse*

During the Victorian age, home was the domain exclusively for women which "the angel in the house" dominated as a specialist of mothering and domestic hygiene. But as Anna Davin has said, "[a]round the begining of this century infant life and child health took on a new importance in public discussion" (9). Interfering in this women's sphere, male politicians of various stripes began to discuss motherhood, because they pursued the improvement of motherhood, child-rearing and infant health as part of a national agenda to ward off the decline of the Empire and the degeneracy of the race. Early twentieth-century British culture featured a vigorous debate over the high infant mortality and declining birth-rate among imperialists, expansionists, eugenists, pronatalists, social purity campaigners, socialists, feminists, and female social activists, among others. William Saleeby, a leading advocate of maternalism and positive eugenics, regarded "the safe-guarding and the ennoblement of motherhood as the proximate end of all political action, the end through which the ultimate ends, the production and recognition of human worth, can alone be attained" (170). George Newman, in his influential book entitled *Infant Mortality: A Social Problem*, also succumbed to maternalism: "the problem of infant mortality is . . . mainly the question of motherhood . . . in the consideration of any measures for reducing the infant mortality, we must first attempt to solve the problem through the mother"(257-8). "Woman's groups also welcomed the new importance that attached to maternity"(Lewis 13), but the child and maternal welfare services that male policy-makers offered by no means met women's real demands for birth control and direct economic assistance. Such is the network of discourse with which Woolf's *To the Lighthouse*, particularly its first part, was involved. Motherhood, however, gradually transformed itself during the first three decades of this century. The tri-part structure of the novel represents well the wax and wane of this ideological climate. Maternity shifts from political to poetical in Woolf's text as in the historical context. This article is an attempt to read *To the Lighthouse* in this ideological context of motherhood. A close examination of the words "fertility" and "milk" in the text will help to throw the ideological change into clear relief.

Political motherhood, that is, motherhood for the nation's sake, sustains the world of the Ramsays in Part 1 and at its center Mrs. Ramsay is represented as a model of its ur-mother figure. Her reproductive capacity, which is the supreme virtue in maternalism, is described in such words as "fecundity," "fertility" and "abundance," and is often contrasted to the "barrenness," "sterility" and "poverty" of male characters and a spinster, Lily Briscoe (*TTL* 37,101). In Part 1 "fertility" means "domestic fertility," that is, Mrs. Ramsay's flooding power of life reproducing a new generation with sound mind and body.

In this ideological context, however, Mrs. Ramsay is caught within the contradictory positioning. She is "both Victorian ur-mother and the force of Empire itself" (Winston 50); "at once colonized and colonizer" (Doyle 153). In short, as a woman, she might be a "victim" of the ideology, sacrificing all her life to eight children, but as a white, middle-class, British, reproductive mother, she represents "the force of Empire."

As Winston and Dickson have thoroughly argued, the frequent comparisons of Mrs. Ramsay to Queen Victoria in the text certainly designate her authority as "the force of Empire." But rather than these allegorical expressions, I would like to put more emphasis on her ambition to be "an investigator, elucidating the social problem" (*TTL* 9). As far as one sees in the text, her habitual visits to the poor seem to be the ordinary scenery of visiting with which respectable Victorian women were engaged in the name of social purification. Mrs. Ramsay, however, dares to differentiate herself from these charitable visitors. Then, what is the difference between a social investigator and a visitor? According to Deborah Epstein Nord, "[t]wo phenomena of the late century—one methodological and one ideological—helped to pave the way for a female-authored social investigation" (212): on the one hand, by adopting the methods of social investigation established by Charles Booth, female social investigators could be more scientific and specialized than visitors; on the other hand "the end of the 19th century also produced an ideological climate receptive to women's efforts at investigation" (213). In brief, both Booth's methodology and the ideology of motherhood enabled the emergence of female investigators. Lynda Nead defines the social investigation as a task to colonize the working class "in the same way the geographical exploration was a strategy of British Colonialism" (150-1). Now, it follows that, by declaring her ambition to be an investigator, Mrs. Ramsay reveals herself as a colonizer of working-class people. Besides, the fact that the milk problem is her primary concern as social investigator further illustrates how politicized her character actually is (*TTL* 58,103). As I previously discussed in my short essay, "Milk Problem in *To the Lighthouse,*"[1] in Edwardian Britain the milk problem was one of the most controversial issues being considered as a key to improve the physical strength of the younger generation. Taking all these things into account, it can be concluded that Mrs. Ramsay represents a forceful mother, a white middle-class woman colonizer who repeats the imperialistic discourse propagating the ideology of motherhood.

As Woolf notably said in "Mr. Bennett and Mrs. Brown," "on or about December 1910 human character changed"; the decade around the First World War witnessed great changes in many fields. Motherhood was one of them. The "Time Passes" section bears the traces of this process of transformation. In this section Mrs. McNab plays quite an important role in mediating old and new motherhood. In the opening paragraph of section 9, under the guise of the description of wild plants and animals insensibly growing over and ruining the house, the text inscribes in itself the possible end of limitless fertility of human race which expansionists propagated. And just after the description, the text asks, "[w]hat power could now prevent the fertility, the insensibility of nature?" (*TTL* 138). And as its answer, "Mrs. McNab's dream of a lady, of a child, of a plate of milk soup" is suggested. What does this fertility mean, especially in relation to WW I and the postwar world? And why can Mrs. McNab's dreaming exert the power to prevent it? What is the connection of a lady and a child with a plate of milk soup?

Obviously "fertility" here has negative implications. The house ruined by "the fertility, the insensibility of nature" in part 2 is a metaphor for the disastrous state of Europe during WWI as a result of the insensibility of "human" nature. The Great War was the destination that expansionist, imperialist ideology, or, in a broader sense, phallogocentrism was bound for, because in spite of the Malthusian economists' caution against the danger of excessive population, which might lead to the exhaustion of resources, epidemic disease, poverty, war and ultimately to the end of the race, the British Empire didn't stop seeking for expansion, exploiting population as power. The tragedy of war, Woolf's text seems to suggest, was the natural consequence of this insensible proliferation of human nature. Historically the great loss of imperial assets in the war gave new stimulus to the question of fertility and child welfare, and the cult of motherhood lost some of its force after the war in Britain, partly because of the gradual decline in infant mortality in 1910s, partly because of their strong aversion to the extreme cult of motherhood in Nazi Germany.

Here, however, rather than exploring historical documents, one should turn to Woolf's literary text that would provide one with more available clues to elucidating the ideological changes. By examining the keywords—Mrs. McNab, dream, and milk—what is to come after the catastrophe should be revealed, for in the process of Mrs. McNab's metaphorical labor to promote the ideological and textual change the text anticipates that "some rusty laborious birth seemed to be taking place" (*TTL* 139).

First, "Mrs. McNab." Why is it that Mrs. McNab's dreaming can be a force to suppress the fertility of nature and save the ruined house from plunging "to the depths to lie upon the sands of oblivion"(*TTL* 139)? Why is she rendered such a specific power? Mrs. McNab is a working class woman who was forced into silence in Part 1. But in Part 2, she is given her voice. Giving voices to working-class women corresponds to a historical fact in 1915, that is, the publication of *Maternity—Letters from Working-Class Women* by the Women's Co-operative Guild. In fact, the publication had a great damaging impact on the ideology of motherhood, because women's fresh voices and complaints about the burden of motherhood disclosed the deceptiveness of men's rhetoric of maternalism. They revealed that the real cause of physical deterioration of the young was not the ignorance of mothers but poverty itself (Davin 44-46). Working women's voices including McNab's gave the impetus to take the mother's voice back from men and to destroy the delusion of maternalism. It is also to be noted that the publication was promoted by Woolf herself.

Secondly, "the dream." Dreaming is not the conscious or rational way of thinking, but "something not highly conscious; something that leered, something that lurched . . ." (*TTL* 139). It represents an alternative mode of thinking, which would subvert phallogocentrism at the basis of western civilization but produce creative feminine writing instead.

Lastly, "milk." Calling up her memory of the Ramsays, Mrs. McNab associates Mrs. Ramsay with milk, because Mrs. Ramsay often kept a plate of milk soup for her (*TTL* 136). The gesture of giving precious milk to a poor old maid implies the hierarchical power relationship of the two persons, for a working-class woman could hardly afford to buy pure milk at the time.[2] But it is more important that Mrs. McNab is designated a role of conveyer of milk from a lady to a child, from Mrs. Ramsay to her spiritual child, Lily, from part 1 to part 3, though she gives a twist to the milk by metaphorically pasteurizing it to kill its bacteria of politics. Having repressed fertility, subverted phallogocentrism and suggested new femininity, Mrs. McNab has prepared all the conditions for Lily to bring forth her own vision, her own style of creativity in the last section. That would be the greatest accomplishment of "some rusty laborious birth" given by Mrs. McNab.

Motherhood, which had been under the control of male politicians, was brought back into the hands of women in the form of "voluntary motherhood" after the war. The prevalence of birth control in 1920s enabled women to choose motherhood, which freed them from the burden of imposed motherhood and opened up new possibilities for female creativity in many fields. Sanger articulated, "[b]eing free, we have a right to expect much of her. We expect her to give still greater expression to her feminine spirit—we expect her to enrich the intellectual, artistic, moral and spiritual life of the world" (70-71).

Now in part 3, ideological and textual conditions favor the fruition of Lily's creative efforts. In part 1, in spite of all her wishes and efforts to capture Mrs. Ramsay, her vision consistently eluded her. The failure results partly from the fact that Lily could never accept certain political aspects of Mrs. Ramsay however she wanted and adored the lady. For example, at the dinner table when Mrs. Ramsay enthusiastically talked about the question of "real butter and clean milk," Lily's attitude toward the lady's eloquence looked rather aloof or even sardonic: "(she [Mrs. Ramsay] was thoroughly roused, Lily could see, and talked very emphatically)"(*TTL* 103). The use of parentheses further distances Lily from the argument and the others. Besides, just after her overheated eloquence was ridiculed by her husband and children, Mrs. Ramsay, finding Lily out of things, tried to draw her in by saying "'Lily anyhow agrees with me,'" but Lily was "a little fluttered, a little startled. (For she was thinking about love)" (*TTL* 103-104). No matter how Mrs. Ramsay expected Lily to be an inheritor of her ambition or at least to be sympathetic with her social concerns, Lily was totally indifferent to them, introspectively thinking about love instead. The reader might further recall the women's responses to Mr. Ramsay's finding an earwig in his milk at breakfast: Lily detached herself from it with laughter, while it *cow*ed Mrs. Ramsay and made Prue *white*—the latter both seen as victims of maternal politics (*TTL* 199-201).

Although Lily rejects the politics of motherhood against Mrs. Ramsay's will, she inherits the poetics of motherhood from her spiritual mother. In the beach scene retrospectively told in part 3, Lily manages to identify herself with Mrs. Ramsay by the same gesture of "making of the moments something permanent" (*TTL* 161). Mrs. Ramsay's moment of silence in this scene gives her a sort of a revelation: "Mrs. Ramsay sat silent . . . Aren't things spoilt then, Mrs. Ramsay may have asked . . . by saying them? Aren't we more expressive thus? The moment at least seemed extraordinarily fertile" (*TTL* 171-2). Contrasted to her aversion to Mrs. Ramsay's eloquence at the dinner table, here, in what she calls "the perfection of the moment," Lily found the silent language of Mrs. Ramsay most expressive and eloquent. Now she realized that it was the very language that she had been seeking for as female artist. That's why the word "fertile" used above is attached the greatest importance in the text by the modifier "extraordinarily." Fertility here serves a completely different function from its previous use. It is no longer the domestic fertility exploiting maternal bodies in part 1 or the threatening fertility to be controlled in part 2, but now in part 3 it is abstracted and represents the richness of female creativity. In the course of ideological and textual change, political motherhood, going beyond voluntary motherhood, is sublimated into poetical motherhood in Woolf's text and in Lily's art.[3]

The milk Mrs. Ramsay feeds Lily is not the one diluted or contaminated with maternal politics but, as Hélène Cixous points out, it is the "white ink" of the radical woman writer's text:

> Even if phallic mystification has generally contaminated good relationships, a woman is never far from "mother" (I mean outside her role functions: the "mother" as nonname and as source of goods). There is always within her at least a little of that good mother's milk. She writes in white ink. (251)

Under the auspices/suppression of Empire and its eugenicist views of motherhood and birth, "women can't write" as Tansley cursed, because they were deprived of their own voice and language, which could never be expressed by means of a phallogocentric system of language. But the end of such an ideological climate after the war together with the physical death of Mrs. Ramsay, who embodied "the politics of motherhood" itself, enable Lily's efforts to give birth to a new art: "the construction of a grammar" (Abel 78) of her own. The language of painting Lily chooses functions in the text as a means of representing "the poetics of motherhood," by which the mother-daughter relationships, a feminine way of acquiring their own language, and the silence of language can all be articulated. As Elizabeth Abel notes, "[c]onstructing Mrs. Ramsay in her own image, Lily fashions the mother she now needs, one who, neither engulfing nor diminishing, actively joins in the creation of a shared imaginative space" (79). Thus, Lily/Woolf managed to skim white ink from good mother's milk and accomplished her work of art by thinking back through her mothers but refashioning a politics into a poetics of motherhood.

## Notes

[1] In the essay, I contextualized the milk problem Mrs. Ramsay discussed within the ideology of motherhood as well as in preventive medicine since 1880s and by examining how politically the milk mattered in the early 20th century, I pointed out the political aspects of the lady.

[2] According to Newman, the average quantity of fresh milk consumption varied widely owing to social conditions—poverty, etc.: "the average consumption among all classes may be taken at one-fifth to one-half a pint per capita per diem, amongst the very poor the average is not more than one-tenth of a pint per capita per diem" (*BMJ* 425). Instead of fresh milk, the poor consumed condensed milk because "condensed milk was cheaper than fresh, and condensed skimmed milk cheapest of all" (Davin 35).

[3] Most of my discussion here is based on my essay already published in Japanese, "*Miruku-to Teikokushugi-to: Woolf ni okeru 'Bosei' no Gensetsu* [Milk and Imperialism: the Discourse of 'Motherhood' in Woolf's text]." *The Rising Generation* 143.12 (1998): 694-696.

## Works Cited

Abel, Elizabeth. *Virginia Woolf and the Fictions of Psychoanalysis*. Chicago: The U of Chicago P, 1989.

Cixous, Hélène. "The Laugh of the Medusa," *New French Feminisms: An Anthology*. Ed. Elaine Marks et al. New York: Schocken Books, 1981.

Davin, Anna. "Imperialism and Motherhood." *History Workshop* 5 (1978): 9-65.

Dickson, Jay. "Elegiac Modernity: Woolf and the Nineteenth Century." *Virginia Woolf: Themes and Variations*. Ed. Mark Hussey and Vara Neverow-Turk. New York: Pace U. P., 1993.

Doyle, Laura. *Bordering on the Body: The Racial Matrix of Modern Fiction and Culture*. New York: Oxford U.P., 1994.

Kato, Megumi. "Milk Problem in *To the Lighthouse*." *Virginia Woolf Miscellany* 50, Fall (1997): 5.

Lewis, Jane. *The Politics of Motherhood: Child and Maternal Welfare in England, 1900-1939*. London: Croom Helm, 1980.

Nead, Lynda. *Myths of Sexuality: Representations of Women in Victorian Britain*. Oxford: Basil Blackwell, 1988.

Newman, George. "Discussion on the Control of the Milk Supply." *The British Medical Journal* 27 Aug. 1904: 421-29.

——. *Infant Mortality: A Social Problem*. London: Methuen and Co., 1906.

Nord, Deborah Epstein. *Walking the Victorian Street: Women, Representations, and the City*. Ithaca NY: Cornell UP, 1995.

Saleeby, William. *Parenthood and Race Culture: An Outline of Eugenics*. London: Cassell and Company, Ltd., 1909

Sanger, Margaret H.. *Woman and the New Race*. New York: Brentano's Publishers, 1920.

Winston, Janet. "'Something Out of Harmony': *To the Lighthouse* and the Subject(s) of Empire." *Woolf Studies Annual* Vol.2, New York: Pace UP, 1996.

Women's Co-operative Guild, comp. *Maternity: Letters from Working-Women*. London: G. Bell and Sons, Ltd., 1915 rpt. Garland Publishing, Inc. 1980.

Woolf, Virginia. *To the Lighthouse*. 1927. San Diego: Harvest, 1981.

## Deborah Wilson

### Between the Arts: Woolf, Pedagogy, and the Persistence of Authority

In *Three Guineas*, Virginia Woolf argues for the value of biography and autobiography as an "aid to the understanding of human motives," since, rather than being "confined to the minute span of actual experience," we can "supplement" that narrowly circumscribed space "by looking at the picture of the lives of others" (7). Those words have encouraged me in the writing of this paper, which is my first foray into the realms of autobiography and pedagogy combined. And although Woolf's motive in *Three Guineas*, the prevention of war, looms much larger than educational philosophy and classroom methodology, on some level, our tasks are similar. For one thing, Woolf discovers in the "witness of biography" unanimous agreement that "the value of education is among the greatest of all human values" (24); yet she goes on to acknowledge that the same "double-faced" set of facts in biography (which "bristles with innumerable conflicts of private opinion") "also prove that education is by no means a positive value":

> It is not good in all circumstances, and good for all people; it is only good for some people and for some purposes. It is good if it produces a belief in the Church of England; bad if it produces a belief in the Church of Rome; it is good for one sex and for some professions, but bad for another sex and for another profession. (26)

Forced to recognize the vested interests imbricated in the current system of education, Woolf nonetheless hopes that education can become a powerful force for the prevention of war—by educating the young "'to hate war . . . to feel the inhumanity, the beastliness, the insupportability of war'" (22); but that hope depends upon a radical transformation, since history and biography both prove that education teaches people to use, rather than to hate force (29).

In a vision that has proven liberating for my own teaching, Woolf then posits an "'experimental . . . adventurous'" education more likely to prevent the abuses of power that lead to war (33). Beginning with some basic exclusions (no chapels, for instance), she advocates a curriculum of "'the arts that can be taught cheaply and practised by poor people; such as medicine, mathematics, music, painting and literature . . . human intercourse . . . and the little arts of talk, of dress, of cookery'" (34). It would aim to combine rather than "'segregate and specialize'" (working toward the cooperation of mind and body); its students would "'love learning for itself'" rather than as career preparation; its teachers ("'good livers as well as . . . good thinkers'") would likewise learn—and all without competition (34). Of course, the passage breaks off when the reader of this letter reminds its dreaming author of the realities: "'What is the use of thinking how a college can be different . . . when it must be a place where students are taught to obtain appointments?'" (35). This is the question I presume we all face in our respective universities, and how to find our way as teachers between these conflicting demands is part of my concern in this brief meditation. Woolf's reader wearily adds to her question, "'Dream your dreams, . . . fire off your rhetoric, but we have to face realities'" (35). In the next several minutes, I want to attempt all three at once.

I recently developed and taught a course on Bloomsbury as the required introductory course in the Master of Liberal Arts program I direct. Like most of its kind, our degree program is a nontraditional, interdisciplinary program which appeals primarily to students who want to further their liberal arts education, yet without being forced into a pre-set curriculum designed for some narrowly conceived professional goal. When I first read Woolf's description of her adventurous college and its curriculum, I thought, "She's describing a (perhaps utopian) interdisciplinary liberal arts program!" My convictions were further strengthened when, later in her argument, she advocates determining how much money and knowledge "'are needed for the full development of body and mind, and which are the real loyalties which we must serve and which the unreal which we must despise'"—all to be determined by means of a "'public psychometer'": "'Go to the public galleries and look at pictures; turn on the wireless and rake down music from the air; enter any of the public libraries which are now free to all'" (81). Again, the answer is the liberal arts—the art, music, and literature that are being systematically stripped from the core curricula of so many universities, and which we find ourselves defending by attaching them to the search for appointments (you know, English makes a great pre-Law degree). But I fear I preach to the choir here and defending the liberal arts is not my primary aim. Because, in addition to an interdisciplinary liberal arts program, I also see in Woolf's experimental college what Paulo Freire calls education as "the practice of freedom—as opposed to education as the practice of domination" (62). My attempts at such a practice in that Bloomsbury course generated complex questions about power and pedagogy that Woolf's ideas are helping me to work through.

I had developed the course to offer students from multiple disciplines sufficiently diverse research topics to pursue—painting, decorative arts, literature, biography, political science, economics—and yet, when the non-English majors (particularly the history and political science students) saw the novels included on the syllabus the first night, they disappeared from the course. The students who remained, none of whom were familiar with Woolf or Bloomsbury, were at best disinterested and at worst resistant to discussion of the visual arts, expressing a preference for the narrative art that Bloomsbury eschewed, while at the same time declaring the art of "significant form" inaccessible, undemocratic and elitist. A former military man who still tended to stand at attention and never called me anything but "ma'am" (in spite of all attempts to dissuade him), became the spokesman for what was a more widely held disbelief in the politics of aesthetics. For him, style could never subvert ideology, and Woolf's resistances to master narratives or patriarchal narrative forms was silly twaddle. Class after class, he worked to shift our discussion to the *really* political writers like George Orwell. The one student who had entered the course with a vague notion of Virginia Woolf's identity and a predisposition to enthusiasm was a newly-out lesbian in her early twenties who found herself deeply disappointed in the difficulty of Woolf's style and the covert-to-invisible nature of lesbianism in Woolf's texts. I frequently felt like those cheerleaders who stomp their feet at the restless, unenthusiastic crowd and whine, "Y'all cheer!"—and I was on the verge of agreeing with another disgruntled colleague who, in response to my grumbling, muttered, "Deborah, you've got to learn: *never teach what you love*."

More significant than the struggle over content, however, was the struggle over pedagogy.

In *Talking Back*, bell hooks advocates a revolutionary feminist pedagogy that would allow us as feminist teachers to "use power in a way that is not coercive, dominating":

> Yet we must acknowledge that our role as teachers is a position of power over others. We can use that power in ways that diminish or in ways that enrich and it is this choice that should distinguish feminist pedagogy from ways of teaching that reinforce domination. (52)

This, to me, was the pedagogy Woolf calls for in *Three Guineas* and, therefore, the pedagogy to which I was committed in this course. One method hooks offers is "to elect not to assume the posture of all-knowing professors," to admit that "we do not have all the answers" (a method Woolf adeptly uses in such texts as *A Room of One's Own*[1]); hooks does, however, recognize the risk of such a method—the accusation from our students that we are "not prepared" (52). My Bloomsbury class sat around a couple of tables we pushed together, and although the result wasn't the utopian round table, I never sat at the "head" or "foot," and I moved my own position at the table from class to class. Nonetheless, discussion tended to be directed toward me, even when I worked to encourage group dialogue rather than a series of one-on-one conversations with the professor and even when I withheld eye contact, nods, or any verbal responses until someone else responded first. The military man I mentioned earlier was often more than willing to step into what he perceived as a power gap.

Let me illustrate by relating part of our discussion of E. M. Forster's *A Passage to India.* Walking into the middle of the friendly preclass chat, I was almost immediately confronted with a question: "So, what are those Marabar caves?"—to which I responded, "What did you do with them in your reading? Didn't you at least attempt some interpretation of those caves before you moved on?" Silence. And more silence. Until one student laughed and said, "I just figured I'd wait until you told us." For the next quarter of an hour or so, they did begin to offer possible meanings and discuss how their ideas did or did not satisfy, until the aforementioned man slammed his book on the table, sighed deeply, and interrupted the speaking student with, "Well, of course the caves represent . . ."—I must admit to having since blanked out whatever else he said, although I do remember that he had with him a copy of *Twentieth-Century Interpretations of* A Passage to India, or some such text, from which he had derived his entire reading. To my amazement, all of the other students seemed visibly to relax as he spoke, and, when he finished, one of the thoroughly socialized Southern women in the room thanked him sweetly for his help. Almost a year after the course ended, one of the other students talked with this man, who confided in her, as bell hooks had anticipated, that I was without question the most ill-read, poorly prepared professor he had ever met.

What, then, of my attempts at an adventurous curriculum and a liberating pedagogy? My frustration and sense of failure grew until I caught myself thinking, "This could be such a great class without this group of students!"—and, suddenly, I saw myself mirrored in the commanding Miss La Trobe in *Between the Acts*, the playwright and director who, experiment gone awry, declares, "O to write a play without an audience" (180). A disturbing image for a feminist pedagogue—the woman with whip in hand who "'makes everyone do something'" (58). Surreptitiously nicknamed "'Bossy'" by her "little troops" (63), La Trobe longs to "expose them, as it were, to douche them, with present-time reality," and then curses them when they begin "slipping the noose" (179-80). How was I to feel about such an identification? According to Sallie Sears's reading of the novel, Miss La Trobe is "the artist as an ameliorating force for social change" (223), who assumes that showing her audience "deplorable truths" will make them "seek to abolish the circumstances that brought them into being" (229). A number of readers make me feel more at ease with La Trobe as my model by identifying her with Woolf herself.[2] Yet Sears acknowledges that La Trobe's audience remains untransformed, "dialogue fails; the relation is one of servitude, resistance, seduction gone awry" (229). And Judith Johnston offers a much more negative view of La Trobe as one who "*nearly* becomes an artist who rejects patriarchal authority" (emphasis added; 264), but instead resumes "total control" by exhorting the audience "with a voice that masters the air and prevents dialogue" (266). Labeling the playwright "an authoritative peace-monger," Johnston argues that La Trobe's desire to "dominate the people's minds" links her with the tyrannical impulses of Mussolini and Hitler, even though hers is a "different message" (266). Miss La Trobe was not, then, the model I wished to emulate, nor the proper faculty member for Woolf's experimental college. What had gone wrong with my experiment?

As a partial answer, I offer two passages, one from *Between the Acts* and one from Paulo Freire's *Pedagogy of the Oppressed.* In the first, we find Miss La Trobe after the recalcitrant audience has departed:

> She could say to the world, You have taken my gift! Glory possessed her—for one moment. But what had she given? . . . And the triumph faded. Her gift meant nothing. If they had understood her meaning; if they had known their parts . . . —it would have been a better gift. (*BTA* 209)

In Freire's description of liberating pedagogy, he insists that "the oppressed must be their own examples in the struggle for their redemption" (*Pedagogy* 36); redemption—understanding, "their parts"—cannot be *given to* them. Even when "members of the oppressor class join the oppressed in their struggle for liberation," Freire notes, "they almost always bring with them the marks of their origin: their prejudices and their deformations, which include a lack of confidence in the people's ability to think, to want, and to know" (42). In spite of the noble desire to bring about transformation, they—that is, we—fail because we "talk about the people, but . . . do not trust them; and trusting the people is the indispensable precondition for revolutionary change" (42).

Freire relates an incident that offers a different way to read my students' desire for and comfort in the totalizing, authoritative interpretations I have wanted to liberate them from—the story of a peasant in a "culture circle" who tells his professor, "Why don't you explain the pictures first? That way it'll take less time and won't give us a headache" (45). His request proves that, not only do we distrust them, they also distrust themselves; and that distrust and dependence, which is the product of domination, cannot be transformed into independence through "libertarian propaganda," nor can "even the best-intentioned leadership . . . bestow independence as a gift" (48). What's called for is trust, dialogue, a working together of student and teacher toward what Freire calls "cointentional education" (51).

Let me stop here to confess that I have rewritten the last two pages of this paper a number of times. In fact, the day before I left Arkansas for the Woolf conference, a colleague who read the previous version offered her advice: "You should be starting where you are stopping." In other words, she claims to agree with the ideas, but she wants to know exactly *how* to implement them. She wants praxis alongside theory. I must admit to similar desires, which have been largely frustrated by the four major proponents of what's called "critical pedagogy." Both Freire and Ira Schor advocate such methods as "collective and collaborative work styles; peer and group instruction and evaluation; as well as self and mutual instruction" (Gore 105). Henry Giroux and Peter McLaren aim to "enable" teachers to develop their own critical pedagogy, but one finds in their writing a "dearth of attention to specific practices" (Gore 42, 107). As Jennifer Gore notes, such "reluctance to articulate specific practices often emerges out of a concerted attempt to avoid prescriptive dogmatism"; yet we are forced to acknowledge that theory alone may not provide sufficient guidance (111).

However, serious difficulties immediately surface the moment one begins to offer prescriptions of classroom practices. In fact, Kathleen Weiler points out a central problem in Freire's liberation pedagogy: that is, his assumption of a universal, undifferentiated "oppressed," an abstraction that elides differences of gender, race, and class, for example (27-29). As Elizabeth Ellsworth insists, oppression must be "understood and struggled against": the terms of classroom practices are "wholly dependent on the Others/others whose presence—with their concrete experiences of privileges and oppressions, and subjugated or oppressive knowledges—I am responding to and acting with in any given classroom" (114-15). That is to say, our practice cannot be "predicted, prescribed, or understood beforehand" because it is and must be "profoundly contextual (historical) and interdependent (social)" (115). It seems we must work out our own practice as individual teachers, class by particular class.

But there are certain principles that can guide us in that ongoing process, principles I have tried to point toward in this paper. And Woolf's texts, which, unlike Freire's, *insist* upon difference, can help us work out those principles in our classrooms as we enter into dialogue with her with students. I want to leave you with another of Woolf's examinations of education to go alongside the image of her experimental college in *Three Guineas*. This passage is from the sketch "A Woman's College from the Outside":

> Elderly women slept, who would on waking immediately clasp the ivory rod of office. Now . . . they lay . . . supported, by the bodies of youth . . .; pouring forth into the garden this bubbling laughter, this irresponsible laughter: this laughter of mind and body floating away rules, hours, discipline: immensely fertilising, yet formless, chaotic, trailing and straying and tufting the rose-bushes with shreds of vapour. (*CSF* 147)

Notice that the "irresponsible laughter" of youth displaces discipline, and, although it is fertilizing, it is also "formless, chaotic, trailing and straying." Making our classrooms a space for "cointentional learning" requires risking the loss of power and control. And, lest I be accused of leaving my audience wandering about in the vapor, I come back to the question of what kind of teachers Woolf's college would hire to replace those elderly women too quick to clasp that ivory rod: "'Musicians, painters, writers, would teach there, because they would learn'" (*TG* 34). That is what a dialogic, liberation pedagogy requires—that we *learn* from as well as teach our students. They must participate in their own liberation; if they will not, the experiment is a failure, no matter what we do. I look again at Woolf's college, where "'lectures are not given, and sermons are not preached'" (*TG* 35)—not even peace-mongering, liberating ones. Otherwise, the students' voices, like the villagers' chorus in *Between the Acts*, may be blown away by our own ideological wind, and our pedagogies may become merely a different version rather than a subversion of domination.

## Notes

1 As Marcus points out, Woolf "deconstructs the lecture as a form" in *A Room of One's Own*, enacting instead the "lecture as conversation (between women) rather than the dictation of the expert to the ignorant" (145).

2 Sears, for instance, equates La Trobe's relation to her audience with Woolf's "conflict about the value of her work" in a world where events were "stripping her" of an "audience" (229); and Schneider goes so far as to call La Trobe "in many ways [Woolf's] surrogate" (109).

## Works Cited

Ellsworth, Elizabeth. "Why Doesn't This Feel Empowering? Working Through the Repressive Myths of Critical Pedagogy." *Feminisms and Critical Pedagogy.* Ed. Carmen Luke and Jennifer Gore. New York: Routledge, 1992. 90-119.

Freire, Paulo. *Pedagogy of the Oppressed.* Rev. ed. Trans. Myra Bergman Ramos. New York: Continuum, 1997.

Gore, Jennifer M. *The Struggle for Pedagogies: Critical and Feminist Discourses as Regimes of Truth.* New York: Routledge, 1993.

hooks, bell. *Talking Back: Thinking Feminist, Thinking Black.* Boston: South End, 1989.

Johnston, Judith L. "The Remediable Flaw: Revisioning Cultural History in *Between the Acts*." *Virginia Woolf and Bloomsbury.* Ed. Jane Marcus. Bloomington: Indiana UP, 1987. 253-77.

Marcus, Jane. *Virginia Woolf and the Languages of Patriarchy.* Bloomington: Indiana UP, 1987.

Schneider, Karen. "Of Two Minds: Woolf, the War and *Between the Acts*." *Journal of Modern Literature* 16:1 (1989): 93-112.

Sears, Sallie. "Theater of War: Virginia Woolf's *Between the Acts*." In *Virginia Woolf: A Feminist Slant.* Ed. Jane Marcus. Lincoln: U of Nebraska P, 1983. 212-35.

Weiler, Kathleen. "Freire and a Feminist Pedagogy of Difference." *Debates and Issues in Feminist Research and Pedagogy*. Ed. Janet Holland and Maud Blair, with Sue Sheldon. Clevedon: Open U, 1995. 23-44.

Woolf, Virginia. *Between the Acts*. 1941. San Diego: Harvest, 1969.

——. *Three Guineas*. 1938. San Diego: Harvest, 1966.

——. "A Woman's College from Outside." *The Complete Shorter Fiction of Virginia Woolf*. Ed. Susan Dick. San Diego: Harvest, 1989.

# Re-examining Discourses of Power

## Tuzyline Jita Allan, Featured Speaker

### Civilization, Its Pretexts, and Virginia Woolf's Imagination

In her essay "On Seeing England for the First Time," Jamaica Kincaid offers two opposing visions of England that complicate the promised denouement of colonial history:

> When I saw England for the first time, I was a child in school sitting at a desk. The England I was looking at was laid out on a map gently, beautifully, delicately, a very special jewel . . . . When my teacher had pinned this map on the blackboard, she said, "This England"—and she said it with authority, seriousness and adoration and we all sat up. It is as if she had said, "This is Jerusalem, the place you will go to when you die but only if you have been good." We understood then . . . that England was to be our source of myth and the source from which we got our sense of reality, our sense of what was meaningful, our source of what was meaningless. (32)

Her Antiguan childhood disrupted by England's Delphic authority, Kincaid responded to "the real England" she visited later on as an adult "with hatred" so strong that, as she puts it, "I wanted to take it into my hands and tear it into little pieces and then crumble it up as if it were clay, child's clay" (37).

Journeying to England from another outpost of Empire, Buchi Emecheta evokes in her autobiography *Head Above Water* a similar sense of dashed desire suffered in the collision between colonial rhetoric of rescue and the reality of rejection: "England gave me a cold welcome," Emecheta writes. "As I said in *Second-Class Citizen,* 'If I had been Jesus, I would have passed England by and not dropped a single blessing.' It felt like walking into the inside of a grave" (29). As with Kincaid, England fails to live up to the talismanic image implanted in the impressionable mind of the colonial child: "Whenever my father pronounced the words, 'United Kingdom,'" Emecheta recalls, "it sounded so heavy, so reverential. It was so deep, so mysterious that my father always voiced it in hushed tones wearing an expression as respectful as if it were God's Holiest of Holies. Going to the United Kingdom must surely be like paying God a visit" (26). Perceived in England as an incongruous presence, Emecheta, like Kincaid, reacts to this classic bit of colonial betrayal with rabid scorn.

Kincaid's and Emecheta's postcolonial acts of retrospection resonate with Woolf's concerns about England's identity as a sustainable paradise. Woolf presses hard the edges of this issue in *Three Guineas*, casting imperial doubt on the promise England held for the daughters of educated men like herself. Speaking to the nation's ruling class of men, Woolf asserts:

> When we meet in the flesh we speak with the same accent; use knives and forks in the same way; expect maids to cook dinner and wash up after dinner; and can talk during dinner without much difficulty about politics and people; war and peace; barbarism and civilization . . . . But . . . those three dots mark a precipice, a gulf so deeply cut between us that for three years and more I have been sitting on my side of it wondering whether it is any use to try to speak across it. (4)

The statement points to Woolf's deepening distrust of Englishness, though she herself was incontrovertibly English. The travesties of gender difference and the unreasoning power of wayward masculinity are indices of her legendary alienation within British society. In *Three Guineas*, published three years before her death, Woolf symbolically removes herself from the killing grounds of British sexist nationalism by claiming alien status. From the margins of a society of outsiders, the mantra of resistance is sounded: "'as a woman I have no country. As a woman I want no country. As a woman my country is the whole world'" (109). This eruption of what might be called "bound-less desire" is clearly a postcolonial act that bears prophetic witness to the imminent demise of Empire and prefigures the transnationalism of postimperial society. Woolf's renunciatory rhetoric thus anticipates Kincaid's and Emecheta's declarations of aversion to England. Like Woolf, these once-colonized women impeach the "motherland" for its long-launched practice of social inequality.

Admiration for Woolf's feminism in *Three Guineas* and other texts has the tendency, however, to overwhelm other concerns raised in her work. Perhaps that is because the benefit of a genuinely curious attitude toward the complexity of Woolf's ideological struggles has yet to be assessed. Happily, feminist scholars are beginning to pay attention to Vron Ware's strong argument in *Beyond the Pale* "that [nineteenth-century] feminist ideology and practice were shaped by the social, economic and political forces of imperialism to a far greater extent than has been acknowledged" (119). In her book's third chapter, provocatively titled "Britannia's Other Daughters," Ware maps "the extent to which feminists defined womanhood against or in line with dominant ideologies of Empire, which demanded particular roles of white women" (xv). For Ware, this information is necessary "to ensure that feminism has a future as a radical movement that can unite women across existing divisions of class, race and culture" (xvii). In other words, while the integrationist imperative of contemporary feminism is both crucial and noble, feminist scholars cannot afford to ignore the historical contexts that underlie individual women's constructions of self and other. In the case of Woolf, Emecheta, and Kincaid, Europe's centuries-long division of the world's population into white and black, master and servant, free and slave, civilized and savage determined the estrangement of these women within an inescapably gendered system. Even as she vigorously tried to relax gender barriers, as an English woman and as a writer, Woolf frequently relied on certain ideological assumptions about English cultural identity that would have prevented a natural alliance between her and Emecheta or Kincaid.

The passage from *Three Guineas* cited above richly illustrates Woolf's double status as woman and English. To fully grasp its significance, it is important to recall Woolf's habit of painting pictures with words in an attempt to burn her message into the consciousness of her readers and listeners. "It is impossible that one should not see pictures," Woolf wrote in the essay "Three Pictures" (*DM* 12). And it is impossible "to interpret" a voice, "to make it intelligible to the mind" (14) without locating it in a body. A painter manqué, Woolf became a wordsmith with the painterly skills of a poet, shaping and fitting words together so that in the end it would seem as if, as she said of the work of the Elizabethan playwrights, "thought plunged into a sea of words and came up dripping" (*CR*1 55). With this in mind, let's go back to the embodied thought, or picture, that emerges from the piece from *Three Guineas*. We see a group of people with a similar background, upbringing, taste, and world view, "a little private circle of exquisite and cultivated people" (*L*6 420), to use Woolf's own words. The "we" in the picture have not only gathered "in the flesh," they are of the same flesh, kinfolk, if not strictly by blood, then through a shared cultural understanding of themselves and their kind as civilized. That is why the group is also defined by its invisible counterpart, the "other" frame of reference marked by class, race, and silence. The "maids" and the teeming masses of racial and cultural outsiders lumped under the term "barbarism" serve to solicit an understanding of the group's rights and privileges. Like Zora Neale Hurston's Janie Crawford in *Their Eyes Were Watching God*, they are both in and outside the picture. But somehow the logic of exclusion is far from finite, and when it repeats itself in this case (the moment of repetition is marked by the three dots), Woolf finds herself on the "other" side, pondering the murderous ambiguity of the margin. Harnessing the margin's nervous energy, Woolf goes on to launch a scathing attack on England's militaristic patriarchy in the rest of *Three Guineas*.

At this point I would like to take a closer look at the territory Woolf calls "my side," the home of "a society of outsiders." What are the psychological, moral, and ideological contours of this liminal landscape? Is it Dostoevsky's "underground" of split personalities which Woolf, speaking of Dostoevsky's fictional world, saw as the home of the soul (*CR*1 179)? Or is it more akin to Richard Wright's version of the underground as a safe haven for the transgressive witness to the tyranny of custom? Is Woolf's exile home a kind of Bantu homeland where radicalism was reduced under apartheid to a harmless practice of "compliance without consent" (Adam and Moodley 129)? Is Woolf's imagined community akin to Gloria Anzaldua's "borderland," the site of cultural crossings and overlapping identities? These questions, in their punishing persistence, point to the deep quandaries that engaged Woolf in narrating the English nation. They are intended to draw attention to what Homi Bhabha refers to as "a particular ambivalence that haunts the idea of the nation, the language of those who write it and the lives of those who live it." This ambivalence, according to Bhabha, "emerges from a growing awareness that, despite the certainty with which historians speak of the 'origins' of the nation . . . [,] the cultural temporality of the nation inscribes a much more transitional social reality" (1). In other words, national identity, like other forms of identity, is far from stable. It is my contention that Woolf's symbolic occupation of the border located both in and outside England is a trope that expands and clarifies her epic narrative of English nationhood. I say "epic" to convey a sense not only of the encyclopedic scope of Woolf's canon but also the very nature of her subject, namely, England's grand national theme of civilization. The story of Woolf's disloyalty to civilization, to borrow Adrienne Rich's often-quoted phrase, is the story of the feminization of English society. And in this regard, Woolf would agree with Benedict Anderson's remark that "in the modern world everyone can, should, will 'have' a nationality, as he or she 'has' a gender" (14). She insisted on the simultaneity of these two categories—gender and national identity—and wrote with withering satire about the coercive civility of England's ruling men. Woolf's symbolic murder of the "angel in the house" is as much an act of civil disobedience directed against a system of gender hierarchy as it is a rite of passage of the artist as a young woman. But, to return to Anderson's aphorism, to have a nationality in the modern world is also to have a race.

It is no surprise that the European construction of whiteness in the eighteenth and nineteenth centuries was laced with various nationalistic agendas that gave powerful expression to the concept of civilization. Norbert Elias sums up this point at the beginning of his book *The Civilizing Process*:

> [W]hen one examines what the general function of the concept of civilization really is . . . one starts with a very simple discovery: this concept expresses the self-consciousness of the West. One could even say: the

> national consciousness. It sums up everything in which Western society of the last two or three centuries believes itself superior to earlier societies or "more primitive" contemporary ones. By this term Western society seeks to describe what constitutes its special character and what it is proud of: the level of *its* technology, the nature of *its* manners, the development of *its* scientific knowledge or view of the world, and much more. (3-4)

In painstaking detail, Elias shows how the civilizing idea traveled lifetimes through religious, courtly, bourgeois, and state formulations, finally depositing itself in the individual psyche for more ill than good. The layers of this history reflect the process-driven character of civilization. No summary can do justice to the book's tremendous sweep, but I will try to isolate a few pertinent points. First, the history of civilization in the West is a history of manners, of the transformation of human behavior from "that which we [now] call uncivilized." That means, as Elias argues, the "terms 'civilized' and 'uncivilized' do not constitute an antithesis of the kind that exists between 'good' and 'bad,' but [instead] represent stages in a development which, moreover, is still continuing" (59). Second, the meaning of civilization varies among different Western nations, evoking in the English and French "pride in the significance of their own nations for the progress of the West and of mankind" (4), while conjuring up the notion of outward progress among Germans, who prefer the term *kultur* to signify the intangible qualities of German identity. Third, civilization and class are old bedfellows, starting with the self-validating courtly/aristocratic attitudes of the seventeenth and eighteenth centuries and including the more recent expressions of anxiety by the professional upper classes. Finally, Elias makes the point popularized by Freud that as the noose tightens around individuals in the postindustrial prisonhouse of civilization, the resulting fears and anxieties become as destructive as the social constraints that produce them. The book's thematic ballast lies in its careful mapping of the undulating zones of Western civilization and in its aim to make any identification with the current view of what is "civilized" and "uncivilized" less simple. Moreover, while the subject of non-Western civilizations are outside its purview, the book establishes a crucial fact of life before the Age of Imperialism, namely that "[t]o a certain extent, the concept of civilization plays down the national differences between peoples; it emphasizes what is common to all human beings or . . . should be"(5). It goes without saying, however, that with Europe's colonial expansion, this idea is lost in the same memory vault that conceals the facts of the uncivilized European past that Elias chronicles.

When Woolf declared in "Mr. Bennett and Mrs. Brown" that "in or about December, 1910, human character changed" (*CE*1 320), she left us, as she does repeatedly in her writing, to surmise its meaning. And, surely enough, we try to cover all the bases: the manifesto for a gendered modernism; an acute case of anxiety of influence, given how she felt about those

Edwardian materialists; a grudging recognition of Freud; an uncannily accurate prophecy, given the fact that the Great War was drumbeats away. Woolf's statement, however, can also be construed as a signifying act that both echoes and subverts John Stuart Mill's axiom that "'mankind have outgrown old institutions and old doctrines, and have not yet acquired new ones'" (qtd. in Houghton 1). Like Mill, Woolf was intent on shaping the spirit of her own age, and in what is essentially a declaration of independence, she tries to dispel with the force of the caesura the chronic uncertainty of her Victorian forebears to make room for a more powerful expression of her desire for a clean break.

But pulling up the bridge was for Woolf a Herculean task, and nowhere is this fact more apparent than in her engagement with the Victorian "invention of Africa," to borrow V. Y. Mudimbe's aptly titled book. The Victorian obsession with change finds a curious correlation in its conceptualization of Africa as a fixed essence. Drawing upon the assumption that Woolf's works are dual-language texts, always already deconstructed, the title of this paper indulges in a willful play on the word "pretexts" to register the double meaning of discursive influence or texts that operate under cover and subversive intentionality with the potential to erase itself. The larger argument of this paper is that while Woolf rejected the running narrative of English nationhood that cast English women on the outer banks of civilization, she sometimes queried but more frequently endorsed the huge elements of that story that dealt with the uncivilized state of the racial other. Hence, regarding the narratives of racial civilization, "pretext" implies both what was said and what was omitted about Africa. If, as Patrick Brantlinger has noted, "Africa grew dark as Victorian explorers, missionaries, and scientists flooded it with light" (173), then it stands to satiric reason that Africa existed before it was "discovered" by Europe. This, of course, is the heart of the matter in Chinua Achebe's *Things Fall Apart* and in the fiction of several other African writers, including Buchi Emecheta, whose feminist deconstruction of the myth of Africa as a void in *The Rape of Shavi* features a society of women that invites comparison with Woolf's fascinating cast of female characters in "A Society."

Historical records, in addition to historical novels, dispute the Victorian de-civilization of Africa, but these had to be exploded to build an image of Africans befitting their subjugation. Peter Fryer puts it more bluntly in his book *Staying Power*:

> It was their drive for profit that led English merchant capitalists to traffic in Africans. There was big money in it. The theory came later. Once the English slave trade, English sugar-producing plantation slavery, and English manufacturing industry had begun to operate as a trebly profitable interlocking system, the economic basis had been laid for all those ancient scraps of myth and prejudice to be woven into a more or less coherent racist ideology: a mythology of race. (134)

By "those ancient scraps of myth and prejudice," Fryer is referring to the markers of difference early Europeans—from antiquity to the Elizabethan era—used to define Africans. The characterizations make up a vibrant hybrid ranging from an exaggerated name-calling of foreigners to a non-judgmental, often respectful view of the Africans encountered during the opening of European trade routes. It is a period when Africans were considered devils, monsters, the cursed children of Ham and at the same time admired as builders of kingdoms that included ancient Ghana, Mali, Songhay, Benin, and Egypt. The superior/inferior binary is a much later construction. While there is a lot of gray area that archeologists and historians are trying to sort out, especially with respect to periodization, the growing evidence points to the conclusion reached by the renowned English historian Basil Davidson:

> [W]ith the exceptions that so vast a subject must allow, the Europeans of the sixteenth century believed that they had found forms of civilization which were compatible with their own, however differently and variously dressed and mannered. A later age would prefer to forget this, and would roundly state that Africa knew nothing but a savage and indeed a hopeless barbarism. We shall do well to remember that familiar European contempt for Africans . . . was an attitude born of the Atlantic slave trade, after about 1650, and later, of the cultures of European capitalism. (*The Search for Africa* 43)

It is common knowledge that Woolf was familiar with and influenced by the dominant ideas about Africa's culture of savagery that barraged British society at the dawn and height of Empire. But before I speak to this issue, I want to raise a question that may very well establish a new tone in Woolfian criticism: Apart from the texts of Africa's divestiture, did Woolf have access to others that did not support the ideological consensus of a barbarous African past, and did this information linger on the edge of her memory long enough to work as a salient, albeit silent, counterpoint to the beliefs that are grist for her representation of racial otherness? Put differently, if indeed Woolf had access to early African history, whether through the classical Greek philosophers and scientists who, according to Herodotus, were students of Ethiopian and Egyptian civilizations; or through the epic of Portuguese discovery written in 1552 and 1563 by João de Barros titled *Decade de Asia*; or yet still through Richard Hakluyt's famous book *Principal Navigations, Voyages, Traffics and Discoveries of the English Nation*, published in 1597, did these facts in any way influence her thinking about Africa and Africans? Can we find clues—in the Dreadnought Hoax, for example? Is this a drama waiting to be reconceived as Judith Shakespeare's Revenge, whose main act is the recuperation of repressed African history? If so, then we could go on to say that in a double subversive move this "play" both critiques British imperialism and reverses through parodic humor the very idea it sets out to rescue. In this context, the performative aspects of Virginia-in-black-face fuel a good deal of speculation. For example, does this mask simultaneously grin at and hide the nation's secrets, looking disapprovingly both outward at an oppressive world and inward at the self that is somewhat complicit in that oppression? Does it evoke the split self of the black mask memorialized by Paul Laurence Dunbar, or the African mask itself, which functions as a border between the temporal and the eternal to allow for a creative and spiritual engagement with the "other" side? Does it evoke black minstrelsy and its promise of a cathartic release through mockery? What should we also make of Virginia's pidgin Swahili: "'Chuck-a-choi, chuck-a-choi'" and "'Bunga-Bunga'"? Uttered through "'the most complete se[t] of nigger lips'" (Lee 283),[1] its immediate goal is obviously mockery. But is it also possible that Virginia, the writer-in-waiting, is trying to break through to the semantic realm of pre-Oedipal language where her artistic sensibilities will ultimately find anchor?

The idea of a positive African influence on Woolf's imagination might seem less incidental if we consider her view of prehistory. The concept represents modernism's most enduring dilemma: how to enlist the primitive in the modernist project of spiritual restoration without legitimizing Africa. A persistent theme in modernist writing is the journey back in time to an Edenic past, in short, to prehistory. Given the Hegelian construction of Africa as the essence of prehistory, the modernist journey back to recapture the lost credibility of the primitive imagination is in effect a passage to Africa. To get around this epistemological bind, the primitive or the primeval is fetishized by the major modernist writers as they try to extract its mystery in a way that would leave behind its African scent. How this conflict is mediated in Woolf's works deserves critical attention. It may be more appropriate, for example, to think of her as engaging prehistoric Africa rather than the Darwinian imaginary, as Gillian Beer argues in her essay "Virginia Woolf and Prehistory." Such a perspective might help to explain the striking similarities between Woolf's description of the landscape in *The Voyage Out* and language used by the very early European travelers to capture Africa's enchanting beauty. (I don't cite the instances here because I intend to explore the idea more fully in a longer work in progress.)

The vast apparatus of colonial ideology remains a strong presence in Woolf's writings, in spite of the ambiguity of representation I have tried to uncover. A plethora of myths about Africa in Woolf's England weighed heavily against the African subject. Rousseau's idea of the "primitive equality of man" hardly struck a resonant chord in a culture dominated by notions of natural selection and manifest civilization. The texts that tell the story of Africa's dispossession run the gamut from anthropological and scientific tracts to travel literature, the latter's evocative power doing, perhaps, the greatest harm. According to Alan Moorehead, author of *The White Nile*, a historical account of the European stampede to discover the sources of the Nile, "In the Victorian Age, explorers' books exerted an extraordinary power over people's minds . . . . One would have thought that there was enough here to inform, confuse, and finally satiate the most besotted student of African travels, but still the public could not have enough" (61-2).

I will not give you the retinue of travel/explorer books, but I will cite a couple of high-profile examples to illustrate the single-minded pursuit of racial difference. Henry Morton Stanley, one of the explorers to search for the sources of the White Nile, is the originator of the term the "Dark Continent." In his book *In Darkest Africa*, published in 1890, he summoned an enduring fantasy:

> [T]he great forest which lay vast as a continent before them, and drowsy like a great beast, with monstrous fur thinly veiled by vaporous exhalations, answered not a word, but rested in its infinite sullenness, remorseless and implacable. (qtd. in Hammond and Jablow 60)

W. Winwood Reade provided "a link between fiction and the explorers' journals" (Hammond and Jablow 68) in his *African Sketchbooks*, a two-volume collection of short stories and novellas based on his travels in West Africa, published in London in 1873, and *Savage Africa*, the accounts of his travels, published in New York in 1864. Both books contain the entire range of conventions pertaining to African representation, but I found the following description of the black woman in *Savage Africa* particularly relevant to my discussion of Woolf's African sources:

> The negress has beauty—beauty in spite of her black skin. . . . And she is gentle and faithful and loving in her own poor way. . . . Where is the intellect, which is the light in the crystal lamp, the genius within the clay? No, no, the negress is not a woman; she is a parody of a woman; she is a pretty toy, an affectionate brute-that is all. (qtd. in Hammond and Jablow 71))

Mary Kingsley, mentioned in *Three Guineas*, sums up the attitudes of colonial women in Africa in her book *Travels in West Africa*, published in London in 1898:

> It is not necessary to treat them brutally . . . but it is necessary to treat them severely, to keep a steady hand over them. Never let them become familiar, never let them see you have made a mistake. When you make a mistake in giving them an order let it be understood that way of doing a thing is a peculiarly artful dodge of your own . . . and if it fails, that it is their fault. (qtd. in Hammond and Jablow 85)

Let me close by making two points: first, an expanded version of this paper will continue to identify the areas in Woolf's work where the texts and ideas I have mentioned exert influence. The second is to underscore the fact that any effort to reveal Woolf as both a product of and a rebel against her culture is to draw a bigger picture of one woman's struggles to ride the lapping waves that mightily separated her world from "others." A historical perspective will reveal why the voice of Empire is audible throughout Woolf's work, just as it reverberates in the works of her contemporaries, including Forster, Lawrence, and Conrad. As Elleke Boehmer points out in her book *Colonial and Postcolonial Literature*, "no matter how cosmopolitan or transnational the interests [of the modernist writers were], a distinct—and perhaps inevitable—cultural and political fixity remains a characteristic of their work. The relativism that was part of modernism was hemmed in by world-wide grids of imperial authority" (144). It was an authority Woolf railed against, especially its "conversion" impulse. "Conversion" was the code word she often used to refer to her nation's crusading brand of civilization (*MD* 100), one that would not have allowed Kincaid, Emecheta, or herself to share their experiences as women or as writers, let alone as British subjects.

**Note**

1 Lee rightly identifies this incident as a subversive move against Empire, but overlooks its blatant racism. She claims that "it was a family affair. . . . It was the younger generation of Stephens thumbing their nose at their aunts' and uncles' book of tradition" (284). Thus, Lee fails to account for the concomitant sense of racial difference that informs the drama.

**Works Cited**

Achebe, Chinua. *Things Fall Apart.* Greenwich, CT: Fawcett, 1959.

Anzaldua, Gloria. *Borderlands/La Frontera: The New Mestiza.* San Francisco: Aunt Lute Books, 1987

Adam, Herbert, and Kogila Moodley. *South Africa Without Apartheid: Dismantling Racial Domination.* Berkeley: U of California P, 1986.

Anderson, Benedict. *Imagined Communities: Reflections on the Origin and Spread of Nationalism.* London: Verso, 1983

Beer, Gillián. "Virginia Woolf and Prehistory." *Virginia Woolf: A Centenary Perspective.* Ed. Eric Warner. New York: St. Martin's, 1984. 99-123.

Bhabha, Homi K., ed. *Nation and Narration.* London: Routledge, 1990.

Boehmer, Elleke. *Colonial and Postcolonial Literature: Migrant Metaphors.* New York: Oxford UP, 1995.

Brantlinger, Patrick. *Rule of Darkness: British Literature and Imperialism, 1830-1914.* Ithaca: Cornell UP, 1988.

Davidson, Basil. *African Civilization Revisited: From Antiquity to Modern Times.* Trenton, NJ: Africa World Press, 1991.

——. *The Search for Africa: History, Culture, Politics.* New York: Random, 1994.

Elias, Norbert. *The Civilizing Process: The History of Manners.* Trans. Edmund Jephcott. New York: Urizen, 1978.

Emecheta, Buchi. *Head Above Water.* London: Ogwugwu Afo, 1986.

——. *The Rape of Shavi*. New York: George Braziller, 1985.
Fryer, Peter. *Staying Power: Black People in Britain Since 1504*. Atlantic Highlands, NJ: Humanities, 1984.
Hammond, Dorothy, and Alta Jablow. *The Africa That Never Was: Four Centuries of British Writing About Africa*. Prospect Heights, IL: Waveland, 1970.
Houghton, Walter E. *The Victorian Frame of Mind: 1830-1870*. New Haven: Yale UP, 1957.
Hurston, Zora Neale. *Their Eyes Were Watching God*. New York: Harper & Row, 1937.
Kincaid, Jamaica. "On Seeing England for the First Time." *Transition: An International Review* 51 (1991): 32-40.
Lee, Hermione. *Virginia Woolf*. London: Chatto & Windus, 1996.
Moorehead, Alan. *The White Nile*. New York: Harper and Brothers, 1960.
Mudimbe, V. Y. *The Invention of Africa: Gnosis, Philosophy, and the Order of Knowledge*. Bloomington: Indiana UP, 1988.
Ware, Vron. *Beyond the Pale: White Women, Racism and History*. London: Verso, 1993.
Woolf, Virginia. *The Letters of Virginia Woolf*. Vol. 6. Ed. Nigel Nicolson and Joanne Trautmann. New York: HBJ, 1980.
——. "Mr. Bennett and Mrs. Brown." *Collected Essays*. Vol. 1. New York: Harcourt, Brace & World, 1967. 319-37.
——. *Mrs. Dalloway*. San Diego: Harvest, 1981.
——. "Notes on an Elizabethan Play." *The Common Reader: First Series*. Annotated ed. Ed. Andrew McNeillie. San Diego: Harvest, 1984. 48-57.
——. "A Society." *The Complete Shorter Fiction of Virginia Woolf*. 2nd ed. Ed. Susan Dick. San Diego: Harvest, 1989. 124-36.
——. *Three Guineas*. New York: Harcourt, Brace, 1938.
——. "Three Pictures." *The Death of the Moth and Other Essays*. New York: Harvest, 1974. 12-16.
——. *The Voyage Out*. London: Duckworth, 1915. New York: Doran, 1920.
Wright, Richard. "The Man Who Lived Underground." *The Norton Anthology of African American Literature*. Ed. Henry Louis Gates, Jr. and Nellie McKay. New York: W. W. Norton, 1997. 1414-50.

## Lois J. Gilmore

### Virginia Woolf, Bloomsbury, and the Primitive

In his book *Culture and Imperialism* Edward Said calls for a contrapuntal reading of Western works. Urging readers to listen for the submerged voices, the encoded experiences, the representations, the attitudes, and the references, Said writes that empire, the imperial context, and the existence of other cultures cannot be ignored. Indeed, Said's idea of the historical connectedness of culture, the dynamic complexity of negotiations between cultures, the worldliness of art (part of the social world, human life, and the historical moments in which they are located and interpreted), and insistence of the historicity of art authorizes attention to spaces where works of art are situated, and where they connect to other aesthetic and political activities. The modernist period is particularly rich in what Said identifies as overlapping territories, intertwined histories, resistance and opposition. Said sees Europe, that is, the culture of Europe as site and idea, as vulnerable to the very overseas domains, the ties that it has tried to ignore. These domains have become "a presence rather strikingly described in terms unmistakably taken from the exotic annals of overseas discovery, conquest, vision. Only now instead of being out there, they are *here,* as troubling as the primitive rhythms of the *Sacre du printemps* or the African icons in Picasso's art" (188). Indeed, the *idea* of Bloomsbury as community—or site—functions as central, catalytic, and synergistic in the cultural exchanges occurring early in this century, such as the movement of African and Oceanic material culture from natural history museums to avant-garde art that becomes a paradigm for the transformations that allowed the widening of scope in art, literature, anthropology.

Virginia Woolf's response to the primitive is arbitrary, ambivalent, troublesome, and largely ironic, embodying notions of the primitive associated with the ethnographic exhibition culture and with notions associated with avant-garde art. In his book *The Predicament of Culture*, James Clifford encapsulates the activity of imperialism as the material culture of these countries wound up in the anthropological museums in Europe. It relates to the imagery in the literature by underscoring something we must all recognize: that writers and artists drew from what Edward Said calls "a huge library of Africanism" available to all through the activity of colonialism. Clifford writes that the word *nègre* could refer to a variety of works during the twenties like "modern American jazz, African tribal masks, voodoo ritual, Oceanic sculpture, and even pre-Columbian artifacts" (136) that became a "collective representation figuring a geographically and historically vague but symbolically sharp exotic world" (*Orientalism* qtd. 136). Indeed, this collective imagery had the power to construct: "A mask or statue or any shred of black culture could effectively summon a complete world of dreams and possibilities—passionate, rhythmic, concrete, mystical, unchained: an 'Africa'" (136-7). Clifford emphasizes the notion that the history of anthropology and modern art should examine collecting as a "changing set of powerful institutional practices" in order to understand how those who invented the disciplines "have *appropriated* exotic things, facts, and meaning. . . . It is important to analyze how powerful discrimination made at particular moments constitute the general system of objects within which valued artifacts circulate and make sense" (220-1).

There is evidence Virginia Woolf was aware of Roger Fry's collection of primitive objects, for several times in her biography of Fry she remarks that his collection of Negro masks moved from one home to another. When Fry moved from Durbins to Holloway in 1919, Woolf notes that the porters "removed the Chinese statues, the Italian cabinets, the negro masks and all the pots and plates that had made the big rooms at Durbins glow with so many different colours in so many different styles" (*RF* 225-6). Fry's awareness of Apollinaire's early and valuable collection of primitive art objects, his ardent support of the objects as art, his connection to French writers and artists, such as Matisse, Picasso and others, his use of the primitive in the products of the Omega Workshops, and his writings provide evidence of his significance in promoting the aesthetic value of these works. The two Post-Impressionist shows in London (1910 and 1912) introduced Britain to the primitive. In her biography of Fry, Woolf creates the excitement Fry felt about his discovery of the primitive elements in, for example, Picasso's work that became new and exciting, and the conviction Fry felt toward his discovery in a climate of ridicule. She writes that in 1910, "He would explain that it was quite easy to make the transition from Watts to Picasso; there was no break, only a continuation" and that his enthusiasm for the cotton goods "made to suit the taste of the negroes" also made the English decorations look "faded and old-fashioned" as did the boldly decorated hats to "delight the untutored taste of negresses" (*RF* 152-53). Woolf reports, "And what magnificent taste the untutored negress had! Under his influence, his pressure, his excitement, pictures, hats, cotton goods, all were connected" (*RF* 152-3). This passage reveals Woolf's characteristic attitude and expression of elevation and devaluation toward the primitive as she denigrates the taste of the "untutored negresses" while elevating the excitement and energy of the designs. Certainly, Woolf spent much time listening to Fry's lectures, and references to goods purchased from natives occur in her 1915 novel *The Voyage Out.*

These provocative and troubling negotiations with the savage "Other" show up in the imagery of her work in ways that suggest the contested naming, labeling, and valuation of the primitive in anthropology and art. In her first novel *The Voyage Out*, Woolf makes limited but significant use of the primitive in both setting and image, creating an ironic subtext to her criticism of imperial attitudes. The visit to the native village contains elements of Britain's exhibition culture, the powerful gaze signifying resistance of the native and raising questions of European influence on native cultures. Images linking empire and the primitive serve to make an ironic statement: a "troop of naked natives whirled darts into the air," an image of the primitive Other residing on Mrs. Ambrose's embroidery. Here the image of the men harks to Conrad's *Heart of Darkness* and anticipates a similar image in Woolf's later novel *The Waves*. These images and others of "primitive carvings" (*VO* 90) scattered through the novel become focused within the expedition to the native village.

Britain's exhibition culture, for example, provided living displays of villages in an effort to popularize and further the educational function of anthropology, according to Annie Coombes, who notes that they became a means of constructing a national identity while solidifying a set of ideologies (208). Coombes writes that discourse of national unity became more visible in the public domain through the "sphere of the 'amusement' section of the International and Colonial Exhibition" (206). She notes that through the "rhetoric of learning through pleasure" the exhibitions achieved popularization of imperial ideology. For example, the most famous exhibition was The Stanley and African Exhibition in London, 1890, which "replicated" Stanley's journey up the Congo River. Furthermore, "far more successfully than the museums whose exhibits could only signify the colonized subject, the exhibitions literally captured these potentially dangerous subjects and reproduced them in a 'safe' and contained, and yet accessible and supposedly open, environment" (192).

In *The Voyage Out,* Mr. Flushing and Mrs. Ambrose devise a journey that is neither "dangerous," "difficult," or "unusual": "Every year at this season English people made parties which steamed a short way up the river, landed, and looked at the native village, bought a certain number of things from the natives, and returned again without damage done to mind or body" (*VO* 264). Here, Woolf creates a play between the native and the travelers through emphasis of the gaze. The travelers can view the squatting women, undiscovered, until they are seen viewing the group. At first the native women take almost no notice of the viewers whose stare continues to follow them, peering insistently into their lives and over their bodies, until one woman changes the power of the Western gaze: "As she drew apart her shawl and uncovered her breast to the lips of her baby, the eyes of a woman never left their faces, although they moved uneasily under her stare, and finally turned away, rather than stand there looking at her any longer" (*VO* 285). Woolf develops the notion of the Other as object, observed and contained, similar to the "living" villages popular in England; however, she also provides the sense of engagement and resistance articulated by Said: the Other looks back at the West.

Virginia Woolf's ambivalent response to primitive art is illustrated in two accounts of a particularly significant art exhibition at the Chelsea Book Club in 1920. During this year, notions about the primitive crystallized around this exhibition. While the exhibition itself successfully brought African sculpture to the attention of the London public through the ensuing debates, it did uncover and reinforce certain negative, embedded attitudes toward colonial peoples. The advertisement for the exhibition of Negro Sculpture appeared in *The Athenæum* and included a quotation from Roger Fry's earlier article appearing in the same magazine: "Some of these are great sculpture, —greater, I think than anything we produced in the middle ages" (516). Clive Bell responds in a subsequent issue, but he is more conservative in his comparisons of Negro sculpture to great Western schools of art than is Fry. Bell asserts that the best examples of the sculpture are aesthetically rich in important qualities. Yet curiously, Bell reflects that his conservative approach in the context of contempt for Negro art and that of excessive praise may offend some: "because I mean to keep my head, I shall doubtless by my best friends be called a fool" (247). Significantly, Bell elevates what he calls the instinctive, un-selfconscious ability of primitive peoples to create sculpture with aesthetic, tactile, vivifying qualities like the smoothness and wholeness of the sculptural surface; then he continues the undercutting of the artist by declaring that "the savage gift is precarious because it is unconscious" (247). The primitive artist, according to Bell, has no critical sense; thus, he will be caught up in producing vulgar pieces under the direction of Europeans.

There is evidence that Virginia Woolf was involved in the discussion and the ambivalent attitudes toward the primitive sculpture. In a letter to Vanessa Bell dated April 15, 1920, Woolf writes of her visit, accompanied by Roger Fry, to the exhibition of sculpture at the Chelsea Book Club where she finds the carvings "dismal and impressive." She writes "I dimly see that something in their style might be written, and also that if I had one on the mantelpiece I should be a different sort of character—less adorable, as far as I can make out, but somebody you wouldn't forget in a hurry (*L2* 429). Woolf continues this theme in her diary entry: "The day before I went to the Niggers' show in Chelsea; very sad impressive figures; obscene; somehow monumental; figures of Frenchmen, I thought, sodden with civilisation & cynicism; yet they were carved (perhaps) in the Congo 100's of years ago" (*D2* 30).

The enigmatic, witty, ironic nature of Woolf's commentary suggests a sense of mystery in her reaction to the exhibition of the objects. Writing to Vanessa about events Woolf knew her sister would find interesting, Woolf adds the comment about Fry's proclivity to enthusiastic, discursive lectures, knowing that the sisters shared this experience of Fry on occasion. The significant statement buried within the commentary concedes that "something in their style might be written," like a touch of sincerity within the ambiguous tone of the passage. The adjectives Woolf uses to describe the nature of the carvings ("dismal and impressive") seem contradictory in that she first dismisses the emotional effects of the sculpture while granting significance to the figures. She follows the description by noting her ambivalence, finally undercutting the effect the sculpture has on her by appropriating the object and diminishing it by making it a trophy on her mantelpiece, mastering and controlling in much the same way that the Victorians appropriated and decontextualized the trophies of nameless artists that they accumulated. Even so, Woolf does not deny that she feels some kind of power the mysterious carvings possess to affect the personality in some way—to provoke and challenge the West; she acknowledges the existence of some subtle power of the primitive. Indeed, the passage implies that Woolf participates in valuation and devaluation of the primitive object—the primitive "Other." Clearly, Woolf was involved in consideration of the primitive.

There is a second recorded encounter with African art for which we have sufficient evidence to suggest that Woolf was familiar with African material culture and that she was involved with interpreting the event in terms of the supposed power within the object itself The episode of Josette Coatmellec's death in the spring of 1924, given some credence by reputable scholars like Frances Spalding, suggests that the primitive objects embody some magical, highly negative power operating on susceptible people of the West as in the early novel *The Voyage Out.* Indeed, the initial scene in *Orlando* further enacts the hegemonic relationship of the West and the Other through the "play" with the head of the nameless Moor, collected, displayed and manipulated as other Europeans had done since the sixteenth century (Hiller 185). Orlando's performance reflects the Western gaze, possession, and obsession with the African head as Michelle Cliff asserts (97).

The erotic nature of the primitive, combined with the sense of the primitive as pre-civilized, becomes clear when one examines the use of the word *assegais* in her 1931 novel *The Waves.* Woolf uses vocabulary naming or associated with the primitive to resonate forward and backward both within and without the text. Primitive references provide a palimpsestic subtext, a coda, to the symphonic movement of the waves, especially in the italicized interruptions or chorus of the novel. Images and language converge in the monologues/dialogues to echo beyond the present tense of the discourse. Woolf weaves word and image into a fabric that includes the primitive within the larger present of the character's awareness and in the echoes to the natural and artificial forces of the setting so beautifully and hauntingly described. Woolf rewrites the aesthetics of representation, as well as transforming the tropes of empire through modernist strategies like juxtaposition, universality, and encyclopedic form. The problematic use of the primitive occurs in *The Waves.* Woolf represents the silent Other as predatory, preliterate, prehistoric in ironic juxtaposition with the civilization the characters inhabit. The primitive provides not only a backdrop of savagery but also an ironic commentary on the reason for empire, a reason for holding off the darkness.

One clue to Woolf's attitude toward the primitive in these aspects lies first in her echoes of Conrad. Virginia Woolf connects with Conrad through the use of a particularized African word and the recognizable imagery of the figures that complicate the African word and image with references to India. The turbaned warriors incongruously ride in some kind of ritualized, sinister pattern within the Western context. Because the first two passages occur within the italicized portions of the novel, they become part of the rhythm of the waves, part of the rhythm of life and death. Woolf writes: "*The wind rose. The waves drummed on the shore, like turbaned warriors, like turbaned men with poisoned assegais who, whirling their arms on high, advance upon the feeding flocks, the white sheep*" (*TW* 75). This passage connects with a later reference to the "assegais": "*Their spray rose like the tossing of lances and assegais over the riders' heads*" (*TW* 108). Woolf subverts the imperial system of control by establishing the power of nature over the West and by following Neville with the italicized passage combining West and primitive, ritualized "Other." The second passage occurs after the monologues of Jinny and Rhoda. Emblems of empire resound within the language of their narratives. Jinny says "I am native here," providing a disruption of imperial hegemony through the incongruity of dislocation. Jinny proposes "let us wander 'whirling' to the gilt chairs" (*TW* 103), echoing and anticipating the image of primitive warriors to come in the next italicized interlude. She marks the end of her monologue with a statement applicable to male adventurers of empire: "There are girls of my own age, for whom I feel the drawn swords of an honourable antagonism. For these are my peers. I am native of this world. Here is my risk, here is my adventure" (*TW* 104). These disjointed, fragmented images mirror the ebb and flow of relationships between the West and the primitive and set up a subtext that turns over the expected hegemonic order by locating it in the West and conflating the space between cultures. The emphasis is on the material culture; Woolf—with subtlety and ambiguity—creates a field of play wherein the primitive resists and opposes. Furthermore, when viewed within the shadow of Conrad, the passages resonate with meaning. Rhoda's voice picks up the tenuous thread of crossings from West to other world as she hears the dancing and drumming "like the dancing and drumming of naked men with assegais," and Louis answers with his own vision of the "ruthless" savages who "dance in a circle" (*TW* 140).

Woolf echoes Conrad's *Heart of Darkness* to emphasize the displacement of the primitive whose presence has crossed into the consciousness of the West. No longer "out there" at the end of a dangerous journey up the river, "they are here" riding the waves of the sea, a sea that in empire sent Marlow into the heart of darkness. No longer observing the primitive Other in the field as travelers, ethnographers, anthropologists, they exist in the history and consciousness of the West. Woolf is commenting on the ironic transposition of the primitive "Other," out of place in the West. Embedded in the passage is a sense of the "trophy" aspect of primitive objects appropriated by the Victorian empire builders. Yet, here the notion of the West as observer of primitive ritual emanates from the description of the passage. Furthermore, Woolf's description of the dance resounds with fear of the one who is not us, the ritualized powers of those who are further back on the evolutionary scale, those who are close to nature and its magical powers. Woolf incorporates notions of primitive man similar to those held by evolutionists, but at the same time she interrogates the beliefs through juxtaposition by providing a connection and inversion to Conrad's questioning of empire.

The power of the primitive to assert the creative nature of the Other rises out of Woolf's images just as the avant-garde artists sought the creative within the African masks and figures, incorporating the images within their paintings. Woolf views this power as a flow, preferring to revise the image of the turbaned warriors by animating them in much the same way that she animates the sea. Here the men whirl and dance in some mysterious, ritualized, cannibalistic rite. Within the sculptural aspect of Conrad's description, within the Negro sculpture on the mantel, Woolf sees life and exercises the novelist's power to give life to objects and ideas. With movement comes power. She works out her objection to the static nature of Conrad's larger-than-life descriptions in *The Waves* by embedding power in the movement of the savages in their dance and by placing the dance within the movement of the waves. By employing simile as the vehicle for linking the West with the primitive Other, Woolf crosses time and space with imagination like Marlow when he says, "And this, also. . . has been one of the dark places of the earth" (Conrad 9). Sound, color, and movement resound in the drumming as the savages tear the "bleeding limbs." The use of the primitive serves to signify the fragmentation of the personality and the fragmentation of civilization within the novel.

The primitive becomes a place, a geographical location contested, according to Said, by the "theoretical mapping and charting of territory that underlies Western fiction, historical writing, and philosophical discourse of the time" (58). The primitive exists in this novel to connect the West with the Other just as Rhoda looks to Africa for renewal: "Life, how I have dreaded you, . . . . Now as I climb this mountain, from the top of which I shall see Africa, my mind is printed with brown-paper parcels and your faces. I have been stained by you and corrupted" (*TW* 203). Later, Rhoda thinks of Percival: "The mule stumbles up and on. The ridge of the hill rises like mist, but from the top I shall see Africa" (*TW* 206). Life, renewal, death merge in the creative aspect of the primitive although this energy is so often denied. *The Waves* marks Woolf's attempt to reconcile the two creative forces.

Finally, Wole Soyinka gives voice to the Other when he marks the "rapport between our viewers and the absent artists, a rapport with the products of an alien culture" which takes him "to the initial end-of-nineteenth-century encounter" to ask the fundamental question in order to analyze what had happened during the period of the 1880s and 1920s: What transformed Western artistic sensibilities that allowed the avant-garde to respond to this very familiar culture that had been available to the West for centuries through the material culture brought back by missionaries, explorers, traders for the vast collections of the West (167-8)? "They had been sketched, painted and later photographed by explorers, discussed in learned conferences and stored in private collections. . . . The entire culture, the very premise of an African or several African civilizations was subjected to anatomical dissections" (168). Soyinka's discussion of the prevalence of the primitive in the West leads to the fundamental matter here: "this Art as symbolic product of the mind, marveled at by Brancusi, Picasso and company, has emerged from that same race to which Hegel . . . denied even the capacity of Reason" (169). While emphasizing the significance of the encounter between the West and the primitive in terms of anthropology and art,

Soyinka gives voice to the problem traced in the modernist writer's use of the primitive. Said concurs by articulating the importance of the primitive to modernist writers, missing in the histories of European aesthetic modernism that "leave out the massive infusions of non-European cultures into the metropolitan heartland during the early years of this century, despite the patently important influence they had on modernist artists like Picasso, Stravinsky, and Matisse, and on the very fabric of a society that largely believed itself to be homogeneously white and Western" (242). The image of Rhoda looking toward Africa suggests the significance of the primitive to writers like Woolf and others who centered in Bloomsbury and who found themselves in an encounter with the primitive.

**Works Cited**

Anscombe, Isabelle. *Omega and After: Bloomsbury and the Decorative Arts.* London: Thames and Hudson, 1981.

Bell, Clive. "Negro Sculpture." *The Athenæum.* August 20, 1920, pp. 247-8.

Cliff, Michelle. "Virginia Woolf and the Imperial Gaze: A Glance Askance." In *Virginia Woolf: Emerging Perspectives.* Ed. Mark Hussey and Vara Neverow. New York: Pace UP, 1994. 91-102.

Clifford, James. *The Predicament of Culture: Twentieth Century Ethnography, Literature, and Art.* Cambridge, Harvard U.P., 1988.

Conrad, Joseph. *Heart of Darkness.* Ed. Robert Kimbrough. 3rd ed. New York: Norton, 1988.

Coombes, Annie. "Ethnography and National Cultural Identities." In *The Myth of Primitivism: Perspectives on Art.* Ed. and comp. Susan Hiller. New York: Routledge, 1991. 189-214.

Fry, Roger. "Negro Sculpture at the Chelsea Book Club." *The Athenæum.* April 16, 1920, pp. 516.

Hiller, Susan, ed. *The Myth of Primitivism: Perspectives on Art.* New York: Routledge, 1991.

Said, Edward W. *Culture and Imperialism.* New York: Alfred A. Knopf, 1993.

——. *Orientalism.* New York: Vintage Books, 1979.

Spalding, Frances. *Roger Fry: Art and Life.* Berkeley: U of California P, 1980.

Woolf, Virginia. *The Diary of Virginia Woolf. Volume Two. 1920-24.* Ed. Anne Olivier Bell with Andrew McNeillie. New York: Harcourt, 1978.

——. *The Letters of Virginia Woolf. Volume Two. 1912-1922.* Ed. Nigel Nicholson and Joanne Trautmann. New York: Harcourt, 1976.

——. *Orlando: A Biography.* New York: Harvest, 1968.

——. *Roger Fry: A Biography.* New York: Harcourt, 1968.

——. *The Voyage Out.* New York: Harcourt, 1920.

——. *The Waves.* New York: Harcourt, 1931.

**Yuko Ito**

# The Masked Reality in Leonard Woolf's Colonial Writings

Leonard Woolf's letters to Lytton Strachey written from 1904 to 1911, which Spotts finds "the frankest" (*Letters* 62) among the surviving letters from his government-agent days as a member of the Ceylon Civil Service, represent Leonard's colonialistic ideal as well as his territorial imagination. These letters and his autobiography constitute the text of a colonial world in a particular period of the British Empire, when the whole system was still maintained. Though he is considered to be an avowed anti-imperialist, his letters show that he struggles between his own imaginary ideal and the reality of his role as a colonialist. Here, this discrepancy itself represents his "frankest" situation. Spotts remarks that in sharing "physical and metaphysical miseries," the exchange of letters between Leonard and Lytton "demonstrate[s] the strength of the friendship between the two at a dark time in their lives and show[s] how each often believed in the other more than in himself" (*Letters* 63). The straightforwardness in their letters could show one of the representative qualities of the Bloomsbury discourse. This paper explores Leonard's inscription of his territorial imagination onto his colonialist ideal, and a conflict in himself as a government agent in Ceylon where his imaginative ideal colonial community is located.

Leonard's fantasy creates his own district as a "prosperous place" which, he says, will be distinguished from the general colonial condition of Ceylon. His ideal attitude to the colony is reflected by a colonial officer, Sir Thomas Maitland: "In this spirit the best officers of the Ceylon Civil Service were watchful in protecting the 'Natives' against possible exploitation by British planters or the bad effects of monopoly activity by British trading firms" (Wilson 34-5). However, this idea of colonial community, which seeks to restrict the power of British monopoly, is also colonized by the reality of colonial policy. Consequently, there exists a contradiction between Leonard's ideal style of government and the real situation, as he recollects in his autobiography: "I would make my District or Province the most efficient, the most prosperous place in Asia. At the back of my mind I knew that this last solution was fantasy. . . . I had been born in an age of imperialism and I disapproved of imperialism and felt sure that its days were already numbered" (*Growing* 247-8).

Thus, Leonard's representation of the colonial world in his letters to Lytton is problematic: the narrator speaks from the viewpoint of his ideal community, but Leonard confronts what he considers degraded self and reality. As a result, the contents of the letters sometimes become a self-mockery of his own degraded self. In this sense, Leonard's text presents a discord between his social subjectivity, and his own ideal self as a colonizer.

Leonard's internalization of his legal function shows him to be a representative of authority: "As I suppose you know I am everything here: policeman, magistrate, judge, & publican" (*Letters* 141). Leonard has located his "I" in the space of the other, but the coherence of his "I" in Britain and in Ceylon had already been dislocated by the colonial authority. In the same manner, it could be said that the character "I" as a colonial subjectivity is dislocated from the narrator "I" who objectifies this character "I." When a letter from the Orient is addressed to a person in Britain, the narrator of the letter—"I"—stages the protagonist of the story—"I"—in a place culturally, ethnically, and physically distanced from Britain. The subject may also be constructed by the Ceylonese people by a corresponding process of exclusion. Leonard speaks of the expectations that people of Ceylon have of him, derived from their experience of colonialism:

> We are all doomed, I imagine. . . . You cannot imagine the fatuity of it [democracy] in Jaffna. Theoretically everyone is told that he is equal with everyone else, while practically we try to be paternal, despotic. . . . Of course when you get out into the jungle & villages it is different; you are still absolute, the villager still comes to you to settle his dispute & help him when his crop fails & your own word is law. . . . The boys are taught to hate us not because we treat them as inferiors, but because we treat them as inferiors & tell them that they are their own equals. (*Letters* 125)

Leonard's terminology speaks both the insolence of false democracy in Ceylon, and (unconsciously) his colonialistic self blamed by the boys, or his anti-imperialist self. This blame ridicules the arrogant consensus of the English nation internalized in the colonizers.

In Leonard's letters to Lytton, the narration can be conceived of as a monologue, wherein the character-speaker is very similar to the author (Leonard), but where significant dislocations also seem to arise. The narrator-"I" in his letters displays the activities of the character-"I" which are, particularly, policed by the colonizer's ideology. The split of the narrator-"I" and the character-"I" in Leonard's letters is caused by the imperative that he should perform the colonizer's ideology. Ideology, in Louis Althusser's words, is a representation of the imaginary relationship of individuals to their real conditions of existence (*Lenin and Philosophy* 152). Althusser identifies the deferred status of reality as being found in the "representational" characteristics of the "imaginary" relationship. The character-"I" as one of the subjects of colonial ideology may be seen to be deferred in the process of representing the imaginary relationship of the colonizer to the colonized. As a result, the character-"I," trapped in the system of an imaginary text of empire, is separated from the narrator-"I" as Leonard's ideal subjectivity. Leonard, as a colonizer, faces the discrepancy between "the empire" which he is forced to represent as a government agent, and "his own colonial community" which he imagines and idealizes in himself.

Leonard has to behave as a servant of authority and must treat the native people as inferior. The mask of the government agent is imposed on him, the mask which makes the colonizer superior to the native people. At the same time, this mask projects the colonial subject as a "represented," "virtual" or "played" presence. The characteristics of this masked performance suggest that the colonizer's role is inappropriate for Leonard, implying the existence of another proper self, a truer self, behind the mask.

In his biography, Leonard says: "in Ceylon we were all always, subconsciously or consciously, playing a part, acting upon a stage. The stage, the scenery, the backcloth before which I began to gesticulate at the Vigors's dinner-table was imperialism" (*Growing* 24-5). Thus his writings sometimes offer an objective view of that stage of imperialism on which he also plays his part.

Leonard analyzes himself in his letter and discovers a certain aspect of his behavior to be degenerate: "Among other things I have been in love lately [with an English woman called Gwen]. I believe really I am mad. It was, I think, pretty degraded for you to be in love with S . But that is nothing to this. . . . I am beginning to think it is always degraded being in love" (128).[1] However, he thinks his love for Virginia is not degraded. He wrote to Virginia on 12 January 1912:

> I am selfish, jealous, cruel, lustful, a liar & probably worse still. I had said over & over again to myself that I would never marry anyone because of this, mostly because, I think, I felt I could never control these things with a woman who was inferior & would gradually enfuriate me by her inferiority & submission. (169)

Notions of inferiority and submission are imposed on colonial women, even when they are English, or on the colonial site, the Orient; and they cause Leonard and, probably, other colonizers to share a sense of degradation in the place where their power is exercised.

The notion of inferiority is also imposed on the landscape in the colony. The colonizers set about bringing order to the undisciplined landscape of the jungle. They persuade the colonized to join in their project to make a disciplined landscape, that is, to collude in their own colonization. In contrast with an aestheticized nature, the jungle is described as a savage form, as a threatening power against the empire. Referring to Leonard's *The Village in the Jungle*, Sir Hugh Clifford praises Leonard's discovery of "the profound truth" in an article in *Blackwood's Magazine*: "The truth is that in all the long history of man in the tropics, the Jungle has always in the end triumphed over mankind. It has triumphed because it is 'unmanageable' . . . . The Jungle has swallowed up empires no less surely or completely than they have been submerged by the sea, or buried by the Egyptian sands" (5-6). Then, he writes of his actual experience in the Malaysian jungle:

> Even those of us who know him [the Malay] best—to our shame be it written—have overlooked the fact that his present attitude towards our energetic policy of development and exploitation is the direct result of the accumulated experience of his race; that his unerring instinct tells him that, for all the fine seeming of our work, it is, after all, only another and a larger 'raid' upon the unconquerable Jungle, and that at the long last the victory must be with the Jungle, as always the victory has been. (7-8)

The jungle is, from the beginning, an unconquerable object. No matter how much of a "larger raid" is carried out, Clifford emphasizes, the jungle is still an enemy to be defeated. Imperial invasion is designed to attack this invulnerable jungle: that could be colonialism's nominal sovereign purpose in persuading the colonized to work with the colonizers. In fact, what the colonizers want to govern is the nation—the territory and people—itself. The jungle is described as the enemy of the colonizer and the native people. It is almost personified and personalized as something substantial, as the colonizers' own property, with its capital letter "J" in Clifford's description. By presupposing and fantasizing nature's victory, colonialism's policy is aestheticized as an epic project, and their heroic subjugation to nature is again aestheticized, and constructed as the colonizer-hero's slavery under nature. That is to say, the colonizers become the victims at a narrative level.

The narrator's viewpoint in describing the native people's fear toward the jungle in Leonard's *The Village in the Jungle* is ambiguous. The narrator projects the fear of the native people, which is also his own fear. The narrator explains from his viewpoint, at the beginning of the novel: "There are people who will tell you that they have no fear of the jungle. . . . such people are either liars and boasters, or they are fools, without understanding or feeling for things as they really are" (2). There could be a fear of the jungle among the native people, but on the other hand, the narrator describes that the native people are assimilated into the jungle: "The spirit of the jungle is in the village, and in the people who live in it. They are simple, sullen, silent men. . . . They are very near to the animals which live in the jungle around them" (11-2). If the jungle signifies both the jungle itself and the native people, the fear of the jungle does not necessarily belong to the native; it might be the narrator's fear of the jungle which he transfers to the native in the narrative.

This could be the fear which the colonizer has to fight against in himself. The fear is mystified as something he is unable to resist, and unconquerable. This mystification is superimposed on the jungle itself, and on the villager as well, by the narrator. However, it could be said that this mystification of the jungle is used by the colonizer as a kind of propaganda to conquer not only the jungle but also the people and the nation.

In criticizing the reality of colonial society in Ceylon, Leonard also describes the degradation of English people. He probably emphasizes that they are, geographically and psychically, remote from his company, or community in England. In his letter to Lytton, he says: "I can only say again, if you only knew how I want to see you! This place . . . is absolutely beautiful and absolutely degraded. The people—the English are hell, the Australians Sodom & Gomorrah" (68). However it seems that his abhorrence is not after all prompted by those people's unspeakable, unbridled decadence, but by their lack of style: "I believe I have made the remark before but I can't help repeating it, that the people in rotten novels are astonishingly life like [sic]. All the English out here are continually saying things of which, if you saw them in a novel, you would say 'people don't say those sort of things'. They are always sentimentally soliloquizing with an astounding pomposity" (81). The English community in Ceylon has assimilated itself into a world of bad fiction and people can only ape a poorly invented dialogue which they take to be the real thing. The presentation of the degraded colonizer (himself included) is a kind of fictional case-history as Leonard compares English people in Ceylon with characters in "rotten novels."

The British Ceylon society has become a carnival performed as a shameless spectacle: "The 'society' of this place is absolutely inconceivable; it exists only upon the tennis-court & G.A.'s [Governmental Agent] house; the women are all whores or hags or missionaries or all three; & the men are, as I told you, sunk. The G.A.'s wife has the vulgarity of a tenth rate pantomime actress; her idea of liveliness is to kick up her legs & to scream the dullest of dull schoolboy 'smut' across the tennis court or the dinner table" (*Letters* 74). The tennis court and the governmental agent's house are stages for the colonizers to play English society within Ceylon society.

By this description, Leonard pretends to cut himself off from the English community in Ceylon. Indeed, Leonard's figuring of the colonial scenes accords with his understanding of the function of law for the benefit of Ceylon. In his autobiography, he says, "I am all and always upon the side of law and order, and my time in Ceylon, where I was on the Government side of the fence, strengthened me in this attitude, simply because without law and order, strictly enforced, life for everyone must become poor, nasty, brutish, and short" (*Growing* 79). Here, he justifies his past activity as an imperialist who acts for the sake of the profit of the empire, not of the natives. "I" on the side of order is his imperialist "I." This imperialist "I" is all the more distanced from the narrator of the autobiography, as he looks back on his days in Ceylon. And in this autobiography, he uses this distance to justify his present-self, as an anti-imperialist. Leonard's ideal colonial community is fantasized, and he shows the existence of this imagined community as an excuse for his own imperialistic activity.

**Note**

[1] According to Spotts, "S" is J. T. Sheppard or Bernard Swithinbank, a Balliol undergraduate to whom Lytton was much attracted at that time (*Letters* 128).

**Works Cited**

Althusser, Louis. *Lenin and Philosophy and Other Essays*. Trans. Ben Brewster. 2nd ed. London: New Left Books, 1977.

Clifford, Sir Hugh. "Mankind and the Jungle." *"Blackwood": Tales from the Outposts*. Ed. Lieut.-Colonel L. A. Bethell. Vol. 8. 1932. Edinburgh: William Blackwood, 1946. 1-12. 12 vols.

Wilson, Duncan. *Leonard Woolf: A Political Biography*. London: Hogarth, 1978.

Woolf, Leonard. *Growing: An Autobiography of the Years 1904 to 1911*. 1961. London: Hogarth, 1977.

——. *Letters of Leonard Woolf*. Ed. Frederic Spotts. London: Bloomsbury, 1989.

——. *The Village in the Jungle*. 1913. London: Hogarth, 1931.

## Judy Suh

### Woolf and the Gendering of Fascism

As we study the relationship between fascism and twentieth-century literature, Virginia Woolf stands in sharp contrast to other canonical high modernists. While the works of Pound and Yeats offer testimony of flirtations with Irish and Italian Fascist movements, Woolf's *A Room of One's Own* and *Three Guineas* mark her as firmly and defiantly anti-fascist. Her complex perception of fascism as the institutionalization of gender relations that had already flourished in the discourses of "civilization" is an unparalleled opportunity for us to gauge the present. Her writing compels us to reflect on forms of fascism that persist within what we now historically perceive as its aftermath. Woolf's work thus functions as a locus for bringing together critical theorists who define fascism as a discourse that exceeds the historical and geographical specificity of mid-century Italy and Germany. In particular, Woolf gives us valuable insight into tactics of anti-fascist writing. It becomes clear, for instance, that her anti-fascism is inseparable from an ironic practice of fascist style. In order to have Woolf's work speak critically to contemporary neo-fascisms, I will therefore foreground her style as a crucial political component of literary practice and analysis.

My analysis will not reproduce a "formalist" approach to Woolf's work, *or* to fascist art, which would dangerously erase the implications of political content. The definition of style here takes its cue from both Woolf's *A Room of One's Own* and Derrida's definition of style in *Spurs: Nietzsche's Styles*. In these texts, style is not isolated to the "literary" or "philosophical" domains. For Woolf and Derrida, style becomes inextricably tied to a thinking of difference—difference that approaches the other without attempting to sublate, assimilate, or annihilate. In *A Room of One's Own*, Woolf refers to this destructive practice of difference as "sterility" and "virility." Rather, in order to resist the state's co-optation of cultural production for its own proliferation, style must be enacted to create possibilities of life that defy the binary categorizations of modernity, especially in its bifurcations of gender. As Woolf notes in *A Room of One's Own,* "No age can ever have been as stridently sex-conscious as our own"(99).

**Woolf and fascist community**

Fascism itself has been described as a species of "flight" from the binary. If fascism, as Benjamin notes, is an "aestheticization of politics," we might describe *its* style as "binding together" oppositions.[1] Both Alice Kaplan and Ze'ev Sternhell have written extensively on fascism's "binding" of such oppositions as: paternal and maternal registers, left and right, modern and antimodern, and populist and elitist discourses.

In some of Woolf's most celebrated theorizations of gender and revolution, we have instances of these binds and overlaps: authenticity invoked by androgyny in *A Room of One's Own*, the overlapping of the classical and modern eras through the figure of Antigone in *Three Guineas*, and in *Between the Acts*, the creation of a cross-class community through the tropes of national pageantry. In this respect, we must become more specific about what we find liberating in Woolf's undoing of humanist oppositions. In fact, Woolf's work mobilizes discourses that are mainstays of fascist self-representation.

At times, Woolf's deployment of fascist discourse is extremely troubling, and the liberating effects within that deployment difficult to extricate. Because her texts constantly engender a dissatisfaction with liberalism's failure to address aspects of life under capitalism, finding locations for "untroubled" political resistance in Woolf becomes a lesson in critical humility. To specify how Woolf's critique of fascism keeps from becoming reactive, I want to propose that Woolf creates an "abyssal" binding and overlapping. What we find undergirding Woolf's constant repetitions and reproductions of fascist style is an abyssal *lack* of fusion and unity—indeed, the reversal, and discursive destruction, of a fascist stitching of oppositions. The flight that Woolf imagines then, is actually a sinking into—i.e., a deep infiltration of fascist discourse in order to fold into its pervasive and fluid domains—multiple sites to inaugurate the resistance to fascism's own currents.

I want to concentrate on the fascist temporal binding that produces the eternal and the "new" or "revolutionary" simultaneously in an "instant of time." The temporal seamlessness produced by this binding gives rise to a community impervious to the thought of death, decay, and fragmentation—a community that obfuscates from its own view the fragility of the human body. The immortality implied in this model of history values the instantaneity of images made possible by the cinema and photography, the fusion of past and future in one full moment of presence.

Many critics have noted the pretense to immediate common affect in the fascist use of radio, cinema, and photography. The instantaneity of the image, and the immediacy and closeness of the voice that mass media makes possible allows the illusion of a political, national unity. In *Between the Acts* as well as in *Three Guineas*, the reproduced voice of the phonograph and photography both form a national community transcending class boundaries that is itself a trope of fascist discourse.

In *Three Guineas*, the narrator discusses the photographs from the Spanish Civil War:

> Those photographs are not an argument; they are simply a crude statement of fact addressed to the eye. But the eye is connected with the brain; the brain with the nervous system. That system sends its messages in a flash through every past memory and present feeling. When we look at those photographs some fusion takes place within us; however different the education, the traditions behind us, our sensations are the same; and they are violent. (11)

Not only does this passage collapse the class distinctions to form a "fusion" across classes, and across "traditions," it also conceives of the human as a calculable entity, with infinitely reproducible affects and reactions. Recalling Nietzsche's discussion of regressive discourses available to intellectual producers in his own milieu, we are reminded of the totalizing conflation of nature and "nation" indicative of various proto-fascisms. However, Woolf heavily qualifies the instantaneity of the photographs' reception. The agreement across classes, educations, and traditions is charged with warnings, and haunted by the underlying thought of "unaestheticized" death. While the "facts" of photography manufacture a community from the base denominator of affect and reaction, for Woolf, these must be channeled to energies that consider the contingency of human communities: "A common interest unites us; it is one world, one life. How essential it is that we should realise that unity the dead bodies, the ruined houses prove" (*TG* 142). Woolf's residually humanist discourse presents a unity founded on ruins, on fragments; in fact, this unity presents itself as a negative. Woolf calls attention to the borders of this tentative unity as necessary and insurmountable, but simultaneously effaced and shadowed by death and ruins.

*Between the Acts*, as well, invokes the tropes of national community in the theatricality of the country pageant. The audience and the players represent various classes; the play itself rehearses the progression of British history. However, the community is ultimately "brought together" by the specter of its own fragmentation, as individuals and as a group. The megaphone, recorded sound, blares not the triumph of the eternal nation, but the following haunted messages: "Look at ourselves, ladies and gentlemen! Then at the wall; and ask how's this wall, the great wall, which we call, perhaps miscall, civilization, to be built by (here the mirrors flicked and flashed) orts, scraps and fragments like ourselves?" (*BTA* 188). The cruelty of this play brings the community of spectators and actors (and by implication, the nation) to the abyss of its own reflection through the sometimes uncritically unifying mechanisms of theater and pageantry.

Woolf's work further problematizes the fascist temporality of the nation that appears in the collapsing of disparate historical moments. The Nazi amalgamation of Classical Greece and modern Germany confronts us with a profoundly ahistorical suture that abolishes the *work* of history. George Mosse, in his study of Nazism and sexuality writes that, "After all, the present-day Germans and the ancient Greeks were considered the twin pillars of the Aryan race . . . National Socialism was careful to annex familiar national symbols and bend them to its purpose" (Mosse 171-2). This is in part the Nazi attempt to demonstrate an eternal "European" community through the fusion of the ancient and the modern. In *Three Guineas*, the figure of Sophocles' *Antigone* allows Woolf to complicate a fusion of ancient Greece and modern Europe:

> But [Antigone] had neither capital nor force behind her. And Creon said: "I will take her where the path is loneliest, and hide her, living, in a rocky vault." And he shut her not in Holloway or in a concentration camp, but in a tomb. And Creon we read brought ruin on his house, and scattered the land with the bodies of the dead. It seems, Sir, as we listen to the voices of the past, as if we were looking at the photograph again, at the picture of dead bodies and ruined houses that the Spanish Government sends us almost weekly. Things repeat themselves it seems. Pictures and voices are the same today as they were 2,000 years ago. (141)

Woolf picks up on the fascist appropriation of "eternal recurrence" that conjures historical repetition as the inevitability of domination and conquest. Customarily, the Hegelian discourse of progression and perfection accompanies the observation of specific regimes' and historical figures' constant re-emergence. In Woolf's view, however, historical repetition serves only to surface "dead bodies" and "ruined houses," not the perfection of the world-spirit that depends on mechanisms of recurrence. The tragedy of Antigone is reborn in the twentieth-century along with Creon's dictatorship. While our temptation is to translate Creon into the figures of Hitler and Mussolini alone, Woolf's concern is also clearly the "mundane" interactions between daughters and fathers. Creon's focus on disobediences *little* and great highlights the iniquities of the state's repressive force, but also the everyday operations of the patriarchal family and its productions of guilt and consent. Here, Woolf's consideration of recurring gender configurations in quotidian English life offers a further occasion to expose fascist features that appear in liberal democracies.

**Woolf and microfascisms**

In Deleuze's work, the micropolitics of modernity pervade the space of the subject's (seemingly private) desires. This pervasion opens up a space for fascism, which unlike other forms of politics, works on the level of affect, desire, belief, and consent. Micropolitics derives its strength from its very fluidity. By flowing into and thus breaking up the integrity of the subject, and of other organizations perceived as integral, the reassertion of the unified subject is a reaction that seems logical but is ultimately futile. In the molecularization of the subject, in its very suppleness and fluidity, Deleuze perceives the potential for fascist domination. However, he also perceives the other possibility present in this molecularization—the possibility of flight from rigid binary aggregates.

What Deleuze describes in *A Thousand Plateaus* as the "micropolitical" resonates with what Woolf in *Three Guineas* describes as "atmosphere." Observing the almost never-discussed factors that result in the discrepancy between men's and women's salaries, Woolf writes, "Atmosphere not only changes the sizes and shapes of things; it affects solid bodies, like salaries, which might have been thought impervious to atmosphere. . . [A]tmosphere is one of the most powerful, partly because it is one of the most impalpable of the enemies with which the daughters of educated men have to fight" (*TG* 53).

Gender, for Woolf, is a social relation where power is most readily visible as "atmospheric." In other words, it is in gender relations that domination works "unofficially" through the production of consent in addition to the "official" direct applications of force, where desire and belief reinforce the institutions of the state, religion, and economy.

Woolf's feminist concentration on "atmosphere," or on that which escapes easy discursive representation, has already detected the importance of *consent* in the establishment of fascist discourses as so-called "legitimate" liberal politics. The politics articulated by Woolf's prioritization of micropolitical acts of domination has already given us a way to think about the collapse of humanist oppositions, especially "civilization" and "barbarity," and those national identities, England and Germany, which act as their embodiment. She writes: "And what right have we, Sir, to trumpet our ideals of freedom and justice to other countries when we can shake out from our most respectable newspapers any day of the week eggs like these?" (*TG* 53).

By defining a feminist politics as an "avant-garde antifascism," Woolf sharply critiques the microfascisms that have existed in embryonic form before official Fascism, and more importantly, describes lines of flight *from* fascism. If fascism's strongest weapons might be described as its appeal to the molecularities of affect, desire, and belief (or the unquantifiable, unspoken areas of political life), our strongest weapons in resisting fascism would be to take those molecularities elsewhere. In *Three Guineas* and *Between the Acts*, groups of people form as momentary and discontinuous communities of spectators who offer a multiplicity of desires. Through them, Woolf suggests a rechanneling of molecularities toward the formation of tentative, precarious, and self-consciously provisional communities, rather than the national or imperial bodies that carry the deadly pretense of eternity.

In this respect, it is important to note that Woolf does not lament the ideological nature of modernity; features of modern sociality must be mobilized as well as confronted. Micropolitical life necessitates the disruption of a linear style of thinking, and in fact makes possible the breakdown of oppositions, and the conception of oppositions in tandem as sociopolitical constructions and not "natural" occurences. Thus, a critical style such as Woolf's does not so much "undo" humanist oppositions; rather it calls attention to the reality that "atmosphere" has *already* killed the unity of humanist categories.

**Note**

1 See Walter Benjamin's "The Work of Art in the Age of Mechanical Reproduction" in *Illuminations*, trans. Harry Zohn (New York: Schocken, 1968).

**Works Cited**

Deleuze, Gilles and Félix Guattari. *A Thousand Plateaus: Capitalism and Schizophrenia*. Trans. Brian Massumi. Minneapolis: U of Minnesota P, 1987.

Mosse, George L.. *Nationalism and Sexuality: Respectability and Abnormal Sexuality in Modern Europe*. New York: Howard Fertig, 1985.

Woolf, Virginia. *Between the Acts*. San Diego: Harvest, 1969.

——. *Three Guineas*. San Diego: Harvest, 1966.

# Metaphors of Material Cultures

## Rachel Bowlby, Featured Speaker

### Meet Me in St. Louis: Virginia Woolf and Community[1]

Ever since Mark Hussey and Georgia Johnston told me about this conference and its theme, the words "Virginia Woolf and communities" have been running around in my head, making plain sense or no sense or some sense just out of reach—that funny alternation of the mechanical and the enigmatic that happens when the same sequence of words keeps repeating itself to you or in you, over and over again. In one sense, a conference on Virginia Woolf and communities is bound to beg, as well as to ask, its own question. The conference is bound to become, itself, a demonstration as well as a discussion of something about the two: Virginia Woolf *as* community, the capacity of her, or her writings, and the history of both, to draw together, from all parts of the world, a gathering of people who share that particular passion.

Despite their ephemeral nature—the three days that might look like a rootless postmodern community-bite—conferences in other ways evoke an old-fashioned idea of community, involving a physical presence in the same place of persons there in the flesh as well as the word. The rest of the time, other possible or virtual Woolf communities exist, of course—not just those to be found on the net, but the more traditional technologies of distanced community: in writing, books, term papers, seminar discussions, talk between friends—to pluck just a few of the forms that for most of us are taken for granted as part of daily Woolfian life. The conference, at once a produced event and a physical assembly of persons in one place, is both less and more of a community than what we might associate with the term. Like all such gatherings, it shows up the perpetual question of what, exactly, a community might be.

This brings me to the second, and most obvious direction that my mental meanderings around Virginia Woolf and communities came to take—Virginia Woolf *on* community. The confusing clatter and break-up of the words in my head became most acute here, because looked at from this angle, just about everything Virginia Woolf ever wrote can come to seem to be about community, or the lack of it—about families, friends, history, language; about different groups or individuals and their conflicts or compacts, their sharings and their divisions.

More practical thoughts suggested I rush to Mark Hussey's magnificent, solve-all-problems CD-ROM and look up when and where Woolf actually used the word "community." For an hour or so I thought I had discovered what I deemed the extraordinary fact that she never used it at all. Quite what this would have proved I'm not sure, but it seemed, as informational discoveries go, to be high on the negative illumination scale. Communicate, communicating, communicative—yes, many times; community, apparently no. Of course I was quite mistaken and in the event, as community after community came cascading onto the screen, all I did prove—not that I needed to—was my own technical incompetence.

But the conflation of communicating and community, whether by me or the CD-ROM, seemed to me one possible starting point for trying to think about Virginia Woolf and community. Of course, communicate and community are in one sense the same word, with the same root in the Latin *communis*—shared, in common. To communicate is to share, to make common; a community has something "in common," whether that something is where they live, village or college or street or city; their interest in Woolf; their sexual or ethnic identity, or indeed their common language, whether the Queen's English or Spice Girl talk.

But despite this fundamental sense of the shared, the in common, in the past twenty years there has been a tendency to think of community and communication in an apparently opposite sense—not as a space of agreement, consensus; but on the contrary, as *dis*agreement—difference and dispute. A community in which there is no argument, no dissensus would be not so much harmony as delusion or wish-fulfillment—or merely the boredom of nothing to say.

These suggestions about community and communication are very closely involved with ideas about language. The newer conceptions of language set themselves against the idea that a model society or community would be one in which everyone "communicated" openly, transparently, cleanly transporting a meaning across from one mind or even one computer screen to another so that it would always be possible to determine exactly what is being said, and communication would be a matter of clarification and information purely—a pragmatic convenience. Instead of this, it is suggested that communication can't be that simple—and we shouldn't want it to be. If it really did happen that smoothly, there would never have been anything to say to each other; we would have been signalling animals, not language animals, perfectly adjusted to each other and to our environment. Our history, our human mess and vitality and mutability, is the history of our missed communications and faulty communities, as much as—and it is also very much this—the history of our agreements and shared assumptions.

While all the novels are ambivalent and exploratory about ideas of community, it seems to me that *Between the Acts* is uncannily close to this idea of community as necessarily a matter of division and misunderstanding as much as harmony. Community seems to be marked by a sense of being somehow both desperately needed and sought and utterly impossible to attain. As in the planned reunions of *The Waves*, the issue of community in *Between the Acts* is focused on a contrived occasion, with the pageant that shows a history of England in the form of literary pastiche. There is no historical or present reality without its distinctive words and its artifices of reconstruction, selection, and presentation. War impends, and also rain. What, in these times, in any times, makes us keep talking this talk and acting these roles? In this novel, it is language, in particular, which is singled out to highlight at once the inevitability and the impossibility of community. The whole pageant section enacts on the page as well as on the ground—literally, in the field—the randomness and brokenness of language's particles. Sentences are cut off; we move to and fro between play and audience and snippets of attempts to make sense; clichés and obvious remarks proliferate in and out of the play. But all these things are as much a sign of survival as of hopelessness. Words are meaningless, ludicrous, talk for the sake of talking; but at the same time "life goes on," and perhaps there is no more to say than that, which is itself already a cliché.

And this—in rural England in June, 1939, at least—is community of a kind. Individuality in *Between the Acts* seems to be characterized by an acknowledgement or assumption of *passivity* in the face of forces that control us—from aeroplanes to cows mooing to city jobs to the words that already say us. It is a bleak assumption, and its only mitigation, its only peace in the face of battles lost before they take place, is in the form of a continuity in which the individual is nothing, is dead. "It'll be there," says Mrs. Swithin, looking out over the view from the country house, "when we're not" (53). "It" in all its forms and forces supersedes "we" in *Between the Acts*.

The difficulty and provisionality of community are explored in different ways in two essays on which I would like to concentrate from now on. "Memories of a Working Women's Guild" and "Reviewing" are quite close in their time of writing, the first dating from 1930 and the second from 1927. One focusing on social class, the other on modern marketing, both could be said, indirectly, to function as critiques of the effects of capitalism—but without much sense, in either case, of a more just community waiting in the wings. As with many of Woolf's essays, the contradictions and swerves of the writing make both of them hard to summarize; and this is part of what makes them provocative, though far from reassuring, in connection with the idea of community.

## The shop window community

> In London there are certain shop windows that always attract a crowd. The attraction is not in the finished article but in the worn-out garments that are having patches inserted in them. The crowd is watching the women at work. There they sit in the shop window putting invisible stitches into moth-eaten trousers. And this familiar sight may serve as illustration to the following paper. (CDB 127)

Here, in the opening to "Reviewing," a shop window contains not new merchandise and mannequins but real women and old clothes; a crowd is attracted by the display of "women at work," not by the fashion of the "finished article." The "familiar sight" is at first sight what the crowd sees—but it could also be what we, as readers, are being shown, the crowd and the window together. And the passage continues by suggesting that this peculiar spectacle is itself being presented only as a window onto another one:

> So our poets, playwrights, and novelists sit in the shop window, doing their work under the curious eyes of reviewers. But the reviewers are not content, like the crowd in the street, to gaze in silence; they comment aloud upon the size of the holes, upon the skill of the workers, and advise the public which of the goods in the shop window is the best worth buying. The purpose of this paper is to rouse discussion as to the value of the reviewer's office. . . . (*CDB* 127)

First, let us note that the crowd in front of the window has become two groups—performers (the reviewers) and audience (the rest). So now we have no less than four removes or stages from work to ultimate reader: those behind the window, then the reviewers, then the public, then finally the viewers of the whole lot, the present readers. There is also the question of the fit between the window-world and the writing world which it is meant to show.

The women in the window differ from the feminine figures usually to be found there because they are working; but they are also unexpected as author-equivalents. They are women and they are in a group, not men alone with their writing. And what they are doing is not new making but repair work—Roland Barthes's metaphor of modern literature as a fabric or weave of citations finds its literal version here. Yet the aim is to produce not a fragmented modernist work in pieces, but its realist antithesis. The moth-eaten gaps are covered over by 'invisible stitches,' so producing that object so despised of contemporary theoretical criticism, an apparently seamless whole.

After this characteristically enigmatic opening, Woolf launches into a brief disquisition on the history and state of the art of reviewing. I can't, of course, cut it up and put it back together again without losing much of the texture and the material—but basically, her point is that reviewers nowadays have so little time and so little space that they don't fulfill a useful function, either in telling the public whether a book is worth buying, or in giving the author constructive advice. There might as well be a simple hit or miss system, whereby the reviewer, having been issued with a précis of the book by a sinister character called the Gutter, would indicate with an asterisk or a dagger whether the thing is worth the money.

Authors, Woolf thinks, dislike bad reviews not because of their effect on sales, but because they hurt; and they hurt not because they criticize, but because other people see them. The author is on display, shown up, put in the window as a target of criticism. Woolf therefore proposes, alongside her wickedly parodic proposal, a serious reform. The author wants real criticism—she assumes. In place of the present public arrangements, why not have private one-to-one consultations? The author would pay three guineas (three guineas always being what Woolfian people are willing to pay for a good cause) for an hour talking to the critic about his work—"the fee," she says, "would be enough to ensure that the interview did not degenerate into tea-table gossip."(*CDB* 138) Somewhere between a counseling session and a tutorial (assuming there's a difference), here is the scene:

> They would talk seriously and privately. . . The consultant would speak honestly and openly, because the fear of affecting sales and of hurting feelings would be removed. Privacy would lessen the shop-window temptation to cut a figure, to pay off scores.(*CDB* 138)

Not an unconscious in sight. There is a full and frank exchange of ideas, untroubled, it seems, by any difficulty of communication, now that the public context is out of the picture. Reading and writing, ideally, come down to a two-person conversation.

The shop window comes back once again, in answer to the question hypothetically put: "what effect would the abolition of the reviewer have upon literature?" To which Woolf answers:

> Some reasons for thinking that the smashing of the shop window would make for the better health of that remote goddess have already been implied. The writer would withdraw into the darkness of the workshop; he would no longer carry on his difficult and delicate task like a trouser mender in Oxford Street, with a horde of reviewers pressing their noses to the glass and commenting to a curious crowd upon each stitch. Hence his self-consciousness would diminish and his reputation would shrivel. (*CDB* 140; Bowlby, *Crowded* 213)

The violent smashing of the dividing glass paradoxically leads to what is now a much more clearly cut separation between the dark, private interior and the exposure of the outside. For the crowd in front of the shop window has degenerated since we last set eyes on it. It's now a "horde," and the reviewers are repulsively sticking their noses against the window. We as readers are presumed to share in looking from a different vantage point, from which this distasteful and rather alarming vulgarity is apparent to us.

This opposition, between the safety and privacy of the interior and the unpleasant exposure of the outside, is so much at the forefront of the passage that it is easy to miss something else which has occurred to the image. For the complaint against the reviewer here has shifted oddly, and against the grain of the main line of argument. Pressed up against the window, he is presented now as being not so much superficial as too nosey, too detailed, altogether over-interested in the process of production—he comments on every single stitch, and that is what the "curious crowd" wants to hear.

The passage continues:

> No longer puffed this way and that, now elated, now depressed, [the author] could attend to his work. That might make for better writers. Again the reviewer, who must now earn his pence by cutting shop window capers to amuse the public and to advertise his skill, would have only the book to think of and the writer's needs. That might make for better criticism. (*CDB* 140)

The reviewer's performance-as-self-advertisement distracts attention from the real work of the writer, who neither performs nor advertises; the exaggerated contrast serves to enhance the sense of the writer's authenticity as a craftsman. In the new, improved version of things, neither writer nor critic would be in the public eye—but ironically, that means that readers—with the exception of the one privileged consultant—seem to get no look-in whatever.

This is Woolf's concluding summary:

> The review, it is contended, increases self-consciousness and diminishes strength. The shop window and the looking-glass inhibit and confine. By putting in their place discussion—fearless and disinterested discussion— the writer would gain in range, in depth, in power. And this change would tell eventually on the public mind. Their favourite figure of fun, the author, that hybrid between the peacock and the ape, would be removed from their derision, and in his place would be an obscure workman doing his job in the darkness of the workshop and not unworthy of respect. (*CDB* 141)

The author of present times here joins the reviewer as a vaunting "figure of fun"; and now the imagery is consciously turned inside out, as shop window and mirror "inhibit and confine," while the closeted interior opens up a "gain in range, in depth, in power." Yet by the time the "obscure workman . . . in the darkness of the workshop" has emerged, or rather disappeared, at the end, it is almost as if Woolf realizes she may have gone too far. Just in time, the last sentences save writing from a complete absence of publication or publicity by bringing back a now reconstructed "public mind" as witness:

> A new interest in literature, a new respect for literature might follow. And, financial advantages apart, what a ray of light that would bring, what a ray of pure sunlight a critical and hungry public would bring into the darkness of the workshop! (*CDB* 141-2)

But then it was Woolf who had smashed the shop window and consigned the poor writer into that darkness in the first place.

In many ways, then, the shop windows of "Reviewing" dramatically show up ambiguities implicit in Woolf's reflections about the connections between creative writing and the mass literary market. In the opening image, it is menders, not original designers or makers, who draw the crowd. Woolf seems to associate the women's reconditioning work with the bad publicity-culture of the present-day literary market, but the spectacle, of skilled craft, actually comes close to her ideal of the writer as an artisan.

To pursue the sense of such ambiguities, let us look briefly at the shop window itself, in relation to other literary windows in Woolf that might be looked at or through. The vulgarity of the big show window with its gaping crowd is at one end of a spectrum which includes many types of window-gazing. For instance, Woolf often evokes a pleasure in looking at a private window open to view but not deliberately on view. An example of this would be a passage from the essay "How should one read a book?" (1926):

> Shall we read [books] in the first place to satisfy that curiosity which possesses us sometimes when in the evening we linger in front of a house where the lights are lit and the blinds not yet drawn, and each floor of the house shows us a different section of human life in being?

Here is the curiosity of the reader before the window, just as in "Reviewing." But in this instance, it is a single reader, and she is like "us." She is loitering, making the house into her own private theatre. She is seeing but unseen, gazing into a private space from the permitting neutrality of a public one, a virtual *voyeuse*.

The window can be even more private than this. In "Reviewing", the shop window scene is contrasted to the inner sanctum where the author and consultant ideally sit in conference:

> The author wants to be told why Mr. Nicolson [i.e. the reviewer] likes or dislikes his work. This is a genuine desire. It survives the test of privacy. Shut doors and windows; pull the curtains. (*CDB* 136; Bowlby, *Crowded* 211)

Such a passage has something in common with the famous androgynous images for the creative process in *A Room of One's Own*, in which the mind goes about its eroticized creative business well concealed from view, literally with "the curtains. . . close drawn" (99). It is the hidden, intimate nature of the writer's work which is emphasized, figured through an image of the privacy of the interior—and there is someone looking on, or rather imagining from outside what is going on, with a child's-eye curiosity. The secret and private atmosphere of these scenes of literary making seems to guarantee their authenticity in relation to the window scenes where the show is deliberate and the spectators are a crowd. Both the writer's practice and the reader's interest are shown as private, almost illicit pleasures—for their eyes alone, and not a bookshop to be seen.

"Reviewing" casts a different light on many of the concerns we will find in "Memories of a Working Women's Guild." In "Reviewing," there is a community, sure enough—but it is a community of two, the the writer and the one constructive reader. Two's community, three's a crowd, and a rather vulgar crowd at that. The book is their point of contact and communication. Multiply the readers and critics, make them into a mass, and what you get is a system of marketing and false representation where books stand no chance of telling their own story because of the distortions imposed by the show window and its analogous forms of mediation and separation.

For this occasion, there's a particular naturalness to the choice of "Memories of a Working Women's Guild," because the essay, you will remember, is itself about a conference. In 1913, Woolf had attended the annual conference, in Newcastle, of the Women's Co-operative Guild with Leonard, who at that time was very heavily involved in the Co-operative movement. Virginia too had some involvement with this—the Woolfs hosted weekly meetings of the Guild in their Richmond home for a time. Perhaps a word or two about co-operation would be useful, if only because it is so difficult now to recapture the sense of radical possibilities in a social movement which in Britain has subsequently faded into almost complete insignificance, even though—or perhaps because—there are still Co-op stores to be found, now indistinguishable from every other supermarket, just a little on the tacky side.

In the early part of the century, the Co-operative movement, which had started in the mid-nineteenth century, was at its height—in Britain and France and, for that matter, in the United States.[2] A grass-roots challenge to the capitalist profit system, co-operation meant the collective organization of both production and consumption, including a system of profit-sharing through the "dividend" paid out according to what you bought in its shops. By the early years of the twentieth century, co-operation had been so successful commercially, with its shops a feature of every high street, that it was regarded as a serious, and indeed an illegitimate competitor by conventional small businesses, who often mounted quite vitriolic campaigns to try to undermine local loyalty to the "Co-op" that was taking away from their own trade.

The cooperative movement had developed along with a whole array of radical social ideals. These included, and were disseminated through, the *education* of the Co-op's (predominantly working-class) members; middle-class involvement in the movement often took the form of lecturing and related activities, and this was one of Leonard's occupations at the time of the conference Virginia attended. The Women's Co-operative Guild, which began in the 1880s, was an offshoot of this, providing forums for women to meet weekly to learn about Co-operative and socialist ideas, and to consider specifically women's issues in that context. An extract from an article in the Co-operative Wholesale Societies Annual for 1910 gives the flavor of this rich conjunction between feminism, radicalism and consumption:

> The consumers' movement, however, cannot afford simply to reward with dividend the woman with the basket. It must educate her, also, as a buyer, a democrat, and a citizen. It must take part in one of the most urgent and beneficent of possible revolutions—the extension of that great name "the people," until the noun stands, as it ought to stand in all public affairs, for the women just as much as for the men. ("Memories" 215)

The essay of 1930 was written, ostensibly as a letter to Margaret Llewellyn Davies, for many years at the head of the Guild, to introduce a volume of autobiographical writings by "Co-operative working women"; some of them speak movingly abut the change in their lives brought about by joining the Guild. But the essay moves, as it were, from Guild to guilt. It is first of all a retrospect, seventeen years afterwards, reconsidering Woolf's own reactions at the time, as a middle-class visitor, to the conference she attended in 1913. It is also, briefly, an introduction to and appreciation of the communications that make up the body of the book.

The piece is one I have always found uncomfortable to read, I think because of its own, stated discomfort, which we'll come to. It is not an easy read, reassuringly celebratory or optimistic; it neither tells a middle-class peer-group about the worthy co-operative women, nor tells co-operative women how much their work or their writing is appreciated. You want her to be saying the right thing, whatever that might be; and yet what she is talking about is the inevitability of the *gap* between her, the lady observer, and the women who are attending the conference as delegates. This gap takes precedence over the solidarity that might be suggested by their co-presence at the congress—and takes precedence even over the supplementary gap, which might have superseded the first one, of fully seventeen years: Woolf plunges us back into the embarrassments of that conference so that like her, it is as if we feel it now in what she calls that "hot June morning" ("Memories" 133) on the bone.

Or do we? I am making too rapid an assumption of identification, whether through feelings or anything else—when the unhappy failure of identifying with a speaker or writer you may very much want to identify with is precisely the problem for Woolf in her own account of that conference. Where we might think that the first thing the author of *A Room of One's Own* would be struck by and warm to, in 1930 if not in 1913, would be the fact that here was an all-women organization, with only women speaking, in fact she initially describes what she saw and heard in terms that would seem more appropriate to a spectacle of masculinity:

> There was something military in the regularity of the proceeding. They were like marksmen, I thought, standing up in turn with rifle raised to aim at a target. . . . There was no beating the bush; there were no phrases of easy eloquence. ("Memories"134)

In common with the narrator of *A Room of One's Own* to the sight of a troop of soldiers marching down Whitehall, Woolf's feeling here is one of alienation; and yet it is women, not men, who are confronting her. These women's five-minute speeches are *pointed* in every sense; they do not *waste words*; bodies and language seem to be subjected to the same uniform discipline which produces this punctiliously accurate performance.

It is only after having described the *form* of the speeches and their delivery, that Woolf goes on to summarize what they were about, listing a whole range of projected social reforms from divorce law to women's suffrage to subsidized maternity care (an area in which the Women's Guild was particularly active and successful at the time). At this point there is a curious move from the visualized bodies of the speakers to a single "mind," called "it," which though far from unanimous—"it was thinking, in short, about every sort of public question, and it was thinking constructively and pugnaciously" (134-5)—is nonetheless represented as a general, a *common* mind, "the mind which lay spread over so wide a stretch of England" (134).

This single, neutral mind stands out not only against the embodied soldierly speakers of the previous paragraph, but against other minds that then appear at the start of the next one, when Woolf refers to "the thoughts that passed through the minds of your guests, who had come from London and elsewhere not to take part, but to listen" (135). And then a little later, "And yet though it was all so reasonable, much of it so forcible, some of it so humorous, a weight of discomfort was settling and shifting itself uneasily from side to side in your visitors' minds" (135). All these minds, explicitly qualified as "middle-class" in the essay's first publication (*Yale Review*, Autumn 1930, p. 123), look alike, it is implied; and yet they are individual minds in the way that the mind of the conference or the speakers is not.

Speaking now in the first person, Woolf then moves on to indicate the problem of her separation from the mind of the speakers:

> All those questions, I found myself thinking. . . which matter so intensely to the people here, questions of sanitation and education and wages, this demand for an extra shilling, or another year at school, for eight hours instead of nine behind a counter or in a mill, leave me, in my own blood and bones, untouched. If every reform they demand was granted this very instant it would not touch one hair of my comfortable capitalistic head. Hence my interest is merely altruistic. . . . There is no life blood or urgency about it. . . . I am a benevolent spectator. (135)

Later, Woolf uses the related phrase, whens she says:

> It was aesthetic sympathy, the sympathy of the eye and of the imagination, not of the heart and of the nerves; and such sympathy is always physically uncomfortable. (139)

In both instances, the benevolent spectator and aesthetic sympathy, what we have is a separation of body and mind, or bodies and mind*s*, in the plural. Eye and imagination—eye being associated with the mental, the subjective, rather than with the bodily—go against heart and nerves; goodwill and looking on—the benevolent spectator—go against life blood and urgency. The spectator or listener, the cerebral outsider, is left "in my own blood and bones, untouched"; yet at the same time, the body intrudes with the conflict of an unease that is born of this very intactness: "such sympathy is always physically uncomfortable." It is as though she is moved by being unmoved.

Aesthetic sympathy and benevolent spectatorship are not easy, relaxed positions. Woolf here regrets the disjunction of body and mind; but it is fundamental to her understanding of the differences between her and them. Related and equally firm oppositions function in regard to that freedom which is characterized for her by what she calls *detachment*:

> Their eyes looked as if they were always set on something actual—on saucepans that were boiling over, on children who were getting into mischief. Their faces never expressed the lighter and more detached emotions that come into play when the mind is perfectly at ease about the present. They were not in the least detached and cosmopolitan. They were indigenous and rooted to one spot. (137)

Here the immediate environment and the present situation get aligned with one another. The women are stuck in one place and one time, immobile, like trees. The word "detached" is used twice, in the sense of independent and disinterested, but also, I think, of *removed.* To be detached and cosmopolitan is to be *away from*, not tied or "rooted" to, the spot you happen to be physically in, the here and now of present concerns. It is the domestic—children and cooking, both represented in terms of trouble and anxiety rather than pleasure or even just background—that works against lightness and free thinking, with an echo of Matthew Arnold's "free play of the mind" in "the lighter and more detached emotions that come into play."

I'm sure I'm not alone in finding that those saucepans can't help clattering up against Queenie Leavis's attack on *Three Guineas* when it first came out in 1938. There, Mrs. Leavis acidly rebukes Mrs. Woolf's assumptions of middle-class detachment with the words: "I myself. . . have generally had to produce contributions for this review with one hand while actually stirring the pot, or something of that kind, with the other" (Majumdar and McLaurin, 409-10). (I've always been intrigued by what "something of that kind" could possibly be referring to—is it, in spite of herself, a more-detached-than-thou assumed forgetting of the names of these trivial things, or is it some mysterious item of Leavisite kitchen equipment not suitable for naming in the pages of *Scrutiny*?) There's still, however, the same assumption in Leavis's swipe that stirring pans is a detraction from thinking or writing.

Writing and stirring may be a touch more awkward (not to say dangerous) to manage than thinking and stirring, at least in any continuing form. But it seems to be assumed that you can't think in the same way that you can't physically write, because your mind is occupied just as your hands are, with the stirring or the children or both. The question isn't raised—by Woolf in "Memories" or, for that matter, by Leavis—about whether the cook or the child-minder (which can be one person at the same time, as the passage suggests) might not also be better, not diminished, as thinker or writer. To stir the pot might not be limiting, rooting the writer to one spot and preventing her from seeing anywhere else; it might also, or instead, have given her different perspectives on what she is thinking or writing about from the lady who never does. "Think of a kitchen table": as Woolf herself implicitly points out in *To the Lighthouse* (28), the speculations of the philosopher on this matter may be limited precisely because they have no roots in the realities of kitchen thinking.

In this context, it is interesting to see that, as in "Reviewing," Woolf seeks in "Memories of a Working Women's Guild" to hold on to, or to promote, a sense of creative writing, detached as it might be, as *work*. "Hold on to" is perhaps not a metaphor in this context, because what she's alluding to is literally the hand that holds the pen. It's a remark made in passing, and a little defensively: "and moreover no working man or woman works harder with his hands or is in closer touch with reality than a painter with his brush or a writer with his pen" ("Memories" 140). Never mind the difference between ladies and working women—all can be resolved because writers and painters are workers too!

By the time Woolf comes to consider the workers' writings that her letter is introducing, the way has been prepared for all sorts of ambivalent responses. On the one hand, "[t]he writing, a literary critic might say, lacks detachment and imaginative breadth, even as the women themselves lacked variety and play of feature" (146)—which leaves open to what extent the writer is identifying herself as or with a literary critic. For "him," women and writing get welded together as homogeneous, fixed, lacking. On the other hand, even by aesthetic standards, "those pages have some qualities even as literature that the literate and instructed might envy" (146). And Woolf ends with a criterion that is more documentary than aesthetic, acknowledging the interest and importance of writing for "these lives . . . still half hidden in profound obscurity" (147).

As we have seen, "Memories of a Working Women's Guild" in effect separates a community of working women, with a collective "mind," from the detached individual "minds" of lady observers. The community seek physical necessities or utilities to alleviate their condition, whereas, the *Yale Review* text puts it: "ladies desire Mozart and Cézanne and Shakespeare; and not merely money and hot water laid on" (129). "Not merely money": with Art and hot water on either side of the divide, the consumerly difference could not be more blatant. Perhaps—I want to think so—there is just a hint of self-mockery in the specification of the purely aesthetic desires of the ladies whose minds are free from material concerns, and whose surplus money is not, implicitly, used for the unnamed vulgar things that, unlike Mozart or Cézanne or Shakespeare, have no value other than their price. But the fact that the ladies' consumption, the sign of their detachment, is itself aesthetic and consciously immaterial, unlike modern washing facilities, once again installs a distinction in relation to the bodily and the aesthetic, aesthetic sympathy "not of the heart and of the nerves".

The ending to "Memories" does not say whether it is the fact of writing or the publication of the writing that is to be welcomed. In the context of "Reviewing," which is concerned not with the worker as writer but with the writer as worker, that distinction, as we have seen, becomes crucial. These essays give no comforting sense of writing as an activity that might make or strengthen a community, or of communication as something that might easily and fruitfully take place across the haphazard gatherings of the street or the differences of social class. So I cannot help wanting to change the perspective and finish, instead, with a passage from *Three Guineas*, in the hypothetical letter addressed to the president of a women's college:

> [The new college] should explore the ways in which mind and body can be made to co-operate; discover what new combinations make good wholes in human life. . . . [The poor college] would be a place where society was free; not parcelled out into the miserable distinctions of rich and poor, of clever and stupid; but where all the different degrees and kinds of mind, body and soul merit co-operated. (34-35)

Let's notice instead the way that "co-operation" comes back as a positive metaphor, and the way that the body and mind whose separation was all-encompassing before, are now brought together in perfect harmony. But of course, you may remember, a sentence later, the letter is broken off as hopelessly idealistic—and there, I think, I had better break off as well. . . .

### Notes

[1] Because this paper was written as a lecture for the conference, and speaks about that context, I have not tried to alter its format from the "here and now" present tense it occasionally needs. I would like to thank conference participants—especially Jessica Berman and Jane Goldman—for a very helpful discussion, both immediately after the paper and in the days (and months) that followed.

[2] Several books on the history of co-operation and its importance in women's history have appeared over the past few years. See Furlough (1991), Gurney (1996), and especially Scott (1998).

### Works Cited

The Co-operative Wholesale Societies Limited. *Annual for 1910.* Manchester: The Co-operative Wholesale Society Limited and Glasgow: The Scottish Co-operative Wholesale Society Limited, [1909].

Furlough, Ellen. *Consumer Cooperation in France: The Politics of Consumption, 1834-1930.* Ithaca: Cornell UP, 1991.

Gurney, Peter. *Co-operative Culture and the Politics of Consumption in England, 1870-1930.* Manchester: Manchester UP, 1996.

Hussey, Mark, ed. *Major Authors on CD-ROM: Virginia Woolf.* Woodbridge, CT: Primary Source Media, 1997.

Majumdar, Robin, and Allen McLaurin. *Virginia Woolf: The Critical Heritage.* London: Routledge & Kegan Paul, 1975.

Scott, Gillian. *Feminism and the Politics of Working Women: The Women's Co-operative Guild, 1880s to the Second World War.* London: UCL P, 1998.

Woolf, Virginia. *Between the Acts.* New York: Harcourt Brace Jovanovich, Inc., 1941.

——. "How should one read a book?" *The Crowded Dance of Modern Life.* Ed. Rachel Bowlby. London: Penguin, 1993. 59-69.

——. "Memories of a Working Women's Guild." *A Woman's Essays.* Ed. Rachel Bowlby. London: Penguin, 1992. 133-47.

——. "Reviewing." *The Captain's Death Bed and Other Essays.* San Diego: Harvest, 1950. 127-45.

——. "Reviewing." Bowlby, *The Crowded Dance* 152-63.

——. *A Room of One's Own.* London: Panther, 1977.

——. *Three Guineas.* San Diego: Harvest, 1966

——. *To the Lighthouse.* Ed. Stella McNichol. London: Penguin, 1992.

## Michael Whitworth

### Woolf's Web: Telecommunications and Community

The World Wide Web, which is often presented as the most modern of communication systems, had its origins in telecommunications of the mid-nineteenth century. The telegraph network spread quickly across the United Kingdom, growing in parallel with the railway companies, which used it to monitor and control the movement of trains. Marvin and particularly Kieve have described how the gradual improvements in the durability of insulating materials allowed longer and more reliable lengths of cable to be laid, and soon the network became pan-European and then world wide. The first telegram cable was laid across the English Channel in August 1850. In February 1865, the first connection was made between England and British India, and in 1878 a further connection was made to Australia. The telephone system began in 1876, when Alexander Graham Bell took out the first patents, and telephone networks were able to capitalize on the technological advances made in telegraphy.

It was a commonplace in the late nineteenth century that, along with flight, telephones and telegraphs had "brought every individual of the nation into immediate and effortless communication with every other" (Marvin 201). News that would have taken days or weeks to travel across the globe could be transmitted almost instantaneously. Freud, anticipating McLuhan's idea of media as the "extensions of man," recognized that the telephone allowed "man" to "hear at distances which would be respected as unattainable even in a fairy tale" (Freud 279). But while telecommunications had the ability to transform human experience of time and space, they did not serve all individuals equally. Their advantages were most immediately available to financiers and governments. The cross-Channel telegraph was used to link the London and Paris stock exchanges within a year of its being laid. The imperial telegraph system, wrote one commentator in 1896, "brought the distant dependencies of the Empire into far closer connection with the mother country," had "strengthened the central Government in repressing insurrections, protecting property, and punishing crime," and "modified the Irish difficulty by bringing Dublin within a few minutes' communication of London" (William Lecky, quoted in Marvin 99). The growth of telecommunications produced conflicting discourses of, on the one hand, universal cooperation and the "kinship of humanity" (Marvin 199) and, on the other, increasingly effective state control.

In the spheres of finance and politics, telegraphy was sometimes claimed to have superseded letter writing, or at least to have relegated the letter to supplementary status. The degree to which the telegram differed from the letter was debated, particularly in the late 1860s, when the government proposed to bring telecommunications under state control as part of the

General Post Office. The private companies, which resisted state ownership, emphasized the differences, while the government's supporters emphasized the similarities. The telegram and the letter, claimed the largest telegraph company, were emphatically "NOT 'in the same category' or in anything approaching the same category" (Electric and International 53). They contrasted a "broker in London" sending prices and information to his "correspondents in the country," and using the "instantaneous communication afforded by the Telegraphic wire" with "a lady in London" who desires "to afford to her country cousins and acquaintances the fullest information upon household, domestic, and family affairs of interest, the particulars of which require to be conveyed in full, but which are not of pressing or immediate importance." The latter would resort to "the cheaper, but less expeditious, machinery of the Post" (Electric and International 53). The Company conceded that the broker would also write a letter summarizing the day's transactions and that the London lady might send a telegram to announce births or deaths, but they presented the distinction between the media as essentially clear cut. Their gendering the two media represents a further attempt to naturalize the distinction. The extent to which the telegram replaced the letter was also debated in the context of the proposed nationalization, and while claims must be treated with a similar caution, it is certain that, for a time, the telegram seemed to be "tread[ing] on the heels of the postal service as a mode of epistolary correspondence" ("The Post" 7).

Woolf grew up in the era of telecommunications. In 1897, she had visited the noisy and impressive Telegraph Department of the General Post Office (*PA* 6). In her novels, she responds ambivalently to telecommunications. She is fascinated by the idea of an invisible network of voices, but she presents actual phone calls as disruptive. She recognizes the potential of the network to create new communities, communities extending beyond the confines of the body and physical movement, but she also recognizes that such virtual communities compete with physically present ones. Moreover, she recognizes that the network is all too easily assimilated to the needs of the patriarchal establishment.

The dual discourses of telecommunications—of authoritarian control versus democratic cooperation—corresponded to two models of telecommunication networks, as either a hierarchical web, radiating from an authoritarian center, or a decentered, rhizomic structure, cutting across established hierarchies. Telecommunications were sometimes represented as joining "every individual" together, but as often were seen as linking the provinces to the metropolitan center, and the colonies to Europe. The *Electrical Review* in 1885 spoke of dramatic events in Europe, such as the defeat of Napoleon, "which change the flow and custom of the world":

> These things are done in a dozen hours, and in another dozen men are talking in their breathless haste and fever of these great events, not only in Paris and Berlin, but in the mosques of Cairo

> and in the streets of Arkangel, in the bazars of Calcutta and on the quays of Rio, by the falls at Ottawa, in the market place of San Francisco . . . . All the corners of the earth are joined, kindled, fused. (Marvin 199)

As Marvin notes, the four corners of the world are occupied only by passive spectators: the action happens in Europe. American writers naturally placed the center of action in New York or other major American cities, but the hierarchical model was the same. Woolf displays a political and metaphysical aversion to such hierarchies, and this, I would like to suggest, influences her attitude to telecommunications.

The authoritarian network is presented most clearly at the end of *Jacob's Room*, where the wires of the Admiralty "shivered with some far-away communication" (*JR* 151). Like the "criss-cross of telegraph wires" in the story "The Introduction," which seemed to Lily Everit to be part of the "massive masculine achievement" (*CSF* 186), these wires serve the authority of the patriarchal state. In "The Introduction" the wires were associated with high towers, churches and parliaments. In *Jacob's Room* they are similarly associated with public monuments such as Big Ben, Nelson's Column, and the equestrian statues of Whitehall and a voice speaks "with inexorable gravity" (*JR* 151). In her note on this latter scene (*JR* 185), Sue Roe identifies "the voice" with the Prime Minister, but in one paragraph at least, the "elderly man"—the Prime Minister—is represented as listening to the voice and making notes; the voice then must belong to a Foreign Office official. The anonymity of the voice stands in stark contrast to the physical frailty of the politicians. Its anonymity has the potential both to undermine and to reinforce its authority. The repetition of "said that . . . said . . . said that" (*JR* 151) suggests that the voice's reports could be merely hearsay and rumor. Yet precisely because the voice has no apparent human source, it has the impersonal authority of the marble statues (Pitt, Chatham, Burke and Gladstone). This paragraph anticipates the grey car scene in *Mrs. Dalloway*, where the "greatness" of the figure in the car is a function of its invisibility. The figure is powerful exactly because it cannot be identified as Queen, Prime Minister, or Prince of Wales. The "voice" speaks with the authority of the marble statesmen, but cannot be identified with any named individual.

While the network predominantly served the political and financial establishment, it had the potential to circumvent their public spaces. This is exploited by the SGS (presumably the "Society for General Suffrage") in *Night and Day*. The Society's office in Bloomsbury is some distance from London's political center in Westminster, but, because it possesses a telephone, Sally Seal believes it to be "the exact spot on the surface of the globe [where] all the subterranean wires of thought and progress came together" (*ND* 223). Mrs. Seal invokes the common figure of the telecommunications network uniting the "globe" around a center. The reference to "subterranean" wires is curious, given that telegraph wires ran so conspicuously at roof level and had become a prominent feature in cityscapes at this time (see for example, Nevinson's *Amongst the Nerves of the World*). The reference suggests that these wires are as much psychological as physical, standing for telepathy rather than telephony. Certainly it suggests that Mrs. Seal distinguishes her network from that of the establishment. But Mrs. Seal's exaggerrated faith in "subterranean wires" is also an element in Woolf's satirical treatment of her.

Woolf stands aloof from the telephone's potential both as an actual instrument of political organization and as a metaphor, not only in her treatment of Mrs. Seal, but also that of Mr. Clacton and Mary. Mr. Clacton, who invokes the telephone as metaphor, believing that the suffragist society should view itself as "a telephone exchange . . . the centre of an enormous system of wires" (*ND* 215), is as ridiculous as Mrs. Seal. Woolf's narrator draws attention to his image, and his mixing of the telephonic metaphor with that of keeping "fingers upon the pulse" (*ND* 215) draws further attention to it. Mr. Clacton's metaphor resembles those which proliferated in the late nineteenth century: for example, the idea that "the cable net" running "through sea after sea, and ocean after ocean" was "the nerve system of our Empire," and "the central brain from which it ramifies" was "the British Capital" (Heaton 910). Woolf implies that Mr. Clacton is exercising a form of imperialism. Notably, he is concerned to bring the provinces "into line" with the metropolis, not to exchange ideas (*ND* 69). Woolf questions the right of any group, even suffragists, to position themselves at the center of a network or the apex of a hierarchy. Even Mary Datchet makes this mistake, viewing London as a cultural center which is revered across the Empire, in "remote Canadian forests" and "the plains of India" (*ND* 38). She sees herself in similar terms, as "the centre ganglion of a very fine network of nerves which fell over England" (*ND* 64). This network, she hopes, will soon begin "feeling and rushing together and emitting their splendid blaze of revolutionary fireworks" (*ND* 64). Again, the narrator draws attention to the mixed metaphor and to Mary's overheated brain. Ironically, Mary is working at a pile of letters, a medium which, according to the late-Victorian telegraph companies, the "very fine network" should have replaced.

In *Night and Day*, Woolf treats the imagery of networks skeptically, but this seems due more to its being hierarchical than being technological. And in important ways, Mary's image of a nerve network anticipates the metaphors that Woolf later used to convey the idea of unanimist unity. These metaphors of filaments, nets, and threads occur frequently in *Mrs. Dalloway* and particularly in her most unanimist novel, *The Waves*. Bernard speaks of "the line" or the "fine filament" that connects him to Neville; Jinny speaks of the "webs of nerve" that float around us "catching in them far-away sounds unheard before" (*TW* 66, 101); Neville speaks of his self as "a net whose fibres pass imperceptibly beneath the world" (*TW* 164). Unanimism was a mystical doctrine, positing immaterial and mysterious links between individuals and ignoring the actual bonds of social class. However, Woolf's unanimist metaphors bear the traces of a material reality. The analogy of the nervous system and the telephone network was not unique to Woolf: Karl Pearson had proposed it in 1892 in *The Grammar of Science*, describing the brain as a central telephone exchange, and, as we noted earlier, it was invoked by Heaton to depict the imperial body politic. Woolf extends the metaphor, but also removes it from the discourse of empire, thinking instead of a network uniting a group of six or seven friends. That her metaphorical "lines" and "filaments" have their basis in actual telephone lines is confirmed by Bernard using one to arrange the Hampton Court reunion and Neville using one to contact his lover (*TW* 161, 136). The case of Louis is more complex. He describes himself as "half in love" with the telephone (*TW* 127), a phrase that echoes Keats's "Ode to a Nightingale," where Keats is "half in love with easeful death" and where the nightingale, like the phone, will "take into the air my quiet breath." The telephone allows Louis to fuse together his many lives, dissolving his status as an Australian and outsider by lacing together the world. But the allusion to Keats suggests that this telephonic activity is a form of easeful death, an annihilation of self. Moreover, Louis's aspiration to resemble Chatham, Pitt, Burke and Peel aligns him with British imperialism. Three out of these four were staring down at the Cabinet in *Jacob's Room*.

The ability of the telephone to unite individuals who are separated in space is won at the cost of its disrupting those who are physically together. Toward the end of *The Years,* Eleanor interrupts her dinner with Peggy to phone Sara. This irritates both Sara, who tries to ignore the ringing, and Peggy, who cannot share Eleanor's "telephone picture" (*TY* 261). Woolf also hints at another pattern of disruption: Eleanor's "telephone picture" of Sara contrasts with the restored picture of Peggy's grandmother, suggesting a larger pattern wherein the telephonic community, the community of the present moment, displaces the "community" of tradition, family heritage, and the dead. For Eleanor, who is uncomfortable being questioned about the past, this development seems entirely welcome, but for Peggy its effects are more ambiguous.

As we have seen, the development of telecommunications changed perceptions of space and time. Not only could different time zones make instant contact, but, figuratively speaking, different eras of history could be brought into simultaneous contact. It was a standard colonialist trope to present the journey from Europe to the colonized nation as a journey into the past. The European metropolis was represented as the center of the web, as the apex of evolution and civilization, while the colonial periphery was represented as being years or centuries behind. Telecommunications did not create this trope, but their speed created new and shocking juxtapositions. They shrank distance without dissolving difference. Just as the telephone threatened the secure bourgeois home with alien voices (Marvin 103), so it threatened the European present moment with a so-called primitive past. In this respect, the scene in *The Years* is not typical. The actual telephone call threatened to separate Peggy from her past, but, figuratively speaking, telecommunications brought past and present into contact.

The complex simultaneity created by the telephone anticipates and informs the simultaneity of modernist works. A scene from the Katharine Hilbery side of *Night and Day* touches on this topic. In chapter 24, the telephone's imperative bell summons Katharine away from her mother's conversation. The Hilbery's receiver is aptly located, placed in an alcove containing "superfluous possessions," "the wreckage of three generations" (*ND* 262). The possessions not only range widely in time, but in place: the alcove juxtaposes Oriental teapots with the works of Walter Scott. It seems to Katharine that "[t]he thread of sound, issuing from the telephone, was always coloured by the surroundings which received it" (*ND* 262). Yet in itself, the voice of this caller "recked nothing of Uncle James, of China teapots, or of red velvet curtains" (*ND* 263). The telephone call and its sound is paradoxically both present and absent, creating incongruities, yet standing outside them.

"How it Strikes a Contemporary," published in 1923, casts interesting light on this scene. Woolf regrets the failure of modern literature to produce masterpieces comparable with those of the nineteenth century. However, she finds consolation in the phenomena of modern life, describing the telephone, "which interrupts the most serious conversations," as having "a romance of its own" (*E*4 356). She doesn't explain this any further, but later in the same paragraph, she characterizes modernity in terms of "apparently fortuitous groupings of incongruous things" (*E*4 357). The latter phrase describes very aptly the scene at the Hilbery's house, but it is unclear why Woolf finds the telephone "romantic." If it is romantic, its romance is tinged with irony, as it facilitates incongruous juxtapositions. If it is romantic, it is a distinctly modernist form of romance. It is, perhaps, the romance of travel, coupled with the irony of staying in the same place. In the same scene in *Night and Day*, as Katharine answers Ralph's call, she imagines the "welter of voices which crowd round the far end of the telephone" and asks, "out of the enormous range of possibilities, whose voice, what possibility, was this?" (*ND* 263). The "welter of voices" extends the suggestion of modernist aesthetics contained in this scene. For a writer like Eliot, the crowding possibilities are predominantly the voices of his predecessors, for Woolf, the memories of her characters, juxtaposed with their present moments.

Recognising this connection between telecommunications and modernist simultaneity allows us to draw two conclusions. Firstly, although many theorists of modernism have seen modernist aesthetics as standing in opposition to bourgeois modernity (for example, Calinescu), it seems this was not always the case. Indeed, some of the most profound formal experimentation in modernism appears indebted to the technology of the period. Secondly, in so far as the experiences of telecommunications were specifically bourgeois experiences—available to governments, to brokers and their clients, and to families like the Hilberys—modernist simultaneity was not expressing universal or philosophical truths, but was reflecting the experiences of a small and privileged group.

**Works Cited**


Calinescu, Matei. *Five Faces of Modernity*. Durham: Duke UP, 1987.

Electric and International Telegraph Co. *Government and the Telegraphs*. London: Effingham Wilson, 1868.

Freud, Sigmund. *Civilization and Its Discontents*. Trans. Joan Rivière. *Civilization, Society and Religion*. Penguin Freud Library. 12. Ed. Albert Dickson. London: Penguin, 1985. 251-340.

Harvey, David. *The Condition of Post-Modernity*. Oxford: Blackwell, 1990.

Heaton, J. Henniker. "An Imperial Telegraph System." *Nineteenth Century* 45 (1899): 906-14.

Kieve, Jeffrey L. *The Electric Telegraph: A Social and Economic History*. Newton Abbot: David and Charles, 1973.

Marvin, Carolyn. *When Old Technologies Were New: Thinking About Electric Communication in the Late Nineteenth Century*. Oxford: Oxford UP, 1988.

McLaurin, Allen. "Virginia Woolf and Unanimism." *Journal of Modern Literature* 9 (1981-2): 115-22.

Nevinson, C. R. W. *Amongst the Nerves of the World*. c. 1930. Museum of London, London.

Pearson, Karl. *The Grammar of Science*. London: Walter Scott, 1892.

"The Post Office and the Electric Telegraph." *British Quarterly Review* 45 (1867): 442-77. *The Post Office and the Electric Telegraph*. London: Jackson, Walford and Hodder, 1867.

Woolf, Virginia. *Jacob's Room*. Ed. Sue Roe. London: Penguin, 1992.

——. *Night and Day*. Ed. Julia Briggs. London: Penguin, 1992.

——. *The Waves*. Ed. Kate Flint. London: Penguin, 1992.

——. *The Years*. London: Penguin, 1968.


**Deirdre Flynn**

# Virginia Woolf's Women and the Fashionable Elite: On Not Fitting In

### Class Cuts in *Mrs. Dalloway*

In a 1915 journal entry, Virginia Woolf remarks that "if the British spoke openly about W.C.'s & copulation, then they might be stirred by universal emotions"(*D*1 5). Woolf here rather surprisingly juxtaposes natural bodily functions with "universal" compassion. She suggests that by bringing naked, physical realities into day-to-day conversation, isolated individuals might be stirred to some intimate sympathy. However, she checks her optimism in the ensuing sentence, noting that "as it is, an appeal to feel together is hopelessly muddled by intervening greatcoats & fur coats" (*D*1 5). In their very material concreteness, "greatcoats & fur coats" vividly obstruct Woolf's utopian fantasy of togetherness. More figuratively, these specific articles of clothing connote social and economic barriers that block hopes of an inclusive conversation among classes; less expensive, heavy overcoats signal a middle-to-lower-middle-class social body, whereas more expensive fur coats mark an upper-class body. Such coded attire, Woolf laments, veils the common core beneath it, dividing people superficially but "hopelessly."

Woolf consistently problematizes this silent divisiveness of clothing in her short stories and novels. She often portrays women characters who feel that their wardrobes isolate them from fashionable, high society. Mabel Waring, for instance, is tortured as she enters Mrs. Dalloway's drawing room in "The New Dress," realizing, "No! It was not *right*" (CSF 170). From this moment, Mabel experiences the "misery which she always tried to hide, the profound dissatisfaction—the sense she had had, ever since she was a child, of being inferior to other people" (*CSF* 170). This particular woman does not fit the ready-made molds of her upper-crust society friends like Rose Shaw, "herself being dressed in the height of fashion, precisely like everybody else, always" (*CSF* 171). Aware that "fashion meant cut, meant style, meant thirty guineas at least" (*CSF* 170), Mabel tries to take a cheaper, alternative approach by having a dress copied from an old Paris fashion book. However, this "pale yellow, idiotically old-fashioned silk dress" does not make her seem more "original," "dignified," and "womanly" than her contemporaries (*CSF* 171). Rather, it displays her "appalling inadequacy" for all to see (*CSF* 170). So, feeling like a "wretched fly," she creeps away early "in the Chinese cloak she had worn these twenty years" (*CSF* 177).

While Mabel cringes at her own inadequacy when surrounded by Mrs. Dalloway's set, Miss Kilman more bitterly attacks "Mrs. Dalloway and all the other fine ladies" (*MD* 188). Indeed, in the novel, *Mrs. Dalloway*, Miss Kilman glowers at the central protagonist's "delicate body, her air of freshness and fashion" (*MD* 189). At the same time, she defends her own "green mackintosh coat" (*MD* 16), thinking, she "had her reasons. First, it was cheap; second, she was over forty; and did not, after all, dress to please. She was poor, moreover; degradingly poor. Otherwise she would not be taking jobs from people like the Dalloways; from rich people, who liked to be kind" (*MD* 186). Miss Kilman's mackintosh here metonymizes her economic and social inferiority. Her poverty not only limits her to one all-purpose mackintosh, but also enslaves her to the richer classes.

Clothing signals clear positions of dominance and subservience, in this respect: the fashionable Mrs. Dalloway enjoys membership in an idealized, dominant group, while the unfashionable Miss Kilman suffers ostracism in a deidealized, inferior group. Clothing thus defines a social group and communicates a group identity. However, it also serves an ideological function.

As Malcolm Barnard argues in *Fashion as Communication*, "Clothing and fashion are part of the process [by] which social groups establish, sustain and reproduce positions of power, relations of dominance and subservience" (40). Moreover, Barnard continues, "they are . . . part of the process [by] which those positions of dominance and subservience are made to appear entirely natural, proper and legitimate . . . not only to those in positions of dominance, but also to those in positions of subservience" (40). The day-to-day display of superiority and inferiority, Barnard here contends, infuses otherwise empty, abstract social positions with experiential substance. For instance, by wearing elegant dresses that fit beautifully at "Buckingham Palace" and "Hatfield" (*MD* 58), women such as Mrs. Dalloway visually manifest their sociopolitical dominance. They also make this dominance seem proper and natural. Poorer women, on the other hand, dress in bland mackintoshes. They see and serve wealthy women, tutoring their daughters (Miss Kilman) or making their dresses (Sally Parker), for example. Having accepted their inferior status, they then hide away from view, in "the Abbey" (*MD* 202) or "at Ealing" (*MD* 58).

But clothing continues to assert positions of superiority and inferiority even after working-class women hide away and leisure-class women "put off their rich apparel" (*MD* 46). Clothing seems, in effect, to get under women's skins, internally pinning them to specific social ranks. Moreover it does so, Woolf suggests, even when women are aware and critical of its divisive power.[1] Just how does clothing effectively communicate class-codes in ways that override intellectual awareness? And what makes it work so well as an apparatus of class ideologies? Through interior monologues that trace Mrs. Dalloway and Miss Kilman's thoughts about their clothing, Woolf begins to answer these questions. In the process, she unveils a complex logic of *ressentiment* that locks women not only socially, but also psychically into a radically hierarchical fashion system.

## *Ressentiment* and the Double-Bind

In her recent article, "Wounded Attachments," Wendy Brown clarifies how *ressentiment* ensnares even the most self-consciously liberal subjects in such a system. She defines *ressentiment* via Nietzsche as "the moralizing revenge of the powerless, 'the triumph of the weak as weak'" (66-7). She juxtaposes this resentment with liberal "*politesse*," or moderate liberalism's constantly avowed respect for "freedom, equality, self-reliance and self-made capacities" (67). Although *politesse* and *ressentiment* might seem radically divergent, according to Brown they converge in "two related constitutive paradoxes of liberalism: that between individual liberty and social egalitarianism" (67). Liberal, capitalist society, Brown argues, demands that its subjects construct themselves according to proscribed "social relations and forces." However, it denies that such "social relations and forces" limit the domain of self-construction. In fact, it goes so far as to claim that all subjects should be able to flourish in a free, open system.

This double-bind, Brown contends, "produce[s] failure turned to recrimination by the subordinated, and guilt turned to resentment by the 'successful'" (67). Whether suffering from failure or guilt, then, all liberal subjects are vulnerable to some strain of *ressentiment.* The subject's inevitable sense of failure or guilt, Brown adds, "must either find a reason within itself (which redoubles the failure) or a site of external blame upon which to avenge its hurt and redistribute its pain" (67). *Ressentiment* offers a viable way to externalize such uncomfortable feelings. This is its "triple achievement," according to Brown: "it produces an affect (rage, righteousness) that overwhelms the hurt; it produces a culprit responsible for the hurt; and it produces a site of revenge to displace the hurt (a place to inflict hurt as the sufferer has been hurt)." Together, Brown adds, "these operations both ameliorate (in Nietzsche's term, "anesthetize") and externalize what is otherwise 'unendurable'"(68).

The fashion system entangles women in precisely this double-bind. It embodies the mythic promise of freedom, equality, self-reliance, and self-construction that Brown critiques. As one seminal, early sociologist of fashion argues, "the contents of fashion . . . are not, as many other psychic contents are, denied absolutely to any one, for a change of fortune, which is never entirely out of the question, may play them into the hands of an individual who had previously been confined to the state of envy."[2] Fashionable clothes, in this light, hold the promise that they might someday be attainable by all. It is only when this promise butts against the reality of an "unavowed dependence on and construction by a variety of social relations and forces" that fashion's liberating potential begins to look suspicious (Brown 67). Fashion, in this light, embodies a promise that makes all liberal subjects vulnerable to feeling either guilty for dressing fashionably or failed for not dressing fashionably. Those who do not fit available, ready-made molds, the myth implies, must simply make themselves into more suitable subjects. Someone like Miss Kilman who reflects that "no clothes suited her. She might buy anything" (*MD* 195), thus holds the double burden of feeling that these clothes should suit her and that, if they do not, it is her own fault because she has failed to make herself fit into them (and *not* because she is too poor to have dresses made to fit her, as a wealthier woman of substance might do). Someone like Mrs. Dalloway, on the other hand, feels guilty about Miss Kilman, thinking "she wore that coat; . . . she was never in the room five minutes without making you feel her superiority, your inferiority; how poor she was; how rich you were" (*MD* 16).

Both Miss Kilman and Mrs. Dalloway capitalize on the secondary gains of *ressentiment* to ease such feelings of guilt and failure. Unable to approach the ideals of feminine beauty and desirability that Mrs. Dalloway embodies, Miss Kilman, on the one hand, feels an "overmastering desire to overcome her; to unmask her. . . . If only she could make her weep; could ruin her; humiliate her; bring her to her knees, crying, You are right!" (*MD* 189). Rage, here, overwhelms pain, finding an easy target in the depersonalized "her" who embodies all the social and economic power Miss Kilman has been denied as a working-class woman. Mrs. Dalloway, on the other hand, seeks relief from some unspecifiable suffering by "bringing back Kilman with a [jubilant] rush." She thinks, "Ah, how she hated her—hot, hypocritical, corrupt; with all that power; Elizabeth's seducer; the woman who had crept in to steal and defile. . . . She hated her: she loved her. It was enemies one wanted, not friends" (*MD* 266). Mrs. Dalloway here locates an ideal site for her dis-ease, while enjoying "real," "satisfying" hatred.

Such active *ressentiment* does more than simply relieve and displace pain, here. It also evokes intensely satisfying emotional responses that, in fact, psychically charge the vast fabric of social hierarchization which is stitched into clothes themselves. In this way, it invests both these hierarchies and the fashion system with tremendous affective capital; it infuses the capitalist machine with psychic life. At the same time, it binds women together around a single axis of desire for fashionable clothing. Paradoxically, however, resentment also divides women, rendering them competitive and thus compelling them to buy the latest clothes so as to catch up with what is deemed desirable. Through this double-maneuver of division and bondage, resentment fuels and maintains the fashion system.[3]

Resentment in this context, is deeply imbricated in the fashion system at both economic and psychosocial levels. Indeed, it psychically reinforces the class hierarchies upon which the fashion system depends. Miss Kilman and Mrs. Dalloway reveal the complex dynamics by which resentment translates a material, economic division into such a deeply felt psychosocial division. Resentment, in effect, enables each of these women to objectify and dehumanize the other, while temporarily centering herself in stark opposition to this other. Mrs. Dalloway, for instance, consistently dehumanizes Miss Kilman, whom she views as an "unfortunate creature," a dried-up "spectre," a "monster," and a "tyrant" (*MD* 16, 190). Thus establishing Miss Kilman as an inhuman object, Mrs. Dalloway constitutes herself, in contrast, as a human subject. In a similar gesture, Miss Kilman effaces Mrs. Dalloway as a human being when, for example, she caustically grumbles, "she should have been in a factory; behind a counter; Mrs. Dalloway and all the other fine ladies!" (*MD* 188). Fusing Mrs. Dalloway with "all the other fine ladies," Miss Kilman here reduces her rival to an object of mass production ("she should have been in a factory") and/or consumption ("behind a counter"). She positions herself as an enlightened, righteous subject *vis-à-vis* this stupid, generic object. *Ressentiment* thus bolsters the oppositional identities in which both Miss Kilman and Mrs. Dalloway take refuge.

### (Ad)dressing the Bodily Ego

However, these identities would be remarkably transient and hollow if they were not filled in, so to speak, by something more substantial than raw, reactionary affect. Clothing appears to offer this psychosocial substance. Freud helps clarify this potential power of clothing when, in *The Ego and the Id* (1923); he privileges "a person's own body, and above all its surface, [as] a place from which both external and internal perceptions may spring" (15). This bodily surface is not, Freud emphasizes, simply a site upon which internal and external perceptions cross paths. Rather, it is a site upon which they engage quite actively. So actively, in fact, that the physical surface actually enters inside the psyche, "as a mental projection" to constitute the subject's ego (16). The ego, Freud thus argues, "is first and foremost a *bodily ego*; it is not merely a surface entity, but is itself the projection of a surface" (16). If the projection of this bodily surface constitutes the ego, then one might conjecture that the clothing with which one drapes this surface could easily get imbricated in the internalization/projection process. It might, in fact, color and shape a bodily ego with the social codes inscribed in its fabric.

The depth of such inscription far surpasses intellectual appreciation, penetrating to the very core of one's identity. It thus helps explain why Woolf herself can not entirely transcend her class-based identity to "lift the greatcoats & fur coats" that muddle an "appeal to feel together." Regardless of her insistent desire to get beyond such apparently superficial vestimentary distinctions, she can not tear them from the depths of her psyche which is, itself, corseted by the very clothing that clings to the "bodily ego."

By drawing attention to the ways in which clothing intimately shapes women's social and psychic identities, Woolf here opens the dialogue to a class dilemma she saw as paramount. She offers no simple solutions, but begins to lift the veils that obscure intricately interwoven social, economic, and psychological factors which support what she views as an oppressive patriarchal, capitalist system. In so doing, she suggests that multiple points of intervention—on social, intellectual, and psychological fronts—might ultimately interrupt the vicious cycle of class indoctrination which so effectively and painfully divides women who, in fact, share adjoining narrow beds.

**Notes**

1 As Bowlby argues in "Woolf and Communities," Woolf herself painfully experiences such internal class-conflict. According to Bowlby, Woolf underscores her frustration when, in "Memories of a Working Women's Guild" (1930), she blames her "comfortable capitalistic head" for the fact that "all those questions . . . which matter so intently to the [working- class] people here, . . . leave me, in my own blood and bones, untouched." Trapped with a "head" that limits her to the detached position of a "benevolent spectator," Woolf is unable to experience a "universal emotion" that would more intimately connect her to women who, she knows (but does not *feel*), actually share her own narrow bed in a capitalist, patriarchal society. Also see Snaith's "Virginia Woolf and Reading Communities: Respondents to *Three Guineas*." Both are reprinted in this volume.

2 See Simmel, 179.

[3] Such a dynamic is at the heart of Simmel's "trickle down theory" of fashion. Rubenstein paraphrases this theory succinctly: "in Western society the aristocracy often had to compete with the rising middle class for social rewards, wealth, prestige, and power. To do so successfully the aristocrats had to maintain visual superiority. A new fashion was thus invented by members of the aristocracy as soon as their existing style was adopted by members of the middle class" (148).

**Works Cited**

Barnard, Malcolm. *Fashion as Communication.* London: Routledge, 1996.

Bowlby, Rachel. "Woolf and Communities." Virginia Woolf & Communities, Eighth Annual Conference on Virginia Woolf. Saint Louis Univ., St. Louis, June 4-7, 1998. (See elsewhere in this volume.)

Brown, Wendy. "Wounded Attachments," *States of Injury: Power and Freedom in Late Modernity.* Princeton: Princeton UP, 1995. 53-76.

Freud, Sigmund. *The Ego and the Id.* Trans. Joan Rivière. New York: W.W. Norton, 1960.

Rubenstein, Ruth. "Commerce and Fashion," *Dress Codes.* San Francisco: Westview Press, 1995. 146-50.

Simmel, Georg. "Fashion," *Fashion Marketing: An Anthology of Viewpoints and Perspectives,* Eds. Gordon Wills and David Midgley. London: Ruskin House, 1973. 171-91.

Snaith, Anna. "Virginia Woolf and Reading Communities: Respondents to *Three Guineas.*" Virginia Woolf & Communities. (See elsewhere in this volume.)

Woolf, Virginia. *Mrs. Dalloway.* New York: HBJ, 1925.

——. *The Diary of Virginia Woolf.* Ed. Anne Olivier Bell, assisted by Andrew McNeillie. Vol. 1. New York: HBJ, 1977.

——. "The New Dress," *The Complete Shorter Fiction of Virginia Woolf.* Ed. Susan Dick. San Diego: Harvest, 1989. 170-7.

**D. A. Boxwell**

## In the Urinal: Virginia Woolf Around Gay Men

What was Virginia Woolf's relationship to the interwar British gay male subcultural community? In the last decade or so of Woolf criticism, some significant readers of Woolf have posited her attitudes either as necessarily critical of male homosexuality (Jane Marcus, Louise DeSalvo, Phyllis Rose) or, at the other end of the spectrum, as gay-affirmative or even "queer" in terms of our own fin de siècle "post-gay" theory and discourse (Christopher Reed and Stephen Barber). This stimulating, even antagonistic, discussion about Woolf and gay men, as it has been evolving, could do still more than it has to accept and explore the material conditions of Woolf's extensive contact with this particular community, a community which was simultaneously Establishment and Outlaw. She published and mentored more than one generation of gay men; she communed socially and relished gossiping with them; she was related, familially, to them; she was artistically inspired by them; she empathically created them in her own fiction, vividly re-creating them in her letters and diaries; and she had platonic love affairs with at least one of them, as well as exasperating love-hate relationships with many of them.

I want to show how two of her diary entries from the 1930s account for the fact that Woolf was not just situated, both professionally and personally, at the edges of a vibrant metropolitan gay male community consisting of overlapping circles centered on many of her male friends and acquaintances; rather, she was, in large measure, immersed in that community and also even at the center of it. Specifically, I analyze how the *topos* of the "male urinal" in these two entries signals her recognition of, and always problematic identification with, the subcultural aspects of a gay male community.

Issues of class and desire circulate around the "male urinal," for it was, as Woolf implicitly recognized, an erotic space of cross-class male-male relations occurring in a community which transcended socioeconomic boundaries. It was also a potentially exotic space to those it normally excluded. On 4 April 1930 she observes that attending a dinner party at Raymond Mortimer's "made on me a tinkling, private, giggling, impression. As if I had gone into a men's urinal" (*D*3 299). An 11 January 1936 entry detailing a visit with E. M. Forster prompts the association of his "bugger crew" with a "liken[ing] to the male urinal" (*D*5 6). These diary entries echo and reinforce a particularly evocative, peculiarly fragrant letter to Ethel Smyth (15 August 1930), in which Woolf writes that the society of gay men caused her to "feel as if I had strayed into the male urinal; a wet, smelly, trivial kind of place" (*L*4 200).

In these two diary entries, the urinal, tropologically, is more than just an "as if" analogy or a simile; rather, the urinal functions metonymically for the aspects of the gay community which both fascinated and repelled her. The urinal is a condensed site of Woolf's knowledge of, and even need for, a gay male community whose literary elite she helped form, and who, in turn, gave her forms of entrée into that community closed to most women. In fact, her diaries and letters are a superb, even unprecedented, yet still largely unrecognized, primary source of information about British gay male culture between the wars. That is, at least, its rarefied, culturally legitimated strata. The "male urinal" functions, in Woolf's inscription, to hint at her knowing, encoded recognition of the less rarefied aspects of that outlaw community's experience.

It is not difficult to nominate the candidates most crucial to Woolf's engagement with the gay community of her time: Lytton Strachey, E. M.

Forster, Duncan Grant, John Lehmann, Goldsworthy Lowes Dickinson, Harold Nicolson, among many others. Raymond Mortimer (1895-1980) is especially noteworthy for his role in Woolf's life as impresario and tutor of gay male culture in its more spectacularizing forms. Mortimer is key to her inscription of the gay men in her orbit as the inhabitants of the "male urinal," which is both repulsive and fascinating to Woolf. In both entries, Raymond Mortimer figuratively transcends his own dandified, tackily bedecked body (as we have so pictured from her diary entries about him) and becomes a performance space called "Raymond's," a location where Woolf saw gay men at their least inhibited, least straight-acting, if you will. Mortimer was a recurring character in Woolf's diaries from 1923 to the end of her life, one of the Bright Young Things produced by Oxford, a one hit wonder with the Beerbohmian 1921 novel *The Oxford Circus* and eventually the literary editor of *The New Statesman and Nation.* He was, most pertinently to Woolf's professional life, an almost obsequiously flattering fan of her novels. As the lover of Harold Nicolson, he was drawn even further into Woolf's orbit in the second half of the twenties, when Woolf became the lover of Nicolson's wife, Vita Sackville-West. There is no doubt that Woolf's frequently acerbic references to Mortimer are less than flattering to him in return (which is a hallmark of her response to most people in the ostensibly private genre of the diary). She habitually refers to his failed efforts at dandyism and his overall status as a second-rater, displacing her lack of complete comfort with him on to Leonard, who, apparently, can't abide his "'slimy'" presence (*D*2 266). In one of her most memorable entries (20 Oct 1934), she observes that "after 10 minutes the Raymond machine clogs," for he has only "an uneasy shallow sandy mind" (*D*4 187). Yet, for all that, Mortimer was appealing to Woolf at some less lofty level, his very grindingly predictable shallowness a liberating, even catalytic, force in her own creativity. There is a palpable sense of delight in her reports of the "animated admirable light & airy & well seasoned talk" she has with him (*D*3 181-2). And, to seek refuge from writer's block on *The Waves* she needed only turn to recording her response to Mortimer's ostentatiously gay after-dinner salon in all its theatricality and perversity, an outrageously carnivalesque version of the male-male desire which is so stratospherically rarefied in *The Waves* itself.

That is perhaps why the invocation of the "male urinal" or "men's urinal" is so arresting on two separate occasions when Mortimer is made legible in her diary. At first glance, Woolf's recurring analogy between Mortimer's drawing room and a public facility for elimination only works to an extremely limited extent. That the urinal seems specifically and redundantly gendered by Woolf as male (in 1936) emphasizes her desire to summon in her imagination the space of greatest and most obvious exclusivity to men—an unequivocal *zone interdite* for women. But whatever else happens in a public rest room for men, the expression of desire through "raucous . . . and . . . obtrusive" gossip, much less the kind of behavior which is relentlessly effeminized by Woolf in the 1930 entry (*D*3 299), is not tolerated, and is, in fact, forbidden in a urinal. As Lee Edelman has observed in his brilliant essay "Men's Room," the male lavatory is structured on principles of a male body's compliance with the cultural regulation of bodily functions and desires. It is a liminally public/private space for all of its users, a zone of social protection afforded by patriarchy but "only so long as he performatively shelters the structural flaw that opens his body by way of its multiple openings (ocular, oral, anal, genital) to the various psychic vicissitudes able to generate illicit desires" (152). In other words, men may be sheltered in the urinal, but they are also most vulnerable to their own, and other men's, desires in this space. And it almost goes without saying that the scoffing presence of a woman is impermissible in a men's room.

As a space of epistemological anxiety and potential for loss of control, moreover, the urinal operates according to differing laws, according to the sexual orientation of the male user. The urinal is perforce a bottomless reservoir of homosexual panic for straight men, who must, nonetheless, perform an insouciant lack of awareness of such panic (hence the chorus of quasi-melodic whistling in any given men's room). As Edelman puts it with characteristically blunt erudition, "the law of the men's room decrees that men's dicks be available for public contemplation at the urinal precisely to allow a correlative mandate: that such contemplation must never take place" (153). But homosexuals (either according to their identity or desires), under the operation of this paradoxical logic, present the greatest perceived threat to this mandate. And this is where Woolf's diary serves to give us insight into interwar British gay male culture. One of the ironic and lasting effects of the Labouchère Amendment of 1885, which outlawed male homosexuality and drove it underground, was the rapid, and de facto, eroticization of the public urinal: ironic, because the urinal, a word that entered the lexicon only in 1851 (*OED*), was the invention of the same Victorian reformist imperative to sanitize metropolitan public spaces, controlling and even rendering invisible bodily functions and drives.

The public urinal, enshrined in camp, theatrical British slang from the turn of the century as the "cottage," has since remained a communal pick-up point or actual locus of sexual activity, however fumblingly furtive, anonymously impersonal, or riskily consummated under police surveillance—all of which have added to the frisson of its appeal for many. In their oral history of interwar homosexuality, *Between the Acts* (a perfectly Woolfian title!) Kevin Porter and Jeffrey Weeks' respondents consistently point out that "in a climate of illegality the most common places for meeting people were public spaces such as parks and public lavatories" (3). There is little doubt, with the benefit of hindsight and the passage of time, that many of the gay men in Woolf's orbit were inveterate practitioners of cottaging, increasingly confirmed by such recent biographies as Peter Parker's account of J. R. Ackerley's life and Peter Alexander's life of William Plomer. Woolf knew she was, at most, only a degree or two of separation from the roundelay of public sex with the working classes which kept tongues wagging in private salons and propped up a vast, and far-reaching, legal system of surveillance, coercion, and retribution which only began to be disestablished in 1967.

Thus, on closer inspection, Mortimer's drawing room, iteratively suffused as it is with the "atmosphere of buggery" (*D*3 299) is not *like* a urinal, nor could it ever be. The atmosphere is far too relaxed, open, and, in every sense of the word, gay. This room is bereft of the panicked undecidability and abjection of the urinal. In her representation of such after-dinner frivolity in 1930, the effeminizing performative elements of gay self-presentation by Strachey, Forster, Mortimer, and Sackville-West would have been epistemologically impossible in a cottage, unless one wanted to be arrested. Instead, Woolf is slyly deploying an analogy with huge metonymic potential to signal to us, and herself, her recognition that these men are sexual subjects, whose very identities are implicated in their erotic desires and practices. The cottage, in the gay male imaginary, if not in the actuality of a Britain governed by repressive state apparatuses, is (as she notes of Raymond's) "entirely secluded, intimate, & set on one object" (*D*3 299). By the 1930s, as the diaries indicate, there was surely little concerning gay male life about which she remained unaware. Woolf's bemused, fascinated scrutiny with the gender and sexual Other made her a complicit, and even eager, audience for even the most reluctant gay male interlocutor. As the diary entry for 9 April 1937 reveals, she "milk[s]" Hugh Walpole, who "was afraid of being a monstrosity" for his "stories," however outrageous (the one she refers to is about "sodomy—a sudden impulse—over the ships side" [*D*5 78]). Indeed, the voyeuristic and liberatory potential of Mortimer's ostentatiously theatrical arena is implicit, but neverthleless clear. As Porter and Weeks point out, for gay men, cottages were places of great textual production and reading. Informational instructions, invitations, and graphic representations of body parts have all kept sanitation inspectors busy with the business of suppressing the "vandalism," which is also an expression of taboo desires.

By voyaging out and into the metonymic realms of gay male culture, especially its outlawed subcultural sexual practices, Woolf could be said to free herself, on at least one occasion, from the blockages induced by her own expectations and experiences. In the same letter to Ethel Smyth in which Woolf evoked the palpable smell and air of the urinal (15 August 1930), she avers she couldn't write unless "perpetually stimulated. Its no good sitting in a garden with a book; or collecting facts. There must be this fanning and drumming" (*L*4 200). In a way, her always problematic alienation from, but inclusion in, the community of literary gay men, so exemplified in Mortimer's drawing room in the spring of 1930, is a fulfilment of a self-analytical observation she made in her diary on 11 September 1923, an observation triggered by noting Mortimer's attempt to seduce Dadie Rylands with a walk "by the fish ponds" at Bindon, Dorset. She wrote that it was "a damp romantic place; & one wh[ich] perhaps I shall never see again, as I told L. I had an odd feeling that it is queer to find such places lying unknown in the country, inland. I can't get hold of it now. I am perhaps encouraged by Proust to search out & identify my feelings, but I have always felt this kind of thing in great profusion" (*D2* 267-8). We are still searching out and identifying Woolf's relationship with gay men, and, fortunately, she left us with a great profusion of texts from which we can learn much about attitudes toward, and the material circumstances of, gay men before Gay Liberation.

**Works Cited**

Barber, Stephen. "Lip-Reading: Woolf's Secret Encounters." *Novel Gazing: Queer Readings in Fiction*. Ed. Eve Kosofsky Sedgwick. Durham: Duke UP, 1997. 410-43.

DeSalvo, Louise. *Virginia Woolf: The Impact of Childhood Sexual Abuse on Her Life and Work*. Boston: Beacon, 1989.

Edelman, Lee. "Men's Room." *Stud: The Architectures of Masculinity*. Ed. Joel Sanders. New York: Princeton Architectural P, 1996. 152-61.

Marcus, Jane. *Virginia Woolf and the Languages of Patriarchy*. Bloomington: Indiana UP, 1987.

Porter, Kevin, and Jeffrey Weeks. *Between the Acts: Lives of Homosexual Men 1885-1967*. London: Routledge, 1991.

Reed, Christopher. "Bloomsbury Bashing: Homophobia and the Politics of Criticism in the Eighties." *Genders* 11 (1991): 58-80.

Rose, Phyllis. *Woman of Letters: A Life of Virginia Woolf*. New York: Oxford UP, 1978.

Woolf, Virginia. *The Diary of Virginia Woolf*. Ed. Anne Olivier Bell, assisted by Andrew McNeillie. Vols. 2-5. New York: HBJ, 1977-1984.

——. *The Letters of Virginia Woolf*. Ed. Nigel Nicolson and Joanne Trautmann. Vol 4. New York: Harvest, 1981.

## Terry DeHay

### Gathering Around the Punch Bowl: Woolf's Alternative Narrative Communities

That Virginia Woolf was interested in the institutions that both form and limit communities is evident from her earliest writing. She seemed uniquely aware of the importance of narration in the formation of community: as recent communitarian theorists, such as James Boyd White, emphasize: "a community is a group of people who tell a shared story in a shared language" (qtd. in Clayton 135). But as much as Woolf agrees with the importance of "shared stories" and "shared language," much of her writing both deconstructs existing concepts of community and explores new possibilities, new alternatives in the formation of community. Once again, Woolf has anticipated in her novels and essays some of the most recent theoretical concerns; as she demonstrates the danger of communities maintained by practices and customs that oppress or marginalize groups based on gender, sexual orientation, nationality, class, she explores the importance of reconfiguring community in the modern world, assessing the impact of social institutions on the formation of identity.

Attempting to find a definition of "community" which would help me understand Woolf's ideas of the importance of community in modern society led me to the current debate between liberalism and communitarism. Political theorists in the 1980s and 90s are responding to some of the dilemmas facing the West in the early part of the century. The disintegration of traditional systems of values was, and still is, confusing and even threatening to some, especially those invested in existing power structures. As in Woolf's oft quoted pronouncement from "Mr. Bennett and Mrs. Brown," "[i]n or about December, 1910, human nature changed," many postmodern theorists have pointed out that the modern era is marked by the "dissolution of landmarks of certainty" (qtd. in Mouffe, "Liberalism" 179). Political and social theorists have responded with investigations into possible models for organizing society that might provide a center that would hold. In the rhetoric of many of these current investigations, there is a tension between the liberalist emphasis on the rights of the individual and the communitarian insistence on the importance of the "good" of the whole. Liberal thought tends to emphasize an early modern concept of the individual as autonomous and rational: " Individuals find their god for another. . . . In a well-ordered society, then, the plans of life of individuals are different in the sense that these plans give prominence to different aims, and persons are left free to determine their good . . .(Rawls 448). Communitarian theory insists on the historical identity of a community based on shared values which are "*handed down from generation to generation rather than invented or negotiated*" (italics in the original, Etzioni 93). However, as Woolf intuits, this tension of "justice (or rights) versus the good, the primary of hermeneutics over universal modes of rationality," is often just two perspectives coming from the same ethical position, based on traditional assumptions about the relationship of the subject to the social whole (Connolly 194). In other words, these two poles of the debate fold in and reinforce each other, using the same primary assumptions about the nature of the "good" which have governed western thought since the Enlightenment: the rights of the individual are limited and defined by what is the "higher good" of the State, as defined and perpetuated by institutions which support the State.

My assertion is that Woolf was far ahead of the current debate, already working to create a synthesis between the individualism of liberalism and the collectivism of the communitarian vision, at the same time challenging the fundamental assumptions of nationalism. The theorists I will refer to in exploring Woolf's concept of alternative communities have also challenged the motives and methods of both liberal and communitarian thinkers and share with Woolf the paradoxical sense that community is both desirable and dangerous, in the same way that liberal individualism seems essential to western democracy as well as potentially destabilizing. Chantal Mouffe states directly that there is a purpose in returning to "a politics of common good based on shared moral values," but she cautions at the same time against a return to the "premodern view of political community," which would promote a shared system of values over the importance of pluralism. Her vision of an alternative community would require a "radical-liberal-democratic political philosophy which revives a sense of civic virtue . . .and public community . . . reformulated in a way that makes them compatible with the defense of individual liberty" ("Liberalism" 187). Focusing primarily on identity formation and the possibility of social action, Stanley Aronowitz looks at two seemingly contradictory sides of "community": one which signifies positive, collective work and decision making; and the other, the "power systems which guard their particular knowledge and its form jealously and [which] frequently repel challenges with considerable ferocity" (*Politics* 156). He notes the danger when a community limits and excludes oppositional or progressive developments. The individual, Aronowitz asserts, must negotiate these poles of collectivity, finding alternative formulations of community that will promote change and social action.

These syncretistic concepts of community developed by Mouffe and Aronowitz provide paradigms to help understand the radical re-visions of community Woolf develops in her work. One of the clearest examples of alternative community is in her novel *Orlando*. When Orlando, as a woman, descends to the streets dressed as a man, she ironically finds access to a community of women off limits to her as a woman: the community of prostitutes. A man's dress allows her to negotiate the boundaries of class that separate her from these women and to discover alternative bases for community. As an honorary member of the community of prostitutes. Orlando discovers that it is based in part on narration, storytelling, among the women, a type of shared community of discourse:

> These poor creatures, she ascertained, for Nell brought Prue, and Prue Kitty, and Kitty Rose, had a society of their own of which they now elected her a member. Each would tell the story of the adventure which had landed her in her present way of life. . . . So they would draw around the Punch bowl which Orlando made it her business to furnish generously, and many were the fine tales they told and many the amusing observations they made for it cannot be denied that when women get together—but hist . . .(219)

The "hist" acknowledges the footsteps of men on the stairs, the silence of the women's stories, and subsequent narration by men of women's lives: "It is well known . . . that when they lack the stimulus of the other sex, women can find nothing to say to each other." The irony is clear; even with the men's interruptions, Woolf's legitimizing of the prostitutes' narrative community is emphatic.

The negotiation between communities that Woolf describes here reveals her sense of the hierarchical arrangement of various communities and underscores the power systems that mediate this relationship. Although the men clearly represent the community defined by the dominant patriarchal values, the prostitutes have established their own system of power that legitimizes their community even while they are subordinated to the other. Through this contrast, Woolf poses the question of what constitutes a community and how one gains/claims membership and legitimacy. Rather than accepting the received "shared values" promoted by communitarian theory, Woolf's writing, like much postmodern social theory, focuses on the historical origin of these values and the role of hegemonic practices and discourse in determining identity. In *Three Guineas*, she defines "society" as a conglomeration of people joined together for certain aims" (104), emphasizing the importance of action/ "aims" in the present over traditions based in the past. She goes on, however, to critique the actual function of community/ "society" as seen from the "outside": "Society is an ill-fitting form that distorts the truth; deforms the mind; fetters the will. Inevitably we look upon societies as conspiracies" (105), which exclude and oppress non-members.

Although in a very different context, Stanley Aronowitz's characterization of the AIDS political action group ACT-UP as, "operating from 'post'modern premises" and "challeng[ing] the ethical legitimacy of the majority," provides a model for a community not based on "doctrinal pronouncements" or distortions, but rather on "a *substantive* . . . claim to representation." He emphasizes that if the majority "accepts or otherwise acquiesces" to the institutionally sanctioned oppression by "the state and its apparatuses . . .citizens are under no obligation to obey the law and rules of conduct prescribed in its name" (362). He also states that the dilemma becomes most acute when individuals claim citizenship within a group or nation, but cannot give "loyalty to its current definition" (375). He acknowledges that the success of these alternative communities is a balancing act: "The wager of postmodern social movements is that they can maintain their strength by hewing to the thin line between oppositional independence to and troubled participation in the institutions of state policy . . ." (381).

Although Aronowitz is writing about the social movements created out of shared concerns and interests in relationship to the AIDS crisis and governmental funding in the 1990s, his basic questions echo Woolf's concerns expressed directly in *Three Guineas,* and frequently in her novels. Both underscore the inevitable tension between the community as defined by the values and goals of a nation ( as many communitarians promote) and those which arise in terms of shared identity and values grounded in the lived material world. The narrator of *Three Guineas* is clearly positioned in this dilemma. On one hand, she identifies with the letter writer's values, reflected in his campaign against fascism. But she also sees him as part of the community which represses women, perpetuating the patriarchal fascism of British social structure. Comparing two quotations defining the restrictive role of women in relationship to the State, the narrator tells the letter writer: "Are they not both the voices of Dictators, whether they speak English or German. . . ." (53). Her analysis of British society echoes Aronowitz's concept of "structural exclusion," inherent in many concepts of community. He identifies the economic and social boundaries of specific communities which establish this exclusion, using the example of blacks in the United States; they are "free" to participate in the "rituals of citizenship," such as voting and military service, but often are excluded from participation socially, politically, and economically in very real material terms (*Politics* 65). For Woolf, the roles British society allowed for women were clearly of this ritualistic nature; all real power was consolidated in the firmly established "traditions" of the patriarchy.

In this context, the scene in *Orlando* in which the prostitutes begin to tell their stories around the punch bowl (they never write them down), until they are silenced by the approach of men, illustrates Woolf's understanding of the furtive and fragile narrative communities of women (and men) that exist outside the patriarchal order. The "shared narratives" of a dominant group, often associated with the nation-state, can effectively silence and marginalize alternative narratives, especially those that contain resistance to or revision of the dominant narratives. Jay Clayton contrasts Boyd's, and other communitarians', emphasis on "teleological and legitimizing dimensions" of national narratives with "the 'micronarratives' of Lyotard, 'unauthorized narratives' in Foucault . . . 'discredited' narratives in Morrison," among other articulations of narratives which stand counter to the hegemonic narrative of the state. As I stated earlier, for the prostitutes around the punch bowl, clearly a marginalized space, their shared story serves as a type of "unauthorized narrative," an alternative "legitimizing force," placing them within a tradition over which they have some control. Clayton also draws a contrast between the inclusive, stable communities, such as the British Empire or the traditional patriarchal family structure which mirrored it, and "contingent affiliations, based on openness to revision, political struggle, and the subversive power of counternarratives and unofficial practices" (135). This latter definition can be used to consider the types of relationships that Woolf explores in many of her works, especially *The Years*, which led to the associative community of "Outsiders' Society" of *Three Guineas*, whose membership requires primarily the shared self-exclusion from British hegemony.

*The Years* is perhaps Woolf's most intriguing exploration of a new concept of community. As in much of her writing, Woolf challenges here the two primary "communities" in British society: the patriarchal family and the nation. By following the development of the characters over time, Woolf demonstrates her vision of the possibility of fluid, flexible communities based not solely on identification, rejecting the rigid communities of family and nation. Characters in the novel move in and out of relationship with each other, new associations develop, change over time. There is a very loose connection between many of the women, which reinforces their familial and gender identification; however, they eventually form and reform into different groups based on more specific material situations, for example the social action group that includes Rose, Kitty, Eleanor and other men and women of different social positions. As the novel progresses, in fact, there is far less emphasis on gender as defining social groupings.

Woolf goes beyond the open social groupings based on categories of identification to a reconceptualization of community, reflecting the "Outsiders' Society" of *Three Guineas,* which is fluid, flexible, but also inclusive. It is based on a redefinition of the subject in relationship to community, similar to Chantal Mouffe's concept of "citizenship": "a new conception of citizenship . . . requires a conception of the social agent . . . as the articulation of an ensemble of subject positions, corresponding to the multiplicity of social relations in which it is inscribed" ("Feminism" 323). For Mouffe, as for Woolf, the goal is to create a "'we' of radical democratic citizens, a collective political identity articulated through the principle of democratic *equivalence*" (325). She seems to agree with Woolf's belief in the "capacity of the human spirit to overflow boundaries and to make unity of multiplicity" (*TG* 143), to erase the "chalk marks, within whose mystic boundaries human beings are penned, rigidly, separately, artificially . . ." (*TG* 105). Mouffe stresses that this "*equivalence* does not eliminate *difference*"; the struggle as she defines it is not to "pursue the interests of women *as* women," but rather "the goals and aims should consist in the transformation of all discourses, practices, and social relations where the category 'woman' is constructed in a way that implies subordination" (Mouffe, "Feminism" 325). Although she does not resolve the dilemma identified by Aronowitz, she does transform it to an active process of change. Like Woolf, she seems to recognize that "power systems" as identified by Aronowitz in a relationship to community are very similar to Foucault's analysis of "power": "it induces pleasure, forms knowledge, produces discourse . . . as a productive network which runs through the whole social body" (61); in itself power is neither positive or negative. Members of all communities, then, can consciously use their power, not to "repel challenges," but rather to confront other systems of power to produce positive results.

Unlike nationhood or any essentialized grouping, Woolf's "we" in *The Years* does not have a fixed center, giving it a fluidity, reflective of her narrative style, which moves from character to character, never actually giving us one main character (although our attention, and therefore, our interest is drawn more often to some characters than others). The beginning chapters of the novel focus on the oppressive nature of the Victorian family, especially for the women as they pace and pose in the dark, stifling atmosphere of the house on Abercorn Terrace, waiting for their mother to die. And her death only increases the restrictions on their lives, as they must take over her role in caring for the father. The women then form a social group based on their shared identity as daughters and their social responsibilities as part of a social class. But as they grow older and enter the larger social context, the differences that are hinted at earlier become more developed, and their social grouping shifts from that of daughters and sisters to women with complex, multiple lives. At this point, they identify with different groupings based more on interests as well as on family and nation.

The emphasis on the adaptable nature of community becomes more directly patterned as the novel develops. Although Woolf gives clear examples of the exclusionary strength of barriers in the formation of community, they often seem at the same time to point to the organic nature of community that is restricted by the artificial identities demanded by class, gender, nationality. Kitty's relationship with the Robsons is one clear example; although she consciously feels separated from the family through her clothing and her judgment of their surrounding, she feels drawn to them by more natural shared values and understanding, and experiences a sense of loss when she returns home, where the difficulty in communication with her mother emphasizes that loss. Much later, Martin's failure to enter into a sense of community with those invited to Kitty's dinner is also very painful to him, leading him first to a self-critique, then to a critique of Kitty and the artificiality of her life. When the narrative focus is on Martin and his failure, we tend to join his critique of Kitty; when it shifts to Kitty, so do we. In fact, what Woolf demonstrates in this narrative play is the flexibility of the reader in relationship to a flexible narrative community.

As the novel progresses, we are given more examples of the possibilities of authentic community. Certainly, the new openness is largely determined by the destruction of the old order, with challenges to the family, the oppression based on gender, and to the very concept of nationality and the primacy of the British Empire. Woolf, like other women writers in the twenties and thirties, very clearly identified the repressive nature of the metanarratives that delineate the lives of individuals in society. The form and content of Woolf's work, the focus on the formation of communities based on affiliation rather than filiation, "bonding rather than bondage," in the words of Barbara Harlow (135), is a reaction to what she identified as fascism on a personal and political level and the desire to "decenter" the patriarchal control and to free individuals "from unreal loyalties" (*TG* 113). One of Woolf's most obvious deconstructive strategies is to reverse this relationship, to deflect focus from inclusive "metanarratives," to the intersecting stories of individuals living in relation to each other. She resists telling *a story,* choosing instead to present multiple stories that converge at specific points, then disperse, moving toward multiple endings. Woolf often uses the narrative technique of the walk or the "stroll" to develop the randomness of individual stories, as in *The Years*, Martin will meet Sally at St. Paul's Cathedral:

"'And who's that?' he thought, looking at someone who was standing against one of the pillars. 'Don't I know her?'" (228). An unlikely couple, they will then have a lunch together and meet Maggie "at the Round Pond at four" (231). Meetings, alliances, dinners, parties, often have a sense of the fortuitous, an element of chance encounter which resists the "plotting" of traditional narrative in favor of reformations of established social patterns.

Woolf uses this disruption of "logical" narratives, the illogical, improbable narrative wanderings of many of her novels, as a strategy for deconstructing existing discursive structure, much as Gayatri Spivak defines "affirmative deconstruction" (20). Spivak sees deconstruction as a means of identifying what has been "left out" of the "great narratives." Every narrative, she states, "has an end in view," and "[w]hen an end is defined, other ends are rejected, and one might not know what those ends are." The post-structural project, she states, is to "know the limits of narratives, rather than establish the narratives as solutions for the future, for the arrival of social justice . . ." (18-9). This resistance to closure is very important to Woolf, and her works tend to move, not to a resolution, but to a "threshold," such as Lily's bold stroke on the canvas, Mrs. Dalloway's moment of recognition, or Eleanor's anticipatory "And now?" in the dawn at the end of *The Years*.

*The Years*, then, chronicles the "deconstruction" of the patriarchal family, providing family members with openings in the social narrative so that they can choose how to live their lives. Some form new relationships, not based on the established institutions of marriage and nation, providing new "traditions" and new possibilities. By modeling the movement from this patriarchal center to a new vision, Woolf's narrative does not reject the relationship of subject to community, but rather resituates the subject, providing alternative "conceptual frameworks," a redefined position in a redefined community. In the contrast to the orginary concept of tradition supported by communitarians, Woolf emphasizes a sense of tradition revised by looking back through women's eyes, consciously retrieving from the past positive models, and rejecting or revising the repressive ones in terms of the present. In this sense, Woolf's subject is not "decentered," but rather asserts the multiple identities that allow her to be part of multiple social groups. As Mouffe writes, "we can conceive of the social agent as constituted by an ensemble of subject positions that can never be totally fixed in a closed system of differences, constructed by a diversity of discourses among which there is no necessary relation, but a constant movement of over-determination and displacement" (318). Individual identity, in these terms, consists of constantly shifting positions which are often in contestation; an individual can inhabit these multiple positions and be dominant in one and subordinate in another.

In *The Years*, Delia's final party is a culmination of a narrative whose characters move in and out of connection, physically, intellectually, and emotionally. The community that forms throughout the novel is contingent, fluid, inclusive. Not only are members of different genders, ages, and class backgrounds; the community also includes foreigners (challenging the community based on nationality); homosexuals (challenging the need for heterogeneous sexuality); and most interestingly, Sally, who in many contexts would be considered "deviant." And although they come together at the "party," they each have other affiliations, belong to other communities. Peggy, for example, is very conscious of this, remaining connected to her community at work, even as she becomes part of the heterogeneous community around her.

Delia's party disperses with the dawn; the prostitutes disperse when they hear men on the stairs. However, for the individuals comprising these communities, one identity does not erase another; one is not more 'real' than another. Woolf demonstrates the possibility of the individual to "negotiate" between different communities, without "losing" her sense of identity. Each community has a metaphorical Punch bowl, a center, to which she can return. Woolf highlights, in comparing Orlando with the prostitutes, that theirs is not an attempt to become part of a patriarchal world of discourse, but rather to preserve their own language separate and apart from it. Like Eleanor, Renny, Sally, Nicholas, North in *The Years,* and like the Outsiders' Society, they function consciously within the dilemma perceived by Aronowitz, identifying with a certain role in relation to the nation, but retaining their own community and identity on the margin. The margin actually becomes a space in which to develop their communities and the power systems which support their identities: "we believe we can help you most . . . by working for our common ends . . .ends . . .outside your society, not within" (*TG* 106). Woolf envisions her "we" as citizens of a radical, democratic community, celebrating difference at the same time as they rejoice in shared stories and values.

**Works Cited**


Aronowitz, Stanley. "Against the Liberal State." In *Social Postmodernism: Beyond Identity Politics*. Eds. Linda Nicholson and Steven Seidman. Cambridge: Cambridge U. P., 1995. 357-383.

——. *The Politics of Identity: Class, Culture, Social Movements*. New York: Routledge, 1992.

Clayton, Jay. *The Pleasures of Babel.* Oxford: Oxford U. P., 1993.

Connolly, William E. "Democracy and Contingency." In *Democracy and Possessive Individualism: The Intellectual Legacy of C. B. Macpherson.* Ed. Joseph H. Carens. Albany: State U of New York P, 1993. 194-219.

Etzioni, Amitai. *The New Golden Rule: Community and Morality in a Democratic Society*. New York: Basic Books, 1997.

Foucault, Michel. "Truth and Power." In *The Foucault Reader*. Ed. Paul Rabinow. New York: Pantheon Books, 1984. 51-75.

Harlow, Barbara. *Resistance Literature*. New York: Methuen, 1987.

Mouffe, Chantal. "Feminism, Citizenship, and Radical Democratic Politics." In *Social Postmodernism: Beyond Identity Politics.* Eds. Linda Nicholson and

Steven Seidman. Cambridge: Cambridge UP, 1995. 315-331.
——. "Liberalism and Modern Democracy." *In Democracy and Possessive Individualism: the Intellectual Legacy of C. B. Macpherson*. Ed. Joseph H. Carens. Albany: State U of New York P, 1993. 175-193.
Rawls, John. *A Theory of Justice*. Cambridge, Mass.: Belknap, 1971.
Spivak, Gayatri. *The Post-Colonial Critic: Interviews, Strategies, Dialogues*. Ed. Sarah Harasym. New York: Routledge, 1990.
Woolf, Virginia. *Orlando*. San Diego: Harvest, 1956.
——. *Three Guineas*. San Diego: Harvest, 1966.
——. *The Years*. San Diego: Harvest, 1965.

**Diana Royer**

## Remaking Virginia: A Caution for Readers

Hermione Lee said that someone writing on Woolf "can start with a theory or a belief and can see her always in terms of it, since, like Shakespeare, she is a writer who lends herself to infinitely various interpretation" (3). Lee opens her recent book *Virginia Woolf* by noting how others have started their biographies of Woolf: with family history; with social and intellectual setting; "by thinking of her as a victim, as someone who is going to kill herself" (3). Lee goes on to mention something many Woolf scholars can understand: "I am also afraid of presuming. All readers of Virginia Woolf's diaries . . . will feel an extraordinary sense of intimacy with the voice that is talking there. They will want to call her Virginia, and speak proprietorially about her life" (4).

At the Eighth annual conference, we discussed Woolf as a member of various communities. I would like to explore the possibility that we sometimes make her a member of a community to which she might not rightfully belong. I want to look at my own work and ask myself if I'm being a sensitive reader or an overreader. Over the past few years I reread Woolf's journals, letters, essays and novels looking for her attitudes toward food and her body, and I came to see her as disliking her physical self and having anorectic tendencies. But am I "speak[ing] proprietorially about her life"? *Did* Virginia Woolf actually have an eating disorder? Or do I want to believe that in order to feel a special connection with her, having once had an eating disorder myself?

In the Spring 1998 issue of *Virginia Woolf Miscellany*, Vara Neverow reviews Eileen Barrett and Patricia Cramer's collection *Virginia Woolf: Lesbian Readings*. Neverow remarks that the collection "reveals how profoundly cultural context determines the way we interpret literary texts. Such a landmark volume could only have come into existence at this particular historical moment, a moment when lesbian studies has finally become an established discipline with its own vocabulary of analysis, its own discursive validity" (6). Neverow predicts that Barrett and Cramer's work "will almost certainly have an impact comparable to that of such transformative works" as those by Herbert Marder, Roger Poole, and Louise DeSalvo. "A common thread links [the earlier] controversial studies" and the latest: Neverow says, "each has radically challenged received notions of Woolf and has generated heated debate" (6). Such ongoing discussion is what we want in Woolf studies, of course. As long as each critic is upfront about his or her approach, is there a problem with reading Woolf through these various critical lenses? After all, aren't literary and cultural studies comprised of theorizing?

Louise DeSalvo writes, in the preface to her 1989 book *Virginia Woolf: The Impact of Childhood Sexual Abuse on her Life and Work*, "My thinking on Woolf has changed over the course of these years largely as a result of the insights from the disciplines of feminist inquiry, the history of the family, Victorian studies, and the changes in psychoanalytic theory that stress personal history rather than internal drives as causative factors in neurosis. These disciplines now make it possible to understand Virginia Woolf's life in the widest possible context" (xvi). Actually, the context would be made wider still. In his 1992 study *Virginia Woolf and Manic-Depressive Illness*, Thomas Caramagno declares, "In this interdisciplinary study of Virginia Woolf I reexamine her madness and her fiction in the light of recent discoveries about the biological basis of manic-depressive illness" (1). He offers this as a corrective to the "outmoded, simplistic Freudian model of this disorder," instead "integrating neuroscience, psychobiography, and literary theory" (1). DeSalvo and Caramagno seem to be coming at Woolf from different directions, external and internal. Ultimately, the two books work together, building a more complete picture of Woolf than either study taken alone. As readers assess all they have read on Woolf, shake out those parts they deem less useful, implausible, or simply wrongheaded and gather up the rest, they may create their own Woolf. Which is the "real" Virginia?

None, of course. Joyce Carol Oates observed in a recent *New York Times Book Review* article titled "Believing What We Read, and Vice Versa" that "language by its nature tends to distort experience. . . . Contemporary biographies and memoirs that purport to replicate conversations and nuances of behavior across decades are clearly fictional in technique, if not in essence." Further, Oates says, "No matter that the subject's life might not have conformed to a pattern or a story, the task is to find it. What biographer will admit that his subject lacks narrative shapeliness? Between an honest but dull book and a not entirely honest but lively one, how many biographers would hesitate?" We can't know the "real" Virginia Woolf, but is it fair to ask which is the most accurate Virginia? I think it is. Distortions can occur, as Oates is not the first to suggest, and injustices can be done to a writer's work. Let me offer as example my recent experience with a different writer.

One of the things I struggle to do as a professor of lower-division literature courses taught primarily to non-English majors with limited backgrounds in literature is to dispel the myths students have acquired along the way from previous teachers and from popular culture. After recently teaching Edgar Allan Poe to some hundred students in four different classes, I swore I would never teach him again. There were a number of problems—students not caring enough to look up words they didn't know and too inexperienced as readers to follow Poe's sentence structures—but the biggest problem, and one I failed to conquer, was students hanging on to the three-D myth of Poe: drunk, drugged, and deranged. No matter that I told them that the root of these stories was in Rufus Griswold's largely fabricated biography, or that writers don't necessarily live out everything they write about, or that I quite logically asked them if they really thought someone could consistently churn out high quality, polished fiction and criticism while wacked on opium; no matter—they knew the "real" Poe. And the essays by such students on his stories were reductive, shallow, and unanalytical. To me this is a clear case of how applying distorted information creates a false image of a writer, allowing the "critic" to simplify or dismiss his work.

I taught Woolf to these same students, and while she was an unfamiliar figure to most of them, and hence they had no favorite myths about her, they did seize on the information provided in the Dover Thrift Edition of *Monday or Tuesday* that she suffered a recurring mental illness and killed herself. I showed them John Fuegi and Jo Francis's *The War Within*, the video portrait of Virginia Woolf, and a popular question afterwards was why did she kill herself? Why was she depressed? There is a fascination with such personal information, something all teachers are aware of and that Hermione Lee noted in particular about Woolf as she was writing the biography. Lee says, "I have noticed that in the course of any conversation about this book I would, without fail, be asked one or more of the same four questions: Is it true that she was sexually abused as a child? What was her madness and why did she kill herself? Was Leonard a good or a wicked husband? Wasn't she the most terrible snob?" (3). I felt similar frustration. Despite my introduction to modernism and stream-of-consciousness style, a number of students decided Woolf's prose style and content were little more than the rambling of an insane mind. When I see students using limited biographical knowledge to respond to literature, I am quick to criticize their methods. But I have to ask myself if I too perform distortions when reading empathically and using my knowledge of a writer's life.

In a paper I gave at a previous Woolf conference, "Food and the Physical Self in Woolf's Life and Fiction," I used a quote from *The Voyage Out* in the title: "Ugly in body, repulsive in mind." I saw Rachel, who has this thought, making connections among the body, food, and intellect, as does the character St. John Hirst. Reading Woolf's journals with antennae up for references to food, body, and intellect, I saw her from an early age associating people unfavorably with animals, making fun of those with big appetites and large bodies. Cousin Katherine demolishes a pineapple at lunch, cousin Dorothea arrives "as fat as a grampus, & blowing like that animal—terrible in her heat, & perspiration; & general cowlike stout appearance" (*PA* 105). I used feminist theory on Woolf's essays and fiction to see her abhorrence of food and body as related to the oppression of patriarchal society, and I used DeSalvo's book to see it as related to abusive family relationships. Woolf's journals note a repugnance for the weight she gained during doctor-prescribed rest cures that Leonard supervised. She feared that when too heavy in body she was slow in mind. I felt that the pattern of her life—forced abstention from work, proscribed feeding—emerged in the patterns of her fiction. As I read the passage in *The Voyage Out* where Hewett kisses the fevered Rachel when he thinks she's asleep and Rachel opens her eyes to see "an old woman slicing a man's head off with a knife" (320), I felt Woolf's word choice of "slicing" was a deliberate allusion to food. Throughout the book Rachel hates the dressing up and the social meals, and I connected this to Woolf herself, who tells us in "A Sketch of the Past" that she felt like "a horse brought into the show ring" for George Duckworth's inspection before social events (151).

Seizing on such comments in her essays, in another Woolf conference paper I proposed to discuss clothing in her novels. First, of course, I read the journals and letters again, looking this time for any mention of apparel. There were lots of references, and I saw the young Woolf embarrassed by clothing (garters falling down) and annoyed by it (preferring to buy books with her allowance rather than hats, stays, and gloves). The older Woolf kept the disdainful attitude toward clothing, complaining about having to shop for it or needing to change for dinner. I returned yet again to patriarchal society and family relations: Virginia Stephen had to cut short her studies and artistic endeavors to dress for tea and evening social events, and she prepared herself in front of a mirror that George Duckworth gave her. A hideous reminder of both Gerald's and George's abuse, I said in my paper, one couldn't find a more perfect association, and, perhaps, an explanation for Woolf's primary discomfort with clothes and appearance.

Maybe so. Maybe not. Perhaps I am using my own past feelings about food and my ongoing feelings about my body as a way to understand Woolf. I see patterns in her life and fiction, but are they *my* patterns, imposed out of a desire to know her, to connect to her? Maybe her mocking others' physiques and eating habits is just Swiftian humor, a poking fun at the human animal that many writers, and many humans in general, do, and not necessarily linked to a personal problem with food. I got sidetracked in that conference paper and never made it through an in-depth look at *The Voyage Out*, *Orlando*, and *The Years*, as I had proposed. Instead I read scholarly works on fashion and especially on the lifestyles and attire of Victorian and Edwardian British citizens of Woolf's social class. I plucked every complaint about clothing out of her letters as further evidence for what she states in "A Sketch of the Past": "Everything to do with dress—to be fitted, to come into a room wearing a new dress—still frightens me; at least makes me shy, self-conscious, uncomfortable" (68). Yes, critics have convinced me that the emotional abuse George Duckworth put her through over clothing probably had something to do with these feelings. But her negative comments on clothing predate his reign over her social excursions. Some critics suggest her discomfort with her body, and by extension clothing, goes back to her childhood sexual abuse. But maybe Woolf was just a person who hated the fuss made over clothing, cared not for fashion. I see a pattern in Woolf's life regarding clothing and a concomitant one in her fiction. I see Woolf's personal attitudes appearing in her characters' minds, and I see her depicting societal attitudes too—such as in *Orlando* where much is said about patriarchy through having Orlando become a woman and wear women's fashion. Maybe this last point on societal attitudes is one I should pay more attention to. Perhaps Woolf's remarks on bodies and clothes have nothing to do with an eating disorder. Perhaps there is a larger self-loathing on Woolf's part, as a human being and thus part of a questionable species.

I've offered this paper not to oppose theory, but as a cautionary example of its possible misapplication. It is exciting to take a theory, apply it to written texts, and see the text respond, falling within the pattern we hoped to find there. In fact, I've long been a proponent of Louise Rosenblatt, whose 1938 study *Literature as Exploration* (still in print) makes such statements as, "The literary work exists in the live circuit set up between reader and text: the reader infuses intellectual and emotional meanings into the pattern of verbal symbols, and those symbols channel his thoughts and feelings. Out of this complex process emerges a more or less organized imaginative experience" (24). Further, Rosenblatt says, "Language is socially evolved, but it is always constituted by individuals, with their particular histories" (25). Later, Stanley Fish proposed, "The critic has the responsibility of becoming not one but a number of informed readers, each of whom will be identified by a matrix of political, cultural, and literary determinants" (87). If, as Norman Holland suggested, "any individual shapes the materials the literary work offers him—including its author—to give him what he characteristically both wishes and fears" (125), we would do well to heed Susan Feagin's observation that "one thing that is missing in most reader-response theory is attention to the notion of warrant: what warrants or justifies one's responding in the particular way one does, to what one does?" (4). I find myself facing a problem: literature, especially modernist literature like Woolf's, invites, even forces us to deal with gaps, to engage with the text, to create it in the act of reading it. How do we do this without damaging it? For I have argued earlier in this paper that readers can corrupt a text. I have no answer to this question. We must create in the act of reading, but we need to be careful that we don't impose a pattern, fill in the gaps with our mental creations, distort any writer's words through unjustified projection. When we do this, we aren't listening to the writer; we are only hearing ourselves.

**Works Cited**

Caramagno, Thomas. *The Flight of the Mind: Virginia Woolf's Art and Manic-Depressive Illness.* Berkeley: U of California P, 1992.

DeSalvo, Louise. *Virginia Woolf: The Impact of Childhood Sexual Abuse on Her Life and Work.* New York: Ballantine, 1989.

Feagin, Susan L. *Reading With Feeling: The Aesthetics of Appreciation.* Ithaca: Cornell UP, 1996.

Fish, Stanley E. "Literature in the Reader: Affective Stylistics." Tompkins 70-100.

Holland, Norman N. "Unity, Identity, Text, Self." Tompkins 118-133.

Lee, Hermione. *Virginia Woolf.* New York: Knopf, 1997.

Neverow, Vara. Rev. of *Virginia Woolf: Lesbian Readings*, ed. Eileen Barrett and Patricia Cramer. *Virginia Woolf Miscellany* 51 (1998): 6-7.

Oates, Joyce Carol. "Believing What We Read, and Vice Versa." *The New York Times Book Review* 26 Feb. 1998: A23.

Rosenblatt, Louise M. *Literature as Exploration.* 1938. New York: MLA, 1995.

Tompkins, Jane P., ed. *Reader-Response Criticism: From Formalism to Post-Structuralism.* Baltimore: The Johns Hopkins UP, 1980.

Woolf, Virginia. *A Passionate Apprentice: The Early Journals, 1897-1909.* Ed. Mitchell A. Leaska. San Diego: HBJ, 1990.

——. "A Sketch of the Past." *Moments of Being.* Ed. Jeanne Schulkind. 2nd ed. San Diego: Harvest, 1985. 64-159.

——. *The Voyage Out.* New York: Signet, 1991.

# Narratological Communities

## Featured Conversation: Artists and Community

### Introductions

True to the traditions of the annual Virginia Woolf conference, the St. Louis organizers experimented with traditional conference structuring. The conference sponsored two featured conversations in an effort to break down conventional patterns by promoting participation by the audience. As best we could, we attempted to give intimacy to the settings and to undermine the spatial constructions of hierarchy by using props and various seating arrangements. To promote audience participation, "conversationalists" opened topics with initial 20-minute staged discussions; they then mediated impromptu discussion from the floor, which was the focus of each event. The three artists in this conversation witnessed to Woolf's creation of community through their artistic responses to Woolf. Their initial conversation opened up to a vigorous response of questions and comments.

*Georgia Johnston*

I always enjoy our annual Virginia Woolf conferences, but of the many memorable papers, panels, and other sorts of events I have attended at these gatherings, the Artists' Conversation which Georgia Johnston organized last summer was certainly the most remarkable. And I do not say that just because I was assigned the happy task of presiding over it!

The charming setting arranged by Georgia already predisposed everyone for something special; an oriental rug, antique lamp, and cozy chairs took away the auditorium feel of the venue. Our three artists, all working in different ways and all from different communities, had one important experience in common: each had been influenced in profound and lasting ways by Virginia Woolf's writing and life. Their initial presentations made us all feel close to them and to their creative processes, so that the conversation did become general, but in a way impossible to retrace here. I remember worrying earlier about the lack of "rehearsal" and yet that turned out to be its strength. What emerged in the presentations had never been said before and the interchanges that followed were spontaneous, surprising, tender and telling.

I can honestly say, as I am not always able to in our academic meetings, that Virginia Woolf would herself have been interested and rather proud, had she been there. I surely was proud, and am now, to introduce you to Marilou Awiakta, poet/philosopher writer from Memphis; Sigrid Nunez, writer from New York, and Suzanne Bellamy, writer and visual artist from Australia.

*J. J. Wilson*

*(Circumstances, unfortunately, prevented Awiakta from being able to contribute to the* Selected Papers. *Pieces by Suzanne Bellamy and Sigrid Nunez follow.)*

## Suzanne Bellamy
### Imagining the Muse

The opportunity to participate in the Artists' Conversation during the Woolf conference in St. Louis with Sigrid Nunez, Awiakta and facilitator J.J. Wilson was a special experience for me, coming as I do from another culture and country. Creating a fireside chat with touches of the Bloomsbury studio ambience—comfy chairs, a rug—helped to break the model of previous conference ways and to invoke the spirit of fusion of forms so central to Woolf herself. We seemed to be transported into a new space, to draw on a powerful conversational mode, bringing the severed parts together both between, within and among those who came. Could it have been a little like this at the Memoir Club?

Sigrid, Awiakta and I had never met before the conference, and so the expansive spirit of J. J. Wilson was the catalyst for blending our separate contributions in such a way as to release new thoughts and links, new insights about the creative process, some wonderful humor, and speculative future pathways. For my part, I chose to tell something of the story of Woolf as a core spirit in my creative life as artist and writer, through turning points and life-changing times, as well as to outline some of my projects inspired by Woolf.

## First Contact

Australia's first woman publisher, Bessie Guthrie, brought me into the world of Virginia Woolf in the early 1970's, when we were in Women's Liberation together in Sydney, and working on a feminist newspaper. I was a young student, she was in her late 60's, a Woolf lover, bibliophile, radical thinker, and activist. Bessie was a critical influence in my life, and when she died in 1977, I inherited her library, including all her Woolf books, which I have continued to add to over the years. It was just at the start of the explosion of new diary, letter, and biographical material, so she missed all that. When I was asked to write an essay about Woolf in my creative life, twenty years later, in 1997, by Patricia Cramer for her book of Lesbian Readings on Woolf, my mind jumped right back to Bessie.

There are so many ways to view the structure of a life, an imagination, creative output, moments of being. After twenty-plus years of writing, reading, creating art work about Woolf, it was a magical moment for me to sit down and write about my life through the lens of my most powerful muse, and the link-people like Bessie Guthrie, who had handed her on to me.

## Life Choices

On reflection, I feel that Virginia Woolf is an incredible model for radical life choices, for leaps into the unknown territory of the self. Several generations of feminists have explored her ideas together, and I have been the beneficiary of all this. She demands that we take ourselves seriously, put work at the center of our lives, test out the limits of our communities, take risks with form in the work and in the ways we relate to each other. I threw myself into this world, and have kept some form of connection to the written words and the evolving story since that time in the early 1970's.

Trained originally as an historian, teaching academic women's studies, I made a choice to break from that pathway and find a life as artist and writer, independent scholar, and activist. Woolf's influence was central. At those inevitable times when this felt like madness, I returned to her work and story for energy and confidence in the project of renewal of the self. Just as she did, I learned to shape my life around the communities I could live within. Early training in ceramics, sculpture and print making, as well as a deep interest in archaeology and prehistory, were all rekindled in me in the context of the international women's movement and its search for new multitudinous visions. Woolf's disciplined eclecticism and intense interest in everything around her has always thrilled and directed me to combine thoroughness with rebellion against specialization. She fed all the parts of her creative imagination, a broad and rich diet—words, images, shapes, colors, sound—as well as multiple levels of consciousness, from the tiny trivia of a daily moment to the cerebral drift of time before memory. She becomes multiple muse, giving method and forms but mainly a pathway to new choices. This relationship between Woolf and me has never failed me in all the years.

Her very practical influence, and that of her broader circle of Bloomsbury and Omega, the painters and critics and activists of her network, also gave me ideas for a sustainable life outside the academy. I moved my studio to the country, created Strike-A-Light Workshops, and now the Mongarlowe Workshops, as working studios as well as focal points for ideas and extended intellectual projects. The inspiration of the Hogarth Press and the creation of one's own control of production has also been a great experiment for me, moving outside the gallery system and when possible placing art work in intellectual contexts, writing about as well as exhibiting forms, traveling to conferences in many countries. These experiments and experiences then fed back into the new work, watching and being within the flow of international feminism. I wrote this story in several places, as "The Pattern Behind The Words" in Pat Cramer and Eileen Barrett's *Virginia Woolf: Lesbian Readings* and as "The Narrow Bridge Of Art and Politics" in Renate Klein and Diane Bell's *Radically Speaking: Feminism Reclaimed.*

### Dual Creativity

As both artist and writer, I have always responded to Woolf's embodiment of this way of seeing in her work. She has the touch of the visual surreal about her which thrills me and is the key to how visual artists can respond so dramatically to her work. It's not so simple as saying she was surrounded by an art movement. Her own way of seeing is so muscular and sculptural for me: she makes her words and thought forms do what other materials can do. She conceives the world of the nonverbal and fills the mind with the stuff of raw creativity. Inviting artists to participate in the forum of ideas and new explorations of Woolf can really grow, building on the brilliant work of the painter Isota Tucker Epes, whom I had the chance to meet in St. Louis. Artists and writers exploring this aspect of Woolf have much to offer here, in all forms—music, drama, as well as all kinds of visual arts.

### Recent Projects

As part of the Artists' Conversation, I enjoyed describing some of my most recent Woolf-inspired projects. A multimedia installation called *The Lost Culture of Women's Liberation, 1969–1974, The Pre-Dynastic Phase* is a mock archaeological dig in 500 years' time of a women's "sacred site," a meeting house in Sydney where the first women's liberation group in Australia met. As a member of the original group, I was able to incorporate authentic material but in a fantasist mode, inspired by *Orlando.* I used Woolf's thinking about how to conceive of historical biography, how to write about one's own time in larger forms, how to play with systems of knowledge themselves bound by their own times, and how to use humor and shifting consciousness. She has become for me the most marvelous theoretical companion.

The conference provided me with a forum to launch the first full catalogue of another long-term project, my *New Hogarth Little Lesbian Book*

*Series*. Small high-fired porcelain books with individual once-only titles, they play on the labyrinthine world of published "knowledge," making me the most prolific lesbian publisher in the world. From the back list, early titles such as *Old Norse Lesbians*, *Lesbian Microwave Cookery*, *The Lesbian Armada*, *Lenin: The Lesbian Question*, *Lesbian Symphonies For Original Lesbian Instruments*, as well as new titles for the conference, including *Miss LaTrobe's Complete Manuscripts*, and various *Lost Diaries* of Woolf herself. A deeply serious comic project, the series is my contribution to archaeology and the world of the collector.

In response to questions and dialogue with the marvelous Isota Tucker Epes, I was also able to explain a little of the process behind the large print series on Woolf I exhibited at the Plymouth conference in 1997. Each of the panelists described what came first in the business of visualizing Woolf, her work, her world, and our vision of her. For me, the print series began as a waking dream in which I saw Virginia, Vita and Vanessa talking to me through the walls of their houses, extending to their ambient creative spaces in general and their intense interwoven narratives with each other. On seeing this in my mind, I wondered how to invent a method, and that became the work at hand, with my trusting that the original sight would flow through to the paper. On the studio journey, the words joined in, passages from novels, letters, and diaries, blending with the burst of wild color in the prints. These conference conversations between makers are so rich, breaking through studio isolation and putting visual artists into a healthy relation to the wonderful broad body of Woolf scholarship. The contribution of this format for the participants alone is incalculable and praiseworthy.

### The Great Spirit

Listening to Awiakta speak about her relationship with Virginia Woolf was a great privilege for me. In moving us as a group to a more spirit-based meditative language, she lifted the conversation into new territory and gave both Sigrid and me a way of saying things we may not have originally planned. I recall Sigrid speaking of the healing quality in Woolf's words for people she had interviewed during her research. For myself, I decided to speak about the particular meditative/imaginative connection I have developed with Woolf as active muse, and about which I wrote for the first time in *Virginia Woolf: Lesbian Readings*. Virginia Woolf as presence is very real for me, in a developing studio-based creative visualization that I have created over many years in which I visit, discuss projects, sit in deck chairs, and have the opportunity to see her at work. I described her studio, flooded with prismatic light, in which she stands at a large, angled drawing board, in the form of a computer-like circuit board. She has dozens of tiny pairs of tweezers and endless little containers of mysterious materials unknown to me. Here she creates moving patterns, using a method she calls mosaic science, intended to alter brain waves by direct seeing, creating what she has named "the pattern behind the words." This is where writing has evolved for her. I

NEW
HOGARTH
LITTLE
LESBIAN
BOOK
SERIES
1998
CATALOGUE

The Little Lesbian Book Series is named in honour of Virginia Woolf's Hogarth Press, and as a contribution to archaeology.
Created and published at Mongarlowe, NSW, Australia. First edition of Complete Catalogue. 1998. Copyright Suzanne Bellamy.

© 1998

The hand-made porcelain books inthis series are fired in a reducing gas kiln to 1300 degrees Centigrade at the studios of Suzanne Bellamy, in Mongarlowe, NSW, Australia. Only one copy of each title is fired. All rights reserved. © 1998.

**1998 CATALOGUE**

LESBIAN ECONOMIC THEORY
NEW LESBIAN FOREIGN POLICY
LESBIAN DOMESTIC POLICY
LESBIAN TV TAKEOVERS
OLD LESBIAN RUGS AND KILIMS
THE LESBIAN SHOPPER
LESBIAN OPTICS
LESBIAN GARDEN DESIGN
LESBIAN TOFU RECIPES
LESBIAN MILLINERY
LESBIAN POST OFFICES
LESBIAN TAX
THE GREAT LESBIAN TREATY
LESBIAN TABLEWARE
GREAT LESBIAN STRIKES
LESBIAN EMAIL STORIES
GREAT LESBIAN RAILWAYS
OLD LESBIAN STAMPS
LESBIAN MINIATURES
LESBIAN SALAD DRESSINGS
LESBIAN COLOUR THEORY
THE LESBIAN FRACTAL
GREAT LESBIAN CITIES
LESBIAN ISLANDS
THE LESBIAN FALAFEL
SUNDRIED LESBIAN FRUIT
LESBIAN PASTA
THE LESBIAN DOLLAR
THE LESBIAN ARMADA
GREAT LESBIAN PYRAMIDS
THE LESBIAN EYE

LESBIAN IKEBANA
THE LESBIAN MILLENIUM
LESBIAN NURSERY RHYMES
LESBIAN DIALECTS
THATCHING THE LESBIAN ROOF
RESTORING LESBIAN ANTIQUITIES
FINE LESBIAN PORCELAIN
THE LESBIAN THERMOMETER
LESBIAN STICKY DATE PUDDINGS
OLD LESBIAN JAMS AND JELLIES
LESBIAN AIR,WATER AND FOOD
PRUNING THE LESBIAN ROSE
NATURAL LESBIAN ELEGANCE
THE 10 LONGEST LESBIAN RIVERS
OLD STONE AGE LESBIAN TOOLS
THE GREAT LESBIAN MERINGUE
DARWIN ON LESBIAN NATURAL SELECTION
EARLY LESBIAN POLITICAL PARTIES
19th LESBIAN BRIDGES
LESBIAN CAVE ART ON VENUS
LESBIAN RUGWEAVING TECHNIQUES
THE HYDROPONIC LESBIAN
LESBIAN COMPANY MERGERS
ENDANGERED LESBIAN SPECIES
LESBIAN EARTHMOVING EQUIPMENT
OLD LESBIAN CHAMBER POTS
THE GREAT LESBIAN MIGRATION
LESBIAN ENGINEERING MIRACLES
REALLY STUPID LESBIAN STORIES
LESBIAN DRAINAGE SYSTEMS
LESBIAN RESTORATION COMEDY

CARBON DATING FOR LESBIAN ARCHAEOLOGISTS
LESBIANS IN THE NAPOLEONIC WARS
THE FOURTH GUINEA - VIRGINIA WOOLF
WOOLF AND STEIN - TEXT OF SECRET TALKS
MRS.RAMSAY'S FAVOURITE RECIPES
SLATER'S PINS - TRADE CATALOGUE
TO THE LIGHTHOUSE - SUMMER BOAT TIMETABLES
VIRGINIA AND VITA - PRIVATE PHOTO ALBUM
LILY BRISCOE - COMPLETE PAINTINGS, COLOUR SEPARATIONS.
THE ACT ITSELF - A SEQUEL - VIRGINIA WOOLF
MISS LATROBE - COMPLETE SCRIPTS AND STAGE NOTES
BLOODROOT - A LESBIAN LEGEND OF THE 20TH CENTURY
THE RETURN OF LESBIAN CULTURAL PROPERTY
PHOENICIAN LESBIAN BOAT BUILDING TECHNIQUES
LESBIAN SYMPHONIES FOR ORIGINAL LESBIAN INSTRUMENTS

**BACKLIST**

OLD NORSE LESBIANS
LESBIA SAPIENS
THE LESBIAN PALATE
LESBIAN BAD TASTE
LESBIAN HERITAGE
LESBIAN VEGETABLES
LESBIAN CABLE KNITS
LESBIAN SPACE STATIONS
LESBIAN TABLE MANNERS
THE LESBIAN MONSOON
LESBIAN GENETICS
LESBIAN SPEED RECORDS
THE LESBIAN SUMMIT
BLOOMSBURY LESBIANS
LESBIAN PASSPORTS
GREAT LESBIAN SOUFFLES
CITY OF LESBIANS
THE RENAISSANCE LESBIAN
FINE LESBIAN CHINA
LESBIAN LINEAR B
LESBIANS OF THE RAJ
LESBIAN VOGUE
LESBIAN HORSE PARADES
THE LESBIAN ALPHABET
LESBIANS IN SPACE
GREAT LESBIAN CURRIES
THE GREAT LESBIAN WALL
LESBIAN FURNISHINGS
THE HUMOURLESS LESBIAN
LESBIAN SACRED TEXTS
LESBIAN PLUMBING

LESBIANS AT THE ROUND TABLE
LESBIAN MICROWAVE COOKERY
LESBIAN MONETARY POLICY
LESBIAN MUSEUM PRACTICE
LESBIAN MARITIME PRACTICES
NEW LESBIAN MONETARY ORDER
LESBIAN ANTARCTIC TERRITORY
LESBIAN FLORA AND FAUNA
CLIMBING THE LESBIAN MOUNT
A LESBIAN PHARMACOPAEA
OVER THE LESBIAN RAINBOW
VENUS OF WILLENDORF DIET
ALBANIAN LESBIANS SPEAKOUT
LESBIAN TICKERTAPE PARADES
LISTS LESBIANS MAKE
GREAT LESBIAN SPONGE CAKES
LESBIAN WEIGHTS &MEASURES
TROUPING LESBIAN COLOURS
ROMANESQUE LESBIAN ART
OLD LESBIAN CLIMBING KILNS
LESBIAN SUPERCONDUCTORS
EUROPEAN LESBIANPARLIAMENT
LESBIAN WORLD ATLAS
LESBIAN PIRATES OF ATLANTIS
TUDOR AND STUART LESBIANS
LENIN-THE LESBIAN QUESTION
LESBIAN LACEMAKING
LESBIAN JOCKEYS
LESBIAN GEOGRAPHY
CYCLADIC LESBIAN COINS
LESBIAN MARCHING BANDS

WILD LESBIANS OF THE SOUTH SEAS
SUSTAINABLE LESBIAN CULTURE IN THE 21ST CENTURY
THE LESBIAN BRAIN AFTER PATRIARCHY
FIRST LESBIAN EXPEDITION TO MARS
LESBIANS AT THE FALL OF TROY
THE LOST CULTURE OF WOMENS LIBERATION, 1969-1974.
SAPPHO - THE COMPLETE WORKS TRANSLATED
THE WELL OF HAPPINESS - A REVISION
SOFTWOOD CUTTINGS FOR THE LESBIAN GARDENER
COPPER REDUCTION FIRING FOR THE LESBIAN POTTER
INDIGENOUS LESBIAN CULTURES OF THE PREDYNASTIC AGE
LESBIAN CHOREOGRAPHY IN THE PARTHENON FRIEZE
MEDIEVAL LESBIAN ILLUMINATED MANUSCRIPTS
LESBIAN MEGALITHS, STONE CIRCLES & FIELD SPIRALS
BONE DENSITY IN PALAEOLITHIC LESBIANS

visit her a little like Candide, ingenuous and trying to be discreet and non-invasive, and she is very kind. I say in my essay, this is a love affair, but "nothing happens," as is correct with the muse, I suspect. Only after many visits did I realize the link between my vision and Woolf's actual experiences setting type at the Hogarth Press with little tweezers, but in crowded gloomy rooms. Her new studio has greatly improved.

In a powerful concluding conversation, Awiakta, Sigrid, and I discussed Woolf's death and her legacy in this expansive way, referring to her quality as an enduring Great Spirit. For me, the integrity and consciousness of her death has great meaning, and that moment of crossover has always seemed to me an explosion rather than an ending, where the seeds of her core scattered, to be nurtured and planted and watered by new generations of creators. I certainly see Virginia Woolf as a massive and active Muse agent. As this lovely session ended in St. Louis, it was clear that a room of Woolf lovers each in their way had developed very curious, interesting, perhaps even a little quirky relationships with their subject, worthy of some investigation in themselves. There seemed to be no end in sight to the quickening power of this great spirit and much new work to come.

**Works Cited**

Barrett, Eileen, and Patricia Cramer, eds. *Virginia Woolf: Lesbian Readings.* NY: New York UP, 1997.

Bellamy, Suzanne. "The Narrow Bridge of Art and Politics." *Radically Speaking: Feminism Reclaimed.* Ed. Diane Bell and Renate Klein. Melbourne: Zed-Spinifex, 1996. 126-34.

## Sigrid Nunez

### "Why are these pages comforting?"

In an appendix to an essay called "Ordinary Time: Virginia Woolf and Thucydides on War," the poet Anne Carson tells how on the day after her mother's funeral she found herself reading in Virginia Woolf's diaries: "looking for comfort I suppose—why are these pages comforting? They led her, after all, to the River Ouse" (Carson 130).

I am reminded of a man I once met, a tax accountant, who told me how Woolf had helped him get through his divorce. Reading volume after volume of the diaries and letters, he said, "I didn't feel so alone anymore. It was almost as if I had someone again."

Woolf's diaries and letters are works of genius, of course, and it is one of the intrinsic properties of works of genius to be a consolation to us. Another poet, Adam Zagajewski, writes: "Only in the beauty created / by others is there consolation" (60). But surely there is another reason for the solace to be taken in reading Woolf: How well she understood bereavement. How well she knew what it is to lose someone.

Writing her diaries, could Woolf have known what a help to others they might one day be? On November 17, 1934, she describes the wild vacillation in her feelings from one day to the next about her work in progress (*The Years*): "A note, by way of advising other Virginias with other books that this is the way of the thing: up down, up down—& Lord knows the truth" (*D*4 262). *Other Virginias!*

I urge creative writing students to read as much as they can of the "life-writing" (to use Woolf's word) of writers and other artists. No better way to get a true sense of the creative life, the "up down, up down" of it. And no better descriptions of the creative process are to be found than in Woolf. (W. H. Auden singled out the famous passage in *The Waves* beginning " There is a square'" and ending " this is our consolation'" [*W* 163] as the best description of the creative process that he knew.)

There is much breast beating in Woolf's diaries—she found fault with herself and her work so easily—but of what could be called whining there is none. And for all that might be (and has been) said of Woolf's egotism, one finds no self-aggrandizing complaints about how hard she has to work, no moaning and groaning over the writer's uniquely hard lot. Dark though they may be with her despair, her appalling sufferings, what "led her . . . to the River Ouse," these pages do not depress us. On the contrary, they do for us what Faulkner believed all writing should do: lift up the heart and so help us to endure.

The absence of romantic posturing and self-pity makes Woolf an ideal model for the struggling artist. Although, as we see it, she is accomplishing miracles, producing one fine book after another in the face of terrible odds, Woolf herself has a way of bringing her creative work down to the level of the ordinary—ordinary in the sense that it is something she does every day, dutifully, without noise, without fuss. Her morning's work, done mostly between breakfast and lunch—and no waiting around for flashes of genius or inspiration. (Woolf doubtless would have agreed with the artist Chuck Close that inspiration is for amateurs.) To those "other Virginias with other books" to whom Woolf addressed her note of advice, this humble, dogged, level-headed approach to writing will be immensely bracing.

We know from a letter to Vita Sackville-West that after the death of her son Julian, the devastated Vanessa found Virginia's daily consolatory visits the only thing she looked forward to, the only thing that really helped. In this letter, written on April 2, 1941, after Virginia had disappeared but before her body had been found, Vanessa recalled "hearing her voice going on and on keeping life going as it seemed when otherwise it would have stopped" (Marler 475).

I too have heard Woolf's voice going on and on. It is her intimate voice, the voice of the diaries, and it has been a comfort to me, as it has been to others, writers and artists and readers in general—women mostly, perhaps, but also some men (like the accountant). Surely it is astonishing that the record of a life riven—and ultimately destroyed—by the anguish and chaos of madness should turn out to offer such balm.

Perhaps it was from her mother that Virginia got her extraordinary ability to console. We do not know exactly what she said to Vanessa to help her through her darkest hour. We know only that it was all the right things.

**Works Cited**

Carson, Anne. "Ordinary Time: Virginia Woolf and Thucydides on War." *Fence* 1.1 (1998): 127-31.

Marler, Regina, ed. *Selected Letters of Vanessa Bell.* New York: Pantheon, 1993.

Woolf, Virginia. *The Diary of Virginia Woolf.* Ed. Anne Olivier Bell, assisted by Andrew McNeillie. Vol. 4. San Diego: Harvest, 1983.

——. *The Waves.* New York: Harvest, 1959.

Zagajewski, Adam. "In the Beauty Created by Others." *Tremor: Selected Poems.* Trans. Renata Gorczynski. New York: Farrar, 1985. 60.

## Barbara Lounsberry

### Virginia Woolf and the Community of Diarists

The theme of this volume, "Virginia Woolf and Communities," spurred me to reflect on the community of diarists—and Woolf's place within this community. I quickly realized that she interacted with not one, but several diary communities across her life.

In 1922, Arthur Ponsonby, who came from a long line of distinguished British diarists and wrote three books on diaries himself, conducted a survey of one hundred educated people chosen at random. He found that twenty-four—or almost one in four persons—had kept or were keeping diaries (41). If Ponsonby's survey provides a glimpse into diary keeping in Britain in 1922, when we look at the community surrounding Virginia Woolf, we find an even greater percentage of diarists than Ponsonby found in his study. Within the Stephen family, diary keeping seems to have been an expected activity: all Virginia's brothers and sisters kept diaries at one time or another, as did her father, his mother, and his sister. The first words we have from Virginia Stephen as a diarist suggest she considers diary writing as something of a group practice: "We have all started to keep a record of the new year—Nessa, Adrian and I," she writes at the age of fourteen (*PA* 5). Hermione Lee tells us that Thoby Stephen "kept a notebook with careful observations and drawings of birds and animals" (223). This journal may have inspired Woolf's later Asheham diary, which she kept in tandem with her Richmond diary solely for recording what she called her "meticulous observations of flowers, clouds, beetles & the price of eggs" (*D*1 179).

As her family circle shrank, and then enlarged to include the Bloomsbury set—and here I am referring to Leon Edel's *House of* [nine Bloomsbury] *Lions*—again we find a community more than half of whose members kept diaries: Virginia, Vanessa, Leonard Woolf, Lytton Strachey, and Duncan Grant. Biographies disclose that many outside the compound (who fed the lions) kept diaries as well: Violet Dickinson (notebooks), Sydney Waterlow, Ottoline Morrell, Dora Carrington, Frances Birrell, Ethel Smyth, Beatrice Webb, Harold Nicolson, Margaret Lushington, Richard Kennedy (who worked at the Hogarth Press), and Wilfred Blunt. Fellow writers who were also diarists included Katherine Mansfield, Vita Sackville-West, David Garnett, André Gide, Evelyn Waugh, Stephen Spender, Siegfried Sassoon, and Cyril Connolly. In short, Virginia Woolf seems to have moved in a habitat where diary writing was common. William Matthews, whose bibliographies of *American Diaries, British Diaries,* and *Canadian Diaries and Autobiographies* are essential for any diary scholar, noted in 1977 that from the sixteenth century onward "the majority of diarists [in English] have been and still are members of the middle classes" ("The Diary" 297). Perhaps this explains the high percentage of diarists in Woolf's social sphere. My point is that diary writing probably did not seem to Woolf an uncommon or extraordinary practice; rather, it was an activity in which many were engaged.

In fact, passages from Woolf's diaries suggest she valued the diary for its communal associations. She began a new diary book on October 8, 1917, justifying the act by explaining that "This attempt at a diary is begun on the impulse given by the discovery in a wooden box in my cupboard of an old volume, kept in 1915, & still able to make *us* laugh at Walter Lamb" (emphasis added; *D*1 55). And Leonard will not only be included in the laughter, but he "has promised to add his page when he has something to say" (*D*1 55). Virginia may have been reading at this time the *Journal* written by the Goncourt brothers—Michael Holroyd tells us she urged Lytton Strachey to read it about this time (415)—and she may be imagining her 1917 diary as a similar diary with two voices. She acknowledges she will have to overcome Leonard's modesty to secure his participation. However, the entry he finally contributes—more than a month later—is one railing at "committees":

> One of the worst Webb meals to which we have been. . . . Mrs. W[ebb] began to talk almost at once about the Reconstruction Committee which she is on. She talked incessantly & every tenth word was "committee". She has apparently succeeded in inventing a committee for babies, a committee for lunatics, a committee for the sick, a committee for the disabled, & a committee for the dead; but the scheme or the Cosmos is not complete because she has so far failed to invent a Committee for the Able-bodied & unemployed. However she still has hopes. (*D*1 74)

This anti-committee entry marks the end of the collaborative diary. Virginia also expressed disappointment at her diaristic culture's lack of community when it came to sharing journals with one another. "The diary habit has come to life at Charleston," she reports on January 3, 1918. "Bunny [Garnett] sat up late on the Old Year's night writing, & Duncan came back with a ledger, bought in Lambs Conduit Street. The sad thing is that we daren't trust each other to read our books; they lie, like vast consciences, in our most secret drawers" (*D*1 95). Woolf no doubt knew that other diary communities existed that were not as reserved as her own. She wrote a review of Ralph Waldo Emerson's journals, and her godfather, James Russell Lowell, may have acquainted her with the Transcendentalists' amiable practice of showing their journals to each other. Woolf likely also read Leonard's and Koteliansky's translation of Gorky's *Reminiscenses of Leo Nikolaevich Tolstoy,* which spoke of Tolstoy's sharing his diary with Chekhov, Gorky, and others.

If she found her own diaristic community more inhibited than Emerson's in America and Tolstoy's in Russia, Virginia could turn for sustenance to the larger community of "diarists read," which she interacted with throughout her life. (See the beginning list of "Diaries Woolf Read" below.) Few of *these* diarists were her contemporaries, but when she sat down to her diary in her "casual half hours after tea" (*D*1 266), she understood she was joining a community of diarists whose work she valued and admired.

I began making a chronological list of the diarists Woolf read from her references in her own diaries and then added to it diarists she acknowledged reading in her letters, diarists she reviewed as indicated in the *Essays of Virginia Woolf* and *Virginia Woolf's Rediscovered Essays: Sources and Allusions*, diarists noted in her *Reading Notebooks*, and diarists various biographers indicated she read. I do not claim that this list is complete. The list reveals, though, that starting with the diaries of Samuel Pepys, whom she adored at the age of fifteen, Woolf read more than fifty diarists and diaries throughout her life, some (such as Lady Anne Clifford's, Fanny Burney's, and James Woodforde's *Diary of a Country Parson*) more than once. This is Woolf's own special community of "diarists read." One notes that her first exposure to diary writing was fortunate, for she cut her teeth on Pepys, often called the greatest diarist in the English language, and Fanny Burney and James Boswell and Walter Scott—all before the age of twenty-two. From 1905 to 1925, her first two decades as a professional writer, she read the diaries of John Evelyn (Pepys's contemporary), Emerson, Stendhal, the Goncourt brothers, and Swift's *Journal to Stella.*

We know that Woolf valued diaries for their unsurpassed ability to capture the everyday life of past ages and that she turned to diaries repeatedly as primary source material when writing specific *Common Reader* essays, *A Room of One's Own, Three Guineas, Flush,* and many of her novels. In her first *Common Reader* volume, she pays tribute to John Evelyn's massive diary and springboards from the diary to provide us with "Lives of the

Obscure." *The Second Common Reader* might be subtitled "In Praise of Diarists," for here Woolf evokes and explores the worlds of Fanny Burney, Dorothy Wordsworth, two country parsons (James Woodforde and John Skinner), and Swift's *Journal to Stella.* As noted before, Woolf wrote reviews of diaries, including Woodforde's, Katherine Mansfield's, Stendhal's, and the Rev. William Cole's. This is what I mean by her interaction with the community of diarists. Indeed, Woolf's interest in diaries seems to have increased as she aged. In the final decade of her life, she read at least twenty-five diaries—more than two a year—as the list below reveals.

Woolf gained much from this community of diarists, which she would draw upon when writing her own diary. When she was fifteen, in April 1897, she called her "dear Pepys . . . the only calm thing in the house" (*PA* 66), and it is not too much to say that he showed her how to move briskly through a diary entry, just as he was briskly scurrying back and forth across London. Pepys's pattern of home to office to a play or a visit to a coffee house and home again was one Woolf would follow. He offered her, at the age of fifteen, a vision of a busy London lifestyle that she would make her own. The echo of his writing style can be heard in the following Woolf diary entry written thirty-six years after she first read him: "So to tea, & I should add so to Westminster to hear The March of the Women, Ethel Smyth; & Rebecca speaking on married womens [sic] earnings. Instead I shall sleep over the fire, reading Tom's criticism, & Michael Field diaries, alone thank God" (*D*4 189). From Pepys she may also have learned to balance the record of her personal life with the larger events of her time—such as reports of war or strikes—and that inclusion of bouts with servants was not amiss. Woolf read the diaries of Lady Holland, the great hostess, when she was just beginning to make a living as a professional writer. "What numbers of likenesses she [strikes] off, and with what assurance!" Virginia exclaimed in admiration (Lee 212). From Fanny Burney, whom she returned to again and again throughout her life, Virginia may have borrowed the idea of writing her diary "at full tilt exactly as the words came into her head" (*CR*2 102)—that is, as an exercise in freewriting. Surely Woolf identified with Burney's family situation: the mixed family of half-brothers and sisters; the mother's early death; the adored, demanding father; the "endless confabulations, and confidences between sisters and brothers" (*CR*2 99). Certainly she is thinking back through this foremother (and perhaps projecting a bit) when she writes that Burney's "awkward manners, concealed the quickest observation, the most retentive memory" (*CR*2 101), and it is from Burney that she adopted the practices of writing her opinion of people when she first met them (*CR*2 97) and stealing to her cabin at the end of the garden (so like Fanny's) as soon as company left to "[write] down every word, every scene" (*CR*2 101).

Woolf, therefore, learned much from and regularly interacted with her personal community of diarists read. These earlier diarists live again through her vivid evocations. In this way Woolf reinvigorates a neglected community.

What then is Virginia Woolf's place within the vast community of diarists? Matthews wrote in 1977 that his volumes listing published British and American diaries reference about 7,000 diaries and that his annotated list of American diaries in manuscript (but never printed) totals about 5,000 more ("The Diary" 286). He quickly notes, however, that this list of 12,000 extant British and American diaries does *not* include diary manuscripts privately owned and in a good many libraries. If Ponsonby's suggestion that one of four persons is a diarist is accurate, there are potentially millions of people in the community of diarists. Matthews, in fact, asserts that "Apart from letter-writing, diary-writing is probably the most wide-spread of all literary activities," and he notes that "writers of the published diaries represent every rank, occupation and interest that make up [hu]mankind" ("The Diary" 297).

In seeking to locate Woolf's place within this most democratic of forms, I find it helpful to distinguish between "life diaries" and "topical diaries." Some of us seek to record our whole lives, either daily or periodically. This type of diary is different from a "topical diary" which limits itself to a specific subject matter or time period: travel diaries (of a specific, limited trip), war diaries, prison diaries, diaries of pregnancy or illness. Virginia Woolf belongs in the community of life diarists. This point is both ironic and important, for Ponsonby tells us that "If a census of diary keepers could be made it would probably be found that divines and soldiers headed the list" (21). Woolf would hardly be at ease in this community!

Nevertheless, Woolf is one of our greatest "life diarists," and, if one wishes to classify diaries further as "literary" and "nonliterary," she is among the greatest of our "literary diarists." An artist who is also a life diarist, she seeks to capture it all—that is, the truth of our lives—and to induce our participation in this effort. Diary entries, one notices, tend to be short notes rather than extended descriptions or reflections. They therefore invite our expansion. Absent entries invite our speculation, and the closure of all diaries is in the reader's hands (not the writer's). Virginia Woolf's diaries provide spaces of many kinds for us to complete. The reader becomes a collaborator in the re-imagined life. To this degree, we should consider the diary one of Woolf's richest private-public sites. That the private act of diary writing was for Woolf also a community occasion can be seen from her opening words to her *Common Reader* essay "Rambling round Evelyn": "Should you wish to make sure that your birthday will be celebrated three hundred years hence," she writes, "your best course is undoubtedly to keep a diary" (*CR*1 80).

## Diaries Woolf Read[1]

| Woolf's Age | Diarist |
| --- | --- |
| 15 | Samuel Pepys, *Diary*, 1825 (*PA* 62, 65-67, 69). |
| 15 | William Cory, *Extracts from the Letters and Journals of William Cory*, selected and arranged by Francis Warre-Cornish, 1897 (*PA* 126). |
| 15 | Frances (Fanny) Burney, *Diary* (Gordon 134). |
| 20 | Walter Scott's diary of a voyage to the lighthouses on the Scottish coast. In Lockhart's life of Scott (*L*1 49). |
| 21 | James Boswell, *Journal of a Tour to the Hebrides with Samuel Johnson*, 1773, 1775 (*PA* 206). |
| 23 | Burney, *Diary and Letters of Madame d'Arblay*, 7 vols., 1842, 1846. Woolf quotes from vol. 1 in "Their Passing Hour," *Academy & Literature* 26 Aug. 1905 (Steele 180; *E*1 61-65). |
| 23 | Bartholomew James, *Journal of Rear-Admiral Bartholomew James*, 1896 (Steele 180). |
| 23 | Mrs. St. George (pseud. of Melesina Trench), *Journal Kept During a Visit to Germany*, 1861 (Steele 180). |
| 25 | William Allingham, *William Allingham, A Diary*, 1907. See Woolf's review, "William Allingham," *TLS* 19 Dec. 1907 (*E*1 154-56). |
| 26 | Charlotte Bury, *The Diary of a Lady-in-Waiting by Charlotte* Bury, 2 vols., 1908. See Woolf's review, "The Diary of a Lady-in-Waiting," *TLS* 23 July 1908 (*E*1 195-200). |
| 26 | Elizabeth Holland, *The Journal of Elizabeth Lady Holland*, 2 vols., 1908. See Woolf's article, "The Journal of Elizabeth Lady Holland," *Cornhill Magazine* Dec. 1908 (Lee 212; *E*1 230-39). |
| 27 | James Boswell. Woolf quotes from Boswell's description of his journal-writing practice in "Boswell's Genius": "I try to keep a journal, and shall show you that I have done tolerably; but it is hardly credible what ground I go over, and what a variety of men and manners I contemplate every day, and all the time I am myself *pars magna*, for my exuberant spirits will not let me listen enough"; Woolf praises Boswell's "intense consciousness of himself," observation, and memory (*E*1 251, 254). |
| 28 | Ralph Waldo Emerson, *Journals of Ralph Waldo Emerson, With annotations,* vols.1-2, 1909-10. See Woolf's review, "Emerson's Journals," *TLS* 3 Mar. 1910 (*E*1 335-40). |
| 35 | Stopford Brooke. Excerpts from his diary are contained in L. P. Jacks' *Life and Letters of Stopford Brooke*, 1917. See Woolf's review "Stopford Brooke," *TLS* 29 Nov. 1917 (*E*2 183-8; Steele 170-1). |
| 36 | Samuel Pepys, *Occasional Papers Read by Members at Meetings* |

| | |
|---|---|
| | *of the Samuel Pepys Club*, vol. 1, 1918. "Papers on Pepys," Woolf's review of *Occasional Papers* appeared in the *TLS* 4 Apr. 1918 (*E*2 233-38). |
| 36 | Edmund de Goncourt, *Journal des Goncourt: Memoires de las vie litteraire*, 9 vols., 1912–1917 (Holroyd 415). |
| 36 | Henry Crabb Robinson, *Diary, Reminiscences, and Correspondence*, 1869 (Silver 153-4, 194). |
| 38 | John Evelyn, *The Diary of John Evelyn*, 1818, 2 vols. 1911. *Diary* excerpts were also included in *The Early Life and Education of John Evelyn, 1620-1641*, which Woolf reviewed in "John Evelyn," *TLS* 28 Oct. 1920 (*E*3 259-68); she reprinted parts of this review in "Ramblng Round Evelyn" (*CR*1 78-85, 249-50). |
| 40 | *Tant' Alie of Transvaal: Her Diary, 1880–1902*, trans. Emily Hobhouse,1923 (*D*2 216). |
| 42 | Anne Chalmers, *Letters and Journals of Anne Chalmers*,1922 (Steele 13; *E*3 398-99). |
| 42 | Stendhal, *Stendhal: Journal,* vol. 1, 1923. See Woolf's review "Stendhal" in *National & Athenaeum* 5 July 1924 (Steele 18, 169-70; Silver 96, 101-3; *E*3 416-18). |
| 42 | James Woodforde, *The Diary of a Country Parson.* vol. 1, 1924 (Silver 103). |
| 42 | Lady Anne Clifford, *Diary*, Intro. Vita Sackville-West, 1923 (Silver 100, 102-3). |
| 43 | Jonathan Swift, *Journal to Stella, A.D. 1710–1713,* 1923. See Woolf's essay "Swift's Journal to Stella," *TLS* 24 Sept. 1925 (Silver 50-2). |
| 44 | Beatrice Webb, *My Apprenticeship*, 1926 (*D*3 62). |
| 44 | Sharon Turner (great grandfather of Saxon Sydney Turner) (*D*3 72). |
| 43-45* | Jules Renard, *Journal*, 17 vols, 1925-1927 (*D*3 264). |
| 45 | Woodforde, *The Diary of a Country Parson*, vols. 1-3. Woolf reviewed vol. 3 for the *New Republic* 17 Aug. 1927 (Silver 89-90). |
| 45 | Katherine Mansfield, *Journal of Katherine Mansfield*, 1927 (*L*3 408; E4 98). |
| 46 | Burney, *Fanny Burney and her Friends: Select Passages from her Diary and Other Writings*, 1890. See Woolf's "Dr. Burney's Evening Party," *New York Herald Tribune* 21, 28 July 1929 (Silver 215-17, 221). |
| 46 | Mary, Countess of Meath. See Woolf's review "The Diaries of Mary, Countess of Meath," *Nation & Athenaeum* 29 Sept. 1928: 832 (Steele 14, 205). |
| 46 to 48 | Burney, *The Early Diary: 1768-1778*, 2 vols., 1889; and *Diary and Letters of Madame d'Arblay*, 7 vols., 1854. Woolf read |

Burney's diaries for "Dr. Burney's Evening Party" (*CR*2 97-112) and "Fanny Burney's Half-Sister," *TLS* 28 Aug. 1930 (Silver 77-8, 81-3).

47 Boswell. Woolf refers to "18 volumes of Boswell's diaries now to be published. With any luck I shall live to read them" (*D*3 237).

47 Dorothy Wordsworth, *Journals*, 2 vols., 1897. See Woolf's essay "Dorothy Wordsworth" in *Nation & Athenaeum* 12 Oct. 1929; also see "Four Figures: Dorothy Wordsworth" in *The Second Common Reader* (Silver 111-2; *L*4 79).

47 Woodforde. Woolf made reading notes on vol. 4 of James Woodforde's *Diary of a Country Parson*, 1929 (Silver 89-90).

47* Charles Greville. Woolf read excerpts from Charles Greville's 91-vol. diary that Lytton Strachey, Ralph Partridge, and Frances Birrell were editing (Holroyd 636-40).

48 The Rev. John Skinner, *The Journal of a Somerset Rector*, 1930. See Woolf's "Two Parsons: II. The Rev. John Skinner" in *The Second Common Reader* (*D*3 340-3).

48 Sarah Stoddart (Mrs. William Hazlitt), "Journal of my Trip to Scotland" in William Hazlitt, *Liber Amoris or the New Pygmalion*, 1894 (Silver 119).

William Cole, *The Blecheley Diary of the Rev. William Cole*, 1931. See Woolf's review "The Rev. William Cole: A Letter," *New Statesman & Nation*, 6 Feb. 1932 (Silver 63).

49 Vera Brittain, "A Woman's Notebook," *Nation & Athenaeum* 17 Jan. 1931: 508-09 (Silver 270).

49 Lady Anne Clifford, *Lady Anne Clifford . . . Her Life, Letters and Work* by George C. Williamson, 1922 (Silver 229-32).

49 Woodforde, *The Diary of a Country Parson*, 5 vols., 1924-1931. Woolf made reading notes on vol. 5, probably when she was preparing "Two Parsons: I. James Woodforde" for *The Second Common Reader* (Silver 89-90).

50 Swift, *Journal to Stella*, 1924. Woolf made reading notes when she was preparing "Swift's 'Journal to Stella'" for *The Second Common Reader* (Silver 230-1, 233).

51 Thomas Creevey, *The Creevey Papers*, 1928. These were selected correspondence & diaries of the Whig MP and gossip Thomas Creevey (*D*4 157).

51 Michael Field, *Works and Days: Extracts from the Journal of Michael Field*, 1933 (*D*4 189).

51 or 52* Woodforde, *The Diary of a Country Parson*, vol. 4, 1929 (Silver 230-1, 233).

52 Alice James, *Alice James: Her Brothers—Her Journal*, 1934 (*D*4 248, 248n9).

53 Dr. Salter, *Dr. Salter: His Diary and Reminiscences from the year*

| | |
|---|---|
| | *1849 to the year 1932*, 1933 (*D*4 339, 339n5). |
| 53 | John Bailey, *John Bailey, 1864–1931, Letters and Diaries*, 1935 (*D*4 339, 339n6). |
| 54 | Wilfred Scawen Blunt, *My Diaries. Being a Personal Narrative of Events, 1888–1914. Part Two: 1900–1914*, 1920 (Silver 249-50). |
| 54 | Ellen Weeton, *Miss Weeton: Journal of a Governess, 1807–1811*, 1936. Quoted in *TG* 137-38 (*D*5 32; Silver 62, 287). |
| 55 | Leo Tolstoy and his wife. Woolf refers to their diary writing (*D*5 55). |
| 55 | Lord and Lady Amberley, *The Amberley Papers: The Letters and Diaries of Lord and Lady Amberley*, ed. Bertrand and Patricia Russell, 1937 (*D*5 62, 62n21). |
| 56 | Scott. "Why not write about [Sir Walter] Scott's diaries?" (*D*5 138). |
| 56 | Eugène Delacroix, *Journal de Eugène Delacroix*, 3 vols., 1932 (*D*5 199, 199n5). |
| 57 | André Gide, *André Gide's Journal 1885-1939*, 1939. (*D*5 227, 227n8, 228) |
| 57 | F. L. Lucas, *Journal Under the Terror*, 1938. Woolf characterizes Lucas's journal as "The unedited truth of . . . day-to-day impressions of a year (1937) in modern Europe" and refers to his wife's nervous breakdown (*D*5 227, 227n8). |
| 57 | The Rev. Francis Kilvert, *Kilvert's* Diary, 3 vols., 1938–1940 (*D*5 228, 228n10). |
| 57 | Charles Ricketts, *Self-Portrait, Taken from the Letters & Journals of Charles Ricketts, R.A.*, 1939 (*D*5 252, 252n12). |
| 57 | Henry, Earl of Pembroke, *Diaries of Henry, Tenth Earl of Pembroke and His Circle, 1734–80*, 1939 (*D*5 252, 252n12). |
| 58 | Henry Williamson, *Goodbye West Country*, 1937. A journal of his thoughts and occupations (*D*5 320, 320n9, 321). |
| 58 | George B. Harrison, *An Elizabethan Journal . . . 1591–1594*, 1928 (Silver 186). |
| 58 | Philip Henslowe, *The Diary . . . from 1591*-1609, 2 vols., 1904-1908 (Steele 48; Silver187-8). |
| 58 & 59* | Clifford, *Diary*, intro. Vita Sackville-West, 1923 (Steele 47; Silver 92-3, 95). |
| 58 | Pepys, *Diaries and Correspondence*, 1849 (Steele 47). |

* I am unable to date Woolf's reading precisely in these cases.

**Notes**

[1] Diary information included in "Diaries Woolf Read" is that listed in the source cited in parentheses. I am indebted to these editors for their efforts to determine the precise texts Woolf read.

**Works Cited**

Gordon, Lyndall. *Virginia Woolf: A Writer's Life.* New York: Norton, 1984.

Holroyd, Michael. *Lytton Strachey: The New Biography.* New York: Farrar, 1994.

Koteliansky, S. S., and Leonard Woolf, trans. *Reminiscences of Leo Nikolaevich Tolstoy by Maxim Gorky.* New York: B. W. Huebsch, 1920.

Lee, Hermione. *Virginia Woolf.* New York: Knopf, 1997.

Matthews, William. *American Diaries: An Annotated Bibliography of American Diaries Written Prior to the Year 1861.* Berkeley: U of California P, 1945.

——. *American Diaries in Manuscript, 1580-1954: A Descriptive Bibliography.* Athens, GA.: U of Georgia P, 1974.

——. *British Diaries: An Annotated Bibliography of British Diaries Written Between 1442 and 1950.* Berkeley: U of California P, 1967.

——. *Canadian Diaries and Autobiographies.* Berkeley: U of California P, 1950.

——. "The Diary: A Neglected Genre." *Sewanee Review* 85 (1977): 286-300.

Ponsonby, Arthur, M. P. *English Diaries: A Review of English Diaries from the Sixteenth to the Twentieth Century.* London: Methuen, 1922.

Silver, Brenda R. *Virginia Woolf's Reading Notebooks.* Princeton: Princeton UP, 1983.

Steele, Elizabeth. *Virginia Woolf's Rediscovered Essays: Sources and Allusions.* New York: Garland, 1987.

Woolf, Virginia. *The Common Reader: First Series.* Annotated ed. Ed. Andrew McNeillie. New York: Harcourt Brace, 1984.

——. *The Diary of Virginia Woolf.* 5 vols. Ed. Anne Olivier Bell, assisted by Andrew McNeillie. San Diego: Harvest, 1978-85.

——. *The Essays of Virginia Woolf.* 3 vols. Ed. Andrew McNeillie. San Diego: Harvest, 1986-89.

——. *The Letters of Virginia Woolf.* 6 vols. Ed. Nigel Nicolson and Joanne Trautmann. New York: Harvest, 1977-82.

——. *A Passionate Apprentice: The Early Journals 1897-1909.* Ed. Mitchell A. Leaska. New York: HBJ, 1990.

——. *The Second Common Reader.* New York: Harvest, 1932.

**Kathryn Miles**

# "That perpetual marriage of granite and rainbow": Searching for "The New Biography" in Virginia Woolf's *Orlando*

One of the most daunting tasks that we face as scholars is reading literature in light of (and often in *spite* of) the mounds of criticism currently in circulation. Reading Virginia Woolf's *Orlando* is an example of this difficulty. In an earlier edition of conference proceedings, for instance, Lisa Haines-Wright and Traci Lynn Kyle rightly noted the avalanche of "handicapped" criticism concerning Woolf's biography-novel (177-8). But in spite of potential handicaps, criticism regarding the text continues to accumulate: *Orlando* has been called a "raffish portrait" and a quasi-biography" (Richter 61-63), and a failure as both a novel and a biography. Avril Horner, on the other hand, praises *Orlando* because it does not "conform to the ideal of biography as an accurate record of one person's life" (71). Similarly, Elizabeth Cooley writes approvingly that Orlando's biography "defies" the rules set up by both him and the biographical canon.

In short, *Orlando* has been poked, prodded, and interrogated from nearly every theoretical angle and perspective. It is, therefore, somewhat sheepishly that I offer yet another reading of Woolf's novel. This reading, however, returns *Orlando* to what I believe is its original theoretical rubric: Woolf's own essays. Specifically, I'd like to offer a reading of *Orlando* that juxtaposes the novel with the theories of biography outlined in Woolf's essay, "The New Biography." Published in 1927, Woolf's treatise posits a theory of biography that seeks to reconcile the binaries of truth and fiction, or put another way, action and thought. As Woolf suggests, in each binary, two "antagonistic" elements exist at opposite ends of the spectrum of biography, and the successful biographer is one who divines a way to marry the two elements. To understand this enormous task, Woolf asks us to "think of truth as something of granite-like solidity and of personality as something of rainbow-like intangibility and reflect that the aim of biography is to weld these two into one seamless whole" (*E*4 473). The only way for a biographer to achieve this seamless whole is by creating a spectrum of truth and personality in which facts, personality, subjectivity, and even a bit of fictional artifice entertain a visible place within the final biographical product.

We might well pause at this point and ask what this marriage of granite and rainbow has to do with theories of Woolf and communities, the theme of the Eighth Annual Conference on Virginia Woolf. We might also ask, as Catherine N. Parke has, how it is that for Woolf, biography was "an art of composition, the art of composing a culture and community" (368). The question is a good one, and one that Woolf acknowledges early in her essay.

As Woolf concedes, the problem of achieving this marriage "is a stiff one" and "we need not wonder if biographers have for the most part failed to solve it" (*E*4 473). This concession allows Woolf to enter into an examination of approaches to biography throughout literary history. Indeed, within Woolf's aesthetics of biography lies a lucid overview of the various ages and approaches to life writing, as dictated by a literary epoch and its community of writers. A sort of genealogy of approaches to biography, one which includes a study of the Elizabethan age, the eighteenth century, the Victorian era, and of course, the age of modernism, Woolf's study provides us with a framework within which we can evaluate the spectrum of "truths" apparent in each generation, each community, of life writers.

Although Woolf's essay offers a highly sophisticated understanding of the art of biography, it is not until the publication of her novel *Orlando* in 1928 that she provides a fictional praxis to underscore her theory. Undeniably biographical in its aims, *Orlando* employs a narrator who consistently reminds us that his primary function is that of the "biographer."[1] And his account of Orlando's life and sexuality, as well as the chosen form of his text, are dictated by this role. As we follow Orlando from the Elizabethan age to the height of modernism, it becomes clear that we are also following the evolution of biography through these ages as well. This dual construction of character, one which includes both biographer and subject, allows Woolf not only to explore thematic elements, such as Orlando's negotiation of gender roles, but also to examine the ways in which various ages of life writers depict such themes. Ultimately, then, the text of *Orlando* exists not as a single narrative, but rather, as four distinct biographies, separated by their adherence to literary ages, and unified only by character and writer.

The first of these accounts proves the devices and techniques employed by the community of Elizabethan biographers. Woolf characterized the sixteenth-century biography as "a series of exploits" in which the biography "told a tale of battle and victory" with "a formal sincerity which is perfectly satisfactory of its kind" (*E*4 474). This is, of course, the very stuff of the first chapter of *Orlando*. The beginning of *Orlando* finds both biographer in the late sixteenth century, and the Orlando we meet here is one who is of a decidedly Elizabethan cast. As Woolf explains in her essay, biographers of this age depict their subjects as prodigies "of learning and courage" (*E*4 474). It is no surprise, then, that her novel begins with a vivid description of the title character's exploits and actions: the very first sentence of the novel, for instance, finds Orlando "in the act of slicing at the head of a Moor which swung from the rafters" (*O* 13). And, when he falls in love with Sasha, we are told that "his manhood woke; he grasped a sword in his hand; he charged a more daring foe than Pole or Moor; he dived in deep water," and so on (*O* 40). This depiction of Orlando's actions intensifies throughout the opening chapters of the text until, exhausted, the biographer declares that Orlando moved "in violent see-saws from life to death stopping at nothing in between, so that the biographer must not stop either, but must fly as fast as he can and so keep pace with the unthinkable passionate foolish actions" (*O* 46).

The ideals of the Elizabethan biography not only exhaust the narrator, they also restrict his account of Orlando's life. Because "the first duty of a biographer" in the Elizabethan age is "to plod, without looking to right or left, in the indelible footprints of truth; unenticed by flowers; regardless of shade," he finds that he is unable to speculate about the personality and veiled elements of Orlando's internal sensibilities (*O* 65). This idea is, of course, akin to Woolf's sentiment in "The New Biography," in which she notes that the Elizabethan biography drapes "robes decorously over its subjects" (*E*4 474). Moreover, given this age's emphasis on exploits, Orlando's biographer admits that to pause "and seek the reasons of things is out of the question" (*O* 37). Thus, without concrete documentation of inner musings, the Elizabethan biographer must remain silent about much of the life of his or her subject. And as Woolf tells us, the result is often dreadfully dull biographies.

Happily, as Woolf explains in "The New Biography," there arose "toward the end of the eighteenth century one of those curious men of genius" capable of breaking up the tedium of Elizabethan biography. (*E*4 474). With the appearance of Boswell, the draperies and formalities of biography fell to the ground, and so rose the second age, the second community, of life writers. Whereas the Elizabethan biography positioned itself close to the granite bedrock of fact, the eighteenth-century biography moved much closer toward the ephemeral, rainbow-like intangibility of personality. Woolf suggests in her essay that eighteenth- and early nineteenth-century biography "concerned itself as much with the lives of the sedentary as with the lives of the active" (474). The resulting texts, therefore, bespoke of inner life and emotion, rather than just a subject's exploits and learning. And as *Orlando* clearly demonstrates, the advent of this age places biographer, biography, and biographical subject in an entirely new role. No longer restricted to factual accounts, the biographer of this era may employ his or her creative and intuitive powers as well as his or her skills as a writer. Admittedly, a biographer is still governed by truth; nonetheless, the "truth" that Woolf refers to here is one mediated by the speculations and surmising of the biographer. What results from this approach is a highly crafted text, one which liberates the subject and is clearly influenced and dictated by the author's fictive prowess. Boswell's *The Life of Johnson* is, of course, the archetypal example of this age's approach to life writing.

In fact, one can't help but be reminded of Boswell's stylized biography when reading the second section of *Orlando*. Boswell's account of Johnson is clearly reconstructed and staged by the biographer, and the text contains obvious elements of fictionality, such as Johnson's meeting with the king. There are obvious allusions to this scene throughout the second chapter of *Orlando*, and one need only read of Orlando's exploits in Turkey to see the real commonalities between the two texts. By associating this chapter of Orlando's life with the community of Enlightenment biographers, Woolf is able to offer the reader a new and more artful account of Orlando's life, one which reveals the thoughts and introspection which lie hidden beneath the draperies of Elizabethan biography.

The second section of *Orlando*, then, is one clearly marked by a self-reflexive awareness held by both biographer and subject. Whereas the narrator was unable to pause and reflect on Orlando's life in the first section, he consistently tells us that in the second that we "may profit" by reflecting on Orlando's many soliloquies upon them, are important facets of biography (*O* 102). This trend indicates not only the narrator's willingness to investigate Orlando's thoughts and personality, but also his willingness to speculate and theorize about such sentiments. The full extent of this willingness is well documented in the fourth chapter of the novel: in this chapter alone, the biographer tells us what Orlando "thought" thirty-one times, what she "felt" or "believed" eleven times, and what she "remembered" or "reflected" an additional ten. Clearly, Orlando's introspective musing and emotion, not Orlando's exploits and action, are the biographer's new focal point. We see the verity of such a reading in pivotal scenes such as Orlando's all-important gender transformation from male to female: a transformation noted only briefly by the biographer, and one qualified by the reminder that, ultimately, "Orlando remained precisely as he had been" (*O* 138).[2]

Scenes such as this remind us that any account of Orlando is a communally subjective one. Interpreted by historical age, skewed by that age's biographical trends, the Orlando that we see is as much a reflection of cultural construction as he/she is a manifestation of inner characterological identifiers. It ought to come as no surprise, therefore, that this section of *Orlando* leads the biographer to admit that "to give an exact and particular account of Orlando's life at this time becomes more and more out of the question" (220). Instead, the biographer explains that he must rely upon the literary trends established by the eighteenth century in lieu of biographical accuracy. But what this account of Orlando's life lacks in evidential support or accuracy, it more than compensates for with its artful presentation and introspective tendencies.

Of course, as soon as the enlightened age of introspection arrives on the biographical scene, it is quickly supplanted by a new, relatively irksome, community of life writers: the *eminent* Victorians. According to Woolf, the "Victorian biography was a parti-coloured, hybrid, monstrous birth" in which the genius of the previous ages becomes "hampered and distorted" and the manner of presentation becomes increasingly clumsy and laborious (*E*4 474-5). Briefly put, the Victorian community of biographers is one which privileges truth of fact and elides personality. To his credit, Orlando's biographer attempts to resist the third age of biography—he notes, for instance, that its "style is tedious"—but he is, nevertheless, eventually compelled to admit that he has joined a community where "lives which no longer express themselves in actions take shape in innumerable words" (*E*4 475).[3] As Woolf suggests in her essay, this community also reflects the Victorian emphasis on sensibility and notions of "goodness," as well as an age which demands that its biographers observe the truth of fact. To do so, a biographer "must toil through endless labyrinths and embarrass himself with countless documents," thereby creating a biography "laden with truth" but artistically wrong-headed (475). Thus, we find within this "age" of *Orlando* that the biographer becomes increasingly interested in that which can be empirically accounted for: detailed accounts of legal briefs, invitations, and other bits of tangible proof begin to clutter the pages of the Victorian account of Orlando's life.

Interestingly, but not surprisingly, it is in this section of *Orlando* where the biographer begins his most overt critique and protest of biographical mores. Admittedly, Orlando's biographer does attempt to join the community of life writers: he attaches repeated caveats to his descriptions of Orlando's musing, he interrupts said musings with more concrete action, and he endeavors to represent the larger-than-life goodness of his Victorian subject. Nevertheless, the biographer is unable to embrace the techniques of this age. For, as he notes in the sixth chapter of the text, "This method of writing biography, though it has its merits, is a little bare, perhaps, and the reader, if we go on with it, may complain" (266). Likewise, he also tells us that his "patience is wearing thin" with the expectations and restrictions of Victorian biography (267), and he concludes that "whatever the *Dictionary of National Biography* may say," the length and nature of a subject's life is far more disputable and vague than it appears in Victorian biography (305-6).

One cannot help but be reminded of the staunchly Victorian aims of Woolf's father, Leslie Stephen, when reading the biographer's complaints about the *DNB*. But it is more than familial ghosts that Woolf is exorcizing here, as her characterization of Victorian life writing also points to the death of the biographical subject at the hands of this community. Although this characterization may seem a bit severe, we quickly discover the verity of it within the pages of *Orlando*. As the narrator explains, Orlando "inclined herself naturally" to the various ages of English history, but "the spirit of the nineteenth century was antipathetic to her in the extreme" (244). And, because she is forced into this age and its biographical trends, Orlando loses her voice and her identity. As the weight of Victorian goodness presses upon her, the Orlando that we have come to know is diminished and eventually eclipsed until, at last, she must admit, and admit repeatedly, "I am dead."[4] And, as the Victorian biographers tell us, if the subject fails to meet the standards of the nineteenth-century biography, "we may conclude that he or she is no better than a corpse and so leave her" (*O* 269).

Of course, we don't actually leave Orlando, and she certainly does not die. In fact, she manages to subvert Victorian convention and maintain her prior identity, an identity which is, indeed, a far cry from that prescribed by Victorian ideology. Orlando's biographer not only allows for this subversion, but he encourages it. Indeed, we might even go so far as to conclude that Orlando's questionable association with any of the ages and communities is quite deliberate. After all, the strength of fit between Orlando's biographer and historical communities is a dubious one: not only does he reject outright the techniques employed by the Victorians, he also treats the tropes and mores of various ages with obvious irony. That we may question the extent to which the biographer truly embodies various biographical approaches, however, seems quite deliberate throughout the work: the biographer is, after all, throughly modern in his approach and historical posture. As he reminds us, he is writing in "the present," that being November 1, 1927, in the opening chapters of the novel, and October 11, 1928, in the work's conclusion.

But more important than the date of composition is the approach dictated by this age. As a modern biographer, the narrator of *Orlando* is able to recognize his own subjective positioning. In the opening chapter of the biography, for instance, he reminds us that our view of Orlando is necessarily fragmented or skewed because the age is "not ours" (27). Similarly, the biographer suggests that, try as one might, a biographical subject will continuously slip "out of one's grasp altogether" (268). He is forced to conclude, then, that nothing can "be seen whole or read from start to finish," including a biographer or biographical subject (307). Such a conclusion allows Orlando's biographer to create a sort of "metabiography" in which he is at once author and critic, actor and audience (Nadel 140).[5] This recognition of subjectivity is, arguably, the biographer's greatest talent. And it certainly situates him nicely within the community of modern and contemporary biographers, biographers who seek to achieve that "queer amalgamation" first suggested by Woolf in "The New Biography." Of course, Woolf concludes her essay by noting that we cannot yet name a biographer who has achieved that amalgamation. Nonetheless, the subsequent publication of *Orlando* offers us the next best thing: a biographer not named, but *created* by Woolf—one whose life writing demonstrates the potential for achieving that "marriage of granite and rainbow." And one whose community we all might rightly endeavor to join.

**Notes**

1 A note regarding the gender of Orlando's biographer is most certainly in order here. While the sex of the biographer is left deliberately unspecified, the biographer does choose to use the traditional "he" as the pronoun of choice when writing self-reflexively. While not prepared to make a determination regarding the true gender of the biographer, I have preserved "his" pronoun usage throughout my paper.

2 There are two excellent essays which treat this transformation and its relationship to community construction. One is Richter's "The Biographer as Novelist," from which I have quoted earlier in my essay. The other is Philipson's "Virginia Woolf's *Orlando*: Biography as a Work of Fiction."

3 Curiously, it is this approach which has been most criticized by contemporary readers. Cooley, for instance, contends that "Orlando's life does not fulfill all the biographical requirements" of exploits and actions (73). She goes on to argue that, because Orlando's life "is relatively unexceptional," it is not the stuff of which biography is made. What Cooley fails to appreciate, however, is that Orlando's life *is* exceptional: exceptionally eighteenth and nineteenth century.

4 Faced with the traditions of the Victorian age, Orlando tells us at one point that "death is better" (248), at another point she states "I'm dead" (259), and again, "I'm dead, Sir!" (250).

5 Both Cooley and Horner arrive at similar conclusions regarding the biographer's subjectivity. Cooley suggests that much of *Orlando* functions as a tool with which Woolf can expose "the paradoxical limits of language" resulting from subjecthood (76). And, according to Horner, Woolf demonstrates her "very subjective attitude to the past" by creating a biographical novel "in which prejudices and anachronisms are writ large in order to call into question the supposed objectivity of the historian" (76).

## Works Cited


Cooley, Elizabeth. "Revolutionizing Biography: *Orlando, Roger Fry*, and the Tradition." *South Atlantic Review* 55 (1990): 71-83.

Haines-Wright, Lisa, and Traci Lynn Kyle. "From He and She to You and Me: Grounding Fluidity, Woolf's *Orlando* to Winterson's *Written on the Body*." *Virginia Woolf Texts and Contexts: Selected Papers From the Fifth Annual Conference on Virginia Woolf.* Ed. Beth Rigel Daugherty and Eileen Barrett. New York: Pace UP, 1996. 177-183.

Horner, Avril. "Virginia Woolf, History, and Metaphors of *Orlando*." *Essays and Studies* 44 (1991): 70-87.

Nadel, Bruce. *Biography: Fiction, Fact and Form.* New York: St. Martin's, 1984.

Philipson, Morris. "Virginia Woolf's *Orlando*: Biography as a Work of Fiction." *From Parnassus: Essays in Honor of Jacques Barzun.* Ed. Dora Weiner and William Keylor. New York: Harper, 1976.

Richter, Harvena. "The Biographer as Novelist." *Essaying Biography: A Celebration for Leon Edel.* Ed. Gloria G. Fromm. Honolulu: U of Hawaii P, 1986.

Woolf, Virginia. "The New Biography." *The Essays of Virginia Woolf.* Ed. Andrew McNeillie. Vol. 4. London: Hogarth, 1988. 473-480.

——. *Orlando.* New York: Harvest , 1956.

**Anna Snaith**

## Virginia Woolf and Reading Communities: Respondents to *Three Guineas*

The representation of Woolf as a writer divorced from the public sphere, writing for and about a cosy côterie still lingers in the public consciousness, surfacing now and again in the media.[1] A relatively unexplored area of Woolf's work—namely the reception of *Three Guineas* by its reading public—is a body of evidence which shows how much Woolf *was* in the real world, how democratic were her notions of audience and how mixed her reading public was in class terms.[2] Charges of elitism and snobbery were and are often levied at *Three Guineas* based on the question of who the text speaks for; the limitation of its focus to the daughters of educated men. Most famously, Q.D. Leavis in her review "Caterpillars of the Commonwealth Unite!" situates herself as an outsider to the text which is "a conversation between her [Woolf] and her friends" (203).[3] Leavis fails to acknowledge the specificity of Woolf's polemic, the strength of argument that results from her consciousness of the limitations of her own class position. Woolf is not attempting to speak for all women, just as her essay "Memories of a Working Women's Guild" is an anti-introduction to a collection of writing by working-class members of the Women's Co-operative Guild which asserts its inability to speak for, to summarize such a collection. The speaker in the essay is a "benevolent spectator," "irretrievably cut off" (*CE*4 136).

In the Monk's House Papers at the University of Sussex there are letters written to Woolf in answer to *Three Guineas*. There are 22 letters from friends and acquaintances and 58 letters from readers unknown to Woolf.[4] The 58 letters will form the focus of this article, for the insight they offer into the constitution of Woolf's reading public, the reception of the text by its common readers, and Woolf's public image.

Anne Olivier Bell has informed me that it was she, not Woolf, who separated the letters into those from friends versus unknown readers (Bell). It is also important to note that Woolf received more letters in response to *Three Guineas* than she kept. However, Woolf either received, or kept, *many* more letters about *Three Guineas* than any other text.[5] This means that either *Three Guineas* engaged its reading public more than the other texts, this in itself disproving Leavis' argument, since the 58 letters are from unknown readers rather than Woolf's friends, or that Woolf kept more responses to *Three Guineas*, indicating that with this text she was particularly interested in the reaction of the reading public.

Woolf returned continually to the idea of a reading public, its sociological purpose, the relationship between audience and author, and the purpose and methodology of criticism and reviewing. In "The Leaning Tower," a paper given to the Workers' Educational Association in 1940, Woolf writes that "Literature is no one's private ground: literature is common ground" (*M* 125). In her diary Woolf describes the essay: it points to "the supersession of aristocratic culture by common readers: also to the end of class literature" (*D5* 267). As Woolf situates herself without rather than within the tower, her notion of the reader and the reading public, then, is thoroughly democratic: literature is for all and all should have access to the reading and writing of it. Gillian Beer's recently collected essays, which can be read as an extended rebuttal to claims of Woolf's elitism, foreground Woolf's interest in the ordinary and the communal, particularly as regards literature, readers and writers. "The deep value which she accords to communality is not a matter only of her sincerely learnt and practised socialism or her forcefully written (if not always practised) solidarity with other women. It has to do with her practice of writing out of the mass" (Beer 50). She wrote *for*, as well as *about*, the common reader, hence her advocating of public libraries in "The Leaning Tower": "This book was not bought; it was not hired. It was borrowed from a public library. England lent it to a common reader" (124). The speaker here is writer and reader, pointing to Woolf's idea that all readers are critics, all readers engage with the text in dialogue.

In no way is the common reader a passive receptacle: "the nonhierarchical quality of the Common Reader is merged with the concept of dialogue" (Rosenberg 56). The artist/audience relationship is a two-way process for Woolf: "the standards we [readers] raise and the judgements we pass steal into the air and become part of the atmosphere which writers breathe as they work" (*CR2* 269). Here, again, the speaker in and writer of the essay has situated herself amongst the readers, signifying Woolf's own ease in moving between reader and writer, obviously because she was both, but also because of how she conceived of the space between a writer and his/her public. In place of the reviewer, restricted by space, time, the profit motive, and the pressures of publicity, Woolf places the common reader: "if behind the erratic gunfire of the press the author felt that there was another kind of criticism, the opinion of people reading for the love of reading, slowly and unprofessionally, . . . . judging with great sympathy and yet with great severity" (270).

Written in 1932, this quotation seems to prophesy the bundle of 58 letters, proof of a reading public, both praising and criticizing. These members of the reading public respond to the text with enough personal and political intensity to prompt a letter to the author, the instigation of a dialogue with both text and author. Woolf replied to many of the letters, often eliciting a second and even third letter from the correspondent. The notion of letters and dialogues invites comparison with the structure of *Three Guineas* itself. Provisional titles included "Answers to Correspondents" and "Letters to an Englishman," the former ironically foreshadowing the way in which epistolary exchange extended beyond *Three Guineas* itself, the letters which Woolf answered both within and without the text. The rhetorical use of an epistolary format suggests exchange, dialogue, an attempt to bridge the ellipsis in the text, the gap which the narrator wonders "whether it is any use to try to speak across" (155). Letters proliferate in *Three Guineas:* without the barrister's letter the text would not have been written, and this exchange sparks off exchanges with the two treasurers, as well as the other voices and testimonies that serve as evidence. The constantly shifting, implied audience occasioned by the multiple voices, foregrounds the importance of audience (and reading public) in that the text becomes a function of the audience.

This diversity of voices is found in the 58 letters, running counter to Leavis' claims that Woolf was writing for an exclusive readership. The gap between the implied audience, the graying gentleman who receives the letter (the text), and the real audience is enormous. The barrister, whom she describes as a type, is diffused by the sequel to the text, or the letters she receives in reply. The 58 letters are from 49 readers, 34 of whom are women. The letters come from all over the United Kingdom, from Suffolk to Scotland, Highgate to Hereford, as well as from California, Michigan, New York, Massachusetts, and British Columbia. Perhaps even more significant than geographical diversity is the variety in class and employment represented in the letters. Three of the 49 respondents identify themselves as working class, one man and two women (46, 58 and Agnes Smith), and three further respondents situate themselves as different from Woolf in terms of class and/or education (2, 11, 44).[6] Of course there are many letters from which it is impossible to determine class background. This means, then, that certain of these letters represent a rare insight into Woolf's working class readership, particularly working class women. Rather than making assumptions about how a working class woman might react to *Three Guineas*, here we have first hand responses. A working class weaver from Yorkshire, Agnes Smith, for example, writes that she was initially concerned about Woolf's lack of treatment of working class women's experience, but in a second letter agreed with Woolf's decision to write from a position of which she had first hand knowledge.[7] The professions of the respondents are equally diverse, including an office worker, teachers, vicars, housewives, an accountant, a librarian, a bookseller, a bus conductor, and a post graduate student from Michigan who was refused approval for a Ph.D. on Woolf on the grounds that Woolf was too modern a subject, and offered Leslie Stephen as consolation.

Many of the female respondents were politically active. Letters were sent from Geraldine Otle, the Registrar and Secretary of the Froebel Society, a women's educational society (1); Annie Colles, a woman working at *The Call*, the first daily paper owned by women (25); and two women who were members of the WSPU: one of whom had been imprisoned five times (Lilian Mitehill, 11), the other a speaker and organizer for the Union (Ellen Crockren, 22). One of the correspondents is Helena Swanwick, pacifist and editor of *The Common Cause* between 1909 and 1912 (5).

The letters are predominantly positive in response, apart from several letters offering factual corrections, several letters from women who object to

Woolf's pacifism, and three misogynist letters from men. One of the latter is the only letter of the 58 which accuses Woolf of not being able to descend from her "Olympian hieghts [sic] to the level of the street" (William Platt, 21). Woolf acknowledged the variety in response, writing to her American publisher, "It has aroused a great deal of interest here—both anger and approval" (*L6* 268) and of course it's possible that she saved more of the positive letters, but the sum total of the 58 letters is overwhelming praise, thanks and corroboration. Women write "No one has expressed our difficulties in making a living better than you" (Geraldine Otle, 1); "I believe you to be the finest contemporary writer, your books will live" (Diana Boyes, 2); "May you long continue to point the way" (Margaret Amiss, 17)[8] and "I had grown so used to accepting the irrelevance of my position [. . . .]You put fresh courage into our dulled hearts" (Dorothy Soden, 26). In most cases praise is linked to personal corroboration: the idea that Woolf has accurately and forcefully described their situation and the inequality they have experienced.

These letters, then, establish the variety of Woolf's reading public, the diversity of class, background and location. Woolf was not just writing for a privileged elite, a côterie of friends; she was inspiring a wide cross section of women, such that they felt compelled to contact her, to elicit discussion. One woman writes that this is the first time she has written to an author or celebrity (Gladys Rossiter, 6). Woolf herself describes the diversification occasioned by the correspondence: she writes in her diary that the response is "unexpected" and that "Not one of my friends has mentioned it. My wide circle has widened"(*D5* 193). She also acknowledges the way in which the readers' letters extend and become part of the text of *Three Guineas* itself. Again in the diary she writes, "my own, now numerous, semi-official 3 Gs letters"(*D5* 173). The words "semi-official" point to the official *Three Guineas* letters, the three that make up the text, so that the responses being semi-official, are in a liminal space, both part of and outside of the text. They are "my own" as she says, obviously only an extension of the text for her, in private, as no one else had access to them. They are *Three Guineas* letters both because they are about the text *Three Guineas*, but they also continue the text by providing more evidence, more corroboration for Woolf's arguments about women, pacifism and fascism. Her interest in the letters and her reading public even extended to her suggestion that she would write another pamphlet on the responses to *Three Guineas* themselves (*D5* 146). The text continues to extend beyond its boundaries.

In spite of the diversity of Woolf's readership, there seems to me to be one extremely important similarity in so many of the letters. That is, how many of them address the issue of the reading public and the readership of *Three Guineas*. The responses obviously provide information as to the constitution of Woolf's readership, but also comment directly on the issue. Close to half of the respondents take up the issue of audience, nearly always in terms of dissemination and access. *Three Guineas* should be made available to more people, they argue, it should be published in new editions so as to make it cheaper. Several of the respondents themselves argue that the text should reach a wider working class audience, further contradiction to Leavis' review. Woolf's ever widening circle should be made even wider.

The first edition of *Three Guineas*, published on June 2, 1938 by the Hogarth Press cost 7s 6d. The second British edition was not published by Penguin until 1977, and sold at 80p. At the same time as *Three Guineas* was being published, Woolf's *Common Reader, Second Series* was being reprinted by Penguin, copies costing 6d. Of course the price of *Three Guineas* and the lack of a cheap paperback edition are a result of its publication by a small press and the sales figures, but what is important is the readers' sense of urgency that it reach a wider audience and that the price may be a prohibitive factor. The strongest praise in the letters is the repeated call for a larger reading public, tying in with Woolf's own democratic notions of access and the common reader.

Five respondents suggest *Three Guineas* should be mandatory reading in comments such as "Every man and every woman who hasn't come across sex-barriers should be presented with a copy at 18" (Margaret Paul, 14); "a book that should be read & digested by every thinking man & woman" (R. A. Harman, 43)[9]; *Three Guineas* should be in "all schools colleges seminaries" (Constance Cheke, 47). John McAdam, a librarian, picks up on Woolf's championing of public libraries as places which are not closed to women, and makes the link between the public library and a wider reading public for *Three Guineas* (12). He also asks if she will write an introduction for Book News, one benefit of which, he tells her, would be that it would "reach a much wider public" of 40,000 to 50,000 readers.[10] Charles Brumwell, a bookseller, informs Woolf that he sees it as his duty to increase sales of *Three Guineas* by recommending it to his customers (18), as does Belinda Jelliffe, who writes: "I am going to do all in my power to get females I know to read it, and to BUY it" (55). Three respondents raise the issue of price. Jane Walker writes that *Three Guineas* ought to have been published as a Penguin Special, noting "it ought to have a far wider public than it will get as a seven & six penny book" (27). Penguin Specials were an offshoot of the 6d Penguin reprints. Also priced at 6d, they were new books commissioned on current international affairs. Penguin made books a "mass medium," made "knowledge more accessible" which is what the majority of readers argue needed to happen to *Three Guineas* (Hare xii,3). A working class woman, Constance Cheke, writes that she would not have bought it if Smiths had not reduced it to two shillings (46). Annie Colles notes that *Three Guineas* should be "broadcast to millions" (25), in other words a change in medium would be a way of increasing accessibility. These persistent calls for an increased readership disprove the charge that the book has little relevance and speaks only for Woolf and her friends, a charge made by Leavis and by more recent voices. The letters testify to the urgency of dissemination: "if only the unconverted would read and could understand all you express" (Otle, 1); "I hope and believe that your book will have far-reaching influence" (Phyllis Preen, 51).[11] The majority of the respondents are highly sensitive to the educational potential of the text, the political power to be found in its argument, the evidence of its research and its expression.

These correspondents feel, then, that *Three Guineas* speaks for them, it represents their position, their experience of the patriarchal system at work in both private and public. Several women articulate this affinity in terms of Woolf's notion of the Society of Outsiders, her model for being simultaneously within and without, for identification and difference. One woman, Dorothy Mather, who sent her daughter to Cheltenham Ladies College but found to her disappointment that it replicated the male public school system, signs herself a "very grateful 'outsider'" (50). Constance Cheke, who states she is "not of your 'class,'" addresses her letter "Dear Fellow Outsider" (46). A third woman, R. Ranken, tells of the encouragement given her by the notion of the Society of Outsiders, to which she belongs because of her crusade against inequality by sunbathing topless on the beaches of Bognor and Sandy Bay (24). The Society of Outsiders suggests diversity within commonality: for example, one woman calls herself a Fellow Outsider but objects to Woolf's pacifism.

These readers are acutely aware of Woolf's own position as outsider, and this identification facilitates connection and creates community—community as inclusive and diverse rather than an exclusive côterie. *Three Guineas* situates these women as outsiders through their engagement with Woolf's ideas rather than as Leavis argues, because it excludes them. They are included rather than excluded through their outsiderness. One woman writes about her fear that the text did not apply to her because she was not a daughter of an educated man, but her fast realization of the many points at which the text collided with her experience and ideas.

Woolf wrote in a letter to Ethel Smyth: "Not a novel, they [the shops] said, and the public won't touch anything controversial about women. And I'm getting the oddest letters, which I shall collect, as a valuable contribution to psychology" (*L6* 247). "They," the shops, are proven wrong; *Three Guineas* does speak to the reading public. Woolf collects the letters because they are an extension of the text, they are part of the huge body of evidence for the links between patriarchy, war and fascism, the links between public and private tyrannies.

The letters are also evidence of Woolf's own public position. While many of the letters note Woolf's own status as outsider, the attacks which she would receive from the press, the subversiveness of her argument, the letters also support Jane Marcus' recent call for a study of Woolf as public intellectual (Marcus 23). The range of letters is evidence of the currency of Woolf's ideas, the circulation of her arguments: "everybody will have to read you among the public that makes opinions" (A. G. Sayers, 9).[12] She is a thinker who was seen as having "popularity & power" (B. M. Bryson, 29). Finally, these letters contradict Leavis' claim that "Woolf is not living in the contemporary world" (203). They are proof of her place in the public/political arena, and that furthermore, Woolf can speak to, while not for, working class women.

**Notes**

1 For example: Lister, "Why are we so interested in the Bloomsbury Group," *Independent*, 24 Sept. 1995: 1373; Toynbee, "Politicians are the true philistines" *Independent*, 18 Oct. 1995: 1211; Taylor, "Definitely not the last tango in Charleston" *Independent*, 15 Nov. 1997: 583.

2 I would like to acknowledge the, as far as I know, only other work on these letters: Silver's article on the reaction to *Three Guineas* in all the letters and the press: "*Three Guineas* Before and After: Further Answers to Correspondents." I want to build on this work by focusing on the 58 letters and the issues they raise about Woolf and her reading public.

3 Other contemporary reviews in line with Leavis' include: Bogan, *New Republic*, 14 Sept. 1938, and Greene, *Spectator*, 17 June 1938.

4 I am currently editing all of these *Three Guineas* letters, those from friends and those from unknown readers, for publication in *Woolf Studies Annual* in 2000.

5 *TG*: 58, *W*: 23, *AROO*: 14, *O*: 10, *TTL*: 6.

6 Monk's House Papers/ *Three Guineas* Letters, University of Sussex, 1-58. All reasonable attempts have been made to trace and contact copyright holders prior to publication. In some case, however, this has proved impossible. If notified, the author will be pleased to rectify any omissions at the earliest opportunity. I would like to thank the Librarian of the University of Sussex for permission to transcribe and quote from these letters, as well as Elizabeth Inglis, Assistant Librarian in the Manuscripts Section, for the help she gave me in my research.

7 These letters are in the 22, not the 58, because the correspondence continued until Woolf's death, therefore Bell considered her a friend, although she was unknown to Woolf when she first wrote in response to *Three Guineas*.

8 Quoted courtesy of Ms. Joan Smith, friend of Ms. Margaret Amiss, correspondent.

9 Quoted courtesy of I. A. (Bunty) Biggs, daughter of Mr. R. A. Harman, correspondent.

10 Quoted courtesy of Ms. Jean Brocklehurst, daughter of Mr. John McAdam, correspondent.

11 Quoted courtesy of Hilary Bishop-Preen, daughter of Phyllis Preen, correspondent.

12 Quoted courtesy of D. M. Sayers, grandson of A. G. Sayers, correspondent. Woolf's replies to A. G. Sayers' three letters can be found in *L6*, 238 and 363. In her replies, Woolf writes that Sayers' letters have given her "great pleasure" (*L6* 238). In her second reply, Woolf acknowledges the success of *Three Guineas*, but wonders whether it made any impression: "I doubt that ideas ever do"(*L6* 363). A. G. Sayers sent Woolf a book of poems written by his son, A. M. Sayers, to which Woolf replies that she hopes that "he [the son] won't be darkened by the

war. We, as publishers, are hoping that people must read; and so there must be writers" (*L6* 363). Here, again, we sce her concerned with the reading public, particularly its decrease due to the Second World War, a concern which clearly underpins her interest in the response to *Three Guineas* in general.

## Works Cited

Beer, Gillian. *Virginia Woolf: The Common Ground.* Edinburgh: Edinburgh University Press, 1996.

Bell, Anne Olivier. Letter to Anna Snaith. 21 February 1998.

Bogan, Louise. *New Republic.* 14 Sept. 1938: 164-5.

Greene, Graham. *Spectator.* 17 June 1938: 1110.

Leavis, Q. D. "Caterpillars of the Commonwealth Unite!" *Scrutiny.* 7.2 (1938): 203-214.

Lister, David. "Why are we so interested in the Bloomsbury Group?" *Independent.* 24 Sept. 1995: 1373.

Marcus, Jane. "Wrapped in the Stars and Stripes: Virginia Woolf in the USA." *The South Carolina Review.* (1996): 17-23.

Monk's House Papers/*Three Guineas* Letters. University of Sussex, 1-58.

*Penguin Portrait: Allen Lane and the Penguin Editors 1935-1970.* Ed. Steve Hare. Harmondsworth: Penguin, 1995.

Rosenberg, Beth Carole. *Virginia Woolf and Samuel Johnson: Common Readers.* London: Macmillan, 1995.

Silver, Brenda, R. "*Three Guineas* Before and After: Further Answers to Correspondents." *Virginia Woolf: A Feminist Slant.* Ed. Jane Marcus. Lincoln: U of Nebraska P, 1983.

Taylor, D. J. "Definitely not the last tango in Charleston." *Independent.* 15 Nov. 1997: 583.

Toynbee, Polly. "Politicians are the true philistines." *Independent.* 18 Oct. 1995: 1211.

Woolf, Virginia. *Collected Essays. Vol. IV.* Ed. Leonard Woolf. London: Hogarth, 1967.

——. *The Common Reader, Second Series.* London: The Hogarth Press, 1974.

——. *The Diary of Virginia Woolf.* Ed. Anne Olivier Bell, assisted by Andrew McNeillie. Vol. 5 London: Hogarth, 1984.

——. *The Letters of Virginia Woolf.* Ed. Nigel Nicolson and Joanne Trautmann. Vol. 6 London: Hogarth, 1980.

——. *The Moment.* London: Hogarth, 1947.

——. *A Room of One's Own and Three Guineas.* Ed. Morag Shiach. Oxford: Oxford U P, 1992.

**Stephanie Harzewski**

# Hypertext as Metaphor: Reading Woolf in the Electronic Age

The exploration of Woolf's thematics—the tension between fragmentation and unity, the necessary yet painful nature of distance, whether aesthetic or interpersonal, and the line between flux and chaos—invokes a parallel investigation into the theoretical and structural nature of hyperfiction. Hyperfiction exists as a literary subculture of hypertext, a term coined by Theodor Nelson in 1965. One can identify the medium of hypertext as nodes (text consisting of blocks of words, images, or sound) linked electronically in often multiple paths or networks. The presence of links in electronic form functions as the defining characteristic of hypertexts. This essay explores some connections, links, if you will, between Woolf's corpus and hyperfiction theory. The act of constructing and reading a hyperfiction, especially a densely linked one, often blurs the line between flux and chaos. It is this line Woolf traverses in her novels. Inclusion of Woolf into the community of print proto-hyperfiction should be interpreted as an extension of one of her great themes—permanence through mutability—an ethic the Electronic Age embraces.[1]

Woolf's pervasive use of the stream-of-consciousness technique invites several connections with hyperfiction. The modernist stream-of-consciousness style permeates a significant amount of hyperfiction, most notably Michael Joyce's *afternoon, a story*, the best-known hyperfiction. On the formal level, Woolf's shifting point of view, characteristic of the stream-of-consciousnes style, complements the multiple narration frequently found in hyperfiction. The experience of reading hyperfiction as a play of flickering, multilinear screens parallels the luminous evanescence of Woolf's formal principles, especially her fluid syntax. However, one must be wary of assuming that a multilinear structure always reflects a stream-of-consciousness rhetorical style for hypertext at large. Just because structurally hypertext often allows for multiple reading paths, that does not mean that the diction and syntax automatically can be classified as stream-of-consciousness.

Suspicion and resistance of textual closure often found in hyperfiction theory evoke similarities with the stream of consciousness trope of the fragment. The fragment philosophically embraces the elusiveness of definite meaning and structurally eschews a hermetic text. Hypertext theorist George P. Landow indirectly connects hypertext with Woolf's ethic of portraying and constructing a life, painting, or play out of "[o]rts, scraps and fragments," as Mrs. Swithin in *Between the Acts* remembers a line from the pageant (*BTA* 215). Landow asserts: "[The] construction of an evanescent entity or wholeness always occurs in reading, but in reading hypertext it takes the additional form of constructing, however provisionally, one's own text out of fragments" (195). One should distinguish between "read-only" hypertexts such as CD-ROMs, in which readers' contributions are limited to choosing their own reading paths, and hypertexts in which users can add text, links, or both (Snyder 19). However, hyperfiction software such as *Storyspace* allows the user to compose nodes into the existing text—to contribute fragments—and consequently to put closure at bay.

Woolf's concept of "moments of being" as incandescent fragments joined to embody a life or work of art can function as a metaphorical complement to creating and navigating links in a hyperfiction. Woolf's classic "moments of being" analogy, "the necklace of memorable days," invites parallels with hypertextual links, potentially connected moments of heightened textual awareness (*AHH* 107). One can interpret the necklace with its linked beads as metonymical not only for Woolf's corpus and but also for hypertext in its emphasis on visual and conceptual connection. Hyperfiction writer and theorist Michael Joyce, perhaps unknowingly, evokes similarities between Woolf's necklace and hypertext: "We want to say of the hypertext . . . 'Look how, like pearls on a string, these nodes glitter on their path . . . .'" (189). While the necklace's string keeps the beads ordered, formatted, so to speak, the eye navigates around it and amplifies the hue of each node.[2] The structure of the necklace, an entity composed of fragments, complicates definite demarcations of part from whole and form from content. Hypertextual linking heightens this theme in that it questions the boundaries of individual texts and illuminates the oscillating, inextricable status of textual web and fragment.

Hypertextual links can be theorized as visual and conceptual structures that weave textual fragments into a web of associative imagery or "word picture[s]," to borrow a phrase from Carole Maso's novel *The Art Lover* (8). Landow asserts that hypertextual links enact associative processes: "The link, the element that hypertext adds to writing, bridges gaps between texts—bits of text—and thereby produces effects similar to analogy, metaphor, and . . . other figures . . . that we take to define poetry and poetic thought" (215). Reading Woolf in the Electronic Age is, among other things, metaphorically a hypertextual act, one that relies on the perception of associations and connections—a subtle network of motifs and images. Jeanette Winterson, in her essay "A Work of My Own," commends Woolf's "rigorous pursuit of the image" (181). Just one example of Woolf's technique of associative color imagery can be found in the flames of the burning bush in the beginning of *A Room of One's Own* that she transforms into the crimson of the red wine drunk at the Oxford luncheon. Her use of these colors ultimately implies that nourished women writers can change the college water jug into wine and resurrect Shakespeare's sister. Woolf's masterful ability to weave image should be claimed as a precursory alliance with the hyperfiction community.

Examining the intersections of Woolf's texts with hyperfiction heightens the significance of Woolf's water imagery, her dominant image. Michael Joyce theorizes hypertext as a narrative of "intertextual confluence" (236). Relatedly, he employs the phrase "networks of woven water" to describe the mapping of intertextual relations in the collaborative hyperfiction *Izme Pass* by Carolyn Guyer and Martha Petry (61). This phrase perhaps embodies a succinct metaphor for Woolf's works as a whole and functions as a contrast with the image of the ornamental gold nugget that Woolf subtly satirizes in *A Room of One's Own*: "I should never be able to fulfil . . . the first duty of a lecturer—to hand you after an hour's discourse a nugget of pure truth to wrap up between the pages of your notebooks and keep on the mantel-piece for ever" (*AROO* 3-4). As in the case of Woolf's theory of the nugget, in its frequent use of multiple narratives, shifting points of view, and the reliance on the fragment as its organizing principle, hyperfiction stylistically attempts to decenter a single, pure "truth." The phrase "networks of woven water" also mirrors Clarissa Dalloway's conception of selfhood. Clarissa while walking the London streets, "on the ebb and flow of things," employs connected water imagery to situate her identity as "being laid out like a mist between the people she knew best, who lifted her on their branches as she had seen the trees lift the mist, but it spread ever so far, her life, herself" (*MD* 9). Carolyn Guyer's hyperfiction *Quibbling* evokes similarities with Clarissa's simile and Woolf's belief in the transience of meaning: "[I]n that rhythmic sense of ebb and flow, of multi- /directional /change, . . . events. . . disappear before they're quite / intelligible but / somehow come to mean something." Throughout her texts, especially *To the Lighthouse*, Woolf implies that the creative process is not rigid but instead parallels the buoyancy, the undulations of water. Likewise, Michael Joyce characterizes hypertext as a rippling stream through which hypertext reader/writer drifts or rows: "Contours alternately take the foreground and then surrender it like water. . . . Capturing the flow this way, channeling it, the reader turns the text to distinctive uses of her own, which she can float upon or navigate through" (244-45). Thus, both Woolf and Joyce assert that the suppleness of water reflects the necessity of a fluid identity in the artistic and personal quest.

Related to the benefit of engaging multiple meanings and storylines, hypertext theorist Jay David Bolter argues that abeyance of final form and interpretation characterizes electronic narrative: "Electronic reading and writing means, above all, holding things in suspension, deferring conclusions, resisting closure. We must be prepared to be perpetual travelers" (17). Hermione Lee similarly comments on the suspended quality of *To the Lighthouse*'s close: "The ending of the novel is poised between arriving and returning, getting somewhere ('he must have reached it') and being finished" (477). Lily Briscoe contemplates the process of painting in terms that parallel the movement of the oar strokes of the Ramsay party as they row to the lighthouse: "as if the pauses were one part of the rhythm and the strokes another, and all were related" (*TTL* 158). This journey-like motif evokes similarities with hypertextual links in their inextricable connection between mobility and caesura. Similarly, Howard Harper's analysis of the structure of *To the Lighthouse* evokes compositional parallels with hypertext theory's trope of the journey:

> [E]ach section of *To the Lighthouse* represents an avenue of the exploration for the narrative consciousness. And again each avenue ends in a moment of heightened awareness which marks the discovery of a significant turning point in the exploration. The narrative consciousness may realize that this avenue can lead no further. Or it may become aware of a new direction to explore. (140)

Perhaps unknowingly heightening the pattern of searching and discovering in *To the Lighthouse* that Harper describes, hypertext theorist Espen Aarseth comments on the dialectic of losing and finding prevalent in hyperfiction: "[The] pair of master tropes [aporia and epiphany] constitutes the dynamic of hypertext discourse . . . [These tropes] control the progress and rhythm of the reader's investigation" (91, 95). While aporia conveys the sometimes frustrated, labyrinthine experience of encountering the same hypertext nodes, epiphanies instead embody, "the link out" (91). Throughout *To the Lighthouse* the reader witnesses Lily's cycles of aporia and epiphany in regard to the process of her painting and status as guest. Her revelation at Mrs. Ramsay's dinner table and the consequent moving of the salt shaker relieves her frustation as an outsider and self-doubt as an artist. Lily's sudden perception of the quality of the widowed Mr. Ramsay's shoes alleviates her reluctance to sympathize as she compliments him. The aporia-like tension between the most useful and actually available materials, whether emotional or intellectual catalysts, inherent in the process of creation and in the search for social communion functions as a theme throughout Woolf's texts. Yet, by pursuing illumination for aesthetic and psychological survival in a difficult world, revelations, though often small and transitory, offer incandescence or epiphanies.

Related to Aarseth's concept of hypertextual aporia, at the turn of the millennium, literacy at large, the canon, and ourselves can invoke the phrase "between the acts" an apt reference point. Michael Joyce conveys a dramatic aporia regarding the closing of the age of print, the ushering in of the Electronic Age, and the ephemera of all epochs: "We . . . are late at the end of something and unable to speak. It is too much to hope for an orderly enough end to accomplish our hopes of transcendence. Yet what chokes and thwarts us is so transitory that to hope for justice seems foolish" (1). About half a century earlier Woolf in *Between the Acts* similarly comments on the the inevitable passage of time and the painful transition from the Victorian era to the twentieth century and the looming of war the play's audience experiences: "They were neither one thing nor the other; neither Victorians nor themselves. They were suspended, without being, in limbo. Tick, tick,

tick went the machine" (178). In her essay "Rupture, Verge, and Precipice/Precipice, Verge, and Hurt Not," an argument for the coexistence and experimental engagement of both print and electronic media, Carole Maso asserts that electronic forms such as hyperfiction will heighten the elusiveness of the signified and the flux of location: "Electronic writing will gives us a deeper understanding of the instability of texts, of worlds" (63). In the preface to her experimental fiction *Aureole,* Maso implies that Woolf theorizes "the liminal space before whatever happens next will happen," perhaps another way of identifying the situation of between the acts (x). It is this aesthetic and psychological condition that the act of navigating a hypertext visually and conceptually attempts to capture. Similarly, Woolf throughout her works evokes this liminality, this intermediate state: Mrs. Ramsay seated at the dinner table waiting for the company to merge yet filled with anticipation as the candles are lit; Mrs. Ramsay's backward glance and foot suspended on the threshold of the dining room as she contemplates exiting a scene fading before her eyes; the party of six at the first luncheon in *The Waves* eagerly waiting for Percival to arrive; and Peter Walsh before he gazes at Clarissa at the close of *Mrs. Dalloway.*

While texts such as *Finnegans Wake*, *Tristram Shandy*, and *In Memoriam* have been claimed by the hyperfiction community as print proto-hypertexts, Woolf has not been similarly identified to date (Landow 182). For some this inclusion is democratic, for others pernicious. It is interesting to speculate on the full ramifications of Woolf's entry into the canon of print proto-hyperfiction. In the largest sense, inclusion of Woolf in this community further blurs definite demarcations between print and electronic mediums. In the print proto-hypertext canon both mediums mutually, reciprocally coexist. Literature is not so much temporarily between the acts but rather perpetually so in that literary paradigms do not occur in a linear sequence with precise boundaries but instead suggest a pattern of interchange. For better or worse, this inclusion politically could enact dramatic effects, especially for feminist literary scholars, at the pedagogical level and in women's studies programs. I am somewhat hesitant to predict that claiming Woolf would produce a domino effect of women writers into the hypertext community. Carole Maso, a disciple of Woolf publishing in print who like Winterson has been represented on the syllabi of Michael Joyce's hypertext courses at Vassar College, employs the phrase "the electronic ladyland" to envison such a community ("Rupture" 56). Nevertheless, we need not forget the range of Woolf's influence on major women writers such as Maso, Winterson, Marguerite Duras, Adrienne Rich, and Alice Walker.

Woolf, as a precursory member, enhances the hyperfiction community more than she depends on such an inclusion for survival in the Electronic Age. David Denby in his introduction to the Signet Classic edition of *Jacob's Room* similarly asserts that "[i]n the end, putting it crassly, we need . . . [Woolf] more than she needs us" (xii). In their best moments Woolf's texts enact their own their theory by embodying an aesthetic practice in which the process of illumination and the vision itself coalesce. Nevertheless, the linking feature of hyperfiction software such as *Storyspace* as a working tool possesses the potential to enhance significantly the tracing of Woolf's imagery and, in the larger sense, to deconstruct visually and literally the boundaries of Woolf's individual texts. Landow asserts that in print proto-hyperfiction, "[h]ypertext . . . makes certain elements . . . stand out for the first time" (182). For Woolf scholars initially encountering hyperfiction, the interlacing of associations navigated in a hyperfiction heightens Woolf's masterful creation of dynamic, confluent images. On the other hand, reading Woolf in the Electronic Age prepares one to read or perhaps to write hyperfiction and complements the metaphoric implications of hypertextual links. The attempt to seek permanence and solidity in a world of fragmentation and mutability—one of Woolf's great themes—parallels the act of claiming Woolf into the hyperfiction community.

## Notes

[1] My concept of "permanence through mutability" finds its source in a variation of a phrase found in Rose's discussion of *Between the Acts*: "The thematic emphasis on permanence and mutability, . . . which permeates *Mrs. Dalloway* and in some ways *To the Lighthouse*, underlies Woolf's last book as well" (226).

[2] I am indebted to Professor Marcia Ian of Rutgers University, New Brunswick, for suggesting this idea to me. In the seminar The Modernist Novel as Theory, taught in the spring semester of 1998, Professor Ian conveyed a paraphrase of this thought in her comments on my final paper of the same title.

## Works Cited

Aarseth, Espen J. *Cybertext: Perspectives on Ergodic Literature.* Baltimore: Johns Hopkins UP, 1997.

Bolter, Jay David. "Alone and Together in the Electronic Bazaar." *Computers and Composition* 10.2 (1993): 5-18.

Bolter, Jay David, Michael Joyce, and John B. Smith. *Storyspace: Hypertext Writing Environment for the Macintosh.* Version 1.2. Diskette. Watertown: Eastgate, 1992.

Denby, David. Introduction. *Jabob's Room.* By Virginia Woolf. 1922. New York: Signet, 1998. v-xiv.

Harper, Howard. *Between Language and Silence: The Novels of Virginia Woolf.* Baton Rouge: Louisiana State UP, 1982.

Guyer, Carolyn. *Quibbling.* Diskette. Watertown: Eastgate Systems, 1993.

Guyer, Carolyn, and Martha Petry. *Izme Pass. Hypertext on the Edge.* Diskette. Davis: U of California, 1991.

Joyce, Michael. *Of Two Minds: Hypertext Pedagogy and Poetics.* Ann Arbor: U of Michigan P, 1995.

——. *Afternoon: A Story.* Diskette. Watertown: Eastgate, 1987.

Landow, George P. *Hypertext 2.0: The Convergence of Contemporary Critical Theory and Technology*. Baltimore: Johns Hopkins UP, 1997.

Lee, Hermione. *Virginia Woolf.* New York: Knopf, 1997.

Maso, Carole. *Aureole*. Hopewell, NJ: Ecco, 1996.

——. "Rupture, Verge, and Precipice/Precipice, Verge, and Hurt Not." *The Review of Contemporary Fiction* 16.1 (1996): 54-75.

——. *The Art Lover: A Novel.* 1990. Hopewell, NJ: Ecco, 1995.

Nelson, Theodor Holm. "A File Structure for the Complex, the Changing, and the Indeterminate." *Proceedings of the 20th National Conference of the Association for Computing Machinery*. New York: Association for Computing Machinery, 1965. 84-100.

Rose, Phyllis. *Woman of Letters: A Life of Virginia Woolf.* New York: Oxford UP, 1978.

Snyder, Ilana. *Hypertext: The Electronic Labyrinth.* Victoria, Austral.: Melbourne UP, 1996.

Winterson, Jeanette. "A Work of My Own." *Art Objects: Essays on Ecstasy and Effrontery*. 1995. New York: Vintage, 1997. 165-92.

Woolf, Virginia. "Moments of Being: 'Slaters Pins Have No Points.'" *A Haunted House and Other Short Stories.* 1944. New York: Harvest, 1972. 103-11.

——. *Between the Acts.* 1941. San Diego: Harvest, 1969.

——. *A Room of One's Own.* 1929. San Diego: Harvest, 1989.

——. *To the Lighthouse.* 1927. San Diego: Harvest, 1989.

——. *Mrs. Dalloway.* 1925. San Diego: Harvest, 1990.

# Constructing Feminine Aesthetic Spaces

**Marianne DeKoven, Featured Speaker**

## The Community of Audience: Woolf's Drama of Public Woman

Virginia Woolf has become such a visible cultural icon that it is difficult to remember her ambivalent relation to the role of public woman.[1] She was deeply ambivalent toward her public stature, simultaneously seeking and avoiding, desiring and fearing, visibility.[2] That ambivalence is not only a significant factor in her relation to increasing fame, but also integral, through a shifting trajectory of accommodation, to her literary practice throughout her career.[3] In her reinventions of literary writing, Woolf launched herself at once out from the conventional feminine private sphere and further into a liberated, subversive feminine privacy, or privatized femininity. At the same time, she worked to represent the public by means of feminine interiority and to insert feminine spaces of the private into reconfigured gendered spaces of the public. Drama or spectacle, particularly in its deployment of the community of audience, emerged for Woolf at the end of her career as best suited to represent these reconfigured spaces.

### I

Woolf's theories of fiction, and her literary writing through most of her career, identify femininity with privacy and interiority, even as she herself increasingly adopted highly visible public roles.[4] "Mr. Bennett and Mrs. Brown" provides one of Woolf's most explicit and powerful accounts of her view of modernist fiction as representation not just of consciousness or psychic process in general, or of interiority as opposed to exteriority in general terms, but of a particular, heretofore suppressed, oppressed and devalued space of feminine privacy.[5]

In her brilliant chapter focusing on "Mr. Bennett and Mrs. Brown" in *Feminist Destinations*, titled "'We're Getting There': Woolf, Trains, and the Destinations of Feminist Criticism," Rachel Bowlby challenges the traditional view of Woolfian modernism as a practice of a bounded interiority, demonstrating that Woolf uses Mrs. Brown in the railway carriage to open up a new representational space where inner and outer interpenetrate. The railway carriage is at once public and private; Mrs. Brown's interiority both encompasses and refers to the new crowds and masses of modernity's public spaces. I find this argument powerfully persuasive, but would argue nonetheless that Woolf's primary move in this essay, as in her fictional practice, is to valorize and inhabit a reconfigured feminine interiority. This interiority is in dynamic conversation with and orientation toward the public, as Bowlby shows, but this public is nonetheless recontained and transformed as the private.

This privacy is very different from the enforced female domesticity that reached its apogee in Woolf's Victorian childhood, the privacy of Coventry Patmore's Angel in the House, whom Woolf so gloriously claimed to have definitively murdered in "Professions for Women." The privacy of Mrs. Brown's interiority is very explicitly an alternative to bourgeois domesticity: a liberated space of freedom from its constraints; a space of valorized femininity redeemed from its denigration of women.[6] But it is also a space that, in refusing not only the female private sphere of bourgeois domesticity but also the hegemonic male public sphere, reinscribes that private/public dichotomy in ways that realign femininity with exclusion from the public sphere.[7] "Mrs. Brown" is finally parallel to "Mr. Bennett" and therefore inevitably in a hierarchical binary that disempowers her, through the Irigarayan logic of the self-same, where the self-present subject is always inevitably masculine.[8]

"Mr. Bennett and Mrs. Brown" is not explicitly feminist, nor does it even address directly the issue of gendered subjectivity. In it, Woolf attacks the failures of the Edwardian meliorative realism she uses Wells, Galsworthy and Bennett to epitomize. She argues instead for the modernist or "Georgian" aesthetics of Forster, Lawrence, Strachey, Joyce, Eliot, and, implicitly, Woolf herself as the only appropriate mode of representation for twentieth-century modernity (this is the essay, of course, in which Woolf makes her famous statement that "on or about December, 1910, human character changed" [96]). In order to make visible the powerful gender content of her analysis in this essay, it is necessary to look carefully at the figurative language Woolf uses to develop her polemics.

This gender content is clearest in Woolf's discussion of Mrs. Brown herself, but it appears as well in her account of post-1910 modernity, which begins with a disclaimer: "I am not saying that one went out, as one might into a garden, and there saw that a rose had flowered, or that a hen had laid an egg" (96). In other words, the changes "in human character" of 1910 that she is about to discuss are more subtle than these clearcut overnight transformations. Note that Woolf chooses here stereotypically feminine imagery—imagery appropriate to Victorian versions of female domesticity and reproductive sexuality—to indicate at once that this change has occurred primarily in the realm of the feminine and also that she is rejecting as metaphors for this change the domesticated female sexuality of roses flowering and hens laying eggs: "I am *not* saying."

She goes on to deploy a highly gendered sequence of objective correlatives to indicate what she *is* saying:

> In life one can see the change, if I may use a homely illustration, in the character of one's cook. The Victorian cook lived like a leviathan in the lower depths, formidable, silent, obscure, inscrutable; the Georgian cook is a creature of sunshine and fresh air; in and out of the drawing-room, now to borrow the *Daily Herald*, now to ask advice about a hat. Do you ask for more solemn instances of the power of the human race to change? Read the *Agamemnon*, and see whether, in process of time, your sympathies are not almost entirely with Clytemnestra. Or consider the married life of the Carlyles and bewail the waste, the futility, for him and for her, of the horrible domestic tradition which made it seemly for a woman of genius to spend her time chasing beetles, scouring saucepans, instead of writing books. All human relations have shifted—those between masters and servants, husbands and wives, parents and children. (96)

This famous sequence concerns itself almost exclusively with the egalitarian revision of gendered hierarchies. Clytemnestra and Mrs. Carlyle are used quite straightforwardly to evoke sympathy for wronged women and to repudiate the "horrible domestic tradition" that entraps bourgeois women, particularly women of genius.

The change in the character of "one's cook," as Rachel Bowlby points out, has very much to do with gender and class. It is an important instance of the conjunction or conflation of class with gender egalitarianism that characterized early twentieth-century leftist ideologies of social change for Woolf and other modernists. The Georgian or modern cook, in emerging from the Victorian cook's subterranean obscurity into "sunshine and fresh air," occupies a space at once inside and outside of the drawing room: a public/private liminality that will become crucial to Woolf's later constructions of a new feminine public space.

In describing the Victorian cook as "leviathan in the lower depths, formidable, silent, obscure, inscrutable," Woolf deploys figuration that points directly to Luce Irigaray's account of the repressed feminine of Western patriarchy, which is typically associated with water, identified as submerged, silent, amorphous, monstrous, and is also characteristically conflated with the working class and with nonwhite race in modernism.[9] Modernity liberates this repressed, oppressed, racialized feminine figure into the "sunshine and fresh air," where she has access to democratic literacy in the form of "the *Daily Herald*" and to the individuated subjectivity interpellated by bourgeois consumerism in "advice about a hat."

The shifts in "all [hierarchical, gendered] human relations" that occurred in 1910 have put Mrs. Brown at the center of the modernist fictional project. In Woolf's narrative, she encounters Mrs. Brown and "Mr. Smith" as she, the Woolfian first-person narrator whom I will call Woolf, enters the railway carriage they already occupy on a journey from Richmond to Waterloo: from suburb to city center, a modernist destination the importance of which Rachel Bowlby makes clear. Mrs. Brown's salient characteristics for Woolfian modernism, characteristics invisible or uninteresting to the Victorians and Edwardians, are her ordinariness, her elderliness, her clean, tidy, threadbare poverty, her "extremely small" size, her "pinched . . . look of suffering, of apprehension" (98).[10]

In Woolf's narrative, based on the strained relations she perceives between the two, she projects Mrs. Brown as suffering with quiet dignity the sexualized, aggressive verbal bullying Mr. Smith has been engaging in just prior to Woolf's entrance into the railway carriage. Woolf accords Mr. Smith a shadowy but characteristically patriarchal power over Mrs. Brown ("some power over her which he was exerting disagreeably" [99]), involving money, property, and family relations. Woolf's story of Mrs. Brown is a story of the oppressive hierarchical gendered "human relations" challenged, if not yet undone, by "1910." In the dignity, centrality, interiority, depth, and complexity it accords Mrs. Brown, this story is also designed to further the project of that undoing.

Such a story would never be written by "the Edwardians." To the utopian H. G. Wells, Woolf imagines, Mrs. Brown would be invisible, because "There are no Mrs. Browns in Utopia. Indeed I do not think that Mr. Wells, in his passion to make her what she ought to be, would waste a thought upon her as she is" (106). In John Galsworthy's meliorative realism, she would have no more material existence in her own right than she does for H. G. Wells: "Burning with indignation, stuffed with information, arraigning civilization, Mr. Galsworthy would only see in Mrs. Brown a pot broken on the wheel and thrown into the corner" (106).

"Mr. Bennett, alone of the Edwardians, would keep his eyes in the carriage" (106). That is why Woolf focuses on Bennett in this essay.[11] Bennett, however, would see only the exterior of Mrs. Brown: how she "wore a brooch which had cost three-and-ten-three at Whitworth's bazaar; and had mended both gloves—indeed the thumb of the left-hand glove had been replaced" (106). With "three-and-ten-three" and "thumb of the left-hand glove," Woolf brilliantly pillories the obsessively detailed banality of Bennett's realism of externals. It is Mrs. Brown's interiority, the "unlimited capacity and infinite variety" (119) of her subjectivity, that Woolf believes only modernist fiction can properly represent. The project of modernist fiction is precisely to place Mrs. Brown at its center and forge an adequate means of representing her elusive privacy. Again, this privacy is in direct conflict with, and rebellion against, Victorian feminine domesticity and subordination. It is in no way a retreat from or denial of either anger or social engagement; it is a profoundly political space of utopian feminist potentiality. Yet it recontains its move into public space as an alternatively privatized femininity, a femininity that represents public experience as and through consciousness and interiority.

Woolf wrote "Mr. Bennett and Mrs. Brown" at the same time that she was working on *Mrs. Dalloway*. Unlike Mrs. Brown, Mrs. Dalloway is wealthy, but in other respects the two characters are remarkably similar. As with "Mrs. Brown," we know Clarissa Dalloway by the title patriarchal marriage assigns her, and that title is the title of the novel. Like Mrs. Brown, Clarissa Dalloway is, despite her own upper-middle-class origins and the wealth, class status, and political importance of her husband, an ordinary woman. She has no great accomplishments or extraordinary personal qualities. Like Mrs. Brown, Mrs. Dalloway is reduced, if not "pinched": in the aftermath of her illness she has become very thin, and has retreated to the "nunlike" single bed in the upstairs bedroom, associating her with the position of a servant and destabilizing, as does the novel as a whole, the hegemonic psychic-social structures of bourgeois marriage. Like Mrs. Brown, Mrs. Dalloway maintains her dignity partly through preserving her privacy, her interiority intact. Much of the novel is devoted to transforming our view of the world precisely by showing it to us through the filter of the rich, complex interiority of this "ordinary" woman. At the same time, Mrs. Dalloway's interiority *is* the world: in her remarkable boundaryless psychic connectedness, she contains, or recontains, the public spaces she passes through and the myriad human others she encounters within her private consciousness. In this regard, *Mrs. Dalloway* accomplishes precisely what Woolf argues in "Mr. Bennett and Mrs. Brown" modernist fiction should accomplish.

*Mrs. Dalloway* is the clearest instance of Woolfian fiction as reinvention of feminine privacy, but that project permeates her work from its inception through the mid-thirties. Rachel Vinrace, protagonist of Woolf's first novel *The Voyage Out*, has an intense inner life that cannot be made to conform or even connect to a superficial and constraining external reality structured by hierarchical gender relations. Language itself, in this early modernist novel, is still far too enmeshed in the late-Victorian universe Woolf devoted her career to re-forming; Rachel is almost entirely inarticulate, unable either to fit into or to affect the highly conventional linguistic games going on around her, whether banal and empty or witty and intellectual. Instead, she finds release and expression only through music. Yet even in this first novel, awkward in many formal respects, Woolf manages to convey through her revolutionary modernist formal innovations the intensity, complexity, authenticity and originality of Rachel's inner life despite Rachel's inability to do so.

In Woolf's great high modernist masterpieces of the late twenties and early thirties following *Mrs. Dalloway—To the Lighthouse, Orlando, A Room of One's Own* and *The Waves*—feminine private interiority becomes the locus of a vast, powerful, original fictional universe.[12] This claim is most easily demonstrated by *To the Lighthouse,* in which Woolf constructs one of the greatest modernist representations of the early twentieth century ("of" meaning both written within and also written about) on the ground of the almost limitlessly rich, monumental interior universes of Mrs. Ramsay's and Lily Briscoe's consciousnesses.

Woolf's deployment of interiority shifts in *Orlando, A Room of One's Own* and *The Waves*, each of which differs from and develops the "Mrs. Brown" model of *Mrs. Dalloway* and *To the Lighthouse* in its own particular way. In *Orlando,* the subversive power of feminine interiority and privacy for modern writing are thematized rather than serving as the substance and location of modernist forms and knowledges—the ground of the fictional universe—as they do in the two novels that preceded it. As a boy and young man, in the first part of the novel, Orlando leads a public life as courtier and ambassador: he has great amorous and political adventures and catastrophes and roams the world at will, but his writing languishes. In the second part of the novel, when she is publicly acknowledged as a woman, Orlando retreats back into the privacy of her ancestral house and, in the modern period, of her great, multiply bisexual love for Shelmerdine; her writing thrives and comes to fruition. This sequence is certainly not the whole story of gender in relation to private and public in this complex novel, but it is clear that the success of Orlando's writing depends on the creation of an unconventional feminine private space alternative both to conventional domesticity and to the hegemonic masculine public spheres that belittle and expel her in her feminine incarnation.

*A Room of One's Own* is in many ways the most interesting instance of Woolf's development of the "Mrs. Brown" principle. The woman writer (as narrative persona) is clearly in deep trouble when she ventures into masculine public spaces: threatened by a Beadle and having the library door slammed in her face at the "Oxbridge" men's college, subjected to Professor von X. and his colleagues' views of the "*The Mental, Moral, and Physical Inferiority of the Female Sex*" in the British Library (31), lecturing publicly in fear, even at the women's college, of Sir Archibald Bodkin leaping in rage out of the linen cupboard.

The most powerful representation of this mortal danger for women writers in the masculine public sphere is Judith Shakespeare, objective correlative and embodiment of the woman writer's fullest potentialities. She is trapped in the sexuate female reproductive body as it is literally abused and murdered within patriarchal gender relations once she moves out on her own into public space. Judith of course is William's equally gifted sister who ventures to London and is immediately impregnated (read raped) by the actor-manager who befriends her—the same "Nick Greene" who uses and belittles

Orlando. She commits suicide—"who shall measure the heat and violence of the poet's heart when caught and tangled in a woman's body?"—and is buried anonymously "at some cross-roads where the omnibuses now stop outside the Elephant and Castle" (48), a prime location of urban public space.

The importance and centrality of Judith Shakespeare in this book is reinforced by the conceit of the Marys: Mary Beton, the narrator, named for her liberating, legacy-bequeathing aunt; Mary Seton, the "Fernham"[13] science don; and Mary Carmichael, the contemporary novelist. This conceit is derived from the traditional "Ballad of Mary Hamilton," which ends "Last night there were four Marys / Tonight there'll be but three / There's Mary Beton and Mary Seton / And Mary Carmichael and me."[14] Mary Hamilton is never mentioned in the book, yet her story, parallel to Judith Shakespeare's, is crucial to its meanings. Mary Hamilton sings her ballad from the gallows on which she is about to die. She is a lady in waiting to the Queen of Scotland; she has been impregnated (again read raped) by the King and has killed the resulting baby. Her voice speaks again the danger to women of the sexuate maternal body in that ultimate hegemonic masculine public space, the domain of the monarchy. It is only in the private interiority of "a room of one's own" that the woman writer is free from that danger, free to allow her mind to claim infinite space and capacity. The fact that Mary Hamilton's name is never mentioned makes her an uncannily powerful presence in the book—the continually returning repressed—a presence, however, lost to most of its current readers, for whom this ballad is no longer common cultural property.

*The Waves* can be seen as the culmination of Woolfian modernist interiority. However, its central character, the consciousness with the greatest complexity, power of vision, scope, insight, and richness of language, is male—Bernard. The other two male characters, Louis and Neville, are close seconds to Bernard in the power, efficacy, and breadth of their language, their privacy, and their interiority. Male rather than female characters occupy the radical territory of Mrs. Brown in this novel, while the silent Percival stands for a hegemonic masculine public sphere almost entirely discredited for Woolf; still far too important, far too powerfully desired and worshiped in the world she creates and represents, but essentially irrelevant to it and verging on the ludicrous.

The three female characters (or the feminine half of the six-sided consciousness) are far more limited than their brothers in every way—in richness of language, in breadth, depth and complexity of consciousness, and scope of vision. They are in many ways feminine stereotypes: Ginny the sexuate body, achieving meaning only in sexual relation to men; Susan the maternal earth mother; Rhoda the selfless, faceless figure of silence and self-annihilation. Woolf accords them powerful, vivid recurring imagery, but, again, far less impact in the realm of Mrs. Brown than either their three male counterparts or their predecessors Rachel Vinrace, Clarissa Dalloway, Mrs. Ramsay, and Lily Briscoe.

It is the male characters—who inhabit the public sphere, but a public now materially transformed by "1910" in ways that Woolf has begun to represent in her fiction—who are able to use the knowledge of Mrs. Brown: their public roles no longer preclude access to Mrs. Brownian interiority, as did those of the "Edwardians." All three men are writers, none with public roles that detract significantly from the rich interiority available to the writing subjectivity. (Louis, Eliot-like, works in a bank, but that work occupies only his most superficial powers.) The female characters have no comparable outlet. They are as inarticulate as Rachel but none of them struggles to articulate as she did or has an alternative language comparable to her music. They are trapped in a feminized privacy that has become too constraining for Woolf.

The writing woman in the novel is enclosed within the fantasy house at Elvedon. She may in some sense be writing the novel but the novel makes no explicit connection between her feminine domestic privacy and the rich interiority it is the novel's primary project to represent. The italicized nature passages that structure the novel may also be seen as located in the realm of the feminine, but, again, they are removed from the novel's central representations of consciousness. The writing woman and the nature passages in a sense occupy residual roles in this novel, looking backward at the feminine privacy that has been at the heart of Woolf's writing since its beginning. After *The Waves*, Woolf's female characters will have to move into, and reconfigure, public spaces in order to move to the center of her fiction again.[15]

*The Years* and its companion *Three Guineas* address very directly the problematic new relation of women to the public sphere opened up by the twentieth century. *The Years* begins with the slow, excruciating death of the Victorian mother. It is structured by the movement of upper-middle-class women like Woolf—the "daughters of educated men," as she labels this class in *Three Guineas*—out of domestic servitude to the patriarch (Colonel Pargiter) in the regime of the Victorian private house, as she calls it in *Three Guineas* (the house at Abercorn Terrace). The newly reconfigured public sphere into which these privileged women move consists of professional employment (Peggy is a doctor), political activism (Delia is an Irish nationalist, Rose is a suffragist), and free independent movement (Eleanor travels around the world alone). In the novel's postwar period, all the central female characters achieve an autonomy that includes control of their bodies, of their sexuality and of their property.

This movement into heretofore hegemonically masculine public spaces and public autonomy, while liberatory and utterly necessary—the Victorian past represents unbearable oppression for women—is in no way triumphal or even predominantly affirmative. The political meetings Eleanor attends and the public charitable work she does are represented by Woolf with considerable irony and distance. Delia and Rose are represented as fanatical, narrow, humorless. Peggy is extremely unhappy, unfulfilled, envious of the older generation that was spared her compromises. Eleanor, the novel's central character who possesses its most capacious sensibility, perceives herself as limited and incomplete. Despite her constitutional optimism, she believes that the only hope lies with future generations and "other" classes (perhaps the Cockney children singing at the end of the party in a language incomprehensible to the sensibilities that constitute the novel). Public space, the traditionally masculine public sphere, is still a mined field for women, even though they now must traverse it, and can finally do so without being blown immediately to bits.[16]

*Three Guineas* makes an attempt to resolve the contradiction between the necessity and the (near) impossibility of women entering the hegemonically masculine public sphere by arguing for a "society of outsiders." The "daughters of educated men," Woolf's own class and therefore the only class of women about whom she feels she can presume to write, must in effect liberate public space from the masculinist tyranny that reaches its epitome in fascism. This violent hierarchical male imperialist militarism is about to destroy Europe, or what Woolf's imaginary interlocutor calls "civilization." He, the solicitor of money from women to help prevent war, argues that the war initiated by fascists is about to destroy democratic civilization, and Woolf herself, his creator, evidently agrees.

In *Three Guineas*, Woolf argues that women must educate themselves, but without acceding to that ludicrous hierarchical procession of men, the highest point or culmination of which is being granted the privilege of wearing "a tuft of horsehair on the left shoulder" (21). Women must enter the professions, but at the lowest levels, avoiding again the corrupt, violent hierarchy of power at the top, the power synonymous with that of fascism and on which it depends. In their societies of outsiders, public and therefore free of the stifling regime of the "private house," yet also free of the public's hegemonic contaminations, upper-middle-class women will constitute what Nancy Fraser calls a "subaltern counterpublic," a space of potential social change. As we will see, it is in *Between the Acts*, her last novel, that Woolf finds a powerful fictional representation of this liminal feminine public/private space.

## II

Gertrude Stein's literary reinvention of feminine interiority looks very different from Woolf's, but in fact there are important similarities. Stein had less ambivalence toward her public role than Woolf did: she savored the popular success she enjoyed on her 1934 American tour, and sought public visibility throughout her career (see Wagner-Martin). Her weekly salons at 27 rue de Fleurus, while initially based on the Steins' art collection rather than on Gertrude's stature as a writer, made her more accessible to a growing, shifting community of practitioners and followers of the new avant-gardes than Woolf was, despite Woolf's participation in fairly visible bohemian, intellectual, literary, artistic and aristocratic segments of London society.

Like Woolf, however, Stein was afraid of public lecturing and reluctant to do it, though Stein's fear was not incorporated into the lectures themselves as Woolf's was in *A Room of One's Own*. Stein's presence as a public woman was made possible for her by its mediation through her attachment to and location within a house (27 rue de Fleurus; later, the house in Belley), and her other links to traditional modes of public-inflected feminine domesticity, such as the salon and the dinner party. It was necessary for Woolf and Stein as modernist women to forge a liminal public/private space in order to be able to enter the masculine public sphere with sufficient presence and credibility to be able at least to imagine, and perhaps also to inhabit, a subaltern counterpublic.

For Stein, the equivalent of Woolf's Mrs. Brown was increasingly her own consciousness. In her early writing, she largely retained the fictional convention of character, assigning complex interiority to named human entities who are distinguishable from one another.[17] In *Three Lives* and the early sections of *The Making of Americans*, character is of pressing concern to Stein. Her project there, like that of the other great modernists including Woolf, is to represent as the deepest truth of human life the unique interiority of exemplary characters. These characters, like Mrs. Brown, are often exemplary in their humble feminine ordinariness; this is particularly the case for the immigrant servant protagonists of "The Good Anna" and "The Gentle Lena," the framing pieces of *Three Lives*' triptych.

In the middle of *The Making of Americans*, and increasingly in the other insistent works of 1906-11, character recedes as a preoccupation for Stein. Interiority, however—a privacy located mainly within domesticity but retrieved from its oppression of women—remains her central preoccupation. Throughout her career, Stein's writing both records and constructs, in a reinvented literary language, a space of interaction of her own consciousness with her immediate environment.[18] This space is located at once within her consciousness, her interiority, and also in a liminal space of fusion of her consciousness with the objects of her attention.

In "Portraits and Repetition," in *Lectures in America*, Stein says of her portrait writing "I must find out what is moving inside them that makes them them, and I must find out how I by the thing moving excitedly inside in me can make a portrait of them" (183). Stein derives or constructs an abstract principle of motion or quintessence of being by concentrating intently on something outside herself; she then focuses her consciousness on this principle or quintessence, incorporating it as an organizing principle for writing. The writing produced in this way recreates interiority as a space of transformative interaction with exteriority, the not-self, which itself breaks down barriers of private and public, mixing indiscriminately domestic interiors with the most official of public locations. Though the writing ultimately resides within the private interiority of Stein's consciousness—"I by the thing moving excitedly in me"—it cannot be produced without the connection to an external object: "I must find out what is moving inside them that makes them them." The result is a liminal private/public space of reconfigured interiority.

Stein's exterior environment usually consists primarily of liberated domestic interiors suffused with the erotic love, intimacy, and mutual support of her relationship with Alice Toklas: a reconfigured privacy comparable to that of Mrs. Brown.[19] The great experimental prose-poem *Tender Buttons*, divided into "Objects," "Food" and "Rooms," is the clearest instance of this characteristic Steinian reconstruction of a liberated domesticity. But Stein's environment also encompasses other people, most of them public figures in the arts, as in the famous portraits of the teens and twenties, as well as public spaces: urban spaces, spaces of nature, of geography, movement or travel, spaces of art.

It is in the publicness of drama that Stein finds the most hospitable vehicle for representing more directly the liminal feminine private/public space which her experimental writing embodies. She wrote hundreds of plays, beginning in the teens and continuing throughout the rest of her career. Among them, *Four Saints in Three Acts* of 1926 is one of the best known. Its fame is due partly to the fact that, as an opera scored by Virgil Thomson, it had a remarkable 1934 US production, and partly to the fact that it is one of her most successful pieces of writing in any genre, with its wit, vividness, aptly startling juxtapositions, and unusual cohesion around recurring motifs.

Saint Therese, the protagonist of *Four Saints*, has two primary recurring motifs that directly construct and represent this private/public liminality: "Saint Therese half in and half out of doors," and "Saint Therese seated and not surrounded." Nothing could be more clearly liminal between the private and the public than "half in and half out of doors." With "seated and not surrounded," Stein establishes a domestic space that is free, open to the air as it were, in no way confining or claustrophobic. Though one *can* be "seated" in a public space, in fact one often is, this posture generally connotes, I would argue, a feminine domestic positioning, as in traditional bourgeois family photographs, with women seated, very much "surrounded" by standing men.

These motifs are developed in ways that make their significance for the purposes of this argument even clearer:

> Saint Therese not seated at once. There are a great many persons and places near together.
>
> Saint Therese once seated. There are a great many places and persons near together. Saint Therese seated and not surrounded. There are a great many places and persons near together.
>
> Saint Therese visited by very many as well as the others really visited before she was seated. There are a great many persons and places

> close together.
>
> Saint Therese not young and younger but visited like the others by some, who are frequently going there.
>
> Saint Therese very nearly half inside and half outside outside the house and not surrounded. (586-7)

"A great many places and persons near together": a crowded public scene, in which Saint Therese is "visited by very many . . . before she was seated." Nonetheless, in her position "half inside and half outside outside the house," she is "not surrounded." Her public/private liminality allows her to enter and be entered by these crowded public scenes without being overwhelmed or made invisible by them. Instead of Woolf's "outsiders' society" partly inhabiting and partly subverting the hegemonic public sphere, Stein has created an inside/outside borderland where, at least in the visionary space of the stage, she can have the best of both worlds.

## III

Drama is capable of enacting a public representation of private experience, and also of enacting in the interior space of a theater, often representing domestic scenes, a public event. In *Between the Acts,* Woolf uses drama as a vehicle for constructing within fiction her own version of this visionary borderland.

Woolf constructs *Between the Acts* around the historical pageant written by the lesbian Miss La Trobe.[20] Patriarchal gender relations, along with the other upper-middle-class conventions, still obtain within the house ostensibly at the center of the text, Pointz Hall, presided over by the gruff patriarch "Old Oliver" and his fascistic heir Mr. Giles Oliver—gender relations and conventions that Woolf represents here with what borders on horror and loathing. The outdoor world of the pageant that decenters the patriarchal bourgeois house, a border space where "[w]ords . . . ceased to lie flat in the sentence" (59), is an ancient village-farm world "in the very heart of England" (16). Liminally civilized and natural, human and nonhuman, it is, in contrast to the house, chaotic, unpredictable, disorderly, full of border and boundary crossings of all kinds: "shiver[ed] into splinters," into "*orts, scraps and fragments,*" like the end of the pageant itself (183, 188).

The outdoors of terrace, garden and field interpenetrate with the barn, literal locus of the action "between the acts" of the pageant. The barn itself is liminally indoors and outdoors, civilized/human and natural/nonhuman:

> The great doors [of the barn] stood open. A shaft of light like a yellow banner sloped from roof to floor. Festoons of paper roses, left over from the Coronation, drooped from the rafters. A long table, on which stood an urn, plates and cups, cakes and bread and butter, stretched across one end. The Barn was empty. Mice slid in and out of holes or stood upright,

> nibbling. Swallows were busy with straw in pockets of earth in the rafters. Countless beetles and insects of various sorts burrowed in the dry wood. . . . All these eyes, expanding and narrowing, some adapted to light, others to darkness, looked from different angles and edges. Minute nibblings and rustlings broke the silence. Whiffs of sweetness and richness veined the air. A blue-bottle had settled on the cake and stabbed its yellow rock with its short drill. A butterfly sunned itself sensuously on a sunlit yellow plate. (99-100)

I quote this passage at length to give a clear sense of its carefully nonjudgemental, egalitarian tone: nibblings and rustlings are on a moral and affective par with a sensuously sunning butterfly, and all coexist with one another, with the trappings of the masculine public sphere (the leftover Coronation festoons of paper roses), with the human feast, and with the humans about to consume it.

Rain comes and goes, utterly unpredictably, helping out with an awkward gap in the performance and thereby justifying the "risk" Miss La Trobe "had run acting in the open air" (181). Swallows sweep in and out of view; cows moo and move in and out of the audience's sightlines, constituting at once a disruption and a part of the pageant: "Then suddenly, as the illusion petered out, the cows took up the burden. One had lost her calf. In the very nick of time she lifted her great moon-eyed head and bellowed. . . . The cows annihilated the gap; bridged the distance; filled the emptiness and continued the emotion" (140-1). A ghost inhabits the lily pool. The gramophone chuffs, its songs along with bits of the dialogue intermittently carried off on the wind ("The breeze blew gaps between their words" [139]). Nature reverses itself as the snake chokes with a toad in its mouth: "birth the wrong way round—a monstrous inversion" as Giles sees it (99). The pageant continually eludes and defeats Miss La Trobe's intentions, acquiring its own unpredictable, erratic, at once ludicrous and beautiful life, force, momentum: "Hadn't she, for twenty-five minutes, made them see? A vision imparted was relief from agony . . . . She hadn't made them see. It was a failure, another damned failure!" (98). Emotions and experiences are lifted out of their orderly social containers and mixed freely, missing more often than hitting any character's intended mark.

It is the levelling and unifying experience of constituting the community of audience and having the fragmentary nature of modern reality revealed to them in the fragmented reflections of their own bodies that enables the characters of the novel to enter and become part of this liminal space "between the acts," where they can "*break the rhythm and forget the rhyme*" (187). In this space, they are able to see themselves not only as "orts, scraps and fragments," but also, in the words of Reverend G. W. Streatfield, "we are members of one another. Each is part of the whole" (192). The Reverend continues:

> "We act different parts; but are the same. . . . Then again, as the play or pageant proceeded, my attention was distracted. Perhaps that too was part of the producer's intention? I thought I perceived that nature takes her part. Dare we, I asked myself, limit life to ourselves? . . . I speak only as one of the audience, one of ourselves. I caught myself too reflected, as it happened in my own mirror . . ." (Laughter) "Scraps, orts and fragments! Surely, we should unite?" (192)

Like those of all the other characters, Streatfield's point of view is limited: he asks pompously, in his religious capacity, "'May we not hold that there is a spirit that inspires, pervades'" (192), and he abruptly switches gears to ask for donations for the "'illumination of our dear old church'" (193). Nonetheless, Woolf allows him to get at her central purposes here. In fact, we must both acknowledge and embrace "scraps, orts and fragments," and at the same time, in public community, "unite": "'I' rejected: 'We' substituted," as Woolf so memorably wrote in her diary on April 26, 1938 (*D5* 135).

It is crucial that the occasion for the construction of this dehierarchized borderland "between the acts" has been provided by a sturdy, middle-aged lesbian woman, who utterly eludes the regime of the private house. Miss La Trobe is highly public in her capacity as writer-director, but she hides in the bushes during the performance; in her combination of ambitious megalomania and abashed insecurity, she is perhaps reminiscent of Stein herself. This liminal space, Stein's "half in and half out of doors," Woolf's "between the acts" of hegemonic masculine public culture (literally, for Woolf, the murderously destructive acts of war—planes are even now flying ominously overhead), is a feminine subaltern counterpublic, inhabited by the great Woolfian and Steinian modernist drama of public woman.

**Notes**

1 Fame during a writer's lifetime is not in any way a precondition of eventual canonicity or even iconicity. But in the twentieth century, with its mass publicity and its short cultural memory, such posthumous fame has become increasingly unusual. Woolf was of course famous both as a writer and as a public personage during her lifetime.

2 Woolf's ambivalence is well known and widely documented; see, for example, Bell.

3 See Snaith for a fascinating analysis of the movement between public and private in Woolf's use of indirect interior monologue. For other, related treatments of public and private spheres and spaces in Woolf, see Hankins, Seeley, Springer, and Squier.

4 See Hewett's unpublished Rutgers University Ph.D. dissertation *Prostituting England: Virginia Woolf and the Liquidation of Cultural Heritage* for a brilliant analysis of the significances of Woolf's extensive involvement in both popular

culture (especially *Vogue*) and mainstream public high culture (especially the BBC). This study makes clear the great extent of Woolf's public visibility.

5 See Caughie for a very different view of the significance of Mrs. Brown: Caughie sees her as signifying Woolf's deployment of character as process, effect, and function in the interaction between narrator and reader.

6 See Marcus for a discussion of the positive significance of virginity for Woolf, a significance that connects to the inviolability of Mrs. Brownian privacy.

7 For a groundbreaking discussion of the hegemonic masculinity of the bourgeois public sphere, and of the crucial notion of "subaltern counterpublics," see Fraser. For a differently illuminating discussion of the repressive nature of the bourgeois public sphere in class terms, and of proletarian counterpublics, see Negt and Kluge.

8 See Irigaray's *Speculum of the Other Woman*, especially "Any Theory of the 'Subject' Has Always Been Appropriated By the 'Masculine,'" and "Plato's Hystera."

9 See Irigaray, "Plato's Hystera," in *Speculum*, and DeKoven, *Rich and Strange.*

10 Dickens might be interested in Mrs. Brown, but he would have to endow her with eccentricities that Woolf would rigorously refuse: the point about Mrs. Brown is precisely that she is thoroughly ordinary.

11 For a discussion of the feminist politics of Woolf's quarrel with Bennett, see Daugherty.

12 Woolf's second and third novels, *Night and Day* and *Jacob's Room*, are in significant ways detours from this project. *Night and Day* can be seen as an antidote to *The Voyage Out*: Woolf's attempt to do a marriage plot with a happy ending, which she achieves by calling on the powers of Shakespearean romance in the person of the goddess-ex-machina Mrs. Hilbery (see DuPlessis for a discussion of the subversion of the marriage plot in *VO*). *Jacob's Room* takes on and decenters, through radical reinventions of fictional form, the centrality of the upper-middle-class educated man: Jacob, the ostensible protagonist, is, as many critics have noted, an absent center. After *Jacob's Room*, Woolf uses those formal innovations to place Mrs. Brown at the center of her work.

13 Interestingly, "Fernham" is very close to the name Gertrude Stein gave her fictional women's college in "Fernhurst," a 1904-5 novella unpublished until 1971.

14 Joan Baez includes this ballad in her first Vanguard album, titled *Joan Baez.* The notes on the back of the album cover list "Mary Hamilton" as Child 173, and describe it as "the tragedy of a maid trapped by the intrigues of aristocratic court life . . . perhaps the best loved of all the ballads."

15 See Abel for an entirely different, though complementary, narrative of this shift in Woolf's career.

16 Form accords with this felt necessity of moving into the public sphere in *The Years*: Woolf moves from the high modernism of *The Waves* to a version of sequential realism, though a realism transformed throughout by modernist formal practices: episodic structure, foregrounding of language and recurring imagery, openended, unresolved scenes, steady shifts of emphasis, decentering of "central" character, multiple, indeterminate meanings.

[17] See DeKoven, *A Different Language*, for a discussion of Stein's chronological stylistic periods. "Insistence," the style of 1908-11, was characterized by gradually shifting incremental repetition, incantatory rhythms, and a reduced, abstract vocabulary. In relation to *A Long Gay Book*, it is likely that Stein was one of the first to use in literary writing the homosexual connotation the word *gay* had acquired by the early twentieth century. According to Wagner-Martin, the portrait "Miss Furr and Miss Skeene," written in 1908, a year before *A Long Gay Book*, "featured a sly repetition of the word *gay*, used with sexual intent for one of the first times in linguistic history" (96).

[18] See North for a fascinating account of Stein's reinvention of literary language in relation to racial masquerade.

[19] See Dydo and Wagner-Martin for biographical-archival material on the crucial importance to her writing of Stein's erotic/domestic relationship with Toklas.

[20] See Abraham for an illuminating discussion of the uses of historical narrative by twentieth-century lesbian writers, including Stein and Woolf.

**Works Cited**

Abel, Elizabeth. *Virginia Woolf and the Fictions of Psychoanalysis.* Chicago: U of Chicago P, 1989.

Abraham, Julie. *Are Girls Necessary? Lesbian Writing and Modern Histories.* New York: Routledge, 1996.

Baez, Joan, *Joan Baez*. New York: Vanguard, 1964.

Bell, Quentin. *Virginia Woolf: A Biography.* New York: HBJ, 1972.

Bowlby, Rachel. *Virginia Woolf: Feminist Destinations.* Oxford: Basil Blackwell, 1988.

Caughie, Pamela. *Virginia Woolf and Postmodernism.* Urbana: U of Illinois P, 1991.

Daugherty, Beth Rigel. "The Whole Contention Between Mr. Bennett and Mrs. Woolf, Revisited." *Virginia Woolf: Centennial Essays.* Ed. Elaine K. Ginsberg and Laura Moss Gottlieb. Troy, NY: Whitston, 1983. 269-94.

DeKoven, Marianne. *A Different Language: Gertrude Stein's Experimental Writing.* Madison: U of Wisconsin P, 1983.

——. "'Excellent Not a Hull House': Gertrude Stein, Jane Addams, and Feminist-Modernist Political Culture." *Rereading Modernism: New Directions in Feminist Criticism.* Ed. Lisa Rado. New York: Garland, 1994. 321-50.

——. *Rich and Strange: Gender, History, Modernism.* Princeton: Princeton UP, 1991.

DuPlessis, Rachel Blau. *Writing Beyond the Ending: Narrative Strategies of Twentieth-Century Women Writers.* Bloomington: Indiana UP, 1985.

Dydo, Ulla, Ed. *A Stein Reader.* Evanston: Northwestern UP, 1993.

Fraser, Nancy. "Rethinking the Public Sphere: A Contribution to the Critique of Actually Existing Democracy." *Justice Interruptus: Critical Reflections on the "Postsocialist" Condition.* New York: Routledge, 1997. 69-98.

Hankins, Leslie. "Virginia Woolf, Literary Tourism and Cultural Site-Seeing."

*Virginia Woolf Miscellanies*. Proceedings of the First Annual Conference on Virginia Woolf. Ed. Mark Hussey and Vara Neverow-Turk. New York: Pace U P, 1992. 71-86.

Hewett, Angela. "Virginia Woolf and the Liquidation of English Culture." Diss. Rutgers U, 1997.

Irigaray, Luce. *Speculum of the Other Woman*. Trans. Gillian C. Gill. Ithaca: Cornell UP, 1985.

Marcus, Jane. "The Niece of a Nun: Virginia Woolf, Caroline Stephen, and the Cloistered Imagination." *Virginia Woolf and the Languages of Patriarchy*. Bloomington: Indiana UP, 1987. 115-135.

Negt, Oskar, and Alexander Kluge. *Public Sphere and Experience*. 1972. Trans. Peter Labanyi, Jamie Owen Daniel, and Assenka Oksiloff. Intro. Miriam Hansen. Minneapolis: U of Minnesota P, 1993.

North, Michael. *The Dialect of Modernism: Race, Language, and Twentieth-Century Literature*. New York: Oxford UP, 1994.

Petersson, Robert T. *The Art of Ecstasy: Teresa, Bernini, and Crashaw*. New York: Atheneum. 1970.

Seeley, Tracy. "Virginia Woolf's Poetics of Space: 'The Lady in the Looking-Glass: A Reflection.'" *Woolf Studies Annual* 2 (1996): 89-116.

Snaith, Anna. "Virginia Woolf's Narrative Strategies: Negotiating Between Public and Private." *Journal of Modern Literature* 22 (1997): 133-48.

Springer, JoAnn. "Unhousing the Self: Virtual Space in *Between the Acts*." *Virginia Woolf and the Arts: Selected Papers from the Sixth Annual Conference on Virginia Woolf*. Ed. Diane F. Gillespie and Leslie K. Hankins. New York: Pace U P, 1997. 218-27.

Squier, Susan Merrill. *Virginia Woolf and London: The Sexual Politics of the City*. Chapel Hill: U of North Carolina P, 1985.

Stein, Gertrude. "Fernhurst." *Fernhurst, Q.E.D., and Other Early Writings*. Intro. Leon Katz. New York: Liveright, 1971.

——. *Four Saints in Three Acts. Selected Writings*. 577-612.

——. *The Making of Americans*. New York: Harcourt, Brace, 1934. 106-11.

——. "Portraits and Repetition." *Lectures in America*. New York: Random, 1935. 165-206.

——. *Tender Buttons*. 1914. Los Angeles: Sun and Moon, 1991.

——. *Three Lives*. 1906-09. New York: Random, 1936.

Wagner-Martin, Linda. *Favored Strangers: Gertrude Stein and Her Family*. New Brunswick: Rutgers UP, 1995.

Woolf, Virginia. *Between the Acts*. New York: Harvest, 1970.

——. *The Diary of Virginia Woolf*. Ed. Anne Olivier Bell, assisted by Andrew McNeillie. Vol.5. San Diego: Harvest, 1985.

——. *Jacob's Room*. San Diego: Harvest, 1978.

——. "Mr. Bennett and Mrs. Brown." *The Captain's Death Bed and Other Essays*. San Diego: Harvest, 1978. 94-119.

——. *Mrs. Dalloway*. San Diego: Harvest, 1925.

——. *Night and Day*. London: Duckworth, 1919. New York: Doran, 1920.

——. *Orlando*. San Diego: Harvest, 1956.
——. "Professions for Women." *Virginia Woolf: Women and Writing*. Ed. Michele Barrett. San Diego: Harvest, 1980. 57-63.
——. *A Room of One's Own*. San Diego: Harvest, 1989.
——. *Three Guineas*. San Diego: Harvest, 1966.
——. *To the Lighthouse*. San Diego: Harvest, 1989.
——. *The Voyage Out*. New York: Harvest, 1948.
——. *The Waves*. San Diego: Harvest, 1959.
——. *The Years*. New York: Harvest, 1965.

## Elisa Kay Sparks

### *The Dial* as Matrix: Periodical Community between Virginia Woolf and Georgia O'Keeffe

In my first talk/article on Woolf and O'Keeffe, presented in 1993, I stated that there was "no evidence of direct influence or contact" between the two women (Sparks, "Match"). However, five years of researching connections between these two modernist artists has now convinced me that it was practically impossible for them *not* to have had at least some awareness of one another's existence. The chief conduit through which they may have heard of each other—aside from unrecoverable gossip—was the thriving network of political and cultural periodicals criss-crossing the Atlantic which both established and reported literary and artistic reputations. Because of its relatively unique position at the forefront of American, British, and Continental modernisms during the particular years when both O'Keeffe and Woolf were just beginning to establish their reputations, *The Dial* magazine, especially during the half dozen years between 1920 and 1926 when it was under the editorship of Scofield Thayer,[1] was very likely the first place they saw each other's names in print, and its publication of works by and about the two women may have either piqued or destroyed subsequent interest in one another as representative modern women artists.

The early twenties saw the appearance of several works by both O'Keeffe and Woolf in *The Dial*, as well as numerous reviews of their works. Between 1921 and 1925, O'Keeffe published four paintings and Virginia Woolf three stories or essays. In addition, there are substantial treatments of O'Keeffe in overviews of American painting in 1921 (2), 1926, and 1927; works by Woolf are reviewed in 1921 (2), 1922, 1923, 1925, 1927, and 1929, in addition to Clive Bell's long retrospective article on her in 1924. And there are numerous other glancing references.[2]

If reading their own notices wasn't enough to make O'Keeffe and Woolf look at the magazine, throughout Thayer's editorship of *The Dial*, articles were constantly being printed by and about their relatives, closest friends, and members of their social and professional circles. Both Paul Rosenfeld and Henry McBride, writers whose columns on music and art appeared in almost every single issue of *The Dial* from 1920-29, were close personal friends of O'Keeffe and her husband, Alfred Stieglitz. Both men, especially Rosenfeld, were members of a circle of liberal intellectuals with pacifist views who wanted to create a new kind of American art, and they regularly reviewed and praised not only the work of O'Keeffe but of other compatriots such as the painters John Marin, Mardsen Hartley, Arthur Dove, and Charles Demuth and writers Waldo Frank and Sherwood Anderson, all of whom were published in *The Dial.*[3]

On Woolf's side of the Atlantic the list of contributors was at least as long. Both Clive Bell and Roger Fry not only wrote articles but were the centers of major aesthetic controversies incited by or covered in the magazine. The "London Letter," a regular feature of *The Dial,* had a distinctly Bloomsburrian cast, being written first by T. S. Eliot and taken over later by Raymond Mortimer. T. S. Eliot was, of course, a friend of Woolf's,[4] and Raymond Mortimer, initially a compatriot of Clive Bell, quickly became an intimate of the Woolfs, visiting fairly frequently both at Monk's House and in London. Nearly every literary friend or rival of Woolf's was at least reviewed in *The Dial*—John Maynard Keynes, E. M. Forster, T. S. Eliot, Leonard, Katherine Mansfield, John Middleton Murry, Bunny Garnett, Lytton Strachey, D.H. Lawrence—and both Duncan Grant and Vanessa Bell had paintings reproduced in the pages of the magazine.

This dense network of mutual acquaintances as well as a concern for their own growing reputations suggests that both O'Keeffe and Woolf would have perused the pages of *The Dial,* at least occasionally. References to *The Dial* in Woolf's diary and letters, however, suggest that the Woolfs did not have a subscription: in August of 1922, Woolf added a postscript to a letter to Ottoline Morrell, "Do you, by any chance, take in the Dial, an American paper, and keep back numbers?" (*L*2 542), and in February of 1926, she mentions in her diary that someone has sent her "a cutting on Hogarth essays from the Dial" (*D*3 58). The likelihood that O'Keeffe saw the magazine more regularly is much higher. In a letter of 1922, she mentions reading Rosenfeld's article on her in *The Dial* (Cowart 171); her husband, Alfred Stieglitz, refers to articles in *The Dial* in letters to Arthur Dove in 1925 and 1927, and Dove recommends a piece by Gertrude Stein in 1926, seeming to assume that Stieglitz had the magazine ready to hand (Morgan, *Dear Stieglitz, Dear Dove* 115, 140, 134).

Knowing that they very probably did not read every word of every issue, what possible impression of one another might Woolf and O'Keeffe have gleaned from reading *The Dial*? Unfortunately, the myths that were already being built around the two women artists seem almost perversely designed to repel them from each other: the presentations of O'Keeffe as a sex-bomb exploding in paint and of Woolf as a repressed doyen of the tea table often disguise the underlying similarities of their methods and motives as women artists. That both women were trying to transcend the reigning cliches of gender in art was hardly apparent since both were presented through the screen of sexually dimorphic stereotypes: Woolf the virgin and O'Keeffe the whore.[5]

Both women were aware of *The Dial* from the beginning of Thayer's editorship. At least a dozen members of the "Round Table" with whom O'Keeffe and Stieglitz dined and discussed art almost every night appeared in the magazine during this first year, some, such as Sherwood Anderson, several times. And we have actual evidence that the new *Dial* made an impact on Woolf, since in December of 1920 she complained to her diary in an end-of the-year self-assessment of her slow "increase in fame" that "I'm not asked to write for the Dial. Lytton is" (*D*2 80). However, early accounts of Woolf and O'Keffe's work published in *The Dial* emphasize the most off-putting aspects of each other's work, failing to highlight what they would have liked in each other: the experimentality of Woolf's work is ignored or muffled and the sexuality of O'Keeffe's work is exaggerated.

For example, Paul Rosenfeld's comment on O'Keeffe in his article on "American Painting" is one of the longest early treatments of the artist. Accompanied by a full-page reproduction of the abstraction "Black Spot," the article praises her for the intensity with which she registers "the manner of perception anchored in the constitution of the woman" (Rosenfeld 666). However, the article completely collapses O'Keeffe's artistic accomplishment into her sexuality by describing her paintings as orgasms on canvas: "Her great painful and ecstatic climaxes make us at last to know something the man has always wanted to know" (666). At times the language is so effusive that one suspects Woolf might have recoiled from O'Keeffe as an even more intense avatar of Vanessa, the woman artist as mother-goddess: "The American woman's work has something leonine, maternal, at once passionate and chaste in its essence. All is ecstasy here, ecstasy of pain as well as ecstasy of fulfillment" (666). The one element of O'Keeffe's painting that might have appealed most to Woolf—her use of color—is undercut both by the over-expansive rhetoric—"A white radiance is in all the bright paint felt by this girl. Her colours sworl [sic] and flame and explode. Everything rushes down in fiery cascade" (666)—and by the fact that this reproduction, like all of O'Keeffe's works published in *The Dial*, is sadly not in color but in black and white.

The first accounts of Woolf's work in *The Dial* are similarly etiolated, concentrating on Woolf's Britishness at the expense of her modernity. For example, in September 1920, Ford Maddox Hueffer mentioned her as a new writer "representing the lingering tradition of George Eliot" (245), a fairly anachronistic remark considering that Woolf was then writing and publishing her most experimental pieces—"Kew Gardens" and the stories that would be collected the next year in *Monday or Tuesday*. And Kenneth Burke's 1921 review of *The Voyage Out* and *Night and Day* also downplays innovation. Reversing the order of composition, Burke discusses *Night and Day* first, stressing its formulaic qualities—"her material is composed from the characteristic English novel accessories" (Burke 573)—and predicting that Woolf's retreat from the more "advanced" vision of *The Voyage Out* presages a dwindling into mere conventionality (Burke 572). While Burke does praise the bold structural juxtapositions of Woolf's first novel, his review gives no hint of how her vision might be coherently connected to a theory of modern art. The militantly American O'Keeffe would certainly not have been interested in reading anything described as a "deadly combination of literature and the drawing room" (575). Indeed, the editors and reviewers of *The Dial* seem to have trouble coping with Woolf's more advanced work. In 1922, the bold novelty of *Monday or Tuesday* is granted only a Briefer Mention which serves to intensify the haze of genteel snobbery surrounding the "arty" Mrs. Woolf when it joins her with Katherine Mansfield, Dorothy Richardson, and T.S. Eliot "to mark the four compass points of ultra-modern tea" (*Dial* 72, 1922, 215).

While there might be some excuse for the American editors and reviewers of *The Dial* to be blinded by a fog bank of preconceptions separating them from Woolf on the other side of the Atlantic, one could hope for a more insightful treatment of Woolf from those closer to home. The 1922 publication of Clive Bell's *Since Cezanne* and the appearance in *The Dial* of David Garnett's 1923 review of *Jacob's Room* and Bell's 1924 essay on Woolf offer explications of Woolf's modernism that might have appealed to O'Keeffe on many levels; however, neither man can resist evoking a certain fastidious femininity, as if to reassure readers that Woolf's newness and independence are adequately socialized and thus under control.

Clive Bell's mention of Woolf in *Since Cezanne* sets the pattern. We know that O'Keeffe had read Bell's earlier book, *Art.* From November 1915 through January 1916, she was preparing a lecture on modern aesthetics for a faculty discussion group at West Texas State Normal College in Canyon Texas, and she wrote her friend Anita Pollitzer that she had been re-reading Bell (Gibore 238). *Since Cezanne* was reviewed in *The Dial* by Raymond Mortimer in August; Stieglitz was reading it that same month because he mentioned it in a letter to Dove (Morgan 82). Bell discusses Woolf in his last chapter, "Plus de Jazz," but his praise of her as a modernist writer "of greater gifts" than Joyce, one who has mastered the literary syncopation of leaving out elements of traditional construction, is a rather undercut by his praise of her "exquisite but old-fashioned qualities" (Bell 224).

If O'Keeffe read the July 1923 of issue of *The Dial*—and it seems likely that she did since it contained a piece by Willard Huntington Wright, an art critic whom she mentions frequently in her letters from 1915–17 (she found Bell "stupid" compared to him, [Gibore 227])—she would at last have had a full chance to appreciate Woolf's modernism by reading both "Miss Dalloway on Bond Street" and David Garnett's review of *Jacob's Room.* Providing a precise gloss on Woolf's short story, Garnett's description of

Woolf's method could have appealed to O'Keeffe: "One thing calls up another, and we skip on to something very different yet queerly linked with what went before" (Garnett 84). O'Keeffe's autobiographical explanation of the creation of "Black Spot" shows how much her own art was committed to trying to capture the inexplicable presences of the unconscious: "I never knew where the idea came from or what it says. They are shapes that were clearly in my mind—so I put them down" (O'Keeffe, facing plate 17). Another connection between the two women artists which O'Keeffe might have recognized is Garnett's comparison of Woolf to Matisse (83), an artist with whom O'Keeffe's friend Henry McBride would compare her in 1927.[6]

The double publication in December 1924 of both "Miss Ormerod" and Clive Bell's essay on Woolf in *The Dial* presented another good opportunity for O'Keeffe to relate to Woolf. One can only speculate on O'Keeffe's reaction to these two pieces, but as a feminist she might have been drawn to Woolf's thumbnail biography of a little girl who sees a grub eaten by its companions and becomes an amateur entomologist, quietly making a life for herself in a world where even the dogs obey "the eldest male person in the room" (Woolf, "Miss Ormerod" 468). And the artist and naturalist who had just determined in the hurry and scurry of modern life to make people stop to see the beauty of flowers by painting them gigantically large might have responded to Woolf's description of the insect world as seen through the lens of a microscope.

In fact, there is much in Clive Bell's account of Woolf's art that O'Keeffe might have found especially relevant, considering that 1924 was the pivotal year she became fed up with the over-sexualized interpretations of her abstract paintings and decided to paint only objective subjects, such as flowers, whose sexual subtext she could plausibly deny. Thus Bell's defense of Woolf's choice of a conventional theme in *Night and Day*, rendered with "high fantasticality and blazing realism" would have resonated with O'Keeffe's decision to paint flowers "big" ( Bell 457; O'Keeffe, note facing pl. 23). His account of Woolf's "abhorrence of symbolism" would have spoken directly to O'Keeffe's contemporary annoyance with her critics; and aside from the fact that she probably would have relished the natural and expressive detail of the long excerpt Bell includes from "Kew Gardens," one can only imagine O'Keeffe's envy at Bell's pronouncement that "an oversexed person will never appreciate the art of Virginia Woolf" (461). Throughout the review of Woolf's work, Bell's emphasis on the individuality of her vision, its painterly qualities, and in particular her search for wholeness and unity in her art, all sound as if they could be descriptions of O'Keeffe's own creative project.

These positive identifications, however, were likely undercut by Bell's long quotation from Woolf's review of a biography of Mary Russell Mitford in which Woolf seems obsessed with ladyhood and niceness and his reference to a letter praising Woolf's vision from "an exquisitely civilized lady of fashion" (464). In retrospect, it is easy to pick out passages that might have resonated for O'Keeffe; at the time of publication, the impression of British gentility would have most likely blinded O'Keeffe to any such reading.

In May 1925, Woolf and O'Keeffe's works, at least, met: two of O'Keeffe's paintings of a small house with a flagpole were immediately followed by Woolf's "Lives of the Obscure" ("The Flagpole [First Painting]" and "The Flagpole [Second Painting]," facing page 380). This unmediated juxtaposition provides the clearest evidence of their affinity that ever appeared in *The Dial,* significantly, the only one not contructed by male critics' accounts of their work.[7] Aside from being by women artists, O'Keeffe and Woolf's pieces are linked formally and thematically as explorations of the relationship between detail and abstraction; both are playful, relativistic, unhinged from the usual rules of genre. Woolf's essay, "Lives of the Obscure," begins by highlighting the importance of the apparently insignificant detail, the significance of mediocre lives which provide the background against which more notable biographies stand out.[8] Although as a whole the essay delights in the invention of telling details from the lives of such tangential identities as Laetitia Pilkington, Ann Gilbert, and Richard Edgeworth, it also evokes a kind of cosmic perspective on the smallness of the individual, celebrating "an obscurity which is not empty, but thick with the star dust of innumerable lives" (*Dial* 384; *CR*1, 108). Placed immediately before Woolf's playful essay, O'Keeffe's two paintings are a clear illustration of the modulation from realistic detail to abstraction which she practiced in many of her painting series.[9] O'Keeffe's first composition of a small shed with a black door opened into blackness, topped by an arrow-shaped weather vane and attached under the roof to parallel electrical wires stretching out of the picture frame, the shed standing behind a white flagpole under a sky full of fluffy clouds, metamorphoses into a second far more whimsical, abstract, and cosmic version in which the flagpole and wires become weirdly elongated. Space seems stretched or exploded; the house itself disappears into folds of clouds which spiral around a mysterious, rectangular entrance to another world, while, loosed from the roof, the arrow points enigmatically away and an almost full moon presides over a scene which both evokes and contradicts the laws of physics.

After this fortuitous joint engagement, O'Keeffe and Woolf's appearances in *The Dial* diverge again, as references to O'Keeffe return to a focus on her sexuality and reviews of Woolf's work continue to emphasize her gentility and fastidiousness. In August 1925, O'Keeffe's still-life of an "Alligator Pear" was placed immediately before an installment of D.H. Lawrence's short story, "The Woman Who Rode Away," re-enforcing O'Keeffe's association with sexuality.[10] Subsequent reviews and mentions of O'Keeffe's work—all by Henry McBride in his regular articles on Modern Art—begin to fixate on the emotionality of women viewers' responses to O'Keeffe's painting. "There were more feminine shrieks and screams in the vicinity of O'Keeffe's works this year than ever before," McBride remarks in May 1926, deciding that as a man he cannot account for

O'Keeffe's appeal: "I begin to think that in order to be quite fair to Miss O'Keeffe I must listen to what the women say of her—and take notes" (437).

Subsequent mentions of Woolf in *The Dial* tend to focus on her aristocracy and charm, continuing a characterization of her femininity as more effete than O'Keeffe's. A brief mention of *Mrs Dalloway* in October 1925 reviews the book as over-animated by "Mrs. Woolf's almost incomparable charm" (352). Conrad Aiken's longer reviews of *To The Lighthouse* and *Orlando* in July 1927 and February 1929 similarly dwell on Woolf's "air of gentility, of sequestration, of tradition" (Aiken 41). And even Mortimer's London Letter of February 1929, praising Bloomsbury for its support of Radclyffe Hall during the obscenity trial for *The Well of Loneliness,* points out how much of a strain on Woolf's fastidiousness it must have been for her to volunteer to testify (138).

The last mention of Woolf in *The Dial,* Aiken's review of *Orlando,* provides a final ironic twist to this account of the two women artists' crossings in the pages of the magazine. In complaining of the excess artificiality of *Orlando,* Aiken proclaims: "Her roses are cloth roses, her scenes are scenes from tapestry" (148). Two years later, O'Keeffe would begin painting calico roses, stuck into the eye holes of the skulls she had picked up in the New Mexico desert. It is a sad probability that these two women modernists, with so much in common in their vision and method, would have been led by the culturally gendered presentations in *The Dial* to discount each other as stereotypes of the kind of femininity they most feared or despised: Woolf the fussy, repressed aristocrat; O'Keeffe the brazen, oversexed American. They each saw the cloth rose in the other's eye—the superficial myths of gender and class—but not the reality of matching bones in their own—the fundamental structural similarity of their experiments in abstraction.

**Notes**

1 For historical information on *The Dial* under Thayer, see especially Joost.

2 For a complete list of all mentions of Woolf or O'Keeffe in *The Dial*, as well as color-coded lists of all contributions by friends, relations, and rivals, see my web site on *The Dial* at http://www.dial.clemson.edu.

3 See Robinson for a description of the "Round Table," 227.

4 Besides eight installments of the London Letter, Eliot contributed twelve articles or reviews to *The Dial* between 1920-29, and both *The Waste Land* and "The Hollow Men" were published in the magazine. There were at least eight major reviews of Eliot's work during this time, and in 1922 he received the Dial Prize.

5 In his new book, *Georgia O'Keeffe and the Eros of Place*, Dijkstra argues persuasively that O'Keeffe's artistic project was to express "*humane* values *beyond* gender" (87).

6 See McBride, 261-3 .

7 It is interesting to speculate on who made the decision to pair Woolf and O'Keeffe in the May issue. During February and March of 1925, Alyse Gregory

was resigning as Managing Editor and negotiations were under way to pay Marianne Moore, who had been volunteering time as an editorial assistant, to take over responsibilities for running the office (Joost 85).

8 The version of "Lives" published in *The Dial* in 1925 differs slightly from that reprinted in *The Common Reader,* chiefly in having a longer introduction.

9 The best known of these series is Jack-in-the-Pulpit, *Georgia O'Keeffe*, pl. 38-42; the same kind of progression can be seen in Shell and Old Shingle series, *Georgia O'Keeffe*, pl. 48-52.

10 This is too early to be a connection between O'Keeffe and New Mexico; she made her first long visit to Taos in 1929. "Alligator Pear" is plate 31 in *Georgia O'Keeffe.*

**Works Cited**

Aiken, Conrad. "The Novel as Work of Art," rev of *To the Lighthouse. The Dial* 83.1 (1927): 41-4.

——. "Orlando." *The Dial* 86.2 (1929): 147-9.

Bell, Clive. "Virginia Woolf." *The Dial* 77.6 (1924): 451-65.

——. *Since Cezanne.* 1922; rpt. Freeport, NY: Books for Libraries Press, 1965.

Burke, Kenneth. "The Modern English Novel Plus." Rev. of *Night and Day* and *The Voyage Out. The Dial* 70.5 (1921) 572-5.

Cowart, Jack, Juan Hamilton, and Sarah Greenough, eds. *Georgia O'Keeffe: Art and Letters.* Washington, D.C.: National Gallery of Art, 1987.

Dijkstra, Bram. *Georgia O'Keeffe and the Eros of Place.* Princeton, NJ: Princeton UP, 1998.

Garnett, David. Rev. of *Jacob's Room. The Dial* 75.1 (1923) 83-6.

Gibiore, Clive, ed. *Lovingly, Georgia.* New York: Simon and Schuster, 1990.

Hueffer, Ford Maddox. "Thus to Revisit" V, *The Dial* 69.3 (1920): 197-9.

Joost, Nicholas. *Scofield Thayer and The Dial: An Illustrated History.* Carbondale: Southern Illinois UP, 1964.

McBride, Henry. "Modern Art." *The Dial* 80.5 (1926): 436-9.

Morgan, Ann Lee, ed. *Dear Stieglitz, Dear Dove.* The American Arts Series. Newark: University of Delaware Press, 1988.

Mortimer, Raymond. "London Letter." *The Dial* 86.2 (1929): 137-41.

O'Keeffe, Georgia. *Georgia O'Keeffe.* New York: Viking, 1976.

Robinson, Roxana. *Georgia O'Keeffe: A Life.* Harper Collins, 1989.

Rosenfeld, Paul. "American Painting" *The Dial* 71.5 (1921): 663-70.

Sparks, Elisa Kay. "'A Match Burning in a Crocus': Modernism, Feminism, and Feminine Experience in Virginia Woolf and Georgia O'Keeffe." *Virginia Woolf: Themes and Variations: Selected Papers from the Third Annual Conference on Virginia Woolf.* Vara Neverow-Turk and Mark Hussey, eds. New York: Pace UP, 1994. 296-302.

Woolf, Virginia. "Lives of the Obscure" *The Dial* 78.5 (1925): 381-90. Rpt. In *The Common Reader: First Series.* Ed. Andrew McNeillie. 1925; Harcourt Brace and Co., 1984.

——. "Miss Ormerod" *The Dial.* 77.6 (1924) 466-74. Rpt. In *The Common Reader: First Series.* Ed. Andrew McNeillie. 1925; Harcourt Brace and Co., 1984.

Jane Goldman

# Artist and Feminist Communities of 1910: Post-Impressionism, Suffrage Aesthetics, and Intersubjectivity in *To the Lighthouse*

This paper, which considers Woolf and community in relation to material taken from my forthcoming book, puts forward a new reading of Woolf's literary Post-Impressionism. It will explore her development of an intersubjective feminist aesthetic from the potent and interconnecting spheres of art and feminism simultaneously erupting in 1910. Drawing both on familiar Bloomsbury aesthetics (including selected statements by Woolf herself) as well as on less well known sources of suffrage aesthetics, it will take as its focus Lily Briscoe's painting practice in *To the Lighthouse.*

While acknowledging orthodox readings of Woolf's Post-Impressionism, which emphasize Roger Fry's Formalism and Clive Bell's theory of Significant Form (both of which may be understood to promote for audiences of visual art access to a sense of community through democracy of form and emotional transcendence), this paper will put forward a contextually-informed, colorist theory of Post-Impressionism, in part drawn from the practices of English Post-Impressionists (such as Vanessa Bell), in part understood in relation to the influence of suffrage agitation on the critical reception of Post-Impressionism. Connecting high art and suffrage aesthetics (the latter associated with a materially different sense of community), it will posit a distinctively feminist model of intersubjectivity—or community—in Woolf's writing.

Lily Briscoe's aesthetic practice, then, is understood to engage the following contradictory elements: the formalist theories of Fry and Bell, the colorist practices of English Post-Impressionists, and the feminist aesthetics of the suffrage movement. Contemplation of her painting, as Woolf represents it, allows for access both to a private, "aesthetic" experience of spiritual community associated with Significant Form, and to the more public, and material, community associated with the historical and political sphere of feminist agitation.

What is at stake in this exploration of Woolf's (and Lily's) Post-Impressionism may be identified, I suggest, in relation to the ongoing debate on "textual politics." I have found Rita Felski's interventions in this debate particularly helpful in clarifying my thoughts on Woolf.

> Feminist theories of "textual politics" grounded in a modernist aesthetics—for example, the celebration of the writings of Virginia Woolf as radically subversive of patriarchal ideology—are thus open to criticism on the grounds that they continue to draw upon static oppositions between realism and modernism without taking into account the changing social meanings of textual forms. The assumption that the political value of a text can be read off from its aesthetic value as defined by a modernist paradigm, and that a text which employs experimental techniques is therefore more radical in its effects than one which relies on established structures and conventional language, is too simple. Such an assumption takes for granted an equivalence between automatized language and dominant ideology and between experimentalism and oppositionality, an equation which is abstract and ultimately formalist in its failure to theorize the contingent functions of textual forms in relation to socially differentiated publics at particular historical moments. . . . It is thus increasingly implausible to claim that aesthetic radicalism equals political radicalism and to ground a feminist politics of the text in an assumption of the inherently subversive effects of stylistic innovation. (Felski 161)

To use Felski's terms, I have been looking at the formalist theories that emerged from the Post-Impressionist exhibitions of 1910 and 1912 "in relation to socially differentiated publics at particular historical moments"; that is, at how Woolf's engagement with formalist aesthetics may be historicized and contextualized; and at the "changing social meanings" of the aesthetic forms she engages. In so doing it becomes possible to read her aesthetics with reference to an historical, materialist feminist politics. Woolf seems to manipulate the male-authored discourse of Post-Impressionist formalism to speak simultaneously to, and in, a feminist community.

I will begin with the orthodox reading of Lily Briscoe's painting in terms of "Significant Form," connecting Woolf's aesthetics with the formalism of Fry and Bell as developed from 1910. I will then return to 1910 to sketch in an alternative, feminist, and colorist, theory of Post-Impressionism with which Woolf's writing simultaneously connects.

In the famous exchange, in "The Window," between William Bankes and Lily Briscoe about her avant-garde painting technique—in her first, prewar, picture—whereby Mrs. Ramsay and her son are rendered as a purple triangle, Bankes represents the untutored type who wants a painting to be like a photograph, and Lily seems to be a disciple of Roger Fry and Clive Bell in putting forward her formalist exposition:

> Her tribute took that form, if, as she vaguely supposed, a picture must be a tribute. A mother and child might be reduced to a shadow without irreverence. A light here required a shadow there. . . . The truth was that all his prejudices were on the other side, he explained. The largest pic-

> ture in his drawing-room, which painters had praised, and valued at a higher price than he had given for it, was of the cherry trees in blossom on the banks of the Kennet. He had spent his honeymoon on the banks of the Kennet, he said. Lily must come and see that picture, he said. But now—he turned, with his glasses raised to the scientific examination of her canvas. The question being one of the relations of masses, of lights and shadows, which, to be honest, he had never considered before, he would like to have it explained—what then did she wish to make of it? (*TTL* 59)

Woolf's letter to Roger Fry, saying "I meant *nothing* by The Lighthouse. One has to have a central line down the middle of the book to hold the design together . . . . I can't manage Symbolism except in this vague, generalised way. Whether its right or wrong I don't know, but directly I'm told what a thing means, it becomes hateful to me" (*L*3 385), which seems to refer to Lily's second version of the picture in "The Lighthouse," is often cited to support orthodox formalist readings of the novel. Her faith "that people would make it the deposit for their own emotions" (*L*3 385) suggests a belief in a sense of common emotional experience, a kind of intersubjectivity, or community, albeit differentiated, or individuated, which is made possible by aesthetic form. But, in telling Fry she "meant *nothing* by The Lighthouse," Woolf may present to him a silence that in other contexts and from other perspectives may speak volumes. We can compare this with the moment in *To the Lighthouse* when Lily explains to her male audience, Mr. Bankes, the "question" of "relations of masses, of lights and shadows" in terms of significant form, "subduing" in the process, "all her impressions *as a woman* to something much more general" (emphasis mine; *TTL* 60).

In this context it is worth considering the famous dish Mrs. Ramsay serves up at her pre-war nuptial banquet. "Boeuf en Daube," it has been acknowledged (Spalding 128), was one of Roger Fry's culinary specialities, but it is a dish the Post-Impressionist painter Lily Briscoe, nevertheless, as we may gather from her opposition to her hostess's promotion of marriage, finds difficult to swallow. Its dominant brown tones seem opposed by Lily's more prismatic palette. Eliza Haywood's advice to women in an eighteenth century man's world seems applicable to the novel's ambiguities here: "whenever we would truly conquer, we must seem to yield" (Haywood 179). If *To the Lighthouse* yields to readings of formalism and significant form, then, it may yet simultaneously disclose a conquering feminism, I will be suggesting. There may be more to Woolf's painterly analogies than the purely abstract "aesthetic emotions" she voices to Fry.

Roger Fry's dismissal, in "The Artist's Vision" (1919), of content and subject matter in favor of a "creative . . . generalised and all-embracing vision" (Fry 52) is echoed in Woolf's references, as noted above, to Lily Briscoe's "general . . . vision". Fry's essay comes nine years after the first

Post-Impressionist exhibition of 1910 (which showed for the first time to a British public a major representation of the work of Van Gogh, Gauguin, and Cézanne).

> The greatest object of art becomes of no more significance than any casual piece of matter; a man's head is no more and no less important than a pumpkin, or, rather, these things may be so or not according to the rhythm that obsesses the artist and crystallises his vision. Since it is the habitual practice of the artist to be on the lookout for these peculiar arrangements of objects that arouse the creative vision, and become material for creative contemplation, he is liable to look at all objects from this point of view. (Fry 52)

Fry's earlier formalist theory was ventriloquized through Desmond MacCarthy for the 1910 exhibition catalogue. MacCarthy sees Post-Impressionism's departure from photographic realism as restoring the poetic qualities of "emotion and associations" lacking in Impressionism:

> Impressionism encouraged an artist to paint a tree as it appeared to him at the moment under particular circumstances. It insisted so much upon the importance of rendering this exact impression that his work often completely failed to express a tree at all; as transferred to canvas it was just so much shimmer and color. The "treeness" of the tree was not rendered at all; all the emotion and associations such as trees may be made to convey in poetry were omitted. . . . And there is no denying that the work of the Post-Impressionists is sufficiently disconcerting. It may even appear ridiculous to those who do not recall the fact that a good rocking-horse often has more of the true horse about it than an instantaneous photograph of a Derby winner. (MacCarthy 96-7)

The "revolutionary" achievement of Manet (and other artists in the exhibition) is understood to be his innovatory colorism: "[Manet] adopted, too, hitherto unknown oppositions of color. In fact he endeavoured to get rid of chiaroscuro" (MacCarthy 12). A Romanticist colorism, I have argued (following Ben Nicolson), is the defining quality of the 1910 exhibition (Goldman 129-30). But a more general formalism has come to dominate our understanding of Post-Impressionism, largely because of the theories associated with the second exhibition.

"Significant Form," although often used interchangeably with Roger Fry's formalism, and often used in discussions of the first Post-Impressionist exhibition, was actually formulated by Clive Bell to promote the work of English artists in the *second* Post-Impressionist exhibition, held in 1912. This was quite different from the first, in that the colorist Romanticism of the 1910 exhibition yielded to a more classical emphasis in 1912, noticeable in the shift of focus from Van Gogh and Gauguin as precursors to Cézanne as main precursor, and also reflected in the new predominance of Cubism (Nicolson 15). The doctrine of "Significant Form" dominates in 1912. This new doctrine emphasizes an emotional understanding of form for its own sake above everything else. The overwhelming concern with color as a main point of definition in 1910 is largely ignored. Yet when one observes the practices of English Post-Impressionists, revolutionised by the first exhibition, it is colorism that predominates. The painting of Woolf's sister, Vanessa Bell, exemplifies this colorism.[1] But according to *theorists* of the new art (Roger Fry and Clive Bell), a more general formalism predominates. From 1912, the term "significant form" begins to become almost synonymous with Post-Impressionism.

In introducing the term "Significant Form" to describe the work of English artists at the second exhibition, Clive Bell also refers to literary art as a point of reference for Post-Impressionism:

> We have ceased to ask "What does this picture represent?" and ask instead, "What does it make us feel?" We expect a work of plastic art to have more in common with a piece of music than with a colored photograph. . . . What I mean by "simplification" is obvious. A literary artist who wishes to express what he feels for a forest thinks himself under no obligation to give an account of its flora and fauna. The Post-Impressionist claims similar privileges: those facts that any one can discern for himself or discover in a text book he leaves to the makers of Christmas-cards and diagrams. He simplifies, omits details, that is to say, to concentrate on something more important—on the significance of form. (Bell 1912: 349-50)

Two years later, according to Clive Bell's influential book, *Art* (1914), "Significant Form" no longer applies specifically to Post-Impressionism but extends to all art. It is "the one quality common to all works of visual art": from "the windows at Chartres" to "Mexican sculpture" to "the masterpieces of Poussin . . . and Cézanne" (Bell 1914: 7-8). For Bell, the power of color is here subsumed in the abstract notion of significant form. He develops the notion of the spiritual dimension of significant form into a full blown religion of art. He closes with a vision of "aesthetic rapture": "the religion of art will serve a man better than the religion of humanity. . . . What he loses in philanthropy he may gain in magnanimity; and because his religion does not begin with an injunction to love all men, it will not end, perhaps, in persuading him to hate most of them" (Bell 1914: 292-4). The theory of "Significant Form" as a kind of aesthetic access to an emotional spiritual experience has some sense of democratic appeal. There is a sense of a transcendent aesthetic community—and that a sensitivity to form and color is all one needs to appreciate it. But this sense of aesthetic, democratic community is always vying in Bell's work with an appeal to cultural élitism: Significant Form, he reassures us, won't ask us to love everybody!

Allen McLaurin's important study, *Virginia Woolf: The Echoes Enslaved* (1973), puts forward a sensitive and sophisticated analysis of Lily Briscoe's art, following Fry's formalism and, more implicitly, Bell's doctrine of Significant Form. Citing the passage given above from Fry's "The Artist's Vision," McLaurin finds that "in [their] discussion Lily speaks for precisely this habitual vision of the artist" whereas "William Bankes is one of those people who, in Fry's terms, would say of a landscape 'What a nice place' instead of 'What a good 'picture'. . . The kind of abstraction that Lily is concerned with is very different from the scientific examination which he is used to." McLaurin connects the formalism of the famous purple triangle that Lily makes of Mrs. Ramsay with Woolf's portrayal of her own parents in the novel which "gives them a formal significance" (McLaurin 192). Clive Bell's theories are evident in this term "formal significance" and where McLaurin suggests (as many have echoed after him): "There is a careful selection and abstraction here which is emotionally significant" (McLaurin 192). Such readings, however, are based on the elision of earlier, colorist definitions of Post-Impressionism (emphasizing the technique of using bright oppositional color planes), and do not take into account the possible feminist import of this colorism. I will now attempt to establish this connection between feminist and Post-Impressionist aesthetics. Before doing so, I must emphasize that I do not dispute the significance of Significant Form for the development of formalist theories, nor for later definitions of Post-Impressionism. But it is interesting for readings of Woolf's work to consider alternative, context-sensitive, cultural readings of Post-Impressionism evident prior to the emergence of the more dominant theory of 1912.

Fry's early formulations on Post-Impressionism and later theoretical developments, along with Clive Bell's more extreme opinions, are not necessarily the most appropriate for investigating Woolf's aesthetic. Woolf, on the contrary, seems to stay with earlier interpretations of Post-Impressionism, developing an interest in color closely related to the aesthetic practice of her sister Vanessa who exhibited at the second Post-Impressionist exhibition. She also seems to draw on suffrage aesthetics. My argument centers on color, which Fry and Clive Bell do not reject as an important factor in Post-Impressionism; but they do come to subsume it in the promotion of "Significant Form," where color loses the kind of impact and definition commanded in other influential theories about the art. Woolf's literary engagement with Post-Impressionism, I suggest, might be differently read with consideration of color as independent of significant form.

This colorist approach is evidenced in the almost universally hostile reviews the 1910 exhibition suffered. The colorism of Van Gogh, Gauguin, Cézanne and Matisse is what really offended people:

> In a typical [Gauguin] hideous brown women, with purple hair and vitriolic faces, squat in the midst of a nightmare landscape of drunken palm trees, crude green grass, vermilion rocks, and numerous glaringly col-

> ored excrescences impossible to identify. . . . Words are powerless to describe an epileptic landscape by Henri Matisse, quite without form, its kaleidoscopic color scheme only bearable from the next room.[2]

I want to bring out as a context for understanding Woolf's engagement with visual arts the connections made in contemporary reviews of Post-Impressionism between the shocking colors and depiction of women in the paintings, and the shocking political colors of the women's suffrage movement which became renowned for its elaborate color coordinated demonstrations in which the colors purple, white and green dominated (Tickner 1987: 265). "Black Friday"—when police turned to brutal tactics against women demonstrators—came only days after the first Post-Impressionist show opened (18 November 1910); Woolf herself, as it opened, attended the two Albert Hall rallies preceding the march (*L*1 438). At the time of the Post-Impressionist show, then, the suffrage movement was making a massive impact, as well as an equally colorful spectacle, on the streets. Consciously or not, reviewers seem to speak both to the exhibition and headline-making suffrage demonstration: disgust at the mud-besmirched and ghastly-colored daughters of Eve seems applicable to both realms. Notions of racial impurity were associated in the minds of the exhibition's detractors with the paintings of Gauguin in particular. The depiction of "native" women in bright contrasting unflesh-like colors seems to have been understood as doubly offensive to reviewers such as Robert Ross. Fearing that artists might "'gauguinise' the European landscape or the Aryan race," he observes that a "later blossom of an unsavoury stock has not only dispensed with chiaroscuro . . . but has dispensed with painting."[3] Such notions of racial impurity associated in the minds of Gauguin's detractors, then, are seen to accompany the abandonment of traditional representation of light and dark ("chiaroscuro") in favor of bright oppositional color planes (colorism). Most furor is aroused where women, perhaps because of their stereotyping as "Nature," are depicted in exotic and "unnatural" colors. Matisse's *La Femme aux Yeux Verts*, for example, was one of the most reviled images.[4]

A different kind of oppositional colorism simultaneously emerges alongside that of Post-Impressionism in 1910—in the feminist public realm where politics and aesthetics meet. The dominant art form is the vibrantly colored suffragist banner and poster. In September 1910, the suffrage artist Mary Lowndes (incidentally, one of the few enthusiastic reviewers of the 1910 Post-Impressionist Exhibition)[5] describes the art of suffrage banner-making in terms *uncannily similar* to those of Post-Impressionist theories: "A banner is not a literary affair, it is not a placard: leave such to boards and sandwichmen." Anticipating the flavor of Clive Bell's 1912 observations on "the makers of Christmas-cards and diagrams," she identifies the non-verbal political significance of feminist colorism, while at the same time drawing on a discourse of aestheticism:

> A banner is a thing to float in the wind, to flicker in the breeze, to flirt its colors for your pleasure, to half show and half conceal a device you long to unravel; you do not want to read it, you want to worship it. Choose purple and gold for ambition, red for courage, green for long-cherished hopes. If above these glories of color you write in great letters 'Troy Town,' that is not now a placard, it is a dedication. (Lowndes 1910: 174)

Andrew McNeillie typically glosses Woolf's infamous date, December 1910, with reference to the Post-Impressionist exhibition and the death of Edward VII (*E*3 437). But 1910 saw other—Suffrage—events we might acknowledge as relevant. The 1910 shift in human relations Woolf famously sees symbolized in the figure of "one's cook": the imagery of a woman servant emerging leviathan-like from the dark depths of the kitchen into sunlight may suggest a shift from women's dark, subliminal, creaturely existence to luminous, colorful liberation: "The Victorian cook lived like a leviathan in the lower depths, formidable, silent, obscure, inscrutable; the Georgian cook is a creature of sunshine and fresh air; in and out of the drawing room, now to borrow the *Daily Herald*, now to ask advice about a hat" (*E*3 422). Her vocabulary is similar to that of Mary Lowndes's 1910 essay on suffrage colorist banner-making: "now into public life comes trooping the feminine; and with the feminine creature come the banners of past times" (Lowndes 173). Incidentally, in the *Daily Herald* of 1913 Christina Walshe declares of the second Post-Impressionist exhibition: "The Post-Impressionists are in the company of the Great rebels of the World. In politics the only movements worth considering are Woman Suffrage and Socialism. They are both Post-Impressionist in their desire to scrap old decaying forms and find for themselves a new working ideal.'"[6] If Woolf's 1910 cook is to be referred in her 1924 retrospective essay to the 1912 Post-Impressionist exhibition as well as the 1910 one, then perhaps Walshe's observations in the *Daily Herald* might also be considered of some relevance along with the now more familiar theories of Clive Bell in the 1912 catalogue.

After the creaturely cook, Woolf gives a "more solemn instance . . . of the power of the human race to change": a revised reading of the *Agamemnon*, in which "sympathies" (usually reserved for the patriarchal order sanctioned by Athena) may now be "almost entirely with Clytemnestra" (*E*3 422), who avenged her daughter's death by murdering her husband Agamemnon on his return from the Trojan War. This classical allusion becomes more potently feminist when considered in relation to suffragist use of such imagery and Lowndes' references to "Troy Town" in 1910. In asking us to "consider the married life of the Carlyles," Woolf returns to the theme of women's servitude, perhaps mindful of the suffragette scorn for Thomas Carlyle (resulting in a cleaver attack on his portrait in the National Gallery) (Atkinson 163). He personifies "the horrible domestic tradition which made it seemly for a woman of genius to spend her time chasing beetles, scouring saucepans, instead of writing books" (*E*3 422).[7]

Contemplation of Lily Briscoe's painting, as Woolf represents it, allows for access both to a private, "aesthetic" experience of spiritual community associated with Significant Form, and to the more public, and material, community associated with the historical and political sphere of feminist agitation. This political resonance, or "social meaning," of Post-Impressionism may inform readings of the Post-Impressionist aesthetics in *To the Lighthouse*, the novel in which Woolf returns to the period of the exhibitions. Think of the purple triangle, and Mrs. Ramsay's green shawl, of the "bright violet" of the jacmanna and the "staring white" of the wall (*TTL* 23)—the novel glitters with feminist colors. Think of Lily's sense of triumph over the patriarchal match-making aspirations of Mrs. Ramsay, as she dips her brush into *green* paint (*TTL* 188-9). Lily's intimate, aesthetic, perhaps "Sapphist," moments with Mrs. Ramsay's ghost, are shot through with the feminist colors that simultaneously position her art in the public sphere—in the contestive public community of feminist politics.

## Notes

1 Gillespie's invaluable work on Woolf's professional and artistic debt to her sister has done much to make us think more carefully about the practice of these women as collaborating artists without necessarily (always and already) filtering their work through the theories of the men of Bloomsbury.

2 Unsigned review, "Paint Run Mad: Post-Impressionism at the Grafton Galleries," *Daily Express*, 9 November 1910; qtd. in Bullen, pp. 105-106.

3 Robert Ross, "The Post-Impressionists at the Grafton: The Twilight of the Idols," *Morning Post*, 7 November 1910; qtd. in Bullen, pp. 101, 103.

4 For example, P.G. Konody, "Art Notes: Post-Impressionism at the Grafton Galleries," *Observer*, 13 November 1910, and the anonymous review in the *Daily Telegraph*, 11 November 1910. See Spalding (plate 46), p. 135.

5 See Lowndes. I discuss in more detail three essays by Lowndes (which appeared in *The Englishwoman* in 1910 and 1911) in relation to Woolf and Post-Impressionism in a forthcoming essay, "Virginia Woolf and Post-Impressionism: French Art, English Theory and Feminist Practice," "Anglophone Modernism and Europe," *Miscelanea: A Journal of English and American Studies*, Vol. 20 (1999), guest eds. Jennifer Birkett and Stan Smith.

6 Christina Walshe, *Daily Herald*, 25 March 1913, qtd. in Spalding, 139.

7 Tuzyline Allan, in her VW-8 conference lecture, connects Woolf's allusion to Carlyle with his racist work, *The Nigger Question*. (See her essay elsewhere in this volume.)

## Works Cited

Atkinson, Diane. *The Suffragettes in Pictures*. London: Sutton, 1996.

Bell, Clive. *Art*. London: Chatto & Windus, 1914.

——. "The English Group," *Second Post-Impressionist Exhibition.* Grafton Galleries, 1912

Exhibition Catalogue, London. Rpt. in J.B. Bullen, ed., *Post-Impressionists in England.* London and New York: Routledge, 1988. 349-51.

Bullen, J.B., ed. *Post-Impressionists in England.* London and New York: Routledge, 1988.

Felski, Rita. *Beyond Feminist Aesthetics: Feminist Literature and Social Change.* London: Hutchinson Radius, 1989.

Fry, Roger. *Vision and Design.* London: Chatto & Windus, 1920.

Gillespie, Diane Filby. *The Sisters' Arts: The Writing and Painting of Virginia Woolf and Vanessa Bell.* Syracuse: Syracuse UP, 1988.

Goldman, Jane. *The Feminist Aesthetics of Virginia Woolf: Modernism, Post-Impressionism and the Politics of the Visual.* Cambridge: Cambridge UP, 1998.

Haywood, Eliza. *The Female Spectator.* London, 1771.

Lowndes, Mary. "On Banners and Banner-Making." *The Englishwoman* 7. 20 (1910): 172-8.

——. "Gauguin—A Personal Impression," *The Englishwoman* 9. 25 (1911): 182-8.

MacCarthy, Desmond. "The Post-Impressionists." *Manet and the Post-Impressionists.* Grafton Galleries 1910 Exhibition Catalogue, London. Rtp. in J.B. Bullen, ed., *Post-Impressionism in England.* London and New York: Routledge, 1988. 94-9.

McLaurin, Allen. *Virginia Woolf: The Echoes Enslaved.* Cambridge: Cambridge UP, 1973.

Nicolson, Benedict. "Post-Impressionism and Roger Fry." *Burlington Magazine,* 93 (1951). 18-21.

Spalding, Frances. *Roger Fry, Art and Life.* Berkeley: U of California P, 1980.

Tickner, Lisa. *The Spectacle of Women: Imagery of the Suffrage Campaign 1907-1914.* London: Chatto & Windus, 1987.

Woolf, Virginia. "Character in Fiction." *The Essays of Virginia Woolf.* Ed. Andrew McNeillie. Vol. 3. San Diego: Harvest, 1988. 420-438.

——. *To the Lighthouse.* Harmondsworth: Penguin, 1992.

**Arianne Burford**

## Communities of Silence and Music in Virginia Woolf's *The Waves* and Dorothy Richardson's *Pilgrimage*

In *Pilgrimage* (1915) and *The Waves* (1931) Dorothy Richardson and Virginia Woolf respectively attempt to invent new languages, breaking rhythms of traditional narratives, through silence and music. My use of "attempt" does not imply that either Richardson or Woolf failed but that from a feminist's perspective the war against words is still necessary. In "The Laugh of the Medusa" (1975) Hélène Cixous states that women need to invent a new language, to reject the language of patriarchy, and "wreck partitions" with this new language. Further, in *Virginia Woolf and the Languages of Patriarchy,* Jane Marcus argues that Woolf disproves critiques which claim that women are outside of language, that Woolf "mastered the language to deconstruct it" (10), adding that Woolf invents a new language based on female desire to "subvert patriarchy" (187). This essay, then, will explore *écriture feminine* in relation to Richardson and Woolf and will show additional ways in which these women writers disrupt patriarchy.

In both Richardson's and Woolf's writing exists the presence of Beethoven—but to different effects. Peter Jacobs discusses Woolf's association with music circles and their influence on her as well as connections between music and her writing. In a letter from Monk's House, Woolf wrote: "It's odd, for I'm not regularly musical, but I always think of my books as music before I write them" (*L*6 426). Before her death, Woolf had planned on investigating "the influence of music on literature" (*L*6 450). Additionally, Woolf owned Beethoven's late quartets and listened to them regularly while writing *The Waves.* In Richardson's *Pilgrimage,* Beethoven's compositions are played on the piano by female characters, and as a form of expression the music functions as an alternative to words. But it is more than Beethoven that connects Richardson and Woolf—using silences and music they both disrupt language. Having written reviews of Richardson, Woolf makes evident in *The Waves* her points of conjunction with as well as departure from Richardson. Both Richardson and Woolf challenge various boundaries such as socio-political constructions of gender and the limitations of conveying or finding meaning through words. The silences, pauses, and music used by Woolf and Richardson interrupt the rhythms of traditional narratives and as part of this project serve a political purpose: these interruptions resist not only authoritative narratives that use words to define and communicate thoughts and feelings but also the very hierarchically structured patriarchal culture that relies upon and uses these words to dictate to, define, and dominate women.[1] While music provides a space for female empowerment and expression in *Pilgrimage*, in *The Waves* music as a means of expression is ultimately rejected for silence and visual imagery. In both *Pilgrimage* and *The Waves*, moreover, silence exists not merely as a space or emptiness but rather as a counter-hegemonic disruption.

Both Richardson and Woolf ironically use "words" to challenge "words" as defined and determined by a patriarchal social structure. The following rhetorical question in *Pilgrimage,* however, takes place in the mind of the main character, Miriam, and thus refutes the use of words in speech: "Why would people insist upon talking about things—when nothing can ever be communicated?" (2: 306). For the women in both texts, words are shown as having lost their importance. In *The Waves*, Susan refers to an attempt to communicate through words and describes herself as physically confined. Also, because of her gender, she says it is difficult "to make even one sentence. What I say is perpetually contradicted. Each time the door opens I am interrupted. . . . I am also a girl, here in this room" (107). Bernard, on the other hand, is dependent on words for his existence: he says that "without words [he] is nothing" (132). As a rebellion against the dismissal of women's voices and the inadequacy of words, Richardson develops a community of understanding (achieved through silence) between Miriam and some women. Further, her critique "Continuous Performance: The Film Gone Male" illuminates her depiction of an understanding within a community of women and her privileging of silence:

> And the film, regarded as a medium of communication, in the day of its innocence, in its quality of being nowhere and everywhere . . . something of the changeless being at the heart of all becoming, was essentially feminine. . . . In becoming audible . . . it is doubtless fulfilling its destiny. But it is a masculine destiny. The destiny of planful becoming rather than purposeful being. (424)

This explains the silence between women in the text as focused on "purposeful being"—a way to understand from within—rather than the "planful becoming" focused on plot that Richardson uses to describe the "masculine" addition of sound to film. Richardson also discusses the loss of audience participation with the addition of sounds to film. In both *Pilgrimage* and *The Waves*, the silences require the reader to fill in the gaps and participate in the characters' experiences. The understanding Richardson depicts between women—which focuses on a silent "purposeful being" and the silences, including the ellipses which function as pauses in the narration—are similar to Woolf's focus on visual imagery in the interludes in that they both disrupt, and thus critique, constant linear progressive movements in conventional narrations. By writing rhythmically, Woolf "wreck[s] partitions" of the boundaries of traditional narratives, which is inclusive of her political agenda. While writing *The Waves,* she stated: "my difficulty is that I am writing to a rhythm and not to a plot" (*L4* 204). Woolf's writing is musical as it disrupts the traditional narrative with counter-rhythms of the "waves"—rhythms of silences, rhythms of sounds, rhythms and interruptions of voices—and yet she also has within her writing harmonies of voices and various continuities.[2] This rhythmic continuity has a similar effect as Richardson's concept of "being": a rejection of linear, event-centered narratives. Patricia Laurence argues: "silence in Woolf's narration is the space where female consciousness does reveal itself" (27). A review Woolf wrote in 1919 connects shared values between her and Richardson: "Her discoveries are concerned with states of being and not with states of doing. Miriam is aware of 'life itself'; of the atmosphere of the table rather than of the table, of the silence rather than of the sound" (*Contemporary Writers* 125). Thus, taken with the passage in which Bernard chooses the coffee table and silence, it is obvious that Woolf is influenced by Richardson's "purposeful being" and aligns herself with the value Richardson gives to silence—as a space—as a new language.

While using words to challenge words, Woolf sets up a male narrator/writer who values words and phrases up until the end, fails in his attempt to "sum up" the narration, and rejects his phrases for silence: "None of those resonances and lovely echoes that break and chime from nerve to nerve in our breasts making wild music, false phrases. I have done with phrases. How much better is silence; the coffee-cup, the table. . ." (295). In *The Sisters' Arts*, Diane Gillespie makes clear a relationship between "still life in words and paint" in this passage, when Bernard, the writer, turns to an object (the coffee cup), using "his eyes to tap what is real" (238). In addition, Woolf turns to visual images as an "alternative language, one that parallels the painters" (*The Sisters' Arts* 238). While writing *The Waves*, Woolf explains the value she finds in painting as a silent form of expression: "But words, words! How inadequate you are! How weary one gets of you! How you will always be saying too much or too little! Oh to be silent! Oh to be a painter!" (*E*3 166).[3]

However, because silence itself is often the result of oppression or marginalization, it is often resisted. For example, in "The Laugh of the Medusa," Helene Cixous states that "[w]omen should break out of the snare of silence" (338). Instead, Richardson resists the very language which has othered the female voice, advocating silence as a way of communicating interiority or "purposeful being." As a result, the very marginalization, insinuated by the "snare of silence," is what Richardson ironically resists. For Richardson as well as for Woolf, "silence" is more a text of resistance and rebellion than a symbolic space of inactivity caused by marginalization.

Furthermore, for both Richardson and Woolf, silences are rhythmic spaces strategically chosen to resist and react against androcentrism. Although the interludes in *The Waves* include sights and sounds, there is an apparent absence of verbalized words, focusing instead on the visual as in painting. For example, the interludes interrupt the monologues of the characters, disrupting the flow of speaking in the narration. The speaking is rhythmic, overlapping like waves, but with pauses in between. However, these pauses are not simply spaces: they are intended political disruptions that are strategically chosen.

Richardson's political agenda includes focusing on "purposeful being": exploring Miriam's consciousness, Richardson writes thoughts or inner dialogues from within a female self, breaking the boundary set by convention that would otherwise write the female body from the exterior. Because Richardson suggests and also enhances the possibilities of women's writing, Jean Radford designates her a "precursor" to *écriture feminine* (112).[4] However, in "Writing the Body" Ann Rosalind Jones necessarily points out some of the various ways in which the notion of *écriture feminine* can be criticized as essentialist. To clarify, it is necessary to point out that while Richardson writes "the female body" she merely provides instances of expressing *a* female body. But such instances do not necessarily define "the female body" as such, rather giving *a* "female body" *a* voice. As a precursor to Cixous, Richardson accomplishes what Cixous later calls for: "Women must write though their bodies, they must invent the impregnable language that will wreck partitions" (342). Woolf, also a precursor to Cixous in this way, credits Richardson with the type of creation of a new language that writes *a* female body: she describes Richardson as creating a sentence that can explore Miriam's consciousness (*Contemporary Writers* 124-25). Woolf's description of Richardson's exploration into Miriam's consciousness connects to Richardson's admiration of the silent films' quality of "purposeful being."

In *Pilgrimage*, Richardson describes Miriam as expressing herself through her body by playing the piano, which is an action of resistance to her marginalization and to her being silenced as a woman:

> The full rich tones of the piano echoed from all over the room; and some metal object far away from her hummed the dominant. She held the chord for its full term. . . . Should she play any more? . . . She had confessed herself . . . just that minor chord . . . any one hearing it would know more than she could ever tell them . . . her whole being beat out the rhythm as she waited for the end of the phrase to insist on what already had been said. (ellipses Richardson's 1:57)

In this passage, Miriam chooses to play Beethoven's *Pathetique*, which begins slowly and includes pauses, silences between each note. In the "adagio cantible," the lower notes repeat themselves as the higher notes become louder and louder. This assertive passage is followed by longer stanzas in "rondo allegro," which repeat themselves increasingly faster and faster. Repetition is part of Miriam's empowerment to "insist," despite the "dominant" background tone. While Miriam expresses herself, a cold, metallic object produces its "dominant" sound. Culturally, Miriam's voice as a woman is a "minor chord," but she is persistent. It is also significant that the ellipses are part of the narration, not only as disruptive gaps but also as signifiers of Miriam's hesitation to reveal herself. In addition, "[s]he did not need to follow the notes on the music stand. Her fingers already knew them" (1:57). This emphasis on memory, especially for such a long complex piece, shows the "music" as already existing inside her and finally breaking the surface, finally expressing through her body. In an interview, Cixous expresses this notion of voice already existing internally: "Our dialogues are often mute. This does not prevent them from taking place" (*Rootprints* 46).

The community in *The Waves* attains silence when its identities are blurred along with the boundary of gender. Louis' statement in *The Waves* defies individual identity: "'I am this, I am that,' which we make, coming together, like separated parts of one body and soul, are false" (137).[5] It is only in the end, when Bernard identifies himself as both male and female, that he rejects words and ultimately embraces silence. He narrates: "I have been talking of Bernard, Neville, Jinny, Susan, Rhoda and Louis. Am I all of them? Am I one and distinct? I do not know. . . . But now . . . we are divided; we are not here. Yet I cannot find any obstacle separating us. . . " (288). These blurrings of rigidly defined, immobile identities suggest the multiplicity of identity in gender, specifically that of the writer that Woolf envisions: "Perhaps to think, as I had been thinking these two days, of one sex as distinct from the other is an effort. It interferes with the unity of the mind" (*AROO* 97).[6] Bernard, the writer who speaks of painful silences, buys a silver-framed picture of Beethoven and ultimately prefers the visual imagery of the coffee-table over his "phrases." Before Bernard does this, however, he acknowledges the voices of Richardson and Miriam: "I heard those songs. I followed those phantoms. I saw Joans, Dorothys, Miriams, I forget their names. . ." (247). Woolf explicitly acknowledges voices of influence and the notion of expression of these voices through music.

Through Bernard's rejection of music and "false phrases" and his privileging of silence, Woolf reconceptualizes Richardson's use of music, specifically her use of Beethoven. Woolf's words express a political agenda: "*Hamlet* or a Beethoven quartet is the truth about this vast mass that we call the world. But there is no Shakespeare, there is no Beethoven; certainly and emphatically there is no God. . ." (*MOB* 72). While for Miriam "Beethoven had always been real," Woolf asserts that there is no place where one can find truth, especially in patriarchal male composition. Further, through the silence—the metaphorical death of Bernard—of the male writer/narrator, Woolf denies him authority. Although she is influenced specifically by Beethoven while writing *The Waves,* Woolf still does not worship "his" composition but rather coopts it for her own purposes.

Music and silence thus function differently for Woolf and Richardson: though Woolf ultimately rejects music, it functions strategically for Richardson's characters. Both authors, however, use music and silence as an interruption. Therefore, silence is more than a gap, a pause, a hesitation, a rhythm, a space for expression that defies words, and a means of understanding "purposeful being" versus "planful becoming": it is all of these as well as a purposeful political strategy that is counter-hegemonic. In these points of conjuncture between Richardson and Woolf, one of which is a focus on "purposeful being," Woolf privileges the language of visual imagery and silence while recognizing the language of music, the songs of Miriam and Dorothy. Still, both Richardson and Woolf attempt to create/invent languages of subversion, "new" languages which, as a futuristic trope in Cixousian terms, necessitate fluency.[7]

**Notes**

[1] Laurence asserts that Woolf's use of silence allows for shifts between interiority and exteriority to reveal "the limitations of language in expressing the conscious mind" (105). DuPlessis argues a case in favor of Richardson's resistance to and rebellion against the traditional narrative ("Woolfenstein . . ." 104; "Beyond. . ." 144). See also Felber (28) and Oxindine (180).

[2] See Laurence on rhythms, spaces, and narration in *Between the Acts* and *The Waves* (170-174). See also Ruotolo (16).

[3] See also Gillespie's "Political Aesthetics" (28).

[4] See Radford. Additionally, see Laurence on the female body, both physical and mental (147-55).

[5] See Minow-Pinkney (157). At the end of *The Waves*, as Harris argues, Woolf challenges the identities of the six characters as separate and immobile and strictly masculine or feminine. Similarly, Porritt argues that Woolf "moves beyond the disarticulated singular self to suggest that the self is actually a plural phenomenon which uses multiple discourses or 'voices' to constitute meaning" (333).

[6] Sypher claims that the concept of androgyny has "limited political value," especially for women in *The Waves* because the writer is male (288); but this assumes that the character is immobile and fixed.

[7] I would like to thank Greg Grewell for the careful reading and encouragement he gave me and my work.

**Works Cited**

Cixous, Hélène. "The Laugh of the Medusa." Trans. Keith Cohen and Paula Cohen. *Feminisms.* Eds. Diane Price Herndl, and Robyn R. Warhol. New Brunswick: Rutgers UP, 1993. 334-49.

——. *Hélène Cixous, Rootprints: Memory and Life Writing.* Trans. Eric Prenowitz. London: Routledge, 1997.

DuPlessis, Rachel Blau. "Beyond the Hard Visible Horizon." *Writing Beyond the Ending: Narrative Strategies for Twentieth Century Writers.* Bloomington: Indiana UP, 1985. 142-61.

——. "Woolfenstein." *Breaking the Sequence: Women's Experimental Fiction.* Princeton UP, 1989. 99-114.

Felber, Lynette. "A Manifesto for Feminine Modernism: Dorothy Richardson's *Pilgrimage.*" *Rereading Modernism: New Directions in Feminist Criticism.*

Ed. Lisa Rado. New York: Garland, 1004. 23-39.

Gillespie, Diane Filby. "Political Aesthetics: Virginia Woolf and Dorothy Richardson." *Virginia Woolf: A Feminist Slant.* Ed. Jane Marcus. Lincoln: Nebraska UP, 1983.

——. *The Sisters' Arts.* Syracuse: Syracuse UP, 1988.

Harris, Andrea L. "'This difference . . . this identity . . . was overcome': Merging Masculine and Feminine in Virginia Woolf's *The Waves.*" *Virginia Woolf and the Arts: Selected Papers From the Sixth Annual Conference on Virginia Woolf.* Eds. Diane F. Gillespie and Leslie K. Hankins. New York: Pace UP, 1997. 350-7.

Jacobs, Peters. "The Second Violin Tuning in the Ante-room: Virginia Woolf and Music." *The Multiple Muses of Virginia Woolf.* Ed. Diane F. Gillespie. Columbia: U of Missouri P, 1993.

Jones, Ann Rosalind. "Writing the Body: Toward an Understanding of *l'écriture feminine." Feminisms.* Ed. Diane Price Herndl and Robyn R. Warhol. New Brunswick: Rutgers UP, 1993. 357-70.

Laurence, Patricia Ondek. *The Reading of Silence: Virginia Woolf in the English Tradition.* Stanford: Stanford UP, 1991.

Marcus, Jane. *Virginia Woolf and the Languages of Patriarchy.* Bloomington: Indiana UP, 1987.

Minow-Pinkney, Makiko. *Virginia Woolf and the Problem of the Subject.* New Brunswick: Rutgers UP, 1987.

Oxindine, Annette. "Sapphist Semiotics in Woolf's *The Waves*: Untelling and Retelling What Cannot be Told." *Virginia Woolf: Themes and Variations: Selected Papers from the Second Annual Conference on Virginia Woolf.* Ed. Mark Hussey and Vara Neverow-Turk. New York: Pace UP, 1993. 171-81.

Porritt, Ruth. "Surpassing Derrida's Deconstructed Self: Virginia Woolf's Poetic Dissarticulation of the Self." *Women's Studies* 21.3 (1992): 323-38.

Radford, Jean. *Dorothy Richardson.* Bloomington: Indiana UP, 1991.

Richardson, Dorothy. *Pilgrimage.* Vol. 1-2 Urbana: U of Illinois P, 1979.

——. "Continuous Performance: The Film Gone Male." *The Gender of Modernism.* Ed. Bonnie Kime Scott. Bloomington: Indiana UP, 1990. 432-5.

Ruotolo, Lucio P. *The Interrupted Moment.* Stanford: Stanford UP, 1986.

Sypher, Eileen B. "*The Waves*: A Utopia of Androgyny?" *Virginia Woolf: Centennial Essays.* Eds. Elaine K. Ginsberg, and Laura Moss Gottlieb. New York: Whitson, 1983. 187-213.

Woolf, Virginia. *A Room of One's Own.* New York: Harcourt, 1929.

——. *Contemporary Writers.* New York: Harcourt, 1966.

——. *Moments of Being.* New York: Harcourt, 1976.

——. *The Essays of Virginia Woolf.* Ed. Andrew NcNeillie Vol. 3. New York: Harcourt, 1965.

——. *The Letters of Virginia Woolf.* Ed. Nigel Nicolson and Joanne Trautmann. Vols. 4 and 6. New York: Harcourt, 1965.

——. *The Waves.* New York: Harvest, 1981, 1982.

# Nita G. Pettigrew (with Julia Gray & Rebecca Weisser)

## First Encounters: Student Responses to Woolf

High school English teachers are very fortunate, indeed. Every day we have the opportunity to work with students who are meeting the great minds of literature for the very first time. Our students are not yet immersed in literary theory; they have not yet been touched by the critics. Our students come to their reading *tabula rasa*, and, if we are clever (and brave), we permit them to address these great writers *mano a mano*—without interference. If we can stay out of their way, if we can resist the daily temptation to put ourselves between the students and the book, we will witness some remarkable first encounters.

Rebecca Weisser's first reading of *Orlando* is a case in point. She read this "biographical" romp without benefit of class discussion or teacher's guidance. In this brief and spirited reflection on her reading, we can hear Rebecca's frustration with the twists and turns of Woolf's "history." But remember, Rebecca read this book without a biographical or critical context; nevertheless, in her second paragraph, Rebecca's gaze settles on a notion at the very heart of Woolf's work. Woolf speaks directly to her, and Rebecca speaks back.

### "Rattigan Glumphoboo: A Very Complicated Spiritual State and the Impossibility of it All" by Rebecca Weisser, Nerinx Hall High School, St. Louis, Missouri

*In* Orlando, *Virginia Woolf devotes six chapters, three hundred twenty-nine pages, and nearly four hundred years to the sole purpose of explaining the meaning of life, and, despite her mammoth effort, fails. What is remarkable, though, is the basis of her novel upon the very fact of the futility of such a journey. For all the time she sees fit to be devoted to such a fruitless pursuit, the questions themselves must be very worthwhile, regardless of the uncertain existence of their answers.*

*In an epic journey that spans two genders, several countries, and four centuries, Orlando embraces and rejects numerous philosophies, none of which are particularly profound, and serve to fulfill only superficial curiosities. The relief, however little there is, of Orlando's particular odyssey comes in the acceptance of "Rattigan Glumphoboo," (O 282) that is, the impossibility of exactly knowing or articulating the entire substance or meaning of anything at all, but that there is an "ecstasy found in the whole, convoluted mess of life." With this revelation, she does what she has always done, and what little else there is left to do: though uncertain, she proceeds. "In short, there was nothing for it but to ask her in and give her a glass of wine." What comes next?*

> *Woolf herself admits, "Alas, we do not know." And it is doubtful that perhaps a few more hundred years' meditation on the subject will give us something more concrete.*

This is the work of an engaged intellect, and as teachers we want to join the dialogue. We want to say, "Tell us more, Rebecca." Reflecting on her first experience at the Virginia Woolf Conference, Rebecca wrote, "Orlando's worlds seemed familiar territory to me, and Woolf's prose differs not so radically from my own mental narration of life. This intense personal resonance made it difficult to articulate my feelings on the work, nearly as difficult a task as explaining myself to a stranger." The conference gave Rebecca an opportunity to explain herself to strangers. As she wrestled with this reading of *Orlando*, Rebecca came to *own* her perception. She has had her vision, and she is on her way to more.

It is especially rewarding to bring Virginia Woolf into the community of high school scholars. But teachers are justifiably wary. We know she is a difficult writer; we think her style might be too difficult for high school students; we wonder how the boys will respond to her. I will confess: it took me twenty-five years to muster the courage to read Woolf with my students. But as I look back, I realize that in the course of my career there has been a shift in the way we think about thinking, a shift in the way we all experience literature.

I first noticed the change shortly after the Beatles came out with their *Sergeant Pepper* album. For several years, I had been teaching "The Love Song of J. Alfred Prufrock"—with much difficulty and little success. Suddenly, in the late Sixties, my students became more responsive to that poem; Eliot's line made sense to them and described a new way of approaching literature:

> It is impossible to say just what I mean!
> But as if a magic lantern threw the nerves in patterns
> on a screen. (Eliot 7)

Since that time, we have all become more comfortable with ourselves as associative thinkers. We know now that good thinking moves in disorderly patterns (rarely A to Z), and that thought is triggered by sensory experience. To be sure, the evolution among educators has been a gradual process, but our experience in the classroom has corroborated the cognitive research pioneered by Howard Gardner and Carol Gilligan almost two decades ago. There *are* multiple ways of knowing, or, as Virginia Woolf might put it, there are multiple ways of *perceiving*.

One of the most popular novels studied by Exeter's seniors is Robert Penn Warren's *All the King's Men*. It is useful to compare this pillar of the canon (and student response to it) with Virginia Woolf's work. Penn Warren's book opens with a long, night drive, at breakneck speed, up a newly paved highway. From the start, we are clearly on a journey. Two journeys, actually: one is an external, episodic, political journey, and the other is an internal evolution toward maturity, the abstract philosophical meandering of an increasingly self-aware narrator. Most students enjoy *All the King's Men*. On one level it's fast paced, full of action. The narrator is a tough talking young man with whom many of our students identify—especially the historians among them, for the fiction is based on fact. Like the highway that opens the novel, there is a linear structure to this tale, and students are rewarded if they pay attention to metaphors and symbols and allusions. They know that the narrator is not trustworthy, but they *do* know *who* the narrator is. As readers, most students feel they are in familiar territory.

There are, however, always a few students who are reticent during discussions of Penn Warren's big book—boys as well as girls. Almost invariably, these same students come alive when we open *Mrs. Dalloway*. Why? Because it's in a different voice; it speaks to a different way of knowing—an associative rather than sequential way of knowing. Woolf requires the reader to collaborate in a way Penn Warren does not.

It doesn't take students long to recognize that Woolf has created a journey that is far more interior than we have previously experienced. At first my students are disoriented; they have trouble tracking the plot. Where's the action? They do not know who or where the narrator is. But before long (if I can manage to stand out of their way) someone will say, "but this is how people really think!" And then we are off and running.

A successful reading of *Mrs. Dalloway* has much in common with a reading of *All the King's Men*. It requires a recognition of the structural journey; it requires the reader's attention to metaphor and allusion. But Virginia Woolf demands something more: the reader must read associatively. The reader must bring the rational self and the sensual self together and read with both. Though Julia Gray is now a sophomore at The Eastman School of Music, her essay demonstrates the rich rewards that come to a student who allows herself to understand through her senses. Here is her (abridged) response to *Mrs. Dalloway*.

**"'Fear No More the Heat of the Sun': A Plunge Into the Metaphors of Life and Death" by Julia Gray, Phillips Exeter Academy '97; Eastman School of Music**

*Synopsis*: Julia Gray's essay emerged out of her own efforts to understand why Woolf wrote the scene in which Clarissa stops at Hatchard's window and reads

> Fear no more the heat o' the sun
> Nor the furious winter's rages. (*MD* 9)

In the course of her essay Julia discovers five scenes in which characters make direct reference to Shakespeare's lines. From the very first line of the book, Julia undertakes a thorough inter-contextual study in which she associates Mrs. Dalloway's youthful sensations with the rich, watery imagery of the text. But Julia is also aware that the imagery shifts when Mrs. Dalloway's thinking shifts. As it happens, Clarissa stops in front of Hatchard's shop window just as her youthful thoughts have drifted to thoughts of aging and death, and, at that moment (Julia notices), we are introduced to the image of the sun's heat. Throughout this study, Julia is aware that Mrs. Dalloway is on a fearsome threshold between youth and age. Julia calls our attention to the comfort Clarissa draws from the quote, and then she begins to trace Clarissa's progressive internalization of the lines, "fear no more the heat of the sun."

We enter Julia's essay as she considers the scene in which Clarissa mends her dress:

> *". . . . Fear no more, says the heart. Fear no more says the heart, committing its burden to some sea. . . . And the body alone listens to the passing bee; the wave breaking. . . ."* (MD *39). Now Clarissa seems to take the plunge that she was poised for in the previous scene. She gives up the burden of life, the pressure of aging, and feels a peace descend upon her. The burden is given over to "some sea," a collective experience, a cycle of experience which "renews, begins, collects, lets fall." Though this sea is not the exhilarating, youthful waters of previous passages, it contains the same idea of connection, of being part of a greater whole that calmed her earlier fears of death. As her heart plunges into this cycle, Clarissa is divided. It is the mind, the heart that gives over—leaving the body separate and alone to listen to the bee, the wave, the dog barking. Her body is again in tune with the intense sensory perceptions that are supposedly lost with age.*
>
> *This moment of peace, of descending quiet reminds us of times in the novel when a cloud passes over the sun: "As a cloud crosses the sun; silence falls on London; and falls on the mind. Effort ceases. Time flaps on the mast"* (MD *49). Such moments seem outside time, outside the pressures and torments of life. Thoughts of aging are relieved, just as the cloud crossing the sun alleviates the heat. Silence falls on London the same way that quiet descends on Clarissa. The heart is left contented . The sentence following the cloud's obstruction of the sun, "Rigid, the skeleton of habit alone upholds the human frame,"* (MD *49) parallels Clarissa's sense of the mind's separation from the body. The simple, habitual action of her body—that is, mending her dress—allows the heart to escape and plunge into relieving waters.*

At this point, Julia turns her attention to the universal significance the line achieves in the mouths of Peter Walsh and Septimus Smith. Again, Julia is responding to a return of the sea imagery. As Peter Walsh walks through London, deciding to attend her party, he philosophizes about the collective truth of the soul; *it is like someone, he thinks, "who fish-like inhabits deep seas and plies among obscurities threading her way between the boles of giant weeds, over sun-flickered spaces and on and on into gloom, cold, deep, inscrutable. . ." (MD 161). Clarissa's soul has entered the strange depths of collective experience, and Peter's words describe the progression that takes place there.*

Septimus Smith is also a part of the collective experience. Julia reminds us that his rooms are described in language that evokes the waters beneath the sea's surface:

> *"Going and coming, beckoning, signaling, so the light and shadow which now made the wall grey, now made the omnibuses bright yellow . . . " (MD 139). This "sun-flickered" space is within Septimus Warren Smith's room, and arguably his mind. He, too, is beneath, submerged within metaphorical waters. It is within this scene that the quote reappears "Fear no more, says the heart in the body; fear no more."*
>
> *This passage is strikingly similar to the previous passage where the quote appeared in Clarissa's narrative. Again, the heart speaks the words, "Fear no more." Again the body, separated and alone, listens to the dog barking far away. The connection between Clarissa and Septimus is thus exposed, or more appropriately—submerged, for that is where the connection lies. Their connection is within the collective sea of life experience, the cycle, the waves of that sea. They are connected by the heart's urging to "fear no more," to "fear no more the heat 'o the sun." The heart urges both to plunge into the present and free themselves from the burden of the past. For Septimus, the only way of alleviating the burden of the past is through committing suicide. It is interesting and very significant that the form of his suicide is itself a plunge.*
>
> *Clarissa, on the other hand plunges into her party. We are reminded of Peter's description of the "fish-like soul" which "shoots to the surface and sports on the wind-wrinkled waves" (MD 161). Clarissa's soul sports on the waves of her party—diving and surfacing, plunging and coming up again.*

Julia examines Woolf's description of the party—full of language of the sea, including, of course, Clarissa's mermaid green dress. And then she turns her attention to that private moment when Clarissa gazes from her own window into the window of the old woman. This is the last allusion to "fear no more the heat of the sun."

> *She notices the old lady at the window going to bed and recalls the terror that she had felt that morning, "the overwhelming incapacity,*

*one's parents giving it into one's hands, this life, to be lived to the end . . ."(MD 185). She describes "an awful fear" in "the depths of her heart." This, of course, is the burden of life, aging, and death that Clarissa has struggled with from the beginning. Through this reflective moment, however, Clarissa realizes her happiness. "It was due to Richard; she had never been so happy. Nothing could be slow enough; nothing last too long. No pleasure could equal, she thought, this having done with the triumphs of youth, lost herself in the process of living, to find it, with a shock of delight, as the sun rose, as the day sank." This passage demonstrates that Clarissa's happiness is now intrinsically linked to her age, to her marriage to Richard, and to the fact that she is "done with the triumphs of youth." She has found life again with "a shock of delight."*

*Clarissa marvels that the party still goes on even as the old woman goes to bed, and despite the fact that the young man had killed himself. She thinks of that young man (Septimus): ". . . she did not pity him, with all this going on." In other words she cannot pity him because she is aware of life's ability to continue on. The words come back to her at this point, "Fear no more the heat of the sun." Clarissa feels a connection with Septimus, "she felt somehow very like him—the young man who had killed himself. She felt glad that he had done it" (MD 186). It is as though Clarissa understands the connection that she and Septimus share. The fact that the old woman—a generic character with not so much as a name—is included in her thoughts serves to broaden further the scope of revelation to include all people.*

*With their hearts repeating those words, both Clarissa and Septimus plunge into present interior moments. It is within those depths that they connect, because it is within those timeless, ageless waters that all souls dwell.*

Julia's essay gives us a perfect example of what can be achieved when we trust ourselves to meet great literature armed only with our senses and our intellects. She is a confident writer, working here on her own, without reference to secondary sources. Her essay—and Rebecca's—gives proof to Eliot's theory of the Objective Correlative, a theory we began to internalize, as a culture, way back in the Sixties.

Virginia Woolf understood the symbiosis between the senses and the intellect. She understood that we come to know first through our senses. Our students were born into a world (post Eliot, post Beatles) that has come to understand and value that symbiosis. Male and female they meet her as kindred spirits.

So where does that leave us, their teachers? Have we no part to play in these early encounters? Of course we do. In fact, our role is crucial: we hover, we prod, we introduce them to writers at just the right moment, and then, if we are truly brave, we stand back and listen. We must have faith in their capacity to meet great writers *mano a mano*, without interference. High school teachers are the fortunate ones: we stand with our students at the water's edge. If we have the courage to stand out of their way, we give our students the courage—and the desire—to plunge deeply and freely into even the most subtle and complex literature.

**Works Cited**

Eliot, T.S. *The Waste Land and Other Poems*. San Diego: Harcourt Brace & Company, 1962.

Woolf, Virginia. *Mrs. Dalloway*. San Diego: Harvest, 1981.

Woolf, Virginia. *Orlando: A Biography*. San Diego: Harcourt Brace & Company, 1956.

## Bonnie Kime Scott
### (with Shari Benstock and Morris Beja)
### *Paris Was a Woman* Conversation

Ideally, con-ferring is what goes on at conferences, and to a limited extent, con-versation takes place whenever an article or project emerges in response to another. But the process is slow, and it goes back and forth infrequently at best. The figurative conversation may be found only in the footnotes, or discovered years later, when we climb out of the contemporaneous vantage point "on the flat, in the crowd, half blind with dust" that Woolf identifies in "Modern Fiction" (*CR*1, 150). Thus the idea of holding a "conversation" at a Woolf Conference had great appeal when Georgia Johnston presented it to me for the 1998 conference in St. Louis. Here was a way of modifying traditional, often inanimate "paper" sessions and keynote "speeches," with their tendency toward solo delivery and pre-fabricated, linear argument. Holding a conversation about film maker Greta Schiller's *Paris Was a Woman*, a documentary that the audience had just viewed, added the possibility of extending the conversation in numerous, unpredictable ways. And I was offered Shari Benstock, who was actually in the film, as a conversationalist, with the added dimension of Murray Beja as moderator.

Conversation is appropriate to the film *Paris was a Woman*, and to Virginia Woolf, whose love of conversation is evident in those she records in her diaries, letters, and novels. My favorite of these is in a letter to Ottoline Morrell, describing a tea at which she brought together Rebecca West and Ethel Smyth: "We discussed religion, sex, literature and other problems, violently, in a roar, to catch Ethel's ear, for three hours" (*L5* 261). Implied conversations are offered in the film's interviews, typically set with the speaker on one side of a café table, or near a desk; the viewer can imagine pulling up a chair. These interviews with many women and a few men of Paris between the wars, plus two interviews with contemporary scholars, help to pace the film and articulate it into segments. It was thrilling to come upon an elderly Gisèle Freund in a broad-shouldered, grey suit, seated beside a small golden table, or Natalie Barney's petite housekeeper and confidante Berthe Cleyrergue, posed by another table which had been neatly outfitted with a lace tablecloth and white flowers, or a seasoned, garrulous Janet Flanner, stationed behind her desk, broadcasting her commentary in a practiced and authoritative radio voice.

The interview, exploited for its conversational potential, was a genre actually cultivated by such women of Paris as Flanner and Djuna Barnes. Barnes, in a typically experimental move, shaded her interviews toward conversations in which it was no longer clear who was the interviewee, or whether it was possible to declare an ending to the interaction.[1] One of the joys of the film *Reds* was that its aged "witnesses," including Dora Russell and Rebecca West, could get into disagreements with one another because they were brought on screen together. In the case of *Paris Was a Woman*, recreation of this kind of conversation may be asking too much, as few of the principals can still be brought together. Schiller substituted instead a very clever editing job, with clips drawn from diverse archival sources. Murray Beja was able to identify, for example, Malcolm Muggeridge's interview of Sylvia Beach from hearing his few surviving questions. Shari Benstock recognized a seminar held at Rutgers University in the 1970s as the source of the Freund and Cleyrergue clips. The poses and sets derived from the Paris sidewalk café could be imitated in the interviews done specifically for the film, including those with scholars Catharine Stimpson and Shari Benstock, and ones with survivors, including the tatoo artist and author, Sam Steward, whose mahogany table was decked with a vase of pink roses, suitable to his explication of Gertrude Stein's "A Rose is a Rose is a Rose." Steward, it turns out, was an alumnus of Murray Beja's academic institution, Ohio State, and Murray had contacted him a decade ago concerning a letter Steward had written to James Joyce in 1927.[2] Our conversations in St. Louis were conducted over comparable café tables. But in the case of our planned rendezvous with Shari Benstock, nature interfered, in the form of flight-defying rains. Thus, we had a hybrid of paper and conversation. Grounded in New England, Shari express mailed a brief statement, from which Murray Beja selected sections. These we worked into a sort of a three-way exchange, joined in eagerly by the audience. This essay is a comparable hybrid, assembled by Scott from notes and statements by Benstock and Beja, with all too sketchy memories of the audience's contributions.

In a way Shari was present in St. Louis through her appearance in the documentary. I regarded her as a very special link to the film both because she was present as a historical and biographical authority throughout, and because the film followed a geographical plotting of women's Paris menages that imitated her 1986 book *Women of the Left Bank.* In the film, Shari was seated in a wicker chair, flowers in the background, and the edge of a book-laden desk barely visible. The camera sought intimate contact with her large eyes, which were accentuated with dark eye-liner, reminiscent of that worn by Nancy Cunard in photos included in the film.

Had she been present, I would have asked Shari about the nature of her participation in the film, and thankfully she anticipated this in her statement. The filming of her segment

> took place over two days at my house in the Berkshires in May 1995. Greta Schiller brought with her a New York City-based film crew who turned my living room into a "set." Greta outlined the project in terms of my participation; I did not know who else was being filmed (apart from Giselle Freund), nor how long the film would be, nor how my contributions would figure in the larger script. Greta had in hand during our conversations and the filming her annotated copy of *Women of the Left Bank* . . . and she drew on it in posing questions to me but she asked me specifically not to refer to it to refresh my memory . . . or to mention any of the women other than the couples that were the focus of the film: Sylvia Beach and Adrienne Monnier, Natalie Barney and Romaine Brooks, Gertrude Stein and Alice Toklas, with attention as well to Djuna Barnes and Thelma Wood, Janet Flanner and Solita Solano, Margaret Anderson and Jane Heap.

These were of course lesbian couples, some discussed as such more extensively than others in the film, with Stein and Toklas featured.

First and foremost, *Paris Was a Woman* celebrates the life that these women writers, painters, photographers, and film-makers made in Paris between the wars. The celebration opens with a female vocalist singing "Sur les quais de vieux Paris," saluting bohemian love as we cruise the Seine in old film clips. We move on to a rapid, dazzling play of still and moving, color and black and white images, and cherish (through Toklas) Stein's rich contralto voice, as it embraces her own written words in sound and rhythmic repetition. Catharine Stimpson, the second feminist authority in the film, seated like Flanner behind a desk, is there to provide insight into lesbian code that for Stein allowed "cow" to represent "orgasm." Stimpson's was the commentary that most successfully addressed the literary techniques of the authors presented. There can be no question that the lesbian celebration accomplished in *Paris Was a Woman* was a triumph with the Woolf Conference audience, as its members entered the conversation—a triumph long awaited on film. *Paris Was a Woman* was delightful in the bright matter-of-factness of its treatment of the women's lives and loves together. Members of the audience were eager to have the video more broadly distributed, and alarmed that we had not been able to obtain a copy readily in St. Louis.

Despite sharing in its celebration, all three conversationalists had some difficulties with the film. Shari noted some limitations in the film's lesbian focus.

> The film and book[3] construct a Left Bank community of gay women who played crucial roles in advancing the cultural innovations associated with Modernism and the avant-garde. But this community was complexly and loosely structured with support systems and competing interests that crossed lines of gender, sexuality, nationhood, class, and political commitments. For example, the tensions between "straight" women (e.g., Maria Jolas and Kay Boyle, who were married and raising children while also contributing in major ways to editing, translating, and publishing their own writing and others' writing) and gay women (e.g., Gertrude Stein, Natalie Barney) were often felt more keenly than the tensions along the fault line of "men" and "Women." Characterizing the Paris expatriate literary community as primarily "gay" erases important differences among its participants.

Murray was troubled by the fact that "what we're shown or made to *see* is often distracting rather than helpful" and is often "quite irrelevant to what we're hearing." For example, interspersed shots from Germaine Dulac's film, *Invitation au Voyage,* were "of real interest in themselves, actually, but that only makes them all the more a problem in terms of our paying attention to what's being *said.*" What was being said during the play of a second, extensive passage from the film was a segment of Djuna Barnes's *Nightwood.*

Both Murray and I were disappointed with the dark portrait of Barnes which I thought focused too much on her break with Thelma Wood (the only portion selected from *Nightwood* for reading), and not enough on her other works, her other connections in Paris, or writing that continued in London and New York. Andrea Weiss's narrative dismisses her last 50 years as those of a "bitter recluse," a characterization that misses (for one thing) a series of animated meetings and letters exchanged with T.S. Eliot and Natalie Barney. We do get glimpses of Barnes's hand-tinted drawings for her *Ladies' Almanack,* but this romp through the garden of Barney's salon, its images better explained, should have played a more central role in the film. Instead the *Almanack* is dismissed as minor work.

My most substantial objection to the film concerns its rendition of the complex story of Sylvia Beach's fortunes and misfortunes in the publication of James Joyce's *Ulysses*, which is simplified to the point of inaccuracy. Beach published *Ulysses* in 1922, when no other publisher dared. She granted Joyce extraordinary freedom in his revisions, as Freund recalls on screen. Beach followed this up with further editions of *Ulysses* and of

Joyce's poetry. But is it fair to say, as script-writer Andrea Weiss does, that his contract for the 1934 Random House American edition was the way Joyce rewarded Beach for her efforts? Did Joyce bankrupt Beach, as the film claims? Joyce and Beach did have a break, urged on Beach by Monnier, around 1931. But this was nine years and many editions after the initial publication of *Ulysses*, and it was encouraged by other loyal assistants to Joyce, including Paul Léon and Maria Jolas. In her extensive study of Beach, *Sylvia Beach and the Lost Generation*, Noel Fitch records no bankruptcy; instead she notes a boom, followed by a bust after each of the editions of *Ulysses* brought out by Beach, and describes continuing royalties paid Beach for ongoing continental editions, as well as income Beach derived from the sale of manuscripts Joyce had given her. One quick image in the film shows "publisher of *Ulysses*" used on a flyer advertising Beach's book shop. It is hard to assess the cash value of this.[4] There was also the pressure of a pirated edition of *Ulysses* flooding the market in the United States. The piracy was difficult to challenge via Beach's small publishing operation in Paris. Hence the New York Random House edition. While films may demand a faster pace than such details allow, they should not gloss over into misrepresentation.

Shari Benstock is selectively quoted calling Joyce a man of "enormous ambition." Statements of ambition can certainly be applied to Stein or Picasso, both of whom are humanized in the film through the use of playful home movies. Picasso struggles with what to do, by way of waving and gesturing, while the camera is trained, seemingly endlessly, upon him. Stein plays with her poodle as if to show its ability at prancing. Nothing is said of Picasso's questionable dealings with women. Unpleasantness is reserved for Joyce, as if the film needed some villain.

In this era of post-colonial studies, even the Parisian focus of the film might be questioned, and here the audience joined in the critique, extending modernism in many directions. *Paris Was a Woman* sustains the idea of an urban modernism of international capitals, even as it discovers a space of female liberation from the heterosexual scripts of patriarchy. Women were involved in trans-Atlantic ventures and rural landscapes that do not fit well into the Parisian community of the film. There was even a migratory modernism, taking authors and artists regularly back to America, or on Continental junkets, conditioned by economic necessity or opportunity. To arrive in Paris was not simply to find paradise, in other words, but to move in and out of alternative subject positions and performances. And many of the important moves that came after World War II destroyed the Paris environment—with women like H.D. and Jean Rhys offering a delayed modernism into the 1960s. Furthermore, the one photo, one sentence mention of "Bricktop," and the leggy film clip of Josephine Baker in the role of a drunken sailor would seem to call for a fuller acknowledgment of the strains of racialism in Paris. Weiss's book version is better able to represent Paris as a crossroads and passage, rather than a settled spot, and thus is able to pull in figures such as H.D. and Bryher, as had Benstock in *Women of the Left*

*Bank*. Indeed, it is only in this way that Virginia Woolf becomes a player in relation to the film.

All three of the conversationalists wondered about a possible shift in the film to Cassis, Woolf's favored spot on the continent, but really a form of the English colony. I defer once again to Shari Benstock:

> Virginia Woolf was, of course, not a part of this community, and certainly not because she was a francophobe. It is difficult to imagine her in this context, primarily I think because of her resistance to Americans and American writing of that period (she was of course reviewing books produced by members of this community, or commenting on them in her diaries and letters). Paris as a place of escape and escapade with Vita, of cross-dressing among the French, is another matter. But living openly as a gay or bisexual woman, living in daily interaction with members of the Paris community (women and men, straight and gay) seems outside the realm of possibility for Virginia Woolf. One can of course see Vita as a guest at Natalie Barney's salon, as indeed she was.
>
> When she began visiting France regularly, [Woolf] followed Vanessa to the south of France for summer holidays. This "community" was one of family and close friends. Here she might have met (but apparently did not have close contact with ) a number of women from the Paris Left Bank community who also vacationed on the south coast between Marseilles and Toulon. Mary Ann Caws has traced Bloomsbury in the south of France very carefully and discussed at length the influences that the little 17th-century fishing village of Cassis and its surrounding vineyards, fjords, and perched chateaux had on Vanessa and Virginia and their friends. This place is resolutely rural, another world entirely from Paris, with its intellectual pretensions. As we know from her diaries and letters, Virginia Woolf loved this place, and loved "motoring" down from Dieppe to Cassis. The occasional punctured tire or engine failure provided her the opportunity to record her impressions of the countryside. Ultimately, Cassis gave her a place to write, and her remarks are about *place*. . . . In the Hotel Cendrillon, Virginia is surrounded by compatriots . . . and she is observing and recording as a writer. And here we might observe that she needs "community" in ways both common to and different from the women presented in *Paris Was a Woman*: unlike Gertrude Stein, Woolf seems not to have needed as a basic element of her writing experience to be surrounded by a different language (French) in order to hear English more clearly in her head; like Edith Wharton, whose home in Hyeres was located twenty miles to the east of Cassis, Woolf found the landscape/seascape of southern France inspiring.

Paris as woman is converted from mistress to muse in this documentary—a muse with a very special and supportive relationship dependent upon women's arrangements with one another. The film assumes the tone of a death knell, with archival footage to match, as Paris ceases to be a woman in the late 1930s, its women divided in their attitudes toward Fascism, and forced into exile or hiding by the German occupation. There is of course a grim parallel in Woolf's own life. One hope is that this documentary serves, not just as a celebration of a golden world of women, but as an encouragement to go back to the rich multi-media archives it has tapped, and to extend and complicate the conversation initiated by *Paris was a Woman.*

**Notes**

1 See for example Barnes's "The Confessions of Helen Westley," as analyzed by Mary Lynn Broe in *The Gender of Modernism* (24-25, 40-45).

2 Beja learned from their conversations that, while still an undergraduate, Steward asked Joyce to help him secure permission to borrow the still-banned *Ulysses* from the university library. He was a friend of both Stein and Toklas, and among his published works are *Chapters from an Autobiography* (San Francisco: Grey Fox Press, 1981), the "racy novel with a streetwalker in it," *Angels on the Bough* (Caldwell, Id.: Caxton Printers, 1936), which helped him lose an academic position, and gay fiction with cult status, written under the pseudonym Phil Andros: *Below the Belt and Other Stories* (Boston: Perineum Press, 1992), and *Different Strokes: Stories* (San Francisco: Perineum Press, 1984). After 20 years, he gave up university teaching to earn the title of tattoo artist, and from that experience wrote *Bad Boys and Tough Tatoos: A Social History of the Tattoo with Gangs, Sailors, and Street-Corner Punks* (New York: Harrington Park Press, 1990).

3 Andrea Weiss, the script writer of the film, authored a book, also titled *Paris Was a Woman*, as a spin-off of the film, using the same and additional images.

4 See my *Joyce and Feminism*, and particularly Chapter 5: "New Free Women in the Company of Joyce" for a more thorough account.

**Works Cited**

Barnes, Djuna. *Ladies Almanack*, 1928. Elmwood Park, IL: Dalkey Archive Press, 1992.

Benstock, Shari. *Women of the Left Bank: Paris 1900-1940.* Austin: U of Texas P, 1986.

Fitch, Noel Riley. *Sylvia Beach and the Lost Generation.* New York: Norton, 1983.

Scott, Bonnie Kime. *The Gender of Modernism.* Bloomington: Indiana U P, 1990.

——. *Joyce and Feminism.* Bloomington: Indiana U P, 1984.

Weiss, Andrea. *Paris Was a Woman: Portraits from the Left Bank.* San Francisco: Harper Collins, 1995.

Judith Allen

# The Rhetoric of Performance in *A Room of One's Own*

*A Room of One's Own* both expresses and enacts its cultural critique by making certain that its readers not only *see* the significance of the women of their culture as "outsiders," but also appropriate that position for themselves. My discussion, using Brecht's theory of performance, examines Woolf's rhetorical and narrative strategies—with a focus on the functioning of language and punctuation—to show how "showing" the reader the process and calling attention to the constructed nature of the text serves to transform those readers—to get them to *see*, and, ultimately, to critique those institutions that had become, in their entrenched familiarity, quite invisible.

I will begin near the end of Woolf's *A Room of One's Own* with a passage not usually highlighted, but one which permits Woolf to take her cultural critique in a multitude of directions. Here, one of her narrators responds to the aridity of Mr. A's new novel:

> But . . . I had said "but" too often. One cannot go on saying "but." One must finish the sentence somehow, I rebuked myself. Shall I finish it, "But—I am bored!" But why was I bored? (104)

After five "buts" in as many sentences, the reader of *A Room of One's Own* is not so much interested in why the narrator is bored, as why she keeps repeating "but." Why does this essay, which, incidentally, also begins its first and last sentences with the word but, seem to reverberate with the significance of that word? Indeed, the essay's sentences do get finished—but with enough equivocation so that "but," along with "perhaps" and "might," becomes, inevitably, the expected conclusion—or rather, the lack of conclusion. In fact, throughout this essay, as the above passage conveys, Woolf's narrators inform their readers of their difficulties and speculate about the forms and methods used to express their experiences.

That the first word of *A Room of One's Own* is "but"[1] does not seem mere chance, for Woolf's narrator in "The Modern Essay" declares that the essay "should lay us under a spell with its first word . . . "(*CR*1 211). One does wonder, however, what kind of "spell" is cast upon the reader when "but" not only begins a text, but is also, in the immediately established dialogue, transferred to the reader's lips by the narrator? By giving this line to the reader, the narrator places herself "in the position of the one asked" (*D*4 361), thus transferring a sense of uncertainty, as well as resistance, to the reader. Interestingly, the varied definitions of "but"—including "except," "outside," and "on the contrary"—to name just a few[2], seem to echo the marginal position of women in our culture; and quite significantly, several of these words are used in *A Room of One's Own* to describe the woman "walking down Whitehall, when from being the natural inheritor of that civilization, she becomes, *on the contrary, outside of it, alien and critical*" (emphasis added; 101).

With the constant intrusion of "but," the text simultaneously resonates with the multiple interruptions in women's lives and the resultant openness created by these breaks. It seems, very simply, that "but" will always negate the state of boredom which Woolf's narrator both describes and questions, for "but" refuses that boredom by leaving things open, creating new possibilities; this coincides, of course, with what Woolf considers a necessary vitality, the essence of life. "But," in its ambiguity, functions as a connective, as a way of continuing and extending, although it also resists that continuity, cuts things off, and most importantly, negates what was said before its appearance. One can assume that something preceded the narrator's opening word, as one always assumes with "but" that something will follow.

"But," in its linkage with the marginality of women, serves to enact their exclusion and oppression with its strategically placed interruptions. Strolling through Oxbridge, thinking about "that wild flash of imagination" in the essays of Lamb (7), the narrator's thoughts move her to speculate about Lamb's thinking regarding Milton's possible revision of *Lycidas*, as well as her own thinking about Thackeray's alterations of *Esmond*, and whether those revisions improved the style or the meaning: "*But* then one would have to decide what is style and what is meaning, a question which—*but* here I was actually at the door which leads into the library itself. I must have opened it, for instantly there issued, like a guardian angel barring the way . . ." (emphasis added; 7). The narrator's quest is now interrupted by "but," as her path was previously intercepted and diverted by the Beadle. "But," by interrupting the sentence as well as her entrance to the library, also interrupts her thoughts and imaginings, her intellectual curiosity, and, most importantly, her desire. What follows "but" is the fact of her exclusion. Her imagination shrinks into the background—as does her all-important freedom. This imaginative freedom, although negated, is, as Wolfgang Iser asserts in another context, still on the page—still visible to the reader, and thus, still a viable option (169).

Also visible to the reader, and explicitly foregrounded by Woolf's various narrators throughout the text, are ellipses and parentheses; interrupting and intruding themselves into sentences, they call attention to the constructed nature of the text, and to the process of writing. In this self-conscious acknowledgment of text as text, there is an implicit recognition of the presence of an audience, of readers. For these readers, an ellipsis may indicate a withholding, a pause, or an omission; it may also express a leap, without logical connections, from one topic to another. This provides the readers with an opportunity to participate, consciously and unconsciously, in the creation of their text—and, as Iser suggests, to fill in the blanks (168). The blanks are spaces of indeterminacy, of possible repression, of unconscious desire, and become spaces for self-conscious questioning, as the narrator, for example, poses questions regarding truth and illusion:

> Why, if it was an illusion, not praise the catastrophe, whatever it was, that destroyed illusion and put truth in its place? For truth . . . those dots mark the spot where, in search of truth, I missed the turning up to Fernham. (15)

And so, the ellipses in *A Room of One's Own*, as Shari Benstock suggests, are used "to signal a falling back or turning away from the socially constructed opposition of truth and illusion within Western thinking, a moment of contradiction and confusion" (124).[3]

Woolf's narrator follows this confusing and attention-getting device by giving her readers some of the evidence she finds during the problematic nature of her quest. She provides varying perspectives which display the contingent nature of one's observations and conclusions. In this case, the houses she observes are "dim and festive now with their red windows in the dusk, but raw and red and squalid, with their sweets and their boot-laces, at nine o'clock in the morning" (15). Here all is contingent upon time. This questioning of truth and illusion is also replicated as the ellipsis blurs textual boundaries. This mark of punctuation, the ellipsis, is talked about as if the dots which structure it were really marks on the road. And the statement that "no conclusion was found on the road to Headingly" (16) similarly blurs boundaries and calls attention to the text as a construct, as readers find themselves questioning that "a conclusion" might be found on the road. The narrator's pursuit of truth continues with a trip to the counter of the British Museum Library where an examination of the catalogue provokes a very different explanation of her next ellipsis: " . . . . . the five dots here indicate five separate minutes of stupefaction, wonder and bewilderment" (26). Her readers may also experience surprise at this confusing interruption of the narrative, as they are addressed directly with the question: "Are you aware that you are, perhaps, the most discussed animal in the universe?" This direct question serves to distance her readers in order to gain their attention, as she continues to investigate her inability to capture the "truth" about women.

Along with the ellipsis, the parenthesis also functions to attract as well as distract her readers by its intrusion into the text. Working as an aside, the parenthesis can add something new that may seem out of place, or abruptly change the direction of the thoughts being conveyed; in another sense, it makes what had been contextualized in a certain way suddenly become the context for the newly added parenthetical statement. One is reminded of the "Time Passes" section of *To the Lighthouse* where catastrophes are scattered, parenthetically, to place them in the context of another kind of destruction; that they are mentioned as Kafka might mention them—so very nonchalantly—also serves to foreground them. This sometimes self-conscious disruption of the narrator's "train of thought," (4) also serves to disrupt the thinking of her readers, moving the reader off the path, as the narrator was moved off the path by the Beadle.

These interruptions by "but," and by the ellipses and parentheses, serve as a partial solution to the narrator's boredom with the discourse of Mr. A's and Mr. B's writings. The compartmentalization of Mr. B's mind seemed to deny access to his feelings, and in his sentences, "it is the power of suggestion that one most misses . . . " (105); this suggestiveness is a call for openness, for contradictions, and a certain wildness. The "smooth lawns"(9) of the men's colleges, perceived as lacking this wildness, are compared to the "wild unkempt grasses"(20) of Fernham, for the roughness and disorder hold more interest. Her boredom is a critique of this smoothness, of the hard and the barren; these qualities are aligned with cultural traditions that exclude women, with language and forms that cannot express women's lives, and with a rigidity that negates creativity.

There is much that acts to counter the rigidity and fixity of patriarchal institutions, the lifeless inscriptions of members of those institutions, and the "spirit of peace" which prevails when one stays "on the paths," or "in the courts and quadrangles of Oxbridge" (6). For the narrator, trespassing, crossing boundaries, or stepping on the forbidden turf are precipitated by a degree of excitement, and by "the mysterious property" of ideas; these thoughts "flashed hither and thither, set up such a wash and tumult of ideas that it was impossible to sit still" (5). When intercepted and chased from the turf onto the gravel, however, these thoughts and ideas—imaged by Woolf's narrator as "my little fish" (another definition of "but")— are sent into hiding. Using "but" in exchange for "fish," and sending it "into hiding," reiterates the banishment of the imagination, for in getting rid of this mode of interruption one smoothes out the text as one smoothes out the turf. This sequestering of ideas, of imagination, where "the roughness of the present seemed smoothed away"(6), is equated with a dull and lifeless quality. The narrator's experience upon passing the chapel door also reflects this lifelessness: "Even the sorrow of Christianity sounded in that serene air more like the recollection of sorrow than sorrow itself; even the groanings of the ancient organ seemed lapped in peace."

Again we have a kind of "peacefulness" linked with lifelessness. The emotion lacking in this serene setting could be found by trespassing on the turf, or by visiting the gardens of Fernham which were "not orderly," but "wild and open," and "windblown and waving" (17). To counter this stifling of ideas, imagination, and creativity, *A Room of One's Own* performs the essayistic—sanctioning mobility, wandering, and the crossing of boundaries. As the narrator wanders, strolling past many magnificent buildings, she speculates about the "unending stream of gold and silver" which must have flowed, and continues to flow, in order to maintain all of this. This "foundation of gold and silver" is linked with "the pavement laid solidly over the wild grasses" (10); and the wild grasses are linked with the life at the women's college. The desire for mobility, and all that it engenders, is evident in the deprivation of this activity; even the fact that there was no "walking tour" (54) for women contributed to the stifling of their thoughts and imaginings.

There is an oscillation between the "rambling" (83) and "strolling"(6) of the narrators—and their minds—and the constraints that try to maintain the nineteenth century's notion that women be silent and still. Subverting society's rule of limiting them to the gravel path, these women must take the wrong turn, duck around the corner, and let the line of their thoughts "dip into the stream" (5). This activity is both their resistance, and their tactic for survival. The desire of a narrator to "expose what was in her mind to the air" (19) expresses her need for freedom. As the narrator thinks about the mysterious qualities of the mind, and just how it functions, she simultaneously enacts this process before her readers; her readers/audience watch her as she thinks about the mind thinking, and her tentative conclusion regarding this state of the mind is "that it seems to have no single state of being." Most importantly, it "is always altering its focus, and bringing the world into different perspectives" (101).

In Woolf's *A Room of One's Own*, its narrators attempt to reveal the inner workings of their minds. Filled with many dialogues which often engage the readers, Woolf's narrators will, without claiming to know anything with certainty, show as well as tell, as the audience joins in on this speculative process.

> . . . I am going to develop in your presence as fully and freely as I can the train of thought which led me to think this. Perhaps if I lay bare the ideas, the prejudices, that lie behind this statement you will find that they have some bearing upon women and some upon fiction. . . . when a subject is highly controversial—and any question about sex is that—one cannot hope to tell the truth. One can only show how one came to hold whatever opinion one does hold. (4)

Woolf's narrator constantly speculates about the reader's response to her assigned topic, and about her effectiveness with the assignment. In her attempt to "show how one came to hold the opinions one holds" (4), to show the process of her thinking, Woolf's self-consciousness regarding language, punctuation, changes of narrative voice, and changes of scene becomes a prominent strategy. This self-consciousness produces an interesting effect on her readers, for it both engages them and distances them, continuing the oscillating movement that repudiates—in yet another way—the rigidity and fixity of forms, institutions, people, and the language used to construct them. In this instance, the oscillation repudiates a fixed stance, a fixed perspective from which we can judge and formulate our opinions.

This distancing of the reader has some resonance with Bertolt Brecht's "estrangement effect." One of the important goals of Brecht's "Epic Theatre," which relates to many of Woolf's novels,[4] and particularly to *A*

*Room of One's Own* and *Three Guineas*, is to have her audience discover the conditions of life. Sallie Sears sees aspects of Brecht's "Epic Theatre" in the context of the audience of Miss La Trobe's play in *Between the Acts* and finds that "it is predicated upon the assumption (so crucial to modernists like Brecht, Artaud, Peter Weiss) that an audience that sees deplorable truths, hitherto unconscious, hidden, or denied, will not only deplore, but seek to abolish the circumstances that brought them into being" (Sears 229). This takes place through an interruption of happenings (as Woolf's narrator is interrupted when she opens the door of the library, or the text is interrupted by a parenthetical comment or a reference to punctuation). The narrator also periodically interrupts her own narrative in order to undermine the illusion her audience has accepted. To accomplish this, the narrator simply points out to the reader that she is creating scenes and fictionalizing, thus causing them to acknowledge that the impervious boundary between fact and fiction is not so easily discernible:

> As I have said already that it was an October day, I dare not forfeit your respect and imperil the fair name of fiction by changing the season and describing lilacs hanging over garden walls, crocuses, tulips, and other flowers of spring. Fiction must stick to facts, and the truer the facts the better the fiction—so we are told. Therefore it was still autumn and the leaves were still yellow and falling, if anything, a little faster then before, because it was now evening (seven twenty-three *to be precise)* and a breeze (from the south-west *to be exact*) had risen. (emphasis added; 16)

The narrator obviously overemphasizes the precision and exactitude of her fictionalizing, in order to call even more attention to the problematic nature of factuality. By self-consciously calling attention to the strategy of fictionalizing Woolf is confronting her audience with the problematic nature of such dichotomizing.

As Woolf foregrounds this playing with "fact" and "fiction," she frequently makes visual—as is the case of the ellipses and parentheses—all those places where the text refers to itself as a text; all of these, in a Brechtian sense, both engage and distance the reader. Relating Brecht's "Epic Theatre" to *Jacob's Room*, Edward L. Bishop finds that the aim is "to make a spectator use his or her critical sense" . . . and that "the process of showing must itself be shown" (157). Bishop also notes that Walter Benjamin's assessment of Brecht can be applied to Woolf, for she is also less interested in the "development of actions" than in the "representation of conditions" (Benjamin 150). Woolf's rhetorical strategies also seem to echo Brecht's "Epic Theatre," for the oscillation I refer to in *A Room of One's Own* seems to resonate with Brecht's aim of "detachment" and "reorientation" (Willett 170-7).

Like the songs, captions, and exposed stagecraft of Brecht's "Epic Theatre," Woolf's use of "but," the ellipses, the parentheses, and the other self-conscious references to the text function to impair the illusion. Calling attention to the constructed nature of the text, to words as words, and to what may have been withheld, serves to distance the audience—to make them, at times, spectators or outsiders—thus enabling them to critique those institutions which continue to structure and have power over their lives, and perhaps to enact some necessary resistance.

## Notes

[1] See earlier references to "but" in the typescript excerpts from *A Room of One's Own*. Here one finds different questions and explanations for the use of "but": "But-were 'buts' beginning again? What did I mean by 'but' this time?" . . . "But–it was the emotion perhaps that made me so uncomfortable" (*WF* 189). Woolf's use of "but" has been discussed in differing contexts by Bowlby, 17-8; Rosenman, 93-94; and Bishop, "Metaphor and Subversive Process in Virginia Woolf's Essays," 574.

[2] "But," as a noun, also refers to a fish, which may fit in with Woolf's fishing metaphor; a "but" in Scotland refers to the outer room, especially the kitchen of a cottage; and, of course, to "butt in" is to interfere, or to thrust against (*OED*). All of these resonate in various ways with Woolf's usage.

[3] Benstock finds that the "ellipsis is not merely a recurrent textual feature of *Three Guineas*, it constitutes the primary structuring device of the text, joining political argument to the rhetorical-grammatical form through which it is elaborated " (124). See her chapter, "Ellipses: Figuring Feminisms in *Three Guineas*" in *Textualizing the Feminine* (123-62). Bowlby also discusses ellipses in a variety of Woolf's works, in "The Dotted Line, " *Virginia Woolf: Feminist Destinations* (160-70).

[4] For other discussions relating Brecht's "Epic Theatre" to Woolf's novels, see Bishop, "The Subject in *Jacob's Room*," 147-75; Johnston, 61-75; and Sears, 212-35.

## Works Cited

Benjamin, Walter. *Illuminations*. Ed. Hannah Arendt. Trans. Harry Zohn. New York: Schocken, 1969.

Benstock, Shari. *Textualizing the Feminine: On the Limits of Genre*. Norman: U of Oklahoma P, 1991.

Bishop, Edward L. "Metaphor and Subversive Process in Virginia Woolf's Essays." *Style* 21 (1987): 573-588.

——. "The Subject in *Jacob's Room*." *Modern Fiction Studies* 38.1 (1992): 147-75.

Bowlby, Rachel. *Virginia Woolf: Feminist Destinations*. Oxford: Basil Blackwell, 1988.

Iser, Wolfgang. *The Act of Reading*. Baltimore: Johns Hopkins, 1978.

Johnston, Georgia. "Class Performance in *Between the Acts*: Audiences for Miss LaTrobe and Mrs. Manresa." *Woolf Studies Annual* 3 (1997): 61-75.

Rosenman, Ellen Bayuk. A Room of One's Own: *Women Writers and the Politics of Creativity*. New York: Twayne , 1995.

Sears, Sallie. "Theater of War: Virginia Woolf's *Between the Acts.*" *Virginia Woolf: A Feminist Slant.* Ed. Jane Marcus. Lincoln: U of Nebraska P, 1983. 212-35.

Willett, John. *The Theatre of Bertolt Brecht: A Study from Eight Aspects.* 3rd ed. London: Methuen, 1967.

Woolf, Virginia. *The Common Reader: First Series.* Annotated ed. Ed. Andrew McNeillie. New York: Harcourt Brace, 1984.

——. *The Diary of Virginia Woolf.* Ed. Anne Olivier Bell, assisted by Andrew McNeillie. Vol. 4. New York: Harcourt, 1982.

——. *A Room of One's Own.* New York: Harcourt, 1957.

——. *Women & Fiction: The Manuscript Versions of* A Room of One's Own. Ed. S.P. Rosenbaum. Oxford: Blackwell, 1992

# Notes on Contributors

**Tuzyline Jita Allan** is an Associate Professor of English and Women's Studies at Baruch College (CUNY). She is co-director of "Women Writing Africa," a Ford Foundation/Feminist Press project, and is co-editing two texts, one on African masculinities and the other on notions of home in postcolonial Africa.

**Judith Allen** is lecturer in English at Penn State University, Abington. She has published articles on Woolf, Montaigne and Woolf, and Joyce, and is currently working on a book on Woolf's essay-writing practice.

**Mónica Ayuso**, born and raised in Argentina, is currently Assistant Professor in the English Department at California State University, Bakersfield. She completed a Doctorate from the University of Florida with a dissertation entitled, "Thinking Back Through Our Mothers: Virginia Woolf in the Spanish American Imagination." She specializes in teaching ethnic, racial, and gender studies.

**Morris Beja**, Professor of English at the Ohio State University, founded the Virginia Woolf Society and is Executive Secretary of the International James Joyce Foundation. Among his books are *Epiphany in the Modern Novel*, *Film and Literature*, and *James Joyce*. He has edited *Mrs. Dalloway* for the Shakespeare Head Press, as well as volumes of essays on Woolf, Joyce, Beckett, and Orson Welles.

**Suzanne Bellamy** is an Australian artist and writer, with a teaching background in history and women's studies. She lives and works in rural New South Wales, operating a sculpture, ceramic, and print studio and exhibits internationally. She spends increasing amounts of time in the USA, most recently as a guest artist at SUNY-Oswego,studying digital design using original images from her print series on Virginia Woolf. She is also currently finishing a *Visual Essay* on the body of clay sculpture she has produced since 1980.

**Shari Benstock** is Professor of English and Women's Studies at the University of Miami, and is Chair of the Department of English. She is the author of *Women of the Left Bank: Paris 1900-1940, Textualizing the Feminine: On the Limits of Genre,* and *No Gifts from Chance: A Biography of Edith Wharton.* She is co-editor of the "Reading Women Writing" feminist book series at Cornell University Press and former editor of *Tulsa Studies in Women's Literature.* Her forthcoming work includes two editorial projects: *Footnotes: On Shoes,* a collection of essays, and *A Handbook of Literary Feminisms,* with an accompanying anthology.

**Rachel Bowlby's** books include *Just Looking* (1985), *Virginia Woolf* (1988; an expanded edition was published in 1997 as *Feminist Destinations*), *Still Crazy After All These Years* (1992), and *Shopping with Freud* (1993). *The Last Shopper,* on how shopping and shoppers' psychology has been imagined in this century, is forthcoming from Faber. She is Professor of Modern Literature at the University of York.

**D. A. Boxwell** is Assistant Professor of English at the Air Force Academy, Colorado Springs. An essay on *Orlando,* camp aesthetics, and 1920s British gay and lesbian culture is forthcoming in the journal *Twentieth Century Literature.*

**Marlene A. Briggs**, a Doctoral Candidate at the University of Ottawa, is currently completing a dissertation on trauma theory, the Great War and twentieth-century British literature. She has presented many conference papers on the Great War, and has planned a book-length project on the contemporary English novel and the Second World War.

**Arianne Burford** earned her B.A. at the University of California in San Diego and is currently working on her Masters Degree at Washington State University. After focusing on teaching as well as on further research for a couple of years, and possibly even attaining a Masters in Spanish Literature, she plans on pursuing her Ph.D. in literature.

**Beth Rigel Daugherty** teaches English and is chairperson of Integrative Studies at Otterbein College. Her publications include articles on Woolf's essays, *Virginia Woolf: Texts and Contexts,* co-edited with Eileen Barrett, and the forthcoming *Approaches to Teaching Woolf's* To the Lighthouse, co-edited with Mary Beth Pringle. She is currently working on a book about Woolf and education.

**Laura Davis** is Associate Professor of English and Assistant Dean, College of Arts and Sciences, Kent State University. Her editing work includes *Conrad's Century: The Past and Future Splendour* (1998) and the previous *Selected Papers* volume, *Virginia Woolf and Her Influences* (1998), co-edited with Jeanette McVicker.

**Terry DeHay** is an Associate Professor and Chair of the Department of English at Southern Oregon State University. She has explored the role of discourse in the formation of alternative communities in articles on African, Latin American, and British Literature.

**Marianne DeKoven** is Professor of English at Rutgers University. She is the author of *Rich and Strange: Gender, History, Modernism*, and *A Different Language: Gertrude Stein's Experimental Writing*. Her current book project concerns the 1960s and the emergence of postmodernism.

**Madelyn Detloff** completed her Ph.D. at the University of California, Santa Barbara. She is currently a post-doctoral fellow at the University of California Humanities Research Institute, where she is working on the manuscript of her book, *The Apocalyptics of Subjection: Trauma, Identification, and Modernist History Making.*

**Deirdre Flynn** is currently completing a Ph.D. in Comparative Literature at the University of California, Berkeley. Her dissertation is entitled, "Modern Authors, Well-Dressed Women: Assembling a Writing Self." Other publications include: "Joyce in Drag," (forthcoming, *Joyce and Commodity Culture*, spring 1999); "La Métaphore Sonore Proustienne," (*Bulletin d'informations proustiennes*, n° 27, 101-112).

**Lois J. Gilmore** has a Ph.D. in English from Temple University and an MA from the University of California, Riverside. She is Professor of Language and Literature at Bucks County Community College, Newtown, PA, where she teaches British Literature and Composition and is Writing Program Director.

**Jane Goldman** lectures in English at the University of Dundee. She is author of *The Feminist Aesthetics of Virginia Woolf* (Cambridge University Press, 1998) and the *Icon Critical Guide to Virginia Woolf* (Icon 1997) and co-editor of *Modernism: An Anthology of Sources and Documents* (Edinburgh University Press and the University of Chicago Press, 1998).

**Julia Gray** is in her second year at the Eastman School of Music, where she is a voice major; she is simultaneously majoring in English at the University of Rochester. This is Julia's second presentation to the Virginia Woolf Conference. Her first essay, included in "Reading Woolf in High School: The First Plunge" is published in the 1997 *Selected Papers*. Julia looks forward to a career that includes Woolf scholarship.

**Stephanie Harzewski** received a master's degree in Women's Studies in 1998 from Rutgers University and plans to enter a doctoral program in English. She has also published an essay on Adrienne Rich's *Diving into the Wreck* and hopes one day to be a Women's Studies and English professor.

**Yuko Ito** is a doctoral student at the Graduate Research Centre for the Humanities, University of Sussex. She is completing a dissertation on some reconstructions of mimesis in the work of the Bloomsbury Group.

**Georgia Johnston** directed the 8th Annual Virginia Woolf Conference. An Associate Professor, she teaches 20th-century literature at

Saint Louis University. She has recently edited the book *Essays on Transgressive Readings: Reading Over the Lines* published by The Edwin Mellen Press.

MEGUMI KATO is a doctoral candidate in English Literature at Sophia University and Research Fellow of the Japan Society for the Promotion of Science. She is researching Woolf's texts in relation to eugenicist discourse from the 1880s to 1930s.

NANCY KNOWLES is facing her preliminary Ph.D. examinations at the University of Connecticut. A fellow of the Redwood Writing Project, she has published an article on Virginia Woolf's use of dome symbolism in the 1998 issue of *Woolf Studies Annual.*

LANA HARTMAN LANDON, an award-winning teacher, has published in a number of scholarly fields. She is past recipient of an NEH Special Study grant for her project "Reading Paintings" and most recently completed a three-year fellowship in Medical Ethics sponsored jointly by the West Virginia Hospital Association and the West Virginia Humanities Council.

BARBARA LOUNSBERRY is Professor of English at the University of Northern Iowa. Her books include *The Art of Fact: Contemporary Artists of Nonfiction* (1990), *The Writer in You* (1994), *Writing Creative Nonfiction: The Literature of Reality* (ed. with Gay Talese, 1996), and *The Tales We Tell: Perspectives on the Short Story* (ed. with Susan Lohafer, 1998).

JEANETTE MCVICKER is Associate Professor of English and current Director of Women's Studies at SUNY College at Fredonia. This is the second volume of *Selected Papers* from the annual Woolf conference she has edited with Laura Davis.

KATHRYN MILES is a doctoral student at the University of Delaware. Her interests include philosophical praxis in the fiction and poetry of Woolf, James, Lawrence and Yeats, as well as the influence of romanticism on British modernists.

MICHELLE N. MIMLITSCH is a Doctoral Candidate in English at the University of California, Los Angeles, where she has taught for four years. Her research interests include both British and American women's literature, and her dissertation deals with women's homefront fiction of the First World War.

VARA NEVEROW is Professor of English and Feminist Theory at Southern Connecticut State University. She currently serves as Director of Graduate Studies in English and Co-Coordinator of the Women's Studies Program. Her publications include the first three volumes of the selected papers of the annual conference on Virginia Woolf, co-edited with Mark Hussey, as well as articles on Virginia Woolf, on composition theory, and on feminist utopian thought. She was the principal organizer of the second annual conference on Virginia Woolf and has also organized eight annual Women's Studies conferences at her university.

**Sigrid Nunez** is the author of three works of fiction: *A Feather on the Breath of God* (1995), *Naked Sleeper* (1996), and *Mitz: The Marmoset of Bloomsbury* (1998), all published by HarperCollins. She is Adjunct Assistant Professor of creative writing at the School of the Arts, Columbia University.

**Nita Pettigrew** teaches English at Phillips Exeter Academy in New Hampshire. She has been teaching for thirty-four years and is pleased to have spent her career reading and writing with high school students. Ms. Pettigrew has received several teaching awards, not least of which was a 1996 NEH grant to study Virginia Woolf with Kathy Hill-Miller in London.

**Diana Royer** is Associate Professor of English at Miami University. She has published on Yusuf Idris, Nathaniel Hawthorne, Edgar Allan Poe, Ambrose Bierce, and Native American topics. She is co-editor with Sherrie A. Inness of *Breaking Boundaries: New Perspectives on Women's Regional Writing* (University of Iowa, 1997).

**Bonnie Kime Scott** is Professor of English and Women's Studies at the University of Delaware, where she serves as Director of Graduate Studies in English. Her revisionary work on modernism includes such books as *Joyce and Feminism, The Gender of Modernism: A Critical Anthology*, and *Refiguring Modernism* (2 vols.), the latter featuring Virginia Woolf. She had just finished editing *The Selected Letters of Rebecca West.*

**Robin Paula Silbergleid** teaches at Indiana University, where she is completing the Ph.D. in English and M.F.A. in Poetry. This essay is part of her dissertation project, an investigation of the relationship between narrative and loss in twentieth-century fiction.

**Laurel Smith** is Professor of English at Vincennes University. She serves on the Executive Boards of the Indiana College English Association and Phi Delta Kappa-Illiana Chapter. Smith's publications reflect her interests in women's studies and poetry. Supported by a recent fellowship from the Indiana Arts Commission, she is completing a collection of her own poems.

**Anna Snaith** is a Lecturer in English at Anglia Polytechnic University in Cambridge, England. She has published articles on Woolf and Mansfield and her book cntitled, *Virginia Woolf: Public and Private Negotiations*, will be published by St. Martin's Press in 1999. She is currently editing the *Three Guineas* letters for publication in *Woolf Studies Annual.*

**Elisa Kay Sparks** teaches English (from Freshman Comp to Feminist Literary Criticism to Science Fiction), Women's Studies, and Women's Art at Clemson University in South Carolina. Her home page at http://hubcap.clemson.edu/~sparks has links to materials for most of her courses as well as to reproductions of some of her prints.

**Judy Suh** is working toward a Ph.D. in English and Cultural Studies at the University of Pittsburgh. She is currently writing on poststructuralist feminist and British modernist critiques of fascism. Woolf will play a central role in her dissertation.

**Pierre-Eric Villeneuve** has a Ph.D. in Semiotics and has published on Woolf in various reviews in French and English. He is currently finishing his book on Woolf's letters to appear in England in 2000. He is an assistant professor at Brock University.

**Rebecca Weisser**, wishing to make a worthy earth from numbers, letters, and Anais Nin, studies voraciously at Washington University in St. Louis and now lives in her own room.

**Michael Whitworth** teaches at the University of Wales, Bangor. He is currently writing a book on modernism and the new physics, and is compiling a bibliography of Sir Herbert Read.

**Deborah Wilson** is an associate professor of English and Director of the Master of Liberal Arts degree program at Arkansas Tech University, where she teaches American studies, Southern literature, and film. Her publications include articles on Woolf, Faulkner, and Welty, and she is currently finishing a book on Gayl Jones.

**J. J. Wilson** has taught English at Sonoma State University for nearly 30 years and has been involved in Woolf studies even longer. She is founding editor of the *Virginia Woolf Miscellany.* In addition to her work on Woolf, she has worked on Dora Carrington and other women artists..

**Marilyn S. Zucker** develops experiential learning opportunities for undergraduates at the University of Washington. This pedagogy, which invites students to become "well-sunned natures" rather than "cloistered disciplinarians," enacts Woolf's basic notions of the interconnection among all realms of meaning, knowledge and experience. Marilyn recently taught American Literature in Portugal as a Fulbrighter and is currently working on a project integrating the arts and humanities with community-based learning.

# Virginia Woolf and Community

## Eighth Annual Virginia Woolf Conference

June 4–7, 1998

### Highlights on Speakers

*Tuzyline Allan*, Associate Professor, CUNY, Baruch College. Her book, *Womanist and Feminist Aesthetics: A Comparative Review* (Ohio UP, 1995), won the 1993 NEMLA Book Award.

*Awiakta*, a Cherokee, Appalachian poet and essayist. Her book of essays, *Selu*, was a Quality Paperback Book Club selection. *Poesie Premiere*, the French literary journal, recently featured a 35-page retrospective of Awiakta's work.

*Suzanne Bellamy*, an Australian sculptor and print-maker.

*Shari Benstock*, Chair of the Department of English at the University of Miami. Books besides *Women of the Left Bank* range from a biography of Edith Wharton (*No Gifts From Chance*) to books she has edited about fashion (*On Fashion*), autobiography (*The Private Self*), and feminism (*Feminist Issues in Literary Scholarship*). Watch for a new book, *Footnotes on Shoes.*

*Rachel Bowlby*, Fellow of St. Hilda's College, Oxford. You can find copies of her many books, *Feminist Destinations and Further Essays on Virginia Woolf* among them, on the book selling tables. Watch for her book in preparation, *What does a shopper want?*

*Marianne DeKoven*, Professor of English at Rutgers University. Her most recent book, *Rich and Strange: Gender, History, Modernism*, won the Choice Award for Outstanding Academic Books.

*Jane Marcus*, Distinguished Professor of English at CUNY Graduate Center and the City College of New York. Just a few of her books are *Virginia Woolf and Cambridge: The Proper Upkeep of Names*; *Art and Anger: Reading Like a Woman*; and *Virginia Woolf and the Languages of Patriarchy.*

*Patricia Moran*, Associate Professor of English at University of California, Davis. You can find her recent book, *Word of Mouth: Body Language in Katherine Mansfield and Virginia Woolf*, on the book selling table.

*Vara Neverow*, Professor of English and Women's Studies at Southern Connecticut State University. She was the first editor, with Mark Hussey, of the Virginia Woolf Conference Proceedings. She was instrumental in beginning these conferences.

*Sigrid Nunez*, a novelist. She has received the Whiting Writer's Award. Read *Mitz, the Marmoset of Bloomsbury.*

*Bonnie Kime Scott*, Professor of English at the University of Delaware. Her books *The Gender of Modernism* and *Refiguring Modernism* (Volumes I and II) have changed the ways modernism is understood and taught.

## Highlighted Events

*Paris Was A Woman*, film based on the book of the same title, about women writers in Paris in the early 20th century.

*Silent Auction.* Come look and bid! Books, memorabilia, and more will be up for auction. The display is in the Pius Memorial Library. Show your badge to get into the library; the display is in the front lobby. To place a bid, write your name, address, item number, and bid on a slip of paper and then put the slip of paper in the box provided. Successful bidders will be notified at the banquet on Saturday, June 6, (or by mail); acceptable forms of paypment include cash or checks made out to Saint Louis University. We gratefully acknowlege Krystyna Colburn's gifts of time, energy, and material; all proceeds form the auction are donated to the Travel Scholarship Fund.

*Xerox Prints* by Eloise Lebov; *Art Work* by Suzanne Bellamy; *South Carolina Review* for sale: in Aunt Hattie's, downstairs BMC.

*Book Selling*: Left Bank Books, one of the few still-independently owned book-stores in St. Louis, will be open for sales in BMC, Aunt Hattie's, Friday, 10-6, and Saturday, 10-7.

## About the Conference

### Conference Funding

The Eighth Annual Virginia Woolf Conference is hosted by Saint Louis University and its Women's Studies Program. Loans from the Arts and Sciences Dean's office helped fund the conference until registration money arrived. An Arts and Sciences Mellon Grant has helped to provide some of the expenses for keynote speakers.

The Women's Studies Program has subsidized the conference, both with time and money, throughout the year. The Dean's Fire Fund has helped with some expenses for keynote speakers. The International Virginia Woolf Society authorizes the conference.

**Travel Scholarship Fund**

Many thanks to the following people and their contributions to the Travel Award Fund:Angela Athy, Morris Beja, D. A. Boxwell, Krystyna Colburn, Margaret Connolly, Peggy Cornelius, Beth Rigel Daugherty, Laura Davis, Isota Tucker Epes, Diane Gillespie, Julia Gray, Lynne Gray, Marjorie Hellerstein, Mark Hussey, Georgia Johnston, Ellen Carol Jones, Jill Kinkade, Patricia Laurence, Vara Neverow, Susanna Rich, Jody Rosen, Diana Royer, Bonnie Kime Scott, Elisa Kay Sparks, Ellen Tremper, Gay L. Vieira, Michael H. Whitworth, J.J. Wilson. *Thank you.* In addition, Wayne Chapman and the *South Carolina Review* are donating part of the proceeds of journals sold at this conference to the travel fund. Krystyna Colburn has designated the proceeds from the Silent Auction go to support this fund. *Thank you to all for your generosity.* (If you would still like to make a donation to the travel fund, you may do so at the registration table. Each year, these funds are given to those in need after the conference is over.)

**Conference Steering Committee**

Without the help of the steering committee (the previous organizers), the Eighth Annual Conference would have driven off the road a number of times. Many thanks to Mark Hussey (1991), Vara Neverow (1992), Jane Lilienfeld (1993), Paul Connolly (1994), Beth Rigel Daugherty (1995), Wayne Chapman and Elisa Sparks (1996), and, especially, Jeanne Dubino (1997), who sometimes dealt with weekly questions.

**Conference Program Commmittee**

To Judith Allen, Penn State, Abington; Suzanne Diamond, Rutgers University; Leslie Hankins, Cornell College; Andrea Harris, Mansfield University; Patricia Moran, the University of California, Davis; and Pierre-Eric Villeneuve, University of Toronto: *THANK YOU.*

**On Location**

Thanks go to students Mandi Schauble and Jennifer Hoef. They were integral in all parts of this conference's organization. Special thanks to Paige Canfield, Beth Dockery, Dru Dockery, Sue Fleming, Cheryl Franz, Nancy Reiter, Margaret Tucker, friends who helped in time of need, especially during the first mailing crisis. Go Rosie the Riveter! Thanks to Beth Dockery, Laura Patton, and Jerry Troxell for putting on stamps. Thanks to Myriam Joseph, of Pius Library, who gave her wisdom and who helped Krystyna Colburn with the Silent Auction display.

And there are more: Thanks to colleagues, friends, and family who have given their time to help at the registration desk: Martha Baker, Toby Benis, Paige Canfield, Richard Dees, Dru Dockery, Martha Finklin, Tony Hasler (and Mrs. Hasler too), Lisa Ives, Helen Mandeville, Colleen McCluskey, Kathleen Nigro, and Hal Parker. There are others who are being gathered even as this program goes to print.

**Main Conference Locations**
The central location for this conference is BMC (Busch Memorial Commons). Classrooms in Ritter Hall (the next building to our north), Tegler Hall (two buildings to our north), and Kelley Auditorium (located in the glass square behind BMC and down a flight up steps) will house conference events. Registration is on the ground (lowest floor) of BMC. The Banquet is on the third (highest) floor of BMC. Thursday and Friday dinners and Sunday lunch will be in the Billiken Club (lowest floor). BMC has a cafeteria (closes at 2 p.m.) at its main floor along with a coffee express (limited hours). Pius Library houses the Silent Auction. Just past the library is Cupples house, open for public viewing. Reinhart Dorm is located 1/2 block South of BMC. Marguerite Dorm is across Grand Blvd, past the clock tower fountain. The recreation center is near the center of campus, parallel to Pius Library.

# Program Schedule

**THURSDAY, JUNE 4, 1998**

| | |
|---|---|
| **11a.m.-8p.m.** | On-site check-in and registration—Busch Memorial Center |
| **2:30-4** | Welcoming Remarks—Tegeler Hall, Carlo Auditorium<br>Shirley Dowdy, Dean of the College of Arts and Sciences<br>Georgia Johnston, Director, Women's Studies Program,<br>Featured Speaker<br>Suzanne Diamond, Rutgers University, Introduction<br>Marianne DeKoven, Rutgers University, "The Community of Audience: Woolf's Drama of Public Women" |
| **4-4:30** | Chairs' meeting—Tegeler Hall 101 |
| **4-4:30** | Coffee Break—BMC Lobbies |
| **4:30-6** | Concurrent Panels I |

1) **Imagining the Nation—Ritter 200**
Ellen Carol Jones, Chair
Penelope Anderson, Bryn Mawr College, "Virginia Woolf's Imagining of Nation through Visionary and Narrative Time"
Stephen Dilks, University of Missouri, Kansas City, "Exploding England: Nationalism and Place in *Between the Acts*"
Tonya Krouse, Brandeis University, "Nationality, Sexuality, Gender:Deconstructing and Proliferating Identities in Virginia Woolf's *Mrs. Dalloway*"

2) **Maternal Politics—Ritter 237**
Carol Ann Niemczura, Chair
Carol Ann Niemczura, Case Western Reserve University, "Surrogacy and Virginia Woolf"
Jill Graham, University of New Brunswick, "A Question of Dependent Relations:Thinking Back Through Mrs. Ramsay"
Megumi Kato, Sophia University, "Politics/Poetics of Motherhood in *To the Lighthouse*"

3) **Ways of Knowing: Creating Epistemologies—Ritter 222**
Terrence Wandtke, Chair
Brad Perri, Iowa State University, "Mrs. Dalloway's Uninvited Guests: Post-Positivist Realism and Communal Knowledge"
Robin Scofield and Robert Wren, University of Texas at Austin, "The Woolfs of Bloomsbury:The Multiplex Marriage"
Terrence Wandtke, Saint Louis University, "Virginia Woolf's Text in a Cinematic Context:Sally Potter's *Orlando* as (Re)Interpretation"

4) **Virginia Woolf in the Age of Mechanical Reproduction—Ritter 223**
Pamela Caughie, Loyola University, Chicago, Chair
Sunny Stalter, Loyola University, Chicago, "The Ways of Seeing: The Cinematic Novel in the Age of Mechanical Reproduction"
Keith Beyer, Loyola University, Chicago, "'The proximity of the omnibuses': Social Movements and Representational Structures in *Jacob's Room*"
Gale Temple, Loyola University, Chicago, "Bloomsbury Politics and the Anti-Patriarchal Trajectory of Popular Culture in *Jacob's Room*"
Christina Heckman, Loyala University, Chicago, "Under 'Chinese' Eyes": Orientalism and Cultural Community in the Novels of Virginia Woolf"

5) **Woolf's Creations of the Dialogic—Tegeler 104**
Douglas Wood, Chair
Douglas Wood, Tulsa Community College, "'Then the Curtain Rose': Anticipation, Transition, and the Postmodern Dialogue in and through *Between the Acts*"
Stephanie L. Johnson, University of Washington, "'A Slave to Her Audience': the Ethical Primacy of the Other in *Between the Acts*"
Gabrielle McIntire, Cornell University, "Heteroglossia, Monologism, and Fascism:Bernard reads *The Waves*"
Andrew John Miller, University of Missouri, Columbia, "'Our Representative, Our Spokesman': Community and Representation in *Between the Acts*"

6) **Woolf, Forster, and Mansfield: A Modernism of Emotion—Tegeler 101**
Patricia Feito, Chair
Michael Kaufmann, Purdue University, Fort Wayne, "Virginia Woolf's Alternative Modernism: The Form of Feeling in *The Waves*"
Patricia Feito, Barry University, "E.M. Forster's Stock in the Body: *Maurice*'s Appropriation of Emotional Value"
Patricia Moran, University of California, Davis, "'Our own particular self': Katherine Mansfield's Politics of Impersonality"

**7) Community Creations of Woolf—Tegeler 103**
Duane Smith, Saint Louis University, Chair
Christine Froula, Northwestern University, "When Woolf Reads Her Biographers: A Dream Vision"
Diane Royer, Miami University, "Remaking Virginia: A Caution for Readers"
Kathryn Miles, University of Delaware, "'That Perpetual Marriage of Granite and Rainbow': Searching for 'The New Biography' in *Orlando*"

| | |
|---|---|
| **6-7:30 p.m.** | Welcoming Dinner Reception (for all conference registrants) Billiken Room, Downstairs BMC |
| **8-9 p.m.** | Featured Reading, Tegeler Hall, Carlo Auditorium<br>J.J. Wilson, Sonoma State University, Introduction<br>Awiakta, "Communing with Virginia Woolf from Cherokee Country: Poetry, Stories, and 'Hums'" |
| **9-9:45 p.m.** | Refreshments, BMC Lobbies |

**FRIDAY, JUNE 5, 1998**

| | |
|---|---|
| **8:15 a.m.-8p.m.** | On-site check-in and registration, BMC Lobbies |
| **7:30-8:30 a.m.** | Continental Breakfast, BMC Lobbies |
| **7:30-8:30 a.m.** | International V. Woolf Society meeting, Ritter 200 |
| **8:30-10 a.m.** | Concurrent Panels II |

**1) Communities of Letters and Diaries—Ritter 200**
Barbara Lounsberry, Chair
D. A. Boxwell, USAF Academy, "In the Urinal: Virginia Woolf Around Gay Men"
Barbara Lounsberry, University of Northern Iowa, "Virginia Woolf and the Community of Diarists"
Shaun Carey, City University of New York, "Absurdity, Alternations, and Variety: Virginia Woolf and the Lesbian Letter"

**2) Foreign Communities—Ritter 237**
Mark Wollaeger, Chair
Karen McLeer, University of Wisconsin, Richland, "The English Adrift: Exploring the Shipboard Community in *The Voyage Out*"
Yuko Ito, University of Sussex, "The Masked Reality in Leonard Woolf's Colonial Writings"
Mark Wollaeger, Vanderbilt University, "Colonizing Communities: Solidarities of Race, Gender, and Sexuality in *The Voyage out*"

**3) Negotiations with Outsiders**, Ritter 222
Karyn Sproles, Chair

Karyn Sproles, James Madison University, "Finding *A Room of One's Own* in Bloomsbury: Virginia Woolf's Feminist Portraits in Miniature"
Karen Volland Waters, Marymount University, "I'm Nobody: Emily Dickinson, Virginia Woolf, and the Outsider's Society"
Judith Allen, Penn State University, Abington, "The Rhetoric of Performance in *A Room of One's Own*"

4) **Musical Influence and Space in Community Formation—Ritter 223**
Traci Kelly, University of Minnesota, Chair
Arianne Burford, Washington State University, "Communities of Silence and Music in Virginia Woolf's *The Waves* and Dorothy Richardson's *Pilgrimage*"
Gwen Anderson, University of South Florida, "Woolf and Lessing Create World Rooms"
Vanessa Manhire, Rutgers University, "'Brilliant, Beautiful, and Absurd': Musical Communities in Woolf's Early Writings"

5) **Psychoanalytical Approaches—Tegeler 101**
Judith Lutzer, Chair
Kathy Cunningham, University of California, Davis, "*The Voyage Out*: A Quest for Mutual Recognition"
Kella Svetich, University of California, Davis, "'The Blessed Island of Good Boots': Fetishism, Footwear, and the Crippled Foot in *To the Lighthouse*"
Judith Lutzer, State University of New York, Stony Brook, "Bloomsbury and Psychoanalysis"

6) **Isolation and Community I—Tegeler 102**
Beth Rigel Daugherty, Chair
Kristen Buck, Idaho State University, "Room with a View: 'The Miraculous Glass Cabinet' as Place of Community in Virginia Woolf's *A Room of One's Own*"
Krystyna Colburn, "Collecting: Virginia Woolf, Elizabeth Bishop, Bessie Head"
Beth Rigel Daugherty, Otterbein College, "Learning Virginia Woolf: Of Leslie, Libraries, and Letters"

7) **Art Talk**, Tegeler 103
Elisa Kay Sparks, Chair

Lois Gilmore, Bucks County Community College, "Virginia Woolf, Bloomsbury, and the Primative"
Elisa Kay Sparks, Clemson University, "*The Dial* as Matrix:Periodical Community between Virginia Woolf and Georgia O'Keefe"
Kathleen Shores Rice, California State University, Long Beach, "Merging Visual and Verbal Creativity: How Art Colors Virginia Woolf's Writing"

| | |
|---|---|
| **10-10:30 a.m.** | Coffee Break, BMC Lobbies |
| **10:30-12 noon** | Film, Kelley Auditorium, ***Paris Was A Woman*** |
| **12-2:30 p.m.** | Lunch on one's own |
| **2:30-3:45 p.m.** | Featured Conversation I, Kelley Auditorium<br>Filming the Left Bank<br>**Shari Benstock**, University of Miami, and **Bonnie Kime Scott**, University of Delaware, with **Morris Beja**, Ohio State University, as moderator |
| **4-5:30 p.m.** | Concurrent Panels III |

1) **Building Literary Traditions—Tegeler 103**
Andrea Zemgulys, Chair
Jennifer Butts, University of Alabama, "Echoing Voices of Virginia Woolf Through the Decades: Her Imagistic and Stylistic Influence in Lessing's *The Summer Before the Dark*, Robinson's *Housekeeping*, and Gilchrist's *The Anna Papers*"
Patricia Laurence, City College of New York, "A Conversation on a Scroll: The Literary Communities of Bloomsbury, England, and the Crescent Moon Society, China"
Matthew Cooper, Webster University, "Woolf's 'Very Clever Men': Writers, Readers, and the Critique of Empire"
Andrea Zemgulys, University of California, Berkeley, "'Lord Macaulay Died Here: Virginia Woolf and the Literary Shrines of London

2) **Isolation and Community II—Ritter 237**
Michelle Mimlitsch, Chair
Michelle Mimlitsch, UCLA, "Powers of Horror and Peace: Abjection and Community in Virginia Woolf's *Between the Acts*"
Lisa Metzgar, Colorado State University, "'All This One Could Never Share': Virginia Woolf and the Conflict between Community and Independence"
John Haegert, University of Evansville, "Woolf's *Mrs. Dalloway* and the Politics of Solitude"

3) **Editing Community Form—Ritter 222**
Sally Greene, Chair
Sally Greene, UNC, Chapel Hill, "'Reverence for her mind and heart': Carl Sandburg's Tribute to Woolf"
Diane Gillespie, Washington State University, "Woolf and the Community of Editors: In Defense of Annotation"
Ted Bishop, University of Alberta, "On Drafting Virginia"
Leslie Hankins, Cornell College, "Film Adaptation and its Discontents: Marketing Woolf for Late 20th-century Film"

4) **First Encounters: Student Response to Woolf—Tegeler 104**
Nita Pettigrew, Phillips Exeter Academy, Chair
Introduction: Mrs. Joan Burtelow, alumna of Nerinx Hall High School
Rebecca Weisser, Nerinx Hall High School, "'Rattigan Glumphoboo':

*Orlando*, A Very Complicated Spiritual Journey"
Julia Gray, Phillips Exeter Academy, '97; Eastman School of Music, "'Fear no more the heat ofthe sun': A Plunge into the Metaphors of Life and Death"
High School Teachers—Responses

5) **Greek Texts and the Birds—Ritter 223**
Rowena Fowler, Chair
Rowena Fowler, University of Bristol, "'Other People's Voices, Singing the Same Song': The Chorus as Communal Voice in *The Waves*"
Lise Schlosser, "'The Twitter of Sparrows': Bird Imagery in Woolf's Later Fiction"
Idris Anderson, Crystal Springs Uplands School, "Virginia Woolf among Classicists: Those Birds Singing in Greek Again"

6) **Mourning: Loss—Tegeler 101**
Robin Silbergleid, Chair
Robin Silbergleid, Indiana University, "'We Perished Each Alone': Loss and Lyricism in Woolf, Young, and Maso"
Sarah Henstra, University of Toronto, "'Some Common Feeling': Elegiac Community in *To the Lighthouse*"
Stefanie Herweck, "Separation and Conquest: Virginia Woolf and the Maternal Center"

7) **Questions of Signification: Life and Art in Woolf's Short Stories—Tegeler 102**
Kathryn N. Benzel, Chair
Ruth Hoberman, University of Eastern Illinois, "Woolf's Short Stories and Collectors"
Susan Rochette-Crawley, University of Northern Iowa, "Virginia Woolf and the Scientific Community"
Kathryn N. Benzel, University of Nebraska, Kearney, "Cloud Chasing in 'Monday or Tuesday'"

**5:30-7 p.m.** Dinner Buffet (white ticket required)—Billiken Club (BMC)

**7-8 p.m.** Woolf Society Players (an on-going tradition), Billiken Club
PLEASE COME even if you opted not to attend the dinner.

**8:15-9:15 p.m.** Featured Speaker, Kelley Auditorium
Introduction, Judith Allen, Penn State, Abington
**Vara Neverow**, Southern Connecticut State University
"Thinking Back Through Our Mothers, Thinking in Common: Virginia Woolf's Photographic Imagination and the Community of Narrators in *Jacob's Room*, *A Room of One's Own*, and *Three Guineas*"

**9:15-10 p.m.** Refreshments, BMC Lobbies

**SATURDAY, JUNE 6, 1998**

**8:15a.m.-8 p.m.** On-site check-in and registration, BMC Lobbies

**7:30-8:30 a.m.** Continental Breakfast, BMC Lobbies

**7:30-8:30 a.m.** Virginia Woolf *Miscellany* meeting, Ritter 200

**8:30-10 a.m.** Concurrent Panels IV

1) **Communities of Language—Ritter 237**
Marijke Rudnick-Smalbraak, Chair
Valerie Brady, Seton Hall University, "Miss La Trobe and Virginia Woolf: A Community of Charwomen/Semioticians"
Marijke Rudnick-Smalbraak, University of Amsterdam, "Writing the Life of the Mind: Virginia Woolf's 'Dialogic' Aesthetics"
Carmine Esposito, University of Connecticut, "A Journey Towards Silence: Martin Heidegger, Virginia Woolf, and the Nature of Language"

2) **Reading Readers and Community—Ritter 222**
Ellen Tremper, Chair
Ellen Tremper, Brooklyn College, "Woolf's Aesthetic Theory: The Relationship of Art to Community"
Pierre-Eric Villeneuve, University of Toronto, "Communities of Desire: Woolf, Proust, and the Reading Process"
Marilyn Zucker, University of Washington, "Virginia Woolf and the French Connection: A Devotion to Language"
Angela Crow, University of Kansas, "Aging with Woolf"

3) **Community's Politics—Tegeler 101**
Karen Levenback, Chair
Karen Levenback, George Washington University, "The General Strike, the Great War, and *To the Lighthouse*"
Judy Suh, University of Pittsburgh, "Woolf and the Gendering of Fascism"
Deborah Cohler, Brown University, "'Still tormented by desires': Woolf, Women's Suffrage, and the Politics of Georgian Femininity"
Matthew Parfitt, Boston University, "Bloomsbury's Ironic Detachment as Political Engagement"

4) **Reading Community in Images of Objects and Machines—Tegeler 102**
Carol Holmberg, Metropolitan State University, Chair
Michelle Levy, University of Toronto, "Virginia Woolf and the Non-human Community"
Stephanie Harzewski, Rutgers University, "Hypertext as Metaphor: Reading Woolf in the Electronic Age"
Michael Whitworth, University of Wales, "Woolf's Web: Telecommunications and Community"

**5) Current Classroom Communities—Tegeler 103**
Helen Power, Chair
Deborah Wilson, Arkansas Technical University, "Between the Arts: Woolf, Pedagogy, and the Persistence of Authority"
Ellen Jay, Wright State University, "Locked Rooms: Writing Divergent Communities"
Helen Power, Washington University, "Virginia Woolf and the Women's Studies Community"

**6) Communities in *Between the Acts*—Tegeler 104**
Jennifer Hoef, Saint Louis University, Chair
Jane de Gay, The Open University, "'The Voices of the poets, answering each other': A Community of Writers, and Writers in the Community, in *Between the Acts*"
Kathryn Harvey, University of Alberta, "'they signify presumably the League of . . . ': Reading Miss La Trobe as a Metaphor in *Between the Acts*"
Margaret Connolly, Villanova University, "Communties and Comedies: If *Between the Acts* Is a Comedy, What Kind of Comedy Is It?"

| | |
|---|---|
| **10-10:15 a.m.** | Coffee Break, BMC Lobbies |
| **10:15-11:30 a.m.** | Discussion Sections. Please go to the discussion room assigned to you in your registration packet. Follow instructions in the room. |
| **11:30 a.m.-1:30 p.m.** | Lunch on one's Own |
| **1:30-3 p.m.** | Concurrent Panels V |

**1) The Privacy of Communities—Tegeler 101**
Laura Davis-Clapper, Kent State University, Chair
Marjorie Hellerstein, "'Freshwater'—Just One Circle of Friends to Anotherr"
Jodie Medd, Cornell University, "Digging up Bloomsburied Sexualities: The Memoir Club Remebers the Drawing Room Revolution"
Annette Teta Snape, New York University, "'. . . we fitted like gloves.' 'But would they ever make a pair?': Strachey and Woolf"

**2) Communities of Representational Heroines—Tegeler 102**
Madeline Moore, "Princess Diana and Mother Teresa: Virginia Woolf and Miyeko Kamiya"

**3) Gendered? Androgynous? Communities—Tegeler 103**
Ann McClellan, Chair
Ann McClellan, University of Cincinnati, "'Dislodging the Weight of Centuries': The Fragmentation of the Female Domestic Ideal in Virginia Woolf's *The Waves*"
Susanna Hoeness-Krupsaw, University of Southern Indiana, "Virginia Woolf's Gynocritics"
Charles Boebel, Manchester College, "The Transcendent Community of

Androgynes in Virginia Woolf's *Orlando*"
A. Camille Ziolek, Wright State University, "Deconstructing Harry (and Sally): Androgyny as an Empty Shell"

**4) Narration/Narrativity—Tegeler 104**
George Piggford, Tufts University, Chair
Robin DeRosa, Tufts University, "'In Front of the Actual Thing': The Anti-Transcendence of Narration in *Mrs. Dalloway*"
Sydney Recht, Fordham University, "Virginia Woolf & Bloomsbury, Zora Neale Hurston & the Harlem Renaissance: Communal Narrative and Attitudes about Community"
Terry DeHay, Southern Oregon University, "Gathering Around the Punch Bowl: Woolf's Alternate Narrative Community"
Thomas M. March, New York University, "The Party and the Collage: Psychoanalysis and Narratology in Virginia Woolf and Anais Nin"

**5) Creating Models of Community—Ritter 223**
Ed Hungerford, Southern Oregon University
Purvi Shah, Rutgers University, "Traveling the Imaginary: Women and Community in *The Voyage Out*"
Christopher Piazzola, University of Montana, "Woolf's Political Pluralism: Alternative Communities in *The Waves* and *Between the Acts*"
Henry Krusiewicz, Midland Lutheran College, "In the Company of the Rhizome: Woolf's Bodies Without Organs in *The Waves*, *Orlando*, *Between the Acts*, and *Flush*"

**6) Woolf and Modernist Women—Ritter 222**
Alisha Rohde, Chair
Sue Thomas, La Trobe University, "Miss Robins and Mrs Brown"
Alan Chong, University of Toronto, "Class Crossings and Parallel Endings: Double Consciousness and Death in Virginia Woolf's *Mrs. Dalloway* and Nella Larsen's *Passing*"
Jeffrey Schwarz, Saint Louis University, "A Life through Death Paradox: Reader Engagement and the Ideologies of Individuality and Society within the Poetry of Stevie Smith"
Alisha Rohde, Ohio State University, "'A Society for Asking Questions': Four Modernist Women Writers Negotiate Their Careers"

**7) Attacking Communities—Ritter 200**
Jane Lilienfeld, Chair
Debrah Raschke, Southeast Missouri State, "Rethinking comunity in *Jacob's Room*: Endorsing transgression and heresy"
Mónica Ayuso, California State, Bakersfield, "Thinking Back Through Our Mothers: Virginia Woolf in the Spanish American Female Imagination"
Jane Lilienfeld, Lincoln University, "Seeking Intertextual Community: Discovering Asymmetrical Parallels in Virginia Woolf's *To the Lighthouses* and Toni Morrison's *Jazz*"

**3-4:15 p.m.** Featured Conversation II, Kelley Auditorium
Artists and Community poet and essayist Awiakta, visual artist Suzanne Bellamy, and novelist Sigrid Nunez, with J.J. Wilson, Sonoma State University, as moderator

**4:15-4:45 p.m.** Coffee Break

**4:45-6:15 p.m.** Concurrent Panels VI

1) **Woolf's Community of Art—Ritter 200**
Gay Vieira, Chair
Jane Goldman, University of Dundee, "Artist and Feminist Communities of 1910: Post-Impressionism, Suffrage Aesthetics, and Intersubjectivity in *To the Lighthouse*"
Emily Blair, University of California, Davis, "'The Silent Kingdom of Paint': Walter Sickert and Vanessa Bell"
Gay Vieira, University of Illinois, Springfield, "The Stephen Sisters' Character Portraits in *Mrs. Dalloway* and *The Conversation*: Portrayal of Woman as Social Hub"

2) **Reading Readers and Communities II—Ritter 222**
Jessica Berman, Chair
Jessica Berman, University of Maryland, Baltimore County, "Exploring Community: Woolf and the Theorists"
Joyce Meier, University of Iowa, "Rewriting the Community of Readers in Virginia Woolf's Artist-Novel *Orlando*"
Anna Snaith, Anglia Polytechnic University, "Virginia Woolf and Reading Communities: Respondents to *Three Guineas*"

3) **Representations—Tegeler 101**
Paul Gauthier, Chair
Nancy Knowles, University of Connecticut, "A Community of Women Looking at Men: The Photographs in Virginia Woolf's *Three Guineas*"
Paul Gauthier, Saint Louis University, "Remodeling Rooms: *A Room of One's Own* as Virginia Woolf's Autoethnographic Responce to E.M. Forster's Female Artist—Lucy Honeychurch—in n *A Room with a View*"
Zelda Austen, Long Island University, "Carrington: The Androgynous Muse"

4) **Virginia Woolf: a visual essay—Ritter 237**
Suzanne Bellamy, Australian Artist, "'Virginia Woolf': A Visual Essay"

5) **A Community of Correspondences—Tegeler 102**
Lana Hartman Landon, Bethany College, and
Laurel Smith, Vincennes University, "A Community of Correspondences: Two Women, Letters, and *The Voyage Out*"

6) **Madness/Sanity—Tegeler 103**
Angela Athy, Chair
Angela Athy, Bowling Green State University, "Questioning Normativity: Virginia Woolf, The 'Mad' Female Modernist"

Roslyn Reso Foy, University of New Orleans, "Sanity and Madness; Art and Life: A Study of Community in Virginia Woolf's *To the Lighthouse* and Mary Butt's *Armed with Madness*"

June Elizabeth Dunn, Southern Connecticut State University, "Mr. Bennett and Dr. Sherlock Holmes: The Question of Crime, Character Witnesses and Conan Doyle in *Mrs. Dalloway*"

**7) Communities in *The Waves*—Ritter 223**

Anne Strothman-Santiago, Chair

Beth Wheeler, Wright State University, "Virginia Woolf and Communities"

Anne Strothman-Santiago, Wright State University, "The Interludes as Community in *The Waves*"

Justyna Kostkowska, Middle Tennessee State University, "'The Facets of The Image Flicker': Woolf's Letters to Vanessa Bell, Vita Sackville-West, and Ethel Smyth as Catalysts for the Poetic Language of *The Waves*"

**7-8:30 p.m.** Banquet (red ticket required)—BMC, St. Louis Room

**8:30-9:30 p.m.** Featured Speaker—BMC, 3rd floor, Argentum Room
Mark Hussey, Pace University, Introduction
Rachel Bowlby, St. Hilda's College, Oxford
"Meet me in St. Louis: Virginia Woolf and Community"

**9:30-10 p.m.** Cash bar and Refreshments—BMC Lobbies

**SUNDAY, JUNE 7, 1998**

**8:15-9:30 a.m.** On-site check-in and registration—BMC Lobbies

**7:30-8:30 a.m.** Continental Breakfast—BMC Lobbies

**7:30-8:30 a.m.** Meeting for next year's conference—Ritter 200

**8:30-10 a.m.** Concurrent Panels VII

**1) Lesbian Communities, Ritter 200**

Patricia Cramer, Chair

Patricia Cramer, University of Connecticut, "The Courtly Love Tradition and Lesbian Romance in *The Years*"

Kurt Koenigsberger, Vanderbilt University, "Radclyffe Hall and the Lecture Hall: Woolf and *The Well* Revisited"

Jody Rosen, City University of New York, "Creating a Community of Women: The Sliding Scale of Female Homoeroticism in Early Modernist Novels"

**2) Traumatic Knowledge—Ritter 222**

Toby Benis, Saint Louis University, Chair

Madelyn Detloff, University of California, Santa Barbara, "Imagined Communities of Criticism: 'Wounded Attachments' to the Icons of H.D.,

Gertrude Stein, and Virginia Woolf"
Jill Kinkade, University of Southern Indiana, "The Muse of Memory: Virginia Woolf and the Modernist Use of Memory"
Marlene Briggs, University of Ottawa, "Veterans and Civilians: Traumatic Knowledge and Cultural Appropriation in *Mrs. Dalloway*"
Maureen Riddle, Rutgers University, "'Horror and Disgust': Bearing Witness to Empire"

3) **The Things of the World: Influence and Image, Ritter 237**
Evelyn Haller, Chair
Evelyn Haller, Doane College, "Virginia Woolf and the Sculptor Barbara Hepworth: A Dual Community of Modernists in the Context of Cornwall"
Shelia Deane, University of Western Ontario, "'Marks and Matter': Knowledge and Ineffability of 'the thing itself'"
Dierdre Flynn, University of California, Berkeley, "Virginia Woolf's Women and the Fashionable Elite: On Not Fitting-in"

4) **Community of the Hogarth Press—Tegeler 101**
Susan Pratt, Chair
Alice Gasque, University of South Dakota, "Virginia Woolf in the USA: Why Anglophones and Americans Like Shakespeare's Sister"
Susan Pratt, Concordia University, "Creating Community and the Hogarth Press"
John Young, Northwestern University, "Advertising in and of *Mrs. Dalloway*"

5) **Roles for Woolf's Women—Tegeler 102**
John McCombe, Chair
Lisa Bryce, Mount Royal College, "Virginia Woolf, Amanda Cross, and Nancy Drew: Cross-referencing the female quest in detective fiction"
John McCombe, Ohio State University, "*The Voyage Out*: *The Tempest* in a Teapot? Woolf's Re-vision of Shakespeare and the Critique of Victorian Female Education"
Andre Furlani, Concordia University, "Virginia Woolf in the Community of Age"

6) **Reproductions of Science and Medicine—Ritter 223**
Jane Fisher, Chair
Kathryn Stinson, "Complementarity and the Voice of the Permeable Self in the Works of Virginia Woolf"
Suzanne Diamond, Rutgers University, "Good Birth, Bad Science, and Textual Counter-Community: Virginia Woolf's Interrogation of Eugenic Pieties"
Kate Marshall, University of California, Davis, "Quantum Woolf: New Physics in *The Waves* and *Between the Acts*"
Jane Fisher, Canisus College, "'Novels . . . devoted to influenza': Communication, Community, and Illness in *Mrs. Dalloway*"

7) **Isolation . . . Community—Tegeler 103**
Liz Gualtieri-Reed, Chair
Liz Gualtieri-Reed, UNC, Chapel Hill, "Catholic Ritual, Feminist Spiritual: the Community of Female creators in Woolf's Novels"

Barbara Weaver, Clemson University, "Community vs. Aloneness in Woolf, Atwood, Didion, and Piercy"

Deborah Weiner, University of Rochester, "'The Writing 'I' Has Vanished. No Audience. No echo. Thats part of one's death': Woolf, Art, and Community under Threat"

| | |
|---|---|
| **10-10:30 a.m.** | Coffee Break—BMC Lobbies |
| **10:30-11:30 a.m.** | Featured Speaker—Tegeler Hall, Carlo Auditorium<br>Introduction, Marilyn Zucker, University of Washington<br>Tuzyline Allan, CUNY Baruch College<br>"Civilization and Its Pretexts in Virginia Woolf's Art" |
| **11:30 a.m.-12:30 p.m.** | Lunch (blue ticket required)—Billiken Club |
| **12:30-1:30** | Featured Conversation, Tegeler Hall, Carlo Auditorium<br>"Politics and *A Room of One's Own*"<br>Jane Marcus, CUNY Graduate School, and Patricia Moran, University of California, Davis with Pierre-Eric Villeneuve, University of Toronto, as moderator |
| **1:30-2** | Plenary wrap-up—Tegeler Hall, Carlo Auditorium |
| **2-3** | Closing refreshments—BMC lobbies |

## At-a-Glance Conference Schedule

**Thursday, June 4, 1998**

| | |
|---|---|
| 11a.m.-8 p.m. | On-site registration |
| 2:30-4 | Welcoming Remarks |
| | **Keynote Speaker: Marianne DeKoven** |
| 4-4:30 | Panel Chairs' meeting, coffee break |
| 4:30-6 | Concurrent Panels I |
| 6-7:30 | Welcoming Dinner Reception |
| 8-9 | **Reading: Awiakta** |
| 9-9:45 | Refreshments |

**Friday, June 5, 1998**

| | |
|---|---|
| 8:15a.m.-8p.m. | On-site registration |
| 7:30-8:30 | International Virginia Woolf Society meeting |
| 7:30-8:30 | Continental Breakfast |
| 8:30-10 | Concurrent Panels II |
| 10-10:30 | coffee break |

| | |
|---|---|
| 10:30-12 | **Movie: *Paris Was a Woman*** |
| 12-2:30 | Lunch on one's own |
| 2:30-3:45 | **Conversation I: Shari Benstock and Bonnie Kime Scott** |
| 4-5:30 | Concurrent Panels III |
| 5:30-7 | Dinner Buffet |
| 7-8 | Woolf Society Players |
| 8:15-9:15 | **Keynote Speaker: Vara Neverow** |
| 9:15-10 | Refreshments |

**Saturday, June 6, 1998**

| | |
|---|---|
| 8:15a.m.-8p.m. | On-site registration |
| 7:30-8:30 | Virginia Woolf Miscellany meeting |
| 7:30-8:30 | Continental Breakfast |
| 8:30-10 | Concurrent Panels IV |
| 10-10:15 | Coffee break |
| 10:15-11:30 | Discussion Sections (follow instructions in program) |
| 11:30-1:30 | Lunch on one's own |
| 1:30-3 | Concurrent Panels V |
| 3-4:15 | **Conversation II: Awiakta, Suzanne Bellamy, and Sigrid Nunez** |
| 4:15-4:45 | Coffee break |
| 4:45-6:15 | Concurrent Panels VI |
| 7-8:30 | Banquet |
| 8:30-9:30 | **Keynote speaker: Rachel Bowlby** |
| 9:30-10:15 | Cash bar and refreshments |

**Sunday, June 7, 1998**

| | |
|---|---|
| 8:15-9:30a.m. | On-site registration |
| 7:30-8:30 | Continental breakfast<br>Meeting for VW Conference 1999 |
| 8:30-10 | Concurrent Panels VII |
| 10-10:30 | Coffee break |
| 10:30-11:30 | **Keynote Speaker: Tuzyline Allan** |
| 11:30-12:30 | Lunch Buffet (ticket required) |
| 12:30-1:30 | **Conversation III: Jane Marcus and Patricia Moran** |
| 1:30-2 | Plenary wrap-up |
| 2-3 | Closing refreshments |

## ANNOUNCEMENTS

******

### Ninth Annual Virginia Woolf Conference!
### Virginia Woolf Turning the Centuries

******

This conference takes Woolf toward the new millenium by inviting participants to focus both on Woolf's work as a feminist historian interested in various periods and transitional markers, and on recent analyses that apply her writings to concerns of the 21st Century.

**Dates:** June 10-13, 1999
**Place:** University of Delaware Campus

Co-directors: Ann Ardis (aardis@udel.edu) and
Bonnie Kime Scott (bscott@udel.edu)

Department of English
University of Delaware
Newark, DE 19716

A web site is under construction.
Check http://odin.english.udel.edu/ for a link.

******

### Directory Out

******

Members of the International Virginia Woolf Society, please stop by the IVWS table in the registration area to pick up a copy of the summer mailing. This includes the directory of members and the 1998 bibliography of Woolf Scholarship. If you are not a member of the IVWS, you can sign up here!

******

### Proceedings

******

Paper presenters, please look in your registration packet for an "invitation to Presenters" to submit papers for consideration in the *Selected Papers*. The volume will be published by Pace University Press. All conference attendees, be sure to fill out the "Paper Evaluation Form" recommending papers for the published volume. Your vote counts.

9 780944 473474